OXFORD TEXTBOOKS IN LINGUISTICS

Series editors
Keith Brown, Eve V. Clark, April McMahon,
Jim Miller, Lesley Milroy

Meaning in Language

OXFORD TEXTBOOKS IN LINGUISTICS

General editors:
Keith Brown, University of Cambridge; **Eve V. Clark**, Stanford University;
April McMahon, University of Sheffield; **Jim Miller**, University of Edinburgh;
Lesley Milroy, University of Michigan

This series provides accessible and authoritative textbooks on the approaches, methods, and theories associated with the main subfields of linguistics.

PUBLISHED

A Practical Introduction to Phonetics (SECOND EDITION)
by J. C. Catford

Principles and Parameters: An Introduction to Syntactic Theory
by Peter W. Culicover

Linguistic Reconstruction: An Introduction to Theory and Method
by Anthony Fox

Semantic Analysis: A Practical Introduction
by Cliff Goddard

Cognitive Grammar
by John R. Taylor

Linguistic Categorization (THIRD EDITION)
by John R. Taylor

IN PREPARATION

The Grammar of Words: An Introduction to Linguistic Morphology
by Professor G. Booij

Pragmatics
by Yan Huang

Meaning in Language

An Introduction to
Semantics and
Pragmatics

Second Edition

Alan Cruse

UNIVERSITY PRESS

OXFORD

UNIVERSITY PRESS

Great Clarendon Street, Oxford OX2 6DP

Oxford University Press is a department of the University of Oxford.
It furthers the University's objective of excellence in research, scholarship,
and education by publishing worldwide in

Oxford New York

Auckland Bangkok Buenos Aires Cape Town Chennai
Dar es Salaam Delhi Hong Kong Istanbul Karachi Kolkata
Kuala Lumpur Madrid Melbourne Mexico City Mumbai Nairobi
São Paulo Shanghai Taipei Tokyo Toronto

Oxford is a registered trade mark of Oxford University Press
in the UK and in certain other countries

Published in the United States by Oxford University Press Inc., New York

British Library Cataloguing in Publication Data

Data available

Library of Congress Cataloging in Publication Data

Data available

ISBN 0–19–926306–X

10 9 8 7 6 5 4 3 2 1

Typeset in Times and Meta
by RefineCatch Limited, Bungay, Suffolk
Printed in Great Britain by
Antony Rowe Limited, Chippenham

To Paule, Pierre, and Lisette

Contents

Typographic conventions

Small capitals
For concepts; occasionally for lexical roots.

Small capitals in square brackets
For semantic components.

Angled brackets
For selectional restrictions.

Bold type
For technical terms when first introduced.

Italics
For citation forms when not set as displayed examples.

Bold italics
For emphasis

Single quotation marks
For quotations from other authors; 'scare quotes'.

Double quotation marks
For meanings.

Question marks
For semantic oddness.

Asterisks
For ungrammaticality or extreme semantic abnormality.

Preface to the first edition

The aim of this book is not to present a unified theory of meaning in language (I am not even sure that that would be a worthwhile project), but to survey the full range of semantic phenomena, in all their richness and variety, in such a way that the reader will feel, on completing the book, that he or she has made face-to-face contact with the undeniably messy 'real world' of meaning. At the same time, it aims to show that even the messy bits can, at least to some extent, be tamed by the application of disciplined thinking. As far as semantic theories are concerned, I have been unashamedly eclectic, adopting whatever approach to a particular problem seems genuinely to shed light on it. If there is a theoretical bias, it is in favour of approaches which, like the cognitive linguistic approach, embrace the continuity and non-finiteness of meaning.

This is not intended to be a 'baptismal' text; it would probably not be suitable for absolute beginners. The sort of readership I had in mind is second- or third-year undergraduates and beginning postgraduates who have completed at least an introductory course in linguistics, and who require an overview of meaning in language, either as preparation for a more detailed study of some particular area, or as background for other studies. I would hope it would be found useful, not only by students of linguistics, but also students of ancient and modern languages, translation, psychology, perhaps even literature.

Most of the material in the book has grown out of courses in general semantics, lexical semantics, and pragmatics, given to second- and third-year undergraduates and postgraduates at Manchester University over a number of years. I owe a debt to generations of students in more than one way: their undisguised puzzlement at some of my explanations of certain topics led to greater clarity and better exemplification; critical questions and comments not infrequently exposed weaknesses in the underlying arguments; and very occasionally, a genuine flash of insight emerged during a classroom discussion.

The final form of the text was significantly influenced by constructive comments at the draft stage by Jim Miller of the University of Edinburgh, an anonymous American reviewer, and John Davey of Oxford University Press, although, of course, full responsibility for remaining imperfections lies with myself.

The organization of the book is as follows. It is in four parts. Part 1 discusses a range of basic notions that underlie virtually all discussions of meaning within linguistics; Part 2 concentrates on aspects of the meanings of words; Part 3 deals with semantic aspects of grammar; Part 4 introduces the core areas of pragmatics, and highlights the relations between meaning and context.

Within Part 1, Chapter 1 provides a very general introduction to questions of meaning, locating the linguistic study of meaning within the wider context of the study of signs and communication in general. Chapter 2 introduces a set of fundamental conceptual tools, mostly drawn from the field of logic, which, because of their wide currency in discussions of semantic matters, constitute indispensable background knowledge for a study of meaning in language. In Chapter 3, a number of concepts are introduced for the description of meanings and differences of meaning. A basic dichotomy (based on Lyons 1977) is introduced between descriptive and non-descriptive meaning and, under each of these headings, important types and dimensions of variation are described. It is rare to encounter any extended treatment of these topics in semantics textbooks, yet a mastery of them is essential to anyone who wishes to talk in a disciplined way about meanings. Chapter 4 discusses the way(s) in which simpler meanings are combined to form more complex meanings.

In Part 2, Chapter 5 provides a general introduction to the study of word meanings, first discussing whether there are any restrictions on what sort of meanings words can bear, then distinguishing the meaning of a word from that of a sentence or discourse, and the meanings of full lexical items from the meanings of grammatical elements. In this chapter the major approaches to lexical semantics are also outlined. In Chapter 6, the focus is on the range of variation observable in a single word form in different contexts, ranging from arbitrarily juxtaposed homonymies to subtle modulations of sense. Chapter 7 introduces a conceptual approach to lexical semantics, beginning with a discussion of whether and to what extent word meanings can be equated with concepts. The discussion continues with an outline of prototype theory, the currently dominant approach to natural conceptual categories, and its relevance for the study of word meanings. Chapters 8 and 9 deal with relations of sense between lexical items which can occupy the same syntactic position—in other words, paradigmatic sense relations, such as hyponymy, meronymy, incompatibility, synonymy, antonymy, complementarity, reversivity, and converseness. Chapter 10 looks at larger groupings of words—word fields—mainly structured by the sense relations examined in the previous two chapters. Chapter 11 describes the main types of process, such as metaphor and metonymy, which enable new meanings to be produced from old ones. In Chapter 12, meaning relations between words in the same syntactic construction, that is, syntagmatic sense relations, are examined. Topics discussed include the nature of normal and abnormal collocations, reasons for a tendency for certain types of words to co-occur, and the nature and consequences of selectional pressures of words on their partners in a string. Chapter 13 outlines the componential approach to the description of word meaning, which specifies meaning in terms of semantic primitives.

The focus in Chapter 14, which constitutes the whole of Part 3, is on the sorts of meanings associated with various grammatical entities. First there is a discussion of the problem of whether there are any constant meanings attached to categories such as noun, verb, and adjective, and functions such as subject and object. There then follows a survey of the sorts of meaning borne by grammatical elements of various sorts, such as number and gender in the noun phrase, tense, aspect, and modality in connection with the verb, degree in the adjective, and so on.

Part 4 covers topics which are usually considered to fall under pragmatics, in that either they involve aspects of meaning which cannot be satisfactorily treated unless context is taken into account, or they are not propositional in nature (or both). Chapter 15 is concerned with reference, that is, establishing connections between utterances and the extralinguistic world. Reference is portrayed as the assigning of values to variables, the variables being signalled by definite expressions and the values being items in the extralinguistic world. Various strategies for indicating (on the part of the speaker) and determining (on the part of the hearer) correct referents are discussed, including the use and interpretation of deictic elements, names, and descriptions. Chapter 16 provides an outline of speech act theory, mainly following Austin and Searle (1969). It discusses the acts that people perform when they are speaking—acts such as stating, requesting, warning, congratulating, commanding, and so on. The range of different types of speech act is surveyed and their nature examined. Chapter 17 deals with conversational implicatures, that is, those aspects of the intended meaning of an utterance which are not encoded in its linguistic structure, but are, as it were, 'read between the lines'. Different types of conversational implicature are described and some proposed explanations of how they arise are considered.

The concluding chapter briefly surveys the areas covered in the book, suggests practical applications of the study of meaning, and highlights areas which are currently poorly understood, and where further research is needed. Each chapter except Chapter 1 and Chapter 5 contains a set of discussion questions and/or exercises, suggested answers to which will be found at the end of the book.

Preface to the second edition

In this revised edition, the original overall plan, purpose and character of the book have not been changed. The revisions are of three principal kinds. The first involves up-dating. Although only three years have elapsed since the publication of the first edition, there have been significant theoretical advances, particularly in lexical semantics. Accordingly, a new chapter has been added (Chapter 14), which outlines new thinking on word meaning. References have also been brought up to date. The second type of revision is the filling in of perceived gaps. There are of course constraints of space, and some omissions are unavoidable, but I have become aware of missing topics which really deserve a mention, such as frames, generalized conversational implicatures and constraints on relevance, to name but three. In the end, of course, the selection is a personal one. The third sort of revision has involved the improvement of existing treatments of topics, sometimes by re-organizing whole chapters, as in the case of Chapters 2 and 18 (originally Chapter 17), in other cases by re-writing short passages to improve clarity and/or consistency.

In preparing this edition, I have benefited from the comments and suggestions of two anonymous referees, although I of course accept full responsibility for the final result.

Part 1
Fundamental Notions

In this first part of the book, a number of fundamental but fairly general notions are introduced, which need to be grasped before the more detailed discussions in later sections can be properly appreciated. Chapter 1 has a scene-setting function, identifying the place of linguistic signs and linguistic communication in the broader domains of semiotics and communication in general. Chapter 2 introduces a number of vital conceptual tools drawn from the field of logic. Chapter 3 surveys the range of different sorts of meaning, and dimensions of variation in meaning. Chapter 4 discusses the notion of compositionality, one of the essential properties of language, and its limits.

Introduction

CHAPTER 1

Introduction

1.1 Communication

Meaning makes little sense except in the context of communication: the notion of communication therefore provides as good a place as any to start an exploration of meaning. Communication can be conceived very broadly, including within its scope such matters as the transfer of information between biological generations via the genetic code, the interaction between a driver and his car, and indeed any sort of stimulus–response situation. Here we shall confine ourselves to what is surely the paradigm communicative scenario, namely, the transfer of information between human beings.

1.1.1 A simple model

Let us begin with a simple model, as shown in Fig. 1.1 (after Lyons 1977). In the model, the process begins with a speaker who has something to communicate, that is, the **message**. Since messages in their initial form cannot be transmitted directly (at least not reliably—I am thinking here of telepathy), they must be converted into a form that can be transmitted, namely, a **signal**. In ordinary conversation this involves a process of **linguistic encoding**, that is, translating the message into a linguistic form, and translating the linguistic form into a set of instructions to the speech organs which when executed, result in an acoustic signal. The initial form of this signal may be termed the **transmitted signal**.

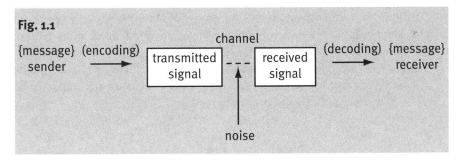

Fig. 1.1

{message} (encoding) → transmitted signal - - - received signal → (decoding) {message}
sender   receiver

channel

noise

Every mode of communication has a **channel**, through which the signal travels: for speech, we have the auditory channel, for normal writing and sign language, the visual channel, for Braille, the tactile channel, and so on. As the signal travels from sender to receiver it alters in various ways, through distortion, interference from irrelevant stimuli or loss through fading. These changes are referred to collectively as **noise**. As a result, the signal picked up by the receiver (the **received signal**) is never precisely the same as the transmitted signal. If every detail of the transmitted signal were crucial for the message being transmitted, communication would be a chancy business. However, efficient communicating systems like language compensate for this loss of information by building a degree of redundancy into the signal. Essentially this means that the information in a signal is given more than once, or is at least partially predictable from other parts of the signal, so that the entire message can be reconstructed even if there is significant loss. It is said that language is roughly 50 per cent redundant.

Once the signal has been received by the receiver, it has to be **decoded** in order to retrieve the original message. In the ideal case, the message reconstructed by the receiver would be identical to the message that the sender started out with. Almost certainly, this rarely, if ever, happens; however, we may presume that in the majority of cases it is 'close enough'. All the same, it is worth distinguishing three aspects of meaning:

(i) sender's meaning: sender's intended message
(ii) receiver's meaning: receiver's inferred message
(iii) sign meaning: This can be taken to be the sum of the properties of the signal which make it (a) more apt than other signals for conveying sender's intended message and (b) more apt for conveying some messages than others.

In the case of an established signalling system like language, the meanings of the signs are not under the control of the users; the signs are the property of the speech community and have stable semantic properties.

1.1.2 Language as a sign system

Any natural human language is a complex sign system, 'designed' to ensure infinite expressive capacity—that is to say, there is nothing that is thinkable which cannot in principle be encoded (provided no limit is placed on the complexity of utterances). Each elementary sign is a stable symbolic association between a meaning and a form (phonetic or graphic); elementary signs may combine together in a rule-governed way to form complex signs which convey correspondingly complex meanings.

1.2 Semiotics: some basic notions

1.2.1 Iconicity

Signs can generally be classified as iconic or arbitrary. **Iconic** signs are those whose forms mirror their meanings in some respect; signs with no natural analogical correspondences between their forms and their meanings are called **arbitrary**. A simple example is provided by the arabic and roman numerals for three: 3 and III. The arabic form gives no clue to its meaning; the roman version, on the other hand, incorporates "threeness" into its shape, and is thus iconic. Iconicity is a matter of degree, and usually coexists with some degree of arbitrariness. Three horizontal lines would be just as iconic as the roman III: the fact that in the roman symbol the lines are vertical is arbitrary, as is the fact that its size corresponds generally to that of capital letters.

Iconicity enters language in several guises. The majority of words in a natural language are arbitrary: the form of the word *dog*, for instance, does not mirror its meaning in any respect. However, the so-called **onomatopoeic** words display a degree of iconicity, in that their sounds are suggestive (to varying degrees) of their meanings:

> bang clank tinkle miaow splash cuckoo peewit curlew
> whoosh thud crack ring wheeze howl rumble (etc.)

The predominance of arbitrariness in the vocabulary is not an accidental feature, but is a crucial 'design feature' of natural language. There is a limited stock of dimensions of formal variation in linguistic signs; if all signs were iconic, there would inevitably be restrictions on what could be expressed. However, a notable characteristic of natural languages is that they show **universal expressivity**, that is, there are no 'no-go areas' of semantic space where language cannot operate.

Some iconicity is also apparent in grammar. For instance, words which belong together tend to occur together. In *The tall boy kissed the young girl* we know that *tall* modifies *boy* and not *girl* because *tall* and *boy* come next to each other in the sentence. In some languages this relationship might be shown by grammatical agreement, which is a kind of resemblance, and therefore also iconic. Another way in which iconicity appears in the grammar is that grammatical complexity by and large mirrors semantic complexity.

1.2.2 Conventionality

Many of the signs used by humans in communication are **natural** in the sense that they are part of genetically inherited biological make-up and do not have to be learned, although a maturational period may be necessary before they appear in an individual, and they may be moulded in various ways to fit particular cultural styles. The sort of signs which are natural in this sense will presumably include facial expressions like smiling, frowning, indications of fear and surprise, and so on, perhaps many of the postural signs and proxemic signs (involving the physical distance between interlocutors) that constitute the so-called 'body language', certain types of gesture, vocal indications of excitement, desire, etc. (whether or not linguistic), and many more. Natural signs are likely to be the most cross-culturally interpretable.

Other signs have conventionally assigned meanings; they have to be specifically learned, and are likely to differ in different communities. Linguistic signs are the prototypical conventional signs. Even onomatopoeic words usually have a significant conventional element; often the iconic nature of the word can only be appreciated, as it were, with hindsight. Take the Turkish word *bülbül*. What does it refer to? A baby's babbling? The noise of a mountain spring? In fact, it means "nightingale". Looking back, one can make the connection. It is not only linguistic signs that are conventional. Obscene or offensive gestures, for instance, can vary quite remarkably cross-culturally: I was once reprimanded for pointing the soles of my feet at the Prime Minister of Iraq (in Arab culture this is disrespectful: my disrespect was entirely inadvertent). Even in Europe, conventional gestures can differ: Greeks are famously—and slightly inaccurately—said to shake their heads to say "Yes" and nod to say "No".

1.2.3 Discreteness

Some signs can vary gradually in their form, and their meanings vary in parallel with the change of form (think of the range between a broad grin and a faint smile); these are called **continuous** signs. Other signs have fixed shapes, and must be chosen from a limited inventory: intermediate forms are not allowed, the range of possibilities is 'chunked'; such signs are described as **discrete**. Linguistic signs are virtually all of the discrete variety. Again, this is not an accidental feature, but has a close connection with iconicity and arbitrariness: continuous signs are necessarily iconic; arbitrary signs are necessarily discrete.

1.3 Language and other communicative channels

The prototypical scenario for linguistic communication is two people engaged in face-to-face conversation. Of course, in such an encounter, language signals are exchanged; but normally so are many other types of signal, and these modify and/or supplement the linguistically encoded message. Let us, then, briefly look at the semiotic environment of language in a typical conversation.

The signs that accompany language can be divided into two major types—**paralinguistic** and **non-linguistic**. The defining characteristic of paralinguistic signs will be taken here to be an extreme dependence on the accompanying language. Either they cannot be produced except during speech (because they are carried on the voice) or they cannot be interpreted except in conjunction with accompanying language. Examples of the first variety are abnormal volume, tempo, pitch, and voice quality; to function as signs, there must be a departure from some (personal) baseline or norm. For instance, abnormally high volume, fast tempo, or high pitch typically signal a heightened emotional state. Examples of the second variety include pausing, emphatic gestures, and gestures which metaphorically depict, for instance, direction of motion.

The functions of paralinguistic signs can be conveniently classified under three headings:

(i) **Punctuation**: there are signs which have functions parallel to those of punctuation in written language, mainly to segment the stream of speech so as to facilitate processing.

(ii) **Modulation**: this involves the addition of an emotive or attitudinal colouring to the linguistically encoded message.

(iii) **Illustration**: some signs 'depict' a key element in the message, such as a direction of movement, or a shape; the depiction may be relatively literal, like the hand movements of someone describing the climbing of a spiral staircase, or metaphorical, as when vertical and parallel hands accompany the setting of limits of some kind.

Paralinguistic signs are typically natural, continuous, and iconic, whereas linguistic signs are for the most part conventional, discrete, and arbitrary.

Not all the signs that occur alongside language are paralinguistic in the sense defined. For instance, one may smile or frown while speaking, and this may well 'modulate' the message. But smiles and frowns (and many other signs) are perfectly interpretable and capable of being produced in the absence of any accompanying language. These are therefore to be considered as non-linguistic.

1.4 Characteristics of language as a signalling system

1.4.1 Double articulation

Simple linguistic signs can be combined to form complex signs which signal complex meanings. But simple signs themselves typically display complexity in their form aspect. Thus, the formal aspect of the unitary sign *cat* is built up from the simpler phonological units /k + æ + t/, which are not individually associated with grammatical or semantic properties. This feature is usually termed **double articulation**. It allows a language to have a very large inventory of elementary signs without overstretching the discriminatory and memory capacities of human language users.

1.4.2 Syntax

Every language has a finite inventory of simple signs, but has an unlimited potential for the expression of meaning. Anything thinkable is expressible, or at least can be approximated to any given degree of accuracy. A major factor making this 'universal expressivity' possible is the possession of a **recursive syntax**. Syntactic rules are essentially rules for combining simpler meanings together in a systematic way to form more complex meanings. There is no theoretical upper limit to the complexity of linguistic signs. This is rendered possible by the recursive nature of syntax, that is, the existence of rules which can be applied indefinitely many times (like the one which yields *This is the dog that worried the cat that killed the rat that ate the corn that . . .*). Such rules are an essential prerequisite for the universal expressivity of language.

1.5 Approaches to the study of meaning

Meaning may be studied as a part of various academic disciplines. There is of course a significant degree of overlap between disciplines, but characteristically all have something idiosyncratic and unique in their approach (the following remarks are merely illustrative).

1.5.1 Philosophy

Linguists typically take the existence of meaning for granted and accept it as an intuitively accessible 'natural kind'. They do not ask questions like *How is it possible for anything to mean something?* or *What sort of relation must hold between X and Y for it to be the case that X means Y?* Such questions are the province of the philosopher, particularly the philosopher of language.

1.5.2 Psychology

Meaning is a major concern of the psychology of language and psycholinguistics. (I shall not attempt to distinguish these.) A distinctive feature here is the experimental study of how meanings are represented in the mind, and what mechanisms are involved in encoding and decoding messages. An example of a fact that could only emerge within a psycholinguistic framework is that in the lexical decision task, where experimental subjects observe strings of letters flashed on a screen and must indicate by pressing the appropriate button whether the string represents a word or not, responses are faster to words with concrete meanings than to words with abstract meanings, even when extraneous factors like length and frequency are rigorously controlled. This observation presumably provides a clue to the role of meaning in word recognition (to the best of my knowledge it is still a puzzle).

1.5.3 Neurology

Psychologists take a 'macro' view of mental states and processes. Neurologists, on the other hand, want to know how these states and processes are implemented at the neuronal level. A psychologist might be broadly compared with a computer programmer, and a neurologist to the designer of computer chips. Meaning, like everything else in mental life (at least if one is a physicalist), must boil down ultimately to connections between neurons.

1.5.4 Semiotics

Semioticians view language as one sign system amongst many, and seek out those features which render it so successful. They are also likely to give emphasis to marginal aspects of linguistic signification. The recent strong interest in iconicity in language represents a significant overlap between the linguistic and semiotic approaches to meaning.

1.5.5 Linguistics

It is not easy to encapsulate the linguistic approach to meaning in language. There are perhaps three key aspects. The first is that native speakers' semantic intuitions are centre-stage, in all their subtlety and nuances: they constitute the main source of primary data. The second is the importance of relating meaning to the manifold surface forms of language. The third is the respect paid not just to language, but to languages.

1.6 The linguistic study of meaning: what are we trying to achieve?

1.6.1 Specifying/describing meanings

A very important task is to discover a way of specifying or describing meanings, whether of isolated words or sentences, or of utterances in context. The position taken in this book is that in general meanings are not finitely describable; so this task boils down to finding the best way to approximate meanings as closely as is necessary for current purposes (lexicographers have long had to confront this problem with regard to words).

1.6.2 How meaning varies with context

The meanings of all linguistic expressions vary with the context in which they occur. For instance, the shade of colour indicated by *redhead* and *red wine* are markedly different; the periods of time denoted by month in (1) and (2) are quite likely to be different:

(1) He's here for a month. (could be four weeks; not dependent on time of utterance)

(2) He's here for the month. (will depend on time of utterance, but could be thirty-one days)

Some variations, like the sex of the doctor in *Our doctor has just married a policeman* and *Our doctor has just married an actress*, can be predicted by general principles; other variants are less predictable, or not at all predictable. Semanticians seek a revealing account of contextual variation.

1.6.3 Kinds of meaning

There are different sorts of meaning, each with different properties, and characterizing such differences is one of the tasks of semantics. For instance, the difference in meaning between (3) and (4) means that they will be not be appropriate in the same range of contexts, but their truth or falsity will be the same in all contexts:

(3) Old Joshua Hobblethwaite popped his clogs last week.
(4) Old Joshua Hobblethwaite passed away last week.

On the other hand, the difference between (4) and (5) means that the range of contexts where one is true will not be the same as the range of contexts where the other is true.

(5) Old Joshua Hobblethwaite fell ill last week.

1.6.4 What happens when meanings combine?

Another vital aspect of semantics is how simple(r) meanings combine to form more complex meanings. To some extent this is a function of grammatical structure: for instance, the way *red* and *hat* combine in *a red hat* is not the same as the way *turn* and *red* combine in *to turn red*. But differences occur even within the same grammatical construction: the mode of combination of *red* and *hat* in *a red hat* is different from that of *long* and *eyelash* in *long eyelashes* (compare the way we interpret *long* in *long eyelashes* and in *a long river*).

1.6.5 Systematicity and structure; possibility of formalization

All semanticians are to some extent looking for regularities and system in the way meanings behave, as this leads to maximally economical descriptions. The most dedicated to this aspect of semantics are those who attempt to model the semantic behaviour of natural language expressions by means of a strict logical or quasi-mathematical formalism. This route will not be followed in this book.

1.6.6 New meanings from old

A striking feature of linguistic expressions is their semantic flexibility: beyond their normal contextual variability, they can be bent to semantic ends far removed from their conventional value, witness *She swallowed it hook, line, and sinker* or *You'll find her in the telephone book*. The study of such extensions of meaning is an important task for semantics.

1.6.7 Role(s) of context

It is usually assumed that linguistic expressions can be assigned some sort of context-independent semantic value, although there is much disagreement regarding exactly what this is. There is also general agreement that context is of vital importance in arriving at the meaning of an utterance. The role of context ranges from disambiguating ambiguous expressions as in *We just got to the bank in time*, through identification of referents (who is *he*, where is *there*, *in time* for what, in *He didn't get there in time*), to working out 'between the lines' messages like B's ignorance of the whereabouts of the corkscrew in:

(6) A: Where's the corkscrew?
B: It's either in the top drawer in the kitchen, or it's fallen behind the piano.

1.6.8 The approach adopted in this book

We are not yet in a position to rule out any approaches which yield insights, even if some such approaches appear at first sight incompatible. This book therefore takes an ecumenical position on many issues. In so far as there is a theoretical bias, it is towards the cognitive semantic position. This means, in particular, that the meaning of a linguistic expression is taken to arise from the fact that the latter gives access to a particular conceptual content. This may be of indeterminate extent: no distinction is made between linguistic meaning and encyclopedic knowledge.

Since this book is not intended to propound a body of theory, but to acquaint non-specialists with the range of semantic phenomena in language, there is a bias towards descriptive coverage at the expense of theoretical rigour.

1.7 Branches of the study of meaning

The following are the main broadly distinguishable areas of interest in the study of meaning. They do not by any means form watertight compartments: there are many points of overlap.

1.7.1 Lexical semantics

Lexical semantics studies the meanings of words; the focus here is on 'content' words like *tiger*, *daffodil*, *inconsiderate*, and *woo*, rather than 'form words'/ 'grammatical' words like *the*, *of*, *than*, and so on. To a non-specialist, the notion of meaning probably has a stronger link with the idea of the word than with any other linguistic unit: words are, after all, what are listed in dictionaries, and the main function of a dictionary is to tell us what the listed words mean. For this reason, lexical semantics perhaps provides the easiest access route into the mysteries of semantics in general, and this is one reason why it has been given a prominent place in this book, and why it comes early.

1.7.2 Grammatical semantics

Grammatical semantics studies aspects of meaning which have direct relevance to syntax. This has many manifestations, which can only be briefly illustrated here. One problem is the meaning of syntactic categories (problematic, because not everyone believes they can be assigned meanings). Consider, for instance, the differences in the meaning of yellow in the following:

(7) She wore a yellow hat. (adjective)
(8) They painted the room a glowing yellow. (noun)
(9) The leaves yellow rapidly once the frosts arrive. (verb)

Another aspect of grammatical semantics is the meaning of grammatical morphemes like the -ed of walked, the -er of longer, the re- and the -al of retrial, and so on.

Clearly this overlaps with lexical semantics, partly because some grammatical elements are words (like the, and of), but more particularly because some aspects of the meanings of full lexical items determine to some degree their grammatical behaviour (for instance, the fact that I am studying that question is grammatical, but not I am knowing the answer to that question).

1.7.3 Logical semantics

Logical semantics studies the relations between natural language and formal logical systems such as the propositional and predicate calculi. Such studies usually aim at modelling natural language as closely as possible using a tightly controlled, maximally austere logical formalism. It is arguable that sometimes such studies shed more light on the formalism used than on the language being modelled; nonetheless, valuable insights have come from this approach. To date, most such studies have concentrated on the propositional/sentential level of meaning, and have rarely attempted to delve into the meanings of words.

1.7.4 Linguistic pragmatics

For present purposes, pragmatics can be taken to be concerned with aspects of information (in the widest sense) conveyed through language which (a) are not encoded by generally accepted convention in the linguistic forms used, but which (b) nonetheless arise naturally out of and depend on the meanings conventionally encoded in the linguistic forms used, taken in conjunction with the context in which the forms are used. This rather cumbersome formulation is intended to allow into pragmatics things like the identity of the individual referred to by *John* in *I saw John today*, and the assumption that the room in question had several lights in *John entered the room; all the lights were on*, at the same time excluding, for instance, the possibility that the person saying *I saw John today* had a private ad hoc arrangement with the hearer that whenever he said *John*, he should be taken to mean "Mary" (since it does not arise naturally out of the normal meaning of *John*), and excluding also the possibility of someone's inferring from a speaker's slurred speech that they were drunk (since this does not depend on the conventional meanings of the words uttered). Pragmatics is usually contrasted with semantics, which therefore deals with conventionalized meaning; obviously, the three divisions discussed above belong to semantics.

Suggestions for further reading

Much fuller accounts of the semiotic environment of spoken language can be found in Argyle (1972), Beattie (1983), Ellis and Beattie (1986), and Clark (1996).

CHAPTER 2

Logical matters

Logical matters

2.1 Introduction

This chapter introduces a set of fundamental conceptual tools, mostly drawn from the field of logic, which, because of their wide currency in discussions of semantic matters, constitute indispensable background knowledge for a study of meaning in language. The level of treatment here is fairly elementary; some of the notions introduced will be refined in subsequent chapters.

2.2 Three levels of meaning

Before we can proceed any further, it is necessary to make a distinction between three 'levels' of meaning, which we shall label **sentence meaning, statement meaning**, and **utterance meaning**. At first sight these might seem to represent academic nitpicking of the worst sort. However, they are absolutely vital for clarity in semantics. For the sake of simplicity of exposition, the distinctions will first of all be explained in connection with declarative sentences only; how the various notions apply to non-declarative sentences will be dealt with later.

2.2.1 Sentence meaning

A sentence is a grammatical unit—that is, it is a string of words of a particular type, whose well-formedness conditions are specified in the grammar of the language. Thus, *The cat sat on the mat* and *John put his hat on the table* are sentences of English; *John put on the table* and *Is the of mother boy swim* are not. We shall not spend too much time on discussing what distinguishes a sentence from other grammatical units, such as a phrase, or a word, except to say that it is the smallest linguistic unit that can be used in an act of 'telling'. Compare the following for normality/oddness:

(1) A: Tell me something nice.
    B: Chocolate.

> A: What do you mean?
> B: Well, chocolate is nice.
>
> (2) A: Tell me something nice.
>   B: Love is a many-splendoured thing.
>   A: Ah! How true!

The oddness of B's reply in (1) consists in the fact that it neither overtly forms a sentence nor permits a plausible sentence to be reconstructed from the context, as in, for instance, (3):

> (3) A: He asked me what I wanted.
>   B: What did you tell him?
>   A: Chocolate.

Here, the full act of telling is reconstructible as *I want chocolate*, which involves a sentence. Henceforward we shall use our intuitions as to what constitutes a sentence.

Notice that we said above that the sentence was 'used in the act of telling': the sentence itself, on its own, does not in fact tell us anything. What does the sentence *The cat sat on the mat* tell us? Is it true? There is no way of knowing, or rather, the question does not make sense: sentences of themselves do not necessarily have truth values (some, arguably, have: *A molecule of water contains two hydrogen atoms and one oxygen atom*). Yet presumably no one would wish to say that *The cat sat on the mat* was meaningless. Let us introduce the notion **sentence meaning** to designate the semantic properties a sentence possesses merely by virtue of being a well-formed sentence, before any question of context or use arises. A sentence possesses this meaning exclusively by virtue of its linguistic make-up, principally, the words it contains, and their grammatical arrangement. (I assume, here, that words have at least some context-independent conventionally assigned semantic properties.) We may assume that the grammar of a language is associated with principles of composition, that is, rules which tell us how to put together the meanings of the constituents of a construction to get the global meaning of the construction. Thus, in *The big cat sat on the small mat* we know, for instance, that *small* relates to *the mat* and not to *the cat*; we know, furthermore, what sort of animal is involved, and that only one of them would be intended as a referent in any actual use of the sentence. And so on. In a fairly obvious sense, the meaning of a sentence will constrain the uses to which it can be put, at least without the setting up of additional ad hoc conventions.

Although a sentence, outside of particular uses, does not have a **truth-value** (that is, it cannot be evaluated as true or false), it does have **truth conditions**, that is, conditions which must hold for the sentence to be used to make a true statement (at least if it is used literally). Thus, before we can truthfully say, on some occasion, *The cat is on the mat*, there must be some relevant feline occupying a specific position relative to an appropriate item of floor covering.

Those aspects of the meaning of a sentence which determine its truth conditions are collectively known as the **propositional content** of the sentence. Two sentences with identical propositional content will yield statements with the same truth values on all occasions of use, as for instance: *John caressed Mary* and *Mary was caressed by John*. By the same token, if two sentences have different propositional content, there will necessarily exist some conceivable situation in which they will yield statements with opposite truth values.

Propositional content does not by any means make up the whole of sentence meaning, as conceived here. For instance, the interrogative meaning of a question is not included, nor the imperative meaning of a command. The force of such words as *yet*, *still*, and *already* is excluded; the following two sentences, for instance, have the same propositional content, since their truth conditions are the same, but one would not want to say that they were identical in meaning (nor are they appropriate in the same circumstances):

(4) John has not arrived.
(5) John has not yet arrived.

Other aspects of meaning which do not fall under propositional content are expressive meaning:

(6) It's very cold in here.
(7) It's bloody cold in here.

and features of register such as the formal/colloquial distinction:

(8) My old man kicked the bucket yesterday.
(9) My father passed away yesterday.

To qualify as part of sentence meaning, a semantic property simply has to be a stable conventional property of some linguistic expression.

2.2.2 Statement meaning

Someone who makes a **statement** uses a (declarative) sentence to assert that some state of affairs (in the most general sense) holds. A statement has a truth-value, so its veracity can be challenged:

(10) A: I saw you with John yesterday.
     B: No, you didn't.

One does not make a statement simply by producing a sentence of declarative form. Someone in a language class, for instance, practising the tenses of English, who says:

The cat sat on the mat.
The cat sits on the mat.
The cat will sit on the mat.

is not making a series of statements, though they are producing a series of sentences. It would not make sense to reply to *The cat sat on the mat* with *No, it didn't*. We shall use the term **statement meaning** to refer to the combination of assertion and what is asserted in the literal, contextualized use of a declarative sentence.

2.2.3 Utterance meaning

An **utterance** will be taken here to be what is produced in an act of linguistic communication, together with its intended meaning. Even a fully elaborated statement meaning may not adequately represent everything the speaker intended to convey by uttering the sentence to which it applies. To take a very simple example, consider the following:

(11) A: Have you cleared the table and washed the dishes?
       B: I've cleared the table.

In normal circumstances, it would clearly be part of B's intended message that s/he had not washed the dishes. Yet this is not the standard meaning of B's words, and cannot be regarded as part of statement meaning. This is even clearer in the following case, where it is obviously the speaker's intention to indicate that A is too late for supper:

(12) A: Am I in time for supper?
       B: I've cleared the table.

These extra aspects of meaning, which are not part of either sentence meaning, or statement meaning are expected to be inferred by the hearer on the basis of contextual information. We shall give the name **utterance meaning** to the totality of what the speaker intends to convey by making an utterance.

In the above cases, utterance meaning subsumes statement meaning, but this is generally the case only for expressions used literally. What a speaker would most likely intend to convey by *Your eyes are deep pools* would not include statement meaning.

2.3 Propositions

Statement meaning was presented above as having two parts—an element of assertion, and something that is asserted. What is asserted, i.e. presented as being true, is called a **proposition**. A proposition is not a specifically linguistic entity (although we shall not dwell too long on the problem of what sort of entity it is, and in what Platonic or other realm it subsists). The same proposition may be expressed by an indefinitely large number of sentences:

John saw Mary.
John saw his sister.

Mary was seen by Peter's uncle.
(etc.)

These can all express the same proposition, provided of course that Mary is John's sister, that John is Peter's uncle, and so on. Propositions have the essential property of being either true or false, and can be asserted, denied, doubted, questioned, believed, inferred, and so on.

A declarative sentence does not express a proposition simply by virtue of being a declarative sentence. For instance, the sentence *The cat sat on the mat* does not, out of context, express a proposition. However, if it is used to make a statement, then it does express a proposition:

(13) A: What did the animals do after you fed them?
     B: Well, the cat sat on the mat.

Here, a particular cat and a particular mat are referred to, and the statement is either true or false. The same proposition could have been expressed by (say) *Kitty sat over there*.

A proposition may be 'entertained', without any stance being adopted towards its truth or falsehood, as for instance in a logic class, where propositions are entertained and their interrelationships studied, as in:

(14) All university lecturers are clairvoyant.
     Alan Cruse is a university lecturer.
     Hence, Alan Cruse is clairvoyant.

However, a proposition on its own cannot actually communicate anything: it is not an item of knowledge. To communicate, it must be accompanied by some indication of its truth or falsehood. For instance, the proposition expressed by *The earth is a polyhedron* tells us nothing unless we know whether it is true or false: a proposition known to be true or false is an item of knowledge. A (minimum) statement is a proposition uttered, as the influential British linguist John (now 'Sir John') Lyons puts it, 'with epistemic commitment', that is, presented as being true. (NB: one frequently encounters references to, for instance, *the proposition "The earth is a polyhedron"*. It is important to bear in mind that this is a kind of shorthand for *the proposition expressed by "The earth is a polyhedron"*. A proposition is not a piece of language, but it can become very cumbersome if this is spelled out on every occasion.)

2.4 Arguments and predicates

So far, we have ignored the internal structure of propositions. It is now time to look 'inside' them. The simplest type of proposition consists of two elements, an **argument** and a **predicate**. Put simply, the argument is what the proposition is 'about', and the predicate is what is attributed to the argument. Take the proposition expressed by *John is tall*, where *John* designates a definite individual. This proposition has two parts: the individual designated by *John*, which functions as argument, and the property designated by *is tall*, which functions as predicate. A simple proposition has only one predicate, but may have more than one argument. So, for example, in the proposition *John likes Mary* (to adopt the shorthand convention), the predicate is *likes*, and *John* and *Mary* are arguments; in the proposition *John gave Mary a rose*, *John*, *Mary* and *a rose* are arguments, and *gave* is the predicate. At this point, a distinction must be introduced between a **syntactic** argument and a **logical** argument. Our concern here is with the latter type. Take the sentence *John gave Mary a necklace*. One way of describing this is to say that *John*, *Mary*, and *a necklace* are arguments of the verb *gave*. But that is a description of a **sentence**, not of a **proposition**. Of course, that sentence could be used to express a proposition with three logical arguments:

(**15**) A: What was that argument about?
         B: John gave Mary a necklace.

It is not clear whether there is any theoretical upper limit to the number of arguments a predicate may take, but the most one is likely to encounter in linguistic semantic discussions is four, exemplified by *Mary paid John £500 for the car*:

Arguments: Mary, John, £500, the car
Predicate: paid (for)

Predicates are commonly described as **one-place, two-place, three-place**, etc. according to the number of arguments they take, so that, for instance, *is poor* is a one-place predicate (*John is poor*), and *teach* is a three-place predicate (*John taught Mary French*). But what does it mean to say that *teach* is a three-place predicate? How do we determine how many places a predicate has? This is in fact a very difficult question, with different possible answers, and we shall not spend too much time on it. One aspect of the problem is immediately obvious when we look at examples such as the following:

(**16**) John teaches Mary French.
(**17**) John teaches French.
(**18**) A: What does John do?
         B: I think he teaches at Lowhampton High.
(**19**) Anybody who teaches teenagers should get double salary.

Do we say that *teach* is three-place in (16), two-place in (17) and (19), and one-place in (18)? While there is some justification for such an analysis, there is intuitively a sense in which the (overt) argument structure of (16) is basic, and irreducible. Logically, for an act of teaching to take place, there must be someone who does the teaching, someone who undergoes the teaching (whether or not they actually learn anything!), and some item of knowledge or skill which it is hoped will be acquired by the latter. Without at least one each of these requirements, the notion of teaching, it might be argued, is not logically coherent. What, then, are we to make of (17) and (19) above? One possibility is to assume a discrepancy between syntactic arguments and logical arguments. Take B's utterance in (18). We could say that the sentence B utters has only one argument, but the proposition he expresses has three, and would be incomplete with any fewer. The 'missing' arguments, present in the proposition expressed, but with no syntactic counterparts, might be *some academic subject* and *pupils at Lowhampton High*. Or perhaps the proposition expressed by B in (18) is not a complete one, but has 'empty slots' to represent the missing arguments. Another possibility would be to say that the logical predicate *teach* in (16) is not the same as the predicate *teach* in (18), the latter requiring only one argument. Notice that if we allow the proposition expressed by a sentence to have more logical arguments than the sentence has syntactic arguments, the problem arises of how to prevent an avalanche of arguments. Acts of reading, teaching, and selling and sneezing take place at particular times and particular places. We may say that unlocated, timeless acts of reading, etc., are logically impossible. It is also necessarily the case that the ambient temperature has such and such a value. Why don't we incorporate these items (and many others) into the propositions expressed, or at least provide slots for them? Intuitively, this would not be correct: there seems to be a maximum number of 'true' arguments. These are interesting problems, but no attempt will be made to solve them here—for present purposes, intuition will suffice.

2.5 Non-declaratives

So far, we have looked only at declarative sentences and their employment in making statements. However, the notions elaborated above apply equally to non-declarative sentences. Take the case of a question. The general notion of sentence meaning is probably unproblematic here. However, in place of statement meaning there will be something fulfilling a parallel role which we can call **question meaning**, which includes both the 'asking' feature and what is asked, which crucially involves a proposition (for more details, see Chapter 17). Any statement made in reply to the question, in addition to having a truth-value, will have something we can call an **answer-value**, according to whether it counts as an answer to the question or not. Recall that the propositional content of a declarative sentence determines what statements it can be used to make, and whether such a statement is true or false in a given situation. Interrogative sentences also have propositional content. The propositional content of an interrogative sentence determines what questions it can be used to make, and hence the answer-values of replies:

(20) A: What day is it today? (said on Tuesday)
        B: It's Monday today. (valid answer, but false)
(21) A: What day is it today? (said on Monday)
        B: It's Monday today. (valid answer, true)
(22) A: Who do you love best?
        B: It's Monday today. (invalid answer)

The same trick can be played with imperatives, involving the notion of **command meaning**. A linguistic response is not always, perhaps not usually, what an imperative sets out to elicit. Generally what is required is an action (in the broadest sense, which covers such cases as *Don't move!*). Actions in response to a command can be judged according to their **compliance-value** with respect to the command (a command can be thought of as involving a proposition representing a desirable state of affairs). Notice that imperative *sentences* do not have command meaning (although they do have propositional content): *Put it there* is an imperative sentence, but it only acquires a command meaning when used in context.

Let us now try to generalize over statements, questions, and commands (regarded not as types of sentence, but as types of language-in-action). These can all be described as types of **illocution** (see Chapter 17 for more extensive discussion). Each instance of an illocution has an **illocution meaning**, which in turn has a proposition component and an **illocutionary** component, such as asserting, questioning, or commanding. Declarative sentences, in general, do not in themselves make statements, interrogative sentences do not ask questions, and imperative sentences do not issue commands. Each of these, however, has propositional content, which governs what illocutions it can be used to perform when properly contextualized, that is, which statements can be made, questions asked, commands issued, etc.

2.6 Sense, denotation, and reference: intension and extension

Language is used to communicate about things, happenings, and states of affairs in the world, and one way of approaching the study of meaning is to attempt to correlate expressions in language with aspects of the world. This is known as the **extensional** approach to meaning.

The thing or things in the world referred to by a particular expression is its referent(s): in saying *The cat's hungry*, I am (normally) referring to a particular cat, and that cat is the referent of the expression the *cat*. The whole utterance attributes a particular state to the cat in question. We can also consider the whole class of potential referents of the word *cat*, namely, the class of cats. This, too, is sometimes called the reference of the word *cat*. But this is clearly different from the designation of particular individuals as in the case of *The cat's hungry*; so, to avoid confusion, we shall follow Lyons and say that the class of cats constitutes the **denotation** of the word *cat*. So, in the case of *The cat's hungry*, the word *cat* denotes the class of cats, but the noun phrase *the cat* refers to a particular cat.

The alternative to an extensional approach to meaning is an **intensional** approach. Take the word *cat*, again. Why do we use it to refer to cats rather than, say, to platypuses or aardvarks or spiny anteaters? One answer is that the word is associated with some kind of mental representation of the type of thing that it can be used to refer to, and aardvarks do not fit the description associated with the word *cat*. This representation constitutes what is called the **sense** of the word (or at least part of it). We shall assume in this book that the main function of linguistic expressions is to mobilize concepts, that concepts are the main constituents of sense, and that sense (and hence concepts) constrains (even if it does not completely determine) reference. (It should be noted that some authors, for instance Lyons, understand sense in a different way. For them, sense is a matter of the relations between a word and other words in a language. So, for instance, the sense of *cat* would be constituted by its relations with other words such as *dog* (a cat is necessarily not a dog), *animal* (a cat is an animal), *miaow* (*The cat miaowed* is normal but *?The dog miaowed* is not).)

2.7 Logical relations between propositions

2.7.1 Entailment

Entailment is the relation which holds between the P and the corresponding Q items in the following:

P	Q
It's a dog.	It's an animal.
John killed the wasp.	The wasp died.
All dogs are purple.	My dog is purple.

Notice that we are assuming that these sentences express propositions; that is to say, the sentences are being used in a particular context with particular reference. We are further assuming that in the first pair *it* refers to the same entity in each case, and in the second pair, the same wasp and the same event are being referred to. To say that proposition P entails proposition Q means that the truth of Q follows logically and inescapably from the truth of P, and the falsity of P follows likewise from the falsity of Q. So, in the first pair of sentences above, if it is true of some entity that it is a dog, then it follows ineluctably that it is an animal, and if it is not an animal, then there is no way it can be a dog. Similarly, in the second pair, if John killed some wasp, then we cannot avoid the conclusion that the wasp died, and if the wasp did not die, then it cannot be the case that John killed it.

Entailment, as used by linguistic semanticists, is to be distinguished from

what logicians call **material implication**. A proposition P materially implies
another proposition Q if and only if (henceforward iff) it is never the case that
P is true and Q false. At first sight this seems to be essentially the same as
entailment. However, there is a crucial difference: the definition of material
implication makes no reference to the meanings of the propositions, merely to
a relation between their truth values; entailment, on the other hand, (sometimes called **strict implication** or **semantic implication**) is essentially a relation
between meanings. To illustrate this point, consider the propositions *It's a dog*
and *All bachelors are unmarried*. It can never be the case that the first is true
while the second is false, so we have a case of material implication. But this is
not entailment, because it is a consequence not of the meaning relations
between the two propositions, but of the fact that the second proposition
cannot under any circumstances (except by altering the meanings of the components) be false. On the other hand, although it is true that *It's a dog* materially implies *It's an animal*, because the former cannot be true while the latter is
false, it is also the case that the former entails the latter, because the truth-
value relation holds by virtue of the relation in meaning between *dog* and
animal. Material implication is essentially of no interest to linguistic semantics, although the status of *All bachelors are unmarried* as being always true is
of interest (see 2.8.4 below).

Two other properties of entailment must be emphasized. The first is that the
relation is not determined by context: it is context-independent, since it
depends entirely on the meanings of the constituent terms in the propositions.
Consider a case where John has in front of him a box of coloured shapes, in
which all the red shapes are round and all the green shapes are square. In such
circumstances, the truth of *John picked a square shape from the box* follows
inescapably from the truth of *John picked a green shape from the box*. But
clearly this relation of truth values does not arise from relations between *green*
and *square*, but from the context: it would in principle have been just as easy to
have all the red shapes square and the green shapes round. On the other hand,
the relation between *It's a dog* and *It's an animal* is independent of any
particular contexts.

The second property is that the truth of the entailed sentence must follow
inescapably from the truth of the entailing sentence. It is not enough for it to
be usually true, or even almost always true; it has to be unthinkable that it
might be false. Consider the relation between *It's a dog* and (i) *It's a pet* and (ii)
It can bark. Most dogs that most people encounter are pets, but there are
such things as wild dogs, so the relationship is merely one of expectation. This
is not entailment. Likewise in the case of (ii), most dogs can bark, but a dog
with a defective larynx does not thereby cease to be a dog, so the relationship
is not logically necessary. Only logically necessary, context-independent
relationships count as entailment.

2.7.2 Contrariety

Propositions P and Q are **contraries** iff the truth of one entails the falsity of the other, but the falsity of one does not entail the truth of the other. In other words, they may not be simultaneously true, although they may be simultaneously false. The following are examples:

P	Q
John killed the wasp.	The wasp is alive.
John killed the wasp.	Mary killed the wasp.
This paint is red.	This paint is green.

It cannot be simultaneously true of some wasp both that John killed it and that it is still alive; on the other hand, if the wasp is actually dead, but it was Bill who killed it, then both *John killed the wasp* and *The wasp is alive* are false.

2.7.3 Contradiction

Propositions P and Q are **contradictories** iff the truth of either one entails the falsity of the other, and the falsity of one entails the truth of the other. In other words, one of the pair must be true. The following exemplify contradictory pairs:

P	Q
The wasp is dead.	The wasp is alive.
John is still singing.	John is no longer singing.
No dogs are brown.	At least some dogs are brown.

If John is still singing, then it is false that he is no longer singing; to this extent, this is like contrariety. However, there is a crucial difference: if it is false that John is still singing, then it must be the case that he is no longer singing, and if it is false that he is no longer singing, then he must be still singing.

2.7.4 Independence

Propositions P and Q can be said to be **independent** iff their truth-values are unrelated:

P	Q
John is retired.	Mary is married.
It is Tuesday today.	It is my birthday.

The relations described in this section have an important role in the analysis of meaning relations between words, as we shall see in later chapters.

2.8 Logical relations between sentences

Most discussions in semantics are conducted in terms not of relations between propositions but of relations between sentences. Although, strictly speaking, relations between propositions are primary, they can be used to define relations between sentences.

2.8.1 Entailment

One frequently encounters in semantic texts statements to the effect that such-and-such a sentence entails some other sentence. This can be taken as a kind of shorthand for something slightly more complex. Saying that sentence S_1 entails sentence S_2 means that in any context where S_1 expresses a true proposition, S_2 also necessarily expresses a true proposition, provided that corresponding definite referring expressions in the two sentences are co-referential. Obviously, in the case of *It's a dog* and *It's an animal*, the two occurrences of *it* must refer to the same entity for the logical relation to hold, and in the case of *John killed the wasp* and *The wasp died*, we must be talking about the same John, the same wasp, and the time references must be the same.

2.8.2 Equivalence

Propositional **equivalence** between two sentences means that in any context, the propositions they express will have the same truth-value (provided, of course, that corresponding definite referring expressions are co-referential). The following are examples of logical equivalence between sentences:

S_1	S_2
John killed the wasp.	The wasp was killed by John.
The wasp is dead.	The wasp is not alive.
It began at 10 o'clock.	It commenced at 10 o'clock.

On every occasion that *John killed the wasp* expresses a true proposition, *The wasp was killed by John* also expresses a true proposition, and vice versa; and on every occasion that *John killed the wasp* expresses a false proposition, *The wasp was killed by John* also expresses a false proposition, and vice versa. A parallel two-way entailment holds between the members of the other two pairs.

2.8.3 Contrariety, contradiction, and independence

Sentential relations of contrariety, contradiction, and independence can be derived from the appropriate relations between propositions in a parallel way to that illustrated above for entailment.

2.8.4 Analytic, paradoxical, and synthetic sentences

2.8.4.1 Analyticity

Analytic sentences are sentences which automatically express true propositions in any context, by virtue of the meanings of their constituent words and their arrangement. The following sentences are therefore analytic

Bachelors are unmarried.
John's uncle is a man.
This proposition is either true or false.

2.8.4.2 Paradox

Paradoxical sentences automatically express false propositions:

Bachelors are married.
John's sister is a man.
This red paint is green.

2.8.4.3 Syntheticity

Synthetic sentences are those which express true propositions in some (conceivable) contexts (although they may be false of the world as we know it) and false ones in others (this is the normal kind of sentence used in communication):

John's sister is married.
This paint is green.
All dogs are brown.

(The last sentence actually expresses a false proposition, but it is not automatically false; it is easy to imagine circumstances in which it would be true.)

2.9 Logical classes

2.9.1 Class relations

2.9.1.1 Identity

Two classes C_1 and C_2 are said to be **identical**, or **equivalent**, iff everything that belongs to C_1 also belongs to C_2, and vice versa. Thus, the class of fathers and the class of male parents are identical, as are the class of pairs of spectacles and the class of pairs of glasses (on the relevant interpretation of glasses).

2.9.1.2 Inclusion

Class C_1 is said to **include** class C_2 if everything that is a member of C_2 is also a member of C_1, but not vice versa. Thus, for instance, the class of animals includes the class of dogs, the class of aardvarks, etc. The class of dogs is described as a **sub-class** of the class of animals, and the class of animals as a **superclass** of the class of dogs. (Inclusion is defined here so as to exclude identity; it can be defined so as to include identity.)

2.9.1.3 Disjunction

Classes C_1 and C_2 are said to be **disjunct** if no member of C_1 is also a member of C_2. The class of cats and the class of aardvarks are disjunct in this sense, as are the class of red things and the class of green things.

2.9.1.4 Intersection

Classes C_1 and C_2 are said to **intersect** if they have some members in common, but each has members which do not belong to the other (i.e. complete intersection, or identity, is excluded here). The class of red things and the class of round things intersect in this fashion, as do the class of architects and the class of amateur musicians. The set of common members to two (or more) overlapping classes is often referred to as the **intersection** of the two (or more) classes.

2.9.1.5 Union

The combined set of members belonging to either of two (or more) classes (including overlapping classes) is called the **union** of the two (or more) classes. Thus the union of the class of dogs and the class of cats is constituted by the class of all entities which are either cats or dogs.

2.9.2 Class relations and propositional relations

There are obvious connections between the class relations described above and the propositional relations described earlier. For instance, the fact that *It's a dog* entails *It's an animal* is straightforwardly related to the fact that the class of dogs is a sub-class of the class of animals. Similarly, the fact that *It's a dog* entails *It's not a cat* is clearly related to the fact that the class of dogs and the class of cats are disjunct.

2.9.3 Mapping

It sometimes happens that the members of one class have a relation of correspondence of some kind with one or more members of a parallel class. This type of correspondence is known as **mapping**. An example will make this clear. It is a well-known fact that a person's fingerprints are uniquely distinctive. If, therefore, we think of the class of persons and the class of fingerprints, there is a straightforward mapping relation between the two classes, in that each member of one class corresponds to a specific member of the other set. This is known as **one-to-one mapping**. Contrast this situation with the two classes FATHERS and CHILDREN. Every member of the FATHERS class corresponds to one or more members of the CHILDREN class, but every member of the CHILDREN class corresponds to a single specific member of the FATHERS class. Here we have **one-to-many mapping** between fathers and children, but **many-to-one mapping** between children and fathers. Yet another elementary mapping relation holds between the class of word forms and the class of meanings. If we allow the possibility of synonymy, then some word forms (e.g. perhaps *begin* and *commence*) will map onto the same meaning, whereas other word forms (e.g. *bank*) will map on to more than one meaning. This is known as **many-to-many mapping**.

2.10 Properties of logical relations

Another useful set of concepts borrowed from logic are to do with relations between individual entities. The entities may be anything at all: objects, people, places, ideas. So can the relations be anything: "brother of", "smaller than", "has played string quartets with", "logically depends on". The logical properties of such relations can be grouped under four headings: **transitivity, symmetry, reflexivity**, and **converseness**.

2.10.1 Transitivity

A relation that is **transitive** is one such that if A is related in this specific way to B and B to C, then it follows inescapably that A stands in the relation to C. Suppose A, B, and C are people, and the relation is "is taller than". Then if A is taller than B and B is taller than C, then A is necessarily taller than C. If a relation is **intransitive**, then if A stands in the relation to B and B to C, then it is logically impossible for A to stand in the relation to C. This is the case with "is the mother of": if A is the mother of B and B the mother of C, then A cannot be the mother of C. A relation may be neither transitive nor intransitive; we shall call such a relation **non-transitive**. If John has played duets with Bill, and Bill has played duets with Tom, then we are not in a position to conclude anything regarding John's musical relations with Tom.

2.10.2 Symmetry

A **symmetric** relation is one such that if A stands in a particular relation to B, then B necessarily stands in that same relation to A. For instance, if A is near to B, then B is near to A. If a relation is **asymmetric**, then if A stands in the relation to B, B cannot stand in the same relation to A. An example of an asymmetric relation is "is taller than". Once again, it is useful to have a designation for relations that are neither symmetric nor asymmetric, such as "is sexually attracted by"; we shall label these **non-symmetric**.

2.10.3 Reflexivity

The property of reflexivity is not of great usefulness in semantic analysis: it is included for the sake of completeness. A relation is **reflexive** if something necessarily stands in that relation to itself. This includes most types of identity relation such as "has the same name as" or "is the same age as". Again, we can recognize **irreflexive** relations like "is taller than", and **non-reflexive** relations such as "knows the weight of".

2.10.4 Converseness

Converseness is a relation between relations. Two relations are converses if one yields the same proposition as the other when the arguments are reversed. By this criterion, "above" and "below" are converses (perhaps more strictly "is above" and "is below"), because *A is below B*, assuming constancy of A and B, expresses the same proposition as *B is above A*. Other examples of (sentences expressing) converse relations are: *A is B's offspring/B is A's parent, A saw B/B was seen by A, A sold B to C/C bought B from A* (it is usual to disregard 'automatic' adjustments in grammatical realization, such as the change from *to* to *from* in the case of *buy* and *sell*). We have defined converseness in terms of two-way entailment between two sentences (e.g. *A is taller than B* and *B is shorter than A*). It is useful to have a relation defined on a one-way entailment. For instance, *A is B's doctor* entails *B is A's patient*, but the reverse entailment does not hold because other practitioners in the medical and paramedical field, such as dentists and speech therapists, also have patients. We shall say that *doctor* is a **semi-converse** of *patient*.

2.11 Quantification

2.11.1 Quantifiers

In standard first-order predicate calculus, propositional functions are constrained by **quantifiers**: these in effect limit the applicability of the predicate to the argument(s). Classical logic only has two quantifiers, the **existential quantifier** and the **universal quantifier**. The existential quantifier says something like this:

There exists at least one 'x' such that 'x sneezed'.

This is typically expressed in logical notation as:

$\exists x \, (sneezed \, (x))$.

This could be roughly translated as *Someone sneezed. A man sneezed* would go into this special logical language as:

There exists at least one individual x such that x is a man and x sneezed.
$\exists x \, (sneezed \, (x) \, \textbf{\&} \, man \, (x))$.

The universal quantifier corresponds roughly to the ordinary language *all*, *every*. Thus *All dogs are animals* would translate as:

For all x, *x is a dog* entails *x is an animal*.
$\forall x \, (dog \, (x) \rightarrow animal \, (x))$.

2.11.2 Scope

In the sentence *Mary ruffled John's hair and kissed him again* we do not know without further contextual evidence, whether it was only Mary's kissing of John that was repeated, or the double action of ruffling the hair and kissing. This is an ambiguity of **scope**: we do not know how much of the previous sentence is included in the range of applicability of *again*. The term *scope* is usually used in connection with quantifiers: *again* is a kind of quantifier over events. An example involving a more traditional quantifier is: *Some women and foreigners must register with the police*. Here we are uncertain whether only some foreigners should register, or whether they all should (which would be the most natural interpretation of *Foreigners must register*). Reversing the order of constituents would remove the ambiguity: *Foreigners and some women must register*. The possibilities for variations of scope of this sort are tightly constrained by syntactic structure. (For a more detailed discussion of quantification, see Chapter 15, section 15.6.)

2.12 Use and mention

Consider the difference between (23) and (24):

(23) Snow has four letters.
       Snow is a noun.
       Snow is a natural kind term.
       Snow is an English word.
       Snow is easy to pronounce.
(24) Snow is white.
       Snow damages crops.
       Snow is frozen water.

The difference between these two sets is usually designated as a difference between **use** (here, of the word *snow*), as in (24), and **mention** (of the word *snow*), as in (23). In the sentences in (23) we are using the word form *snow* to identify a word of the language, and we then proceed to say something about that word; in the sentences in (24) we are using the word form to identify a substance in the world, prior to predicating something of it. A simple way of distinguishing the two is to enclose the language unit in question within inverted commas. If this makes a negligible effect on the meaning, then it is a case of mention:

'*Snow*' has four letters.
'*Snow*' is an English word.
*'*Snow*' is white.
*'*Snow*' damages crops.

Mention may involve any stretch of language:

'*Go to home*' is ungrammatical.
*Go to home is ungrammatical.

This brings us to the end of our brief survey of useful logical notions, and provides an elementary toolkit which will be drawn upon, and sometimes further refined, as and when the occasion demands.

Discussion questions and exercises

1. Considering the following as logical predicates, mark them as one-, two-, three-, or four-place (1, 2, 3, 4) (think in terms of the intuitive maximum number of arguments):

   yawn   steal   thank   pay   be tall   be taller than   meet   put   imagine daydream   cost   understand   explain

2. Sentence, statement, utterance, and proposition

In the light of the definitions given in this chapter, of which of the above can the following be said? Assume we are talking about declaratives, and that statements and utterances inherit the properties of entities they embody.

X was inaudible.
X was uninformative.
X was false.
X was in a foreign accent.
X was ungrammatical.
X was insincere.

3. In which of the following pairs of sentences do the members, on their most likely interpretation, have the same propositional content? Look for situations where they would make different statements, ask different questions, or issue different commands:

   (a) (i) Take your hands off me! (said by a woman to a man)
        (ii) Take your filthy paws off me! (ditto)
   (b) (i) I always get my bread from Gregg's, because it's cheaper.
        (ii) I always buy my bread from Gregg's, because it's cheaper.
   (c) (i) Don't you find him rather skinny?
        (ii) Don't you find him rather thin?

(d) (i) Have you read the stuff he wrote about telepathy?
(ii) Have you read the garbage he wrote about telepathy?
(e) (i) She was there at the start of the race.
(ii) She was there at the beginning of the race.
(f) (i) John hasn't turned up.
(ii) John hasn't turned up yet.
(g) (i) Old Joshua Hobblethwaite died last week.
(ii) Old Joshua Hobblethwaite passed away last week.

4. In which of the following does the (i)-sentence entail the (ii)-sentence? Are there any problems?

(a) (i) X is a cat.
(ii) X has four legs.
(b) (i) X is a cat.
(ii) X is an animal.
(c) (i) X is a cat.
(ii) X is a quadruped.
(d) (i) X is a quadruped.
(ii) X has four legs.
(e) (a) X is a quadruped.
(ii) X is an animal.
(f) (i) X is a pet.
(ii) X is an animal.

(g) (i) X is a pet.
(ii) X is alive.
(h) (i) X is not dead.
(ii) X is alive.
(i) (i) X has stopped smoking.
(ii) X doesn't smoke any more.
(j) (i) X taught Y Z.
(ii) Y learnt Z.
(k) (i) X killed Y.
(ii) Y is not alive.
(l) (i) X watched Y.
(ii) Y was doing something.

5. Mark the relationship between the members of the following pairs of sentences as either (logical) EQUIVALENCE, CONTRARIETY, CONTRADICTION, OR CONVERSENESS:

(a) (i) Proposition P is true.
(ii) Proposition P is false
(b) (i) John likes Mary.
(ii) John dislikes Mary.
(c) (i) Mary agrees with the statement.
(ii) Mary disagrees with the statement.
(d) (i) Mary borrowed the book from John.
(ii) John lent the book to Mary.
(e) (i) John killed the wasp.
(ii) The wasp is still alive.
(f) (i) John is not married.
(ii) John is a bachelor.

6. Classify the following relations with regard to their TRANSITIVITY (i.e. as TRANSITIVE, INTRANSITIVE, or NON-TRANSITIVE) and their SYMMETRY (i.e. as SYMMETRIC, ASYMMETRIC, or NON-SYMMETRIC):

parent of   ancestor of   brother of   related to   sibling of   friend of   near to   to the right of   far from   resembles

Suggestions for further reading

The treatment here has been very informal. A similar elementary treatment, but with more practical exercises, will be found in Hurford and Heasley (1983). Lyons (1995) develops the philosophical background more fully, but still at an elementary level. Those requiring initiation into logical formalization will find an accessible introduction in Allwood et al. (1977). Lyons (1977) gives a more detailed treatment of many of the topics touched on here. There is some discussion of the problem of the number of arguments in Kearns (2000: ch. 8). Cann (1993), McCawley (1981), and Larson and Segal (1995) are only for those who are really serious about the application of logic to language.

CHAPTER 3

Types and dimensions of meaning

Types and dimensions of meaning

3.1 Introduction

The purpose of the present chapter is to survey (albeit somewhat superficially) the range of possible varieties of meaning in language. Before we can do this, we need some idea of what is to count as meaning. There are many different opinions on this question, but the matter will not be argued in detail here, since many of the divergent views are simply a question of terminology—one is, to some extent at least, free to stipulate what is to count. In this book a broad characterization of meaning will be adopted: meaning is anything that affects the relative normality of grammatical expressions. This is an example of a **contextual** approach to meaning, because relative normality is a concept which applies only to combinations of elements; that is to say, it implies that meaning is to be studied by observing the interactions between elements and other elements, in larger constructions such as sentences. It follows from this characterization that if two expressions differ in meaning, this will show up in the fact that a context can be found in which they differ in normality; conversely, two expressions with the same meaning will have the same normality in all contexts. So, for instance, we know that *dog* and cat differ in meaning (to take a crudely obvious case) because (for example) *Our cat has had kittens* is more normal than *?Our dog has just had kittens*. Likewise, we know that *pullover* and *sweater* are at least very close in meaning, because of the difficulty in finding contexts in which they differ in normality (for further discussion of synonymy, see Chapter 8). (Note that 'mention' contexts, such as *Pullover/ ?Sweater has eight letters*, do not count.) It also follows from the characterization adopted here that the **normality profile** of a linguistic item, that is to say its pattern of normality and abnormality across the full range of possible contexts, gives in some sense a picture of its meaning. It does not, however, tell us what meaning *really is*. This is a deep and controversial question; it will be generally assumed in this book that meaning is in essence conceptual (see Chapter 6), but is most easily studied through language.

3.1.1 Semantic anomaly versus grammatical anomaly

For the characterization of meaning given above to work, we need to be able to separate semantic anomaly from grammatical anomaly. This is another contentious issue, but I believe it is possible to get some grip on it. The account given here largely follows that given in Cruse (1986).

The most commonly encountered criterion for separating the two types of anomaly is **corrigibility**: it is claimed that grammatical anomalies are typically corrigible in the sense that it is obvious what the 'correct' version should be, whereas semantic anomalies are typically not corrigible. Thus, *Me seed two mouses* can easily be corrected to *I saw two mice*, whereas there is no obvious way of amending *The noiseless typewriter-blasts squirmed faithfully*. However, while this may be generally true, it is not difficult to find easily corrigible anomalies which intuitively are clearly semantic: *This hole is too large for John to crawl through*.

There is a basic drawback with the notion of corrigibility, which is that it is presupposed that one knows what was originally intended. A better approach is to ask what is the minimum change to the sentence (or whatever) that will remove the anomaly. There are three possibilities (assuming that the anomaly has a single source):

(i) The anomaly can only be cured by replacing one (or more) of the full lexical elements (i.e. a noun, verb, adjective, or adverb). In this case we can be reasonably certain that we are dealing with a semantic anomaly:

(1) John is too   *small to get through this hole.
         √big

(ii) The anomaly can only be cured by changing one or more grammatical elements (affixes, particles, determiners, etc.), but not by changing a full lexical item. In this case we can be sure that the anomaly is grammatical:

(2) Mary   *be going home.
         √is

(iii) The anomaly can be cured either by grammatical or by lexical adjustment. In this case we need to know whether the lexical possibilities form a natural semantic class or not: if they do, the anomaly can be taken as semantic. Compare (3) and (4):

(3) *Mary went home tomorrow./√Mary will go home tomorrow.
         (grammatical adjustment)
     Mary went home   *tomorrow.
                  √yesterday
                  √last week.
                  (etc.)
     (lexical adjustment)

Here, the items which remove the anomaly share a component of meaning, namely, an indication of past time.

(4) *Le livre est sur le table./√Le livre est sur la table.
    (grammatical adjustment)
  Le livre est sur le   *table.
                          √fauteuil.
                          √plancher.
                          √buffet.
                          √rocher.
                          √frigo.

In this case the items which remove the anomaly have nothing in common semantically, and the anomaly of (4) can hence be diagnosed as grammatical.

There is one more possible diagnostic criterion: a semantic anomaly can often be improved by manipulating the context, whereas this is usually not possible with pure syntactic anomalies:

(5) The chair saw Mary.
    (Mary has a persecution mania. She believes all her accidents are due to malevolent forces. No doubt the chair saw her, computed her path across the room, and placed itself just where she would trip over it.)

No amount of contextual elaboration can reduce the anomaly of *The mans possess three car*.

3.1.2 Types of anomaly

We have so far treated anomaly as a unitary phenomenon, without trying to distinguish different sorts. It is quite a useful analytic tool, even without further refinement, as most speakers have sensitive intuitions regarding the normality or oddness of a bit of language. But it is sometimes useful to make a distinction between different types of anomaly. The following are the main varieties (they are only illustrated here: more detailed discussion will be found in Chapter 12).

3.1.2.1 Pleonasm

John chewed it with his teeth.
It was stolen illegally.
Mary deliberately made a speech.

These examples give a feeling of redundancy: how else can you chew something, if not with your teeth? How can anybody make a speech accidentally? We shall look further into the reasons for pleonasm in a later chapter: for the moment an intuitive grasp is sufficient.

3.1.2.2 Semantic clash

The balloon rose ever lower.
The hamster was only slightly dead.
Singing hypotenuses melted in every eye.

Here there is a sense of ill-matched meanings clashing, giving rise to paradox, contradiction, a need to look for figurative readings (interpretability varies).

3.1.2.3 Zeugma

We couldn't pick any apples this year because we chopped them down last winter.
John expired on the same day as his TV licence.

A sense of punning is an unmistakable symptom of zeugma. The essence of zeugma is the attempt to make a single expression do two semantic jobs at the same time.

3.1.2.4 Improbability

The puppy finished off a whole bottle of whisky.
The throne was occupied by a gun-toting baboon.

In the last analysis, there is probably a continuum between improbability and dissonance. For present purposes, we shall distinguish improbability by the fact that *I don't believe it!*, *How extraordinary!*, *That's a lie!*, etc. are appropriate responses.

3.2 Descriptive and non-descriptive meaning

Several scholars have proposed ways of classifying meaning into types, and the various proposals by no means agree in their details. But there is one type of meaning on which there is substantial agreement, and we shall start by separating this type from all the rest, although, as we shall see, the division is not quite so clear-cut as it may at first seem. The type of meaning in question is given various labels, such as **ideational, descriptive, referential, logical**, or **propositional**. These are characterized in different ways by different scholars, but there is substantial overlap in respect of the sort of meaning they are referring to; we shall adopt Lyons's term '*descriptive*' as being the best suited to our purposes. The prototypic characteristics of this type of meaning are as follows (these points are not necessarily independent):

(i) It is this aspect of the meaning of a sentence which determines whether or not any proposition it expresses is true or false (see the discussion in Chapter 2). This property justifies the labels '*logical*' and '*propositional*' for this type of meaning.

(ii) It is this aspect of the meaning of an expression which constrains what the expression can be used to refer to; from another point of view, it is this type of meaning which guides the hearer in identifying the intended referent(s); this is the motivation for the label '*referential*'.

(iii) It is **objective** in the sense that it interposes a kind of distance between the speaker and what he says. It is **displaced** in the sense introduced by the American structural linguist Charles Hockett, that is, it is not tied to the here-and-now of the current speech situation.

(iv) It is fully conceptualized. That is to say, it provides a set of conceptual categories into which aspects of experience may be sorted. Such a categorization effectively 'describes' the experiences and licenses further inferences about their properties, and so on.

(v) Descriptive aspects of the meaning of a sentence are 'exposed' in the sense that they can potentially be negated or questioned. A reply from an interlocutor such as *That's a lie* or *That's not true* targets the descriptive meaning within a statement.

Let us see how these criteria operate with a sentence which contains both descriptive and non-descriptive meaning:

(6) A: What's the matter?
    B: Somebody's turned the bloody lights off.

Taking point (i) first, in B's utterance, *bloody* makes no contribution to the truth or falsity of the statement. That is to say, *Somebody's turned the lights off* and *Somebody's turned the bloody lights off* are true and false in exactly the same range of situations. On the other hand, of course, in a situation where *Somebody's turned the lights off* is true, *Somebody's turned the lights on* would be false; therefore what *off* signifies is part of the descriptive meaning of the utterance.

With respect to points (ii) and (iv), it is clear that *Somebody's turned the lights off* functions to inform A what has happened: it describes an event, in terms of shared conceptual categories such as TURN OFF and LIGHT. The word *bloody*, however, has no descriptive function: it does not specify a sub-category of lights, nor give any help to the hearer in identifying the lights in question. It has a function which is entirely non-descriptive, which we will come to later.

As far as point (iii) is concerned, the descriptive meaning of the sentence can be displaced in the sense that it can be used to refer to events distant in time and space from the speech event:

(7) Somebody will go there and turn the lights off.

Notice, however, that the exasperation expressed by *bloody* cannot be displaced. In fact, in B's utterance in (6), while the descriptive meaning designates a previous event, *bloody* expresses B's exasperation at the moment of utterance.

Finally, the meaning of *bloody* is not amenable to straightforward contradiction. If someone replies *That's a lie* to B's statement, that would mean, not that B is not exasperated, but that the lights had not been turned off; that is to say, only the descriptive meaning would be denied. A reply such as *They are not bloody lights* cannot mean "You are misleading me by expressing exasperation"; such a reply would be, to say the least, unusual, but it could have a metalinguistic meaning such as "You shouldn't have used the word *bloody*".

We shall adopt the above criteria for our conception of descriptive meaning, with two modifications, or provisos. The first is that we shall require not that descriptive meaning should be categorically determinant for truth values/conditions, but merely that it should be directly relevant to truth in the sense of rendering the truth of a proposition more or less likely. For instance, the truth of "Fido is an animal" may be said to be crucial to the truth of "Fido is a dog", in that if Fido is not an animal, then he/it can in no wise be a dog. However, "Fido can bark" is not crucial in this way: it is quite conceivable that a particular dog may not be able to bark. But if "Fido can bark" is false, that makes it less likely that Fido is a dog. Of course, "Fido can bark" is part of a normal description of a normal dog, so the inclusion of such matters under the heading of descriptive meaning is not so perverse.

The second proviso is that we shall not require of descriptive meaning that it be within the normal scope of negation, questioning, etc., provided that it is of the type that can normally be negated, or whatever. In other words, we shall distinguish between descriptive meaning which is, as it were 'ring-fenced' against contradiction, and meaning which cannot be contradicted because it is the wrong type (usually because it does not present a proposition). For instance, *It's a dog* will normally be taken to indicate that (the referent of) *it* is an animal, that is, its being an animal is part (in some sense) of the meaning of *It's a dog*. But if someone points to a creature and says *Is that a dog?*, they are unlikely to be asking whether or not the referent of *that* is an animal.

With these provisos, let us proceed to an examination of a number of dimensions along which descriptive meaning may vary.

3.3 Dimensions of descriptive meaning

3.3.1 Intrinsic dimensions

Intrinsic dimensions are semantic properties an element possesses in and of itself, without (overt) reference to other elements.

3.3.1.1 Quality

What we shall call **quality** is at one and the same time the most obvious and important dimension of variation within descriptive meaning and the one about which we shall say the least. It is this which constitutes the difference between *red* and *green*, *dog* and *cat*, *apple* and *orange*, *run* and *walk*, *hate* and *fear*, *here* and *there*. Pure differences of quality are to be observed only between items which are equal on the scales of intensity and specificity (see below). A rough-and-ready check on difference of quality is whether one can say *not X but Y* and *not Y but X* without oddness:

(8) It's not here, it's there.
It's not there, it's here.

(9) I didn't run, I walked.
I didn't walk, I ran.

(10) Her dress is not red, it's green.
Her dress is not green, it's red.

These may be contrasted with the following, where there is a semantic difference, but not one of a descriptive nature:

(11) ?That's not my father, that's my Dad.
?She didn't pass away, she kicked the bucket.

Notice that items which differ in specificity will pass only half of this test:

(12) It's an animal, but it's not a dog,
*It's a dog, but it's not an animal.

Differences of quality can be observed at all levels of specificity. We may think of hierarchies of semantic domains of varying scope, or, alternatively, of different **ontological types**. A typical set of ontological types at the highest level of generality is the following:

THING QUALITY QUANTITY PLACE TIME STATE PROCESS EVENT ACTION RELATION MANNER

These represent fundamental modes of conception that the human mind is presumably innately predisposed to adopt. At lower levels of generality, we find (among other types) hierarchically arranged sets of conceptual categories:

Living things: animals, fish, insects, reptiles . . .
Animals: dogs, cats, lions, elephants . . .
Dogs: collies, alsatians, Pekinese, spaniels. . .

3.3.1.2 Intensity

Descriptive meaning may vary in **intensity**, without change of quality. For instance, one would not wish to say that *large* and *huge* differ in quality: they designate the same area of semantic quality space, but differ in intensity. It is characteristic of intensity differences that they yield normal results in the following test frame(s):

(13) It wasn't just X, it was Y.
I wouldn't go so far as to say it was Y, but it was X.

If these are normal, then Y is more intense than X:

(**14**) It wasn't just large, it was huge.
(cf. ?It wasn't just huge, it was large.)
I wouldn't go so far as to say it was huge, but it was large.

(**15**) I wasn't just scared of her, I was terrified of her.
I wouldn't go so far as to say I was terrified of her, but I was scared of her.

From (14) and (15) we can conclude that *huge* is more intense than *large*, and *terrified* more intense than *scared*. (Note that virtually any pair of items can be made to seem normal in this frame, given a suitably elaborated context: the test is intended to work in a zero context.)

Variation in intensity is of course possible only in certain areas of quality space. But it is not confined to those areas designated by gradable adjectives (i.e. is not confined to the domain of QUALITIES). Examples from other areas are:

(**16**) It wasn't just a mist, it was a fog.
I wouldn't go so far as to say it was a fog, but it was a mist.

(**17**) He didn't just beat her, he thrashed her.
I wouldn't go so far as to say he thrashed her, but he did beat her.

3.3.1.3 Specificity

Differences of descriptive **specificity** show up in various logical properties. These differ according to the exact type of specificity involved (see below). For one major type of specificity, these properties include, for instance, unilateral entailment (in appropriate contexts):

(**18**) *It's a dog* unilaterally entails *It's an animal.*
It's not an animal unilaterally entails *It's not a dog.*

Note also that *dogs and other animals* is normal, but not *?animals and other dogs*.

From all this, we can conclude that *dog* is more specific than *animal* (alternatively, *animal* is more **general** than dog). Similarly, *slap* is more specific than *hit*, *scarlet* is more specific than *red*, *woman* is more specific than *person*. In all these cases one can say that one term (the more general one) designates a more extensive area of quality space than the other. The American linguist Ronald Langacker (one of the pioneers of cognitive linguistics) likens difference of linguistic specificity to viewing something from different distances: the less specific the greater the distance (Langacker 1993). For instance, from a great distance a dog may just look like an object; from closer in, one can see it is an animal, but not what kind of animal; closer still, and the fact that it is a dog becomes clear, but perhaps not what variety of dog; and so on.

It is possible to distinguish several types of specificity. All the cases illustrated above involve **type-specificity**, that is to say, the more specific term denotes a subtype included within the more general type. But there is also **part-specificity**, illustrated by, for instance, *hand:finger* (where *finger* is the more specific), *bicycle:wheel*, *university:faculty*. *John injured his finger* is more specific than *John injured his hand*. The logical consequences of this type of specificity are different to those for type-specificity. Unilateral entailment appears (in general) only with locative expressions:

(19) *The boil is on John's elbow* unilaterally entails *The boil is on John's arm*.
John lectures in the Arts Faculty unilaterally entails *John lectures in the university*.

A third type of specificity is **intensity-specificity**, where one range of degrees of some property is included in another range. For instance, one reading of *large* includes all ranges of intensity of "greater than average size". Hence *It's huge* entails *It's large*, but *It's large* does not entail *It's huge*. The logical properties here are the same as for type-specificity.

3.3.1.4 Vagueness

We shall say that the meaning of a word is **vague** to the extent that the criteria governing its use are not precisely statable. Before examining this notion in greater detail, it is necessary to make as clear a distinction as possible between it and certain other notions with which it is often coupled in discussions, if not actually confused. The first of these is **generality**. Although someone who says *I saw a reptile* is not giving as much information as someone who says *I saw a snake*, they are not being any more vague. That is to say, the notion "reptile" is as clearly delimitable as the notion "snake"; it is just that it denotes a more inclusive class. Another notion which must be distinguished from vagueness is **abstractness**. For instance, the notion of "entailment" is abstract, but is relatively well defined, and therefore not vague.

Under the heading of vagueness we shall distinguish two different sub-dimensions. The first is **ill-definedness**, and the second is **laxness**. These can vary independently. Ill-definedness is well illustrated by terms which designate a region on a gradable scale such as *middle-aged*. Age varies continuously: *middle-aged* occupies a region on this scale. But at what age does someone begin to be middle-aged, and at what age does one cease to be middle-aged and become old? There is quite an overlap between *middle-aged* and *in their fifties*, but the latter is significantly better defined: we know in principle how to determine whether someone is in their fifties or not. General terms may be better defined than more specific terms. For instance, *animal* is arguably better defined than *pet*: at what degree of domestication does a cat on a farm qualify as a pet?

The second subtype of vagueness is **laxness** (vs. **strictness**) of application. For some terms, their essence is easily defined, but they are habitually applied in a loose way. This seems to be a characteristic of individual words. For instance, the notion of a circle is capable of a clear definition, and everyone is capable of grasping the strict notion, even if they cannot give a correct mathematical specification. But the word *circle* is habitually used very loosely, as in, for instance, *The mourners stood in a circle round the grave*. No one expects the people to form an exact circle here, yet there is no sense of metaphorical or extended use. Contrast this with *odd number*, which not only is clearly definable but is always applied strictly, so that, for instance, it would not do to call *2.8* an odd number, on the grounds that it was 'near enough to 3'.

3.3.1.5 Basicness

Another dimension along which descriptive meanings can vary is that of **basicness**: some meanings are considered more basic than others. This is a complex topic and cannot be fully explored here. There are several different interpretations of the notion. We shall look at three broad ways of thinking of basicness.

In many, extremely varied approaches to language and meaning a distinction is made between words or features which are close to concrete everyday experience and those which, though in some way ultimately derived from these, are to various degrees remote from actual bodily experience. For instance, the meaning of *cold* can be directly experienced through the senses, but the meaning of *gradable* as applied to adjectives (e.g. *a little bit/slightly/ quite/rather/very/extremely cold*) cannot, though there is undoubtedly a connection of some sort between bodily experiences of coldness and the abstract notion of gradability. The distinction we are making here corresponds to one meaning of *concrete* (has spatio-temporal location) as opposed to *abstract* (does not have spatio-temporal location). A standard picture of meaning within the philosophy of language identifies a set of words, known as the **observation vocabulary**, whose meanings are fixed by their relations with observable properties of the environment. The meanings of words not belonging to this set are fixed by a network of inferential or other relations to the meanings of other words, including those belonging to the observation vocabulary. We can take observation vocabulary items to be the more basic. A general assumption is that the concrete/observable/basic terms will be the first learned, probably the first to arise in the evolution of human language, the most accessible in psycholinguistic terms, the most likely to be points of convergence between widely different languages, and so on. Cognitive linguists believe that cognition is built up as it were from concrete to abstract, and concrete domains function as source domains for metaphorical processes involved in creating abstract domains.

Another way of looking at more and less basic meanings is in terms of **independence** and **dependence**: one meaning may presuppose, or depend on, another. As an example of dependency, consider the case of *acceleration*. This presupposes/depends on the notion of *speed*, which in turn presupposes the yet more basic notion of *movement*, down to the most basic notions of all:

physical object, *location*, *change* and *time*. Notice that *acceleration* is not more specific than *speed*, in the way that *dog* is more specific than *animal*, or *finger* than *hand*, but it is more complex, in that it builds on more basic meanings.

A natural way of thinking about this type of dependency is in terms of constituency: the dependent meanings, being more complex, are built up out of the more basic meanings. For instance, if we define *acceleration* as "rate of change of speed with time", we incorporate the simpler notion "speed" into the definition. A similar definition of *speed* would not need to make any reference to a notion of "acceleration" (e.g. "rate of change of location with time"). In a similar way, the meaning of *stallion* is built out of the more basic meanings "male" and "horse". On this view, the most basic meanings are the so-called **semantic primes**—elementary notions out of which all other meanings are built. There is no agreement on any set of primes. (This topic will be discussed in more detail in Chapter 13.)

Yet another interpretation of the notion of basicness is the cognitive psychologists' concept of a **basic-level category**. This is treated in more detail in Chapter 7. Briefly, basic-level categories are easier to use than other categories: examples are APPLE, ROSE, COW, CAR, BUTTERFLY, as opposed to FRUIT, FLOWER, ANIMAL, VEHICLE, or INSECT on the one hand, or RUSSET, HYBRID TEA, JERSEY COW, HATCHBACK, or SWALLOWTAIL on the other.

3.3.1.6 Viewpoint

A number of linguistic expressions encode as part of their meaning a particular **viewpoint** on the events or states of affairs designated. Perhaps the most obvious example of this is provided by deictic expressions (see Chapter 16 for more details), such as *this*, *that*, *here*, *there*, *now*, and *then* which are usually claimed to encode the viewpoint of the speaker at the moment of utterance. So, for instance, if *the book on the table* was a valid description for any speaker in a particular context, it would be valid for anyone present; however, the validity of *this book here*, as a description of the same book, would clearly depend on the position of the speaker relative to the book in question.

There are less obvious manifestations of viewpoint. Consider (20) and (21):

(20) Samantha is in front of the holly bush.
(21) Samantha is behind the holly bush.

We cannot interpret either of these without knowing the reference point assumed by the speaker. One variable is where the speaker is located relative to Samantha and the holly bush. For instance, one obvious interpretation of (20) is that the speaker and Samantha are on the same side of the holly bush, and of (21) that the speaker and Samantha are on opposite sides of the holly bush. Langacker calls this sort of reference point a **vantage point**. But things aren't so simple. Suppose Samantha is where she is because she doesn't want to be in a photograph. It would be quite natural for a speaker on the same side of the bush as Samantha to report her whereabouts using (21), effectively adopting the photographer's vantage point. A different sort of case is illustrated in (22) and (23):

(22) The caterpillar crawled up Samantha's leg.
(23) The caterpillar crawled down Samantha's leg.

The prepositions *up* and *down* encode opposite vertical directions relative to the canonical orientation of human beings. But suppose the caterpillar crawled from Samantha's knee to her ankle, while Samantha was lying on her back with her legs in the air. In this situation, the caterpillar's trajectory could be correctly described either with (22) or (23). This is not so much a matter of vantage point, because Samantha herself could use either *up* or *down*. This is a matter of what Langacker calls **orientation**. A human leg has an inherent orientation, whereby "towards the hip" is *up* and "towards the foot" is *down*. This is the orientation assumed in (23). But there is also orientation relative to the earth, whereby further away from the earth's centre is *up* and the opposite direction *down*. This is the orientation assumed in (22).

3.3.2 Relative dimensions

Under the next three headings, we shall look at parameters which relate not so much to complete meanings as to semantic features which form part of a complete lexical sense. (The notion of decomposing meanings into features or components is discussed in greater detail in Chapter 13. Here we take a fairly naïve view.)

3.3.2.1 Necessity and expectedness

The first parameter is **necessity**. The simple view of this parameter is to make a sharp dichotomy between necessary and contingent logical relationships, and use entailment to determine whether or not a feature is necessary. On the basis of the following we could say that "being an animal" is a necessary feature of dog, whereas "ability to bark" is not:

(24) X is a dog entails X is an animal.
        X is a dog does not entail X can bark.

As a first step towards moving away from a simple dichotomy, I would like to try to undermine the reader's confidence in the notion of entailment. How confident are we in our ability to say definitively whether some sentence A entails another sentence B? Consider the following putative entailments:

(25) *X stopped singing* entails(?) *X did not continue singing.*
(26) *X is a cat* entails(?) *X is an animal.*
(27) *X is pregnant* entails(?) *X is female.*
(28) *X is a physical object* entails(?) *X has weight.*
(29) *X is a quadruped* entails(?) *X has 4 legs.*
(30) *X is Y's wife* entails(?) *X is not Y's daughter.*

Presumably most speakers will have the greatest confidence in the entailment in (25): this seems to depend not on the structure of the world as we know it, but purely on the meanings of *stop* and *continue*: there is no conceivable world or universe in which the words mean what they mean in current English and this entailment does not hold. In (26)–(30), however, the solidity of the entailment is less certain.

Take (26), first. The well-known 'robot cat' scenario is relevant here. It goes something like this. Suppose one day it was discovered that cats were not animals, as everyone has always thought, but highly sophisticated self-replicating robots. Other supposed animals retained their biological status. Under such circumstances, would we be more ready to respond to the information with (31) or (32)?

(31) Aha! So there are no such things as cats, after all!
(32) Aha! So cats are not what we thought they were!

The vast majority of ordinary speakers unhesitatingly opt for (32), which at the very least suggests that animalhood is not a necessary criterion for cathood, since speakers are inclined to retain the name *cat*, but change their ideas about the referents.

This interpretation is strengthened by contrast with cases where speakers are not so accommodating. Suppose that it were discovered that there were no male horses; what we had been used to think of as stallions actually belonged to a different species, and foals were produced parthenogenetically. Under these circumstances, would we be more ready to exclaim (33) or (34)?

(33) Aha! So there are no such things as stallions!
(34) Aha! So stallions are not what we thought they were!

This time, a majority of speakers is happier with (33), although less overwhelmingly than in the previous case, from which it appears that maleness and equinity *are* criterial to stallionhood (or, strictly, at least one of them is). It seems there are two different types of common noun, one with **referential stability** in the face of radical changes in the nature of the conceptual category, and the other without such stability. The first type are known as **natural kind terms** and the latter, as **nominal kind terms**.

In the case of sentence (27) above, the argument against entailment is slightly different. Lyons points out that according to certain authorities, the biotechnology exists to implant a fertilized embryo into the body of a man, in such a way as to allow it to develop, and ultimately, be born. Would we be prepared to apply the term *pregnant* to such a man? (Most people are so prepared, even if reluctantly.) If so, the relationship in (27) is contingent on the way our world usually is—it is not a logical relationship.

People are less sure about examples like (28), which involve seemingly fundamental scientific truths. Is it conceivable that the fundamental laws of physics might have been different? When faced with such a notion, the majority of people concede that they could, thus destroying the logical necessity of the relation.

Example (29) involves a different point. If a cat loses a leg in an accident, does it cease to be a quadruped? The majority view is that it does not, which is slightly disturbing in that "having four legs" is obviously part of the **definition** of a quadruped. However, the matter is fairly easily resolved (but it leaves the entailment in (29) in tatters): what the definition defines is not **any** quadruped, but a **well-formed** quadruped.

Example (30) is slightly dubious. In one sense it is not a logical relationship, but one contingent on particular social rules, which could well be different in different societies. On the other hand, the relation arises from a legal definition (in one society). (One could perhaps say that for the logical relation to hold one would have to say:

(35) *X is Y's legal wife under English law* entails *X is not Y's daughter*.

Even then it is not certain that the relation is a logically watertight one. Suppose that neither X nor Y knew that X was Y's daughter, and they got married in good faith. Would it not be the case that X would be Y's legal wife unless and until it could be proved that she was his daughter?)

It seems clear that some of the relations illustrated in (26)–(30) are stronger than others, and that it would be more useful to recognize a scale of degrees of necessity. In fact we can go the whole hog and extend the scale to cover negative necessity, in other words, impossibility. A convenient and rough way of measuring degree of necessity is by means of the *but* test. It operates as follows:

(36) It's a dog, but it's an animal. (tautology)
It's a dog, but it's not an animal. (contradiction)
("is an animal" is a **necessary** feature of *dog*)

(37) It's a dog, but it barks. (odd—tautology)
It's a dog, but it doesn't bark. (normal)
("barks" is an **expected** feature of *dog*)

(38) It's a dog, but it's brown. (odd)
It's a dog, but it's not brown. (odd)
("brown" is a **possible** feature of *dog*).

(39) It's a dog, but it sings. (normal description of an abnormal dog)
It's a dog, but it doesn't sing. (odd—tautology)
("sings" is an **unexpected** feature of *dog*)

(40) It's a dog, but it's a fish. (contradiction)
It's a dog, but it's not a fish. (tautology)
("is a fish" is an **impossible** feature of dog)

Finer distinctions are possible (and worthwhile), especially in the upper reaches of the *expected* region of the scale of necessity. Lyons (1981) suggests **natural necessity** for expectations based on the nature of the physical universe, and **social necessity** for expectations based on human laws and social conventions. Cruse (1986) has **canonical necessity** for such cases as (29); this could conceivably be extended to include cases like (27), since a male pregnancy, although not a logical contradiction, would be some sort of aberration—that is, it would be non-canonical. Obviously if the process became more common, "female" would fall down the necessity scale to being a merely expected feature of *pregnant*.

3.3.2.2 Sufficiency

Sufficiency is a kind of converse of necessity. We normally speak of the *joint sufficiency* of a set of features (for instance, the features "male", "horse" are jointly sufficient to guarantee that anything possessing them is a stallion). We may interpret the notion as it applies to a single feature in terms of diagnosticity, an obviously gradable notion. For instance, the feature "breathes" is not very diagnostic for BIRD, since many other creatures breathe. The feature "two legged" is much better, but applies also to humans. A maximally diagnostic feature for BIRD is "feathered", since no other creature has feathers. Notice that all of these have the same degree of necessity (i.e. canonical). The *but* test can be made to give results for diagnosticity comparable to those for necessity. Thus "canonically four-legged" is what might be called **logically diagnostic** for *quadruped*, since *X canonically has four legs, but it's a quadruped* is a tautology and *X canonically has four legs but it isn't a quadruped* is a contradiction. "canonically feathered" comes out as **naturally diagnostic** in that while there are no known creatures with feathers other than birds (i.e. that is a feature of the world as we know it), the idea of, say, a feathered mammal is not a logical contradiction (cf. Angela Carter's (1984) *Nights at the Circus*): so, *X has feathers but it's a bird* is an odd use of *but*, whereas *X has feathers but it isn't a bird* is a normal description of an odd state of affairs.

3.3.2.3 Salience

Things which are **salient** stand out from their background in some way, and have a superior power of commanding attention. This property may be shown by one linguistic element vis-à-vis other elements in a larger expression, or by one feature of the meaning of a word vis-à-vis other features of the same word. I would like to distinguish two types of salience (without, however, wishing to deny their interrelationships).

One way of interpreting the notion of salience is in terms of the ease of access of information. Obviously, features which are easy to get at are going to play a larger role in semantic processing in real time than those which are harder to get at. Certainly, many of the so-called prototype effects observable between items and categories seem to depend on ease of access, and it would be reasonable to expect the same to be true of features. When people are asked to list the characteristics of some entity, under time pressure, there is a strong tendency for certain features to be mentioned early in everyone's lists. This is presumably because they are the easiest features to access.

A type of salience which is at least partly different from simple ease of access is degree of foregrounding or backgrounding. One reason for thinking it is different from simple ease of access is that it can be manipulated by speakers. This is most usually discussed in dichotomous terms as the **figure–ground effect**. For many purposes, this may be adequate, but I prefer to think in terms of continuously variable **foregrounding** vs. **backgrounding**. The effect can be very easily illustrated by one use of verb aspect in English: the continuous aspect is regularly used to indicate a background against which information signalled by a simple tense verb is highlighted. Thus, in (41) the highlighted part of the message is "John watched the programme", which is presented against the background of another activity of John's, whereas in (42) the prominence relations are reversed:

(41) John watched the programme while he was having supper.
(42) John had his supper while he was watching the programme.

Various syntactic devices have the function of highlighting/backgrounding information. For instance, in (43) the spotlight is thrown back onto what was backgrounded in (41), without changing the aspect of the verbs:

(43) It was while he was having supper that John watched the programme.

One of the symptoms of backgrounding is that backgrounded information is not in the scope of, for instance, negation or questioning. In (44) and (45), for instance, the fact that John watched the programme is not questioned or negated, but is taken for granted, assumed by the speaker to be known as a fact to the hearer, or, as the technical term has it, **presupposed**:

(44) Was it while he was having supper that John watched the programme?
(45) It wasn't while he was having supper that John watched the programme.

Differences of relative prominence can also be observed within a simple sentence. Consider the difference between *John resembles Bill* and *Bill resembles John*, and between *Bill is taller than John* and *John is shorter than Bill*. The sentences in each pair may be mutually entailing, but they do not mean the same thing. In each one, the less prominent direct object is presented as a kind of standard against which the more prominent subject is assessed.

Less obviously, there can be prominence differences in the features of the meaning of a single word. For instance, (a) *blonde*, *woman*, and *actor* all designate human beings, and this is part of their meaning, but it is backgrounded; what they highlight, respectively, is hair colour, sex, and profession. Hence, if some one says *It wasn't a blonde that I saw*, the likeliest interpretation is that both [HUMAN BEING] and [FEMALE] are outside the scope of the negative, and only [FAIR-HAIRED] is being negated.

3.4 Non-descriptive dimensions

3.4.1 Expressive meaning

Consider the difference between (46) and (47):

(46) Gosh!
(47) I am surprised.

Sentence (46) is subjective, and does not present a conceptual category to the hearer: it **expresses** an emotional state in much the same way as a cat's purr or a baby's cry. Its validity is restricted to the current state of the speaker: it cannot be put into the past tense. No proposition is expressed: the hearer cannot reply *Are you?* or *That's a lie!* (which are perfectly possible responses to (47)). Sentence (46) is also prosodically gradable, in that greater surprise is expressed by both greater volume and greater pitch range. By contrast, (47) expresses a proposition, which can be questioned or denied, and can be expressed equally well by someone else or at a different place or time: *You are surprised* (said by hearer); *He was surprised* (said at a later time). It offers conceptual categories (CURRENT SPEAKER, SURPRISED), under which a given state of affairs can be subsumed. In a sense, of course, (46) and (47) 'mean the same thing', which suggests that the difference between descriptive and expressive meaning is a matter not of semantic quality (area of semantic space) but of mode of signification.

Some words possess only expressive and no descriptive meaning and to these we can assign the term **expletives**:

(48) It's freezing—shut the bloody window!
(49) Oh, hell! Wow! Oops! Ouch!

Notice that expressive meaning does not contribute to propositional content, so the action requested in (48) would not change if *bloody* were omitted: *a bloody window* (in this sense) is not a special kind of window.

Some words have both descriptive and expressive meaning:

(50) It was *damn* cold. (cf. *extremely*, which has only descriptive meaning)
(51) Stop *blubbering*. (cf. *crying*)

Questions and negatives only operate on the descriptive meaning in such sentences, so, for instance, *It wasn't all that cold* in reply to (50) would deny the degree of cold indicated, but would not call into question the speaker's expressed feelings. Evaluative meaning has a variable status: sometimes it seems to be propositional:

(52) A: Don't read that—it's a rag.
     B: No, it isn't, it's a jolly good paper.

There is no doubt that *rag* expresses contempt for the newspaper in question, but B's reply is not at all odd, which suggests that there is also an element of objective conceptualization. In the set *horse, nag, steed*, my intuitions are that the difference between *horse* and *steed* is purely expressive (you can't say: *?It's not a steed, it's just a horse*), but the difference between *horse* and *nag* is propositional/descriptive.

The expressive words we have considered so far cannot be used unexpressively. However, some words seem to be potentially, but not necessarily expressive. With one type of such words, the expressivity appears only when appropriate intonation and stress are added:

(53) *still, yet, already*
Does she still live in Manchester?
Has the postman been yet?
The railway station had already been closed when we came to live here.

These sentences all seem to be expressively neutral, but feeling can be added prosodically:

(54) Are you ***still*** here?
Surely she hasn't gone ***already***?
You mean you haven't done it ***yet***?

What in Chapter 10 are called implicit superlatives (e.g. *huge, tiny, beautiful, brilliant*) are expressively neutral if not stressed, but seem to be able to acquire an expressive element if stressed. They contrast remarkably in this respect with their non-superlative counterparts:

(55) It was absolutely ***huge***.
?It was absolutely ***large***.
(56) It was absolutely ***tiny***.
?It was absolutely ***small***.

Out of a set of near-synonyms, it sometimes happens that some but not others can be expressively stressed:

(57) *baby* vs. *infant, child, neonate*
Mother and baby are doing well.
Oh, look! It's a ***baby***! Isn't he lovely?
?Oh, look! It's a ***child/infant/neonate***! Isn't he lovely?

Some words (called in Cruse 1986 **expressive amplifiers**) can be used with neutral expression, but can also pick up and amplify any expressiveness in their context without needing any prosodic assistance, and in this respect they often contrast with synonyms (which frequently are Latinate). For instance, there is little or no difference between (58) and (59), whereas there is a more palpable difference between (60) and (61):

(58) I want you to go on with the treatment for a few more weeks.
(59) I want you to continue with the treatment for a few more weeks.
(60) They went on banging on the wall for ages.
(61) They continued banging on the wall for ages.

3.4.2 Dialect and register allegiance: evoked meaning

Put briefly (and simplistically), dialectal variation is variation in language use according to speaker, and register variation is variation within the speech of a single community according to situation. Usages characteristic of a particular dialect or register have the power of evoking their home contexts and, in the case of register variants, of actually creating a situation. Such associations, which have no propositional content, are called **evoked meaning** in Cruse (1986). Evoked meaning may be very powerful. It would be almost unthinkable for publicity material for tourism in Scotland to refer to the geographic features through which rivers run as *valleys*, although that is precisely what they are: the Scottish dialect word *glen* is de rigueur, because of its rich evoked meaning.

Three main types of dialect can be distinguished: geographic, temporal, and social. The first type is self-explanatory; dialects of the second type vary according to the age of the speaker (who now speaks of the *wireless*, even though modern radios have far fewer wires than their forebears?); the third type vary according to the social class of the speaker.

A well-known division of register is into **field**, **mode**, and **style**. *Field* refers to the area of discourse: specialists in a particular field often employ technical vocabulary to refer to things which have everyday names. For instance, doctors, when talking to other doctors, will speak of a *pyrexia*, which in ordinary language would be called a *fever*, or just a *temperature*. Of course, the apparent sameness of meaning between an expert word and an everyday word is sometimes illusory, since the technical term may have a strict definition which makes it descriptively different from the everyday term. This is true, for instance, of our use of the term *utterance* in the last chapter, which can scarcely occur in everyday language without sounding pompous; its closest correspondent in ordinary language would probably be *what X said*, which is much more loosely defined.

Mode refers to the difference between language characteristic of different channels, such as spoken, written, (in the old days) telegraphic, and perhaps nowadays e-mail. For instance, *further to* is more or less exclusive to written language, whereas *like* (as in *I asked him, like, where he was going*) is definitely spoken. (Problems with the taxonomy show up in the fact that *further to* is probably also characteristic of business correspondence—a matter of field—and *like* is definitely informal, and is at least partly also a matter of the next sub-dimension, style.)

Style is a matter of the formality/informality of an utterance. So, for instance, *pass away* belongs to a higher (more formal) register than, say, *die*, and *kick the bucket* belongs to a lower register. But things are more complicated than that. Take the sexual domain. Looking at descriptively equivalent expressions, *have intercourse* with is relatively formal, *have sex with/go to bed with/sleep with* are fairly neutral, but while *bonk, do it with*, and *fuck* are all informal, there are significant differences between them. *Did you do it with her?* might be described as 'neutral informal'; however, *bonk* is humorous, whereas *fuck, screw*, and *shag* are somehow aggressively obscene (although probably to different degrees). In the same humorous-informal category as *bonk*, we find *willie* (cf. *penis*), *boobs* (cf. *breasts*), and perhaps *pussy* (cf. *vagina*).

Discussion questions and exercises

1. Types of anomaly

Attempt to identify the types of anomaly present in the following as grammatical or semantic, and if semantic, whether dissonance, pleonasm, zeugma or improbability (a given item may contain more than one type):

    (a) Your misfortune is better than mine.
    (b) What happened tomorrow was a bad disaster.
    (c) Someone's coming! Quickly, conceal in the wardrobe!
    (d) Dogs, on average, are heavier than bitches, but are easier to breed than cats.
    (e) Two of the mice in the front row weren't in tune.

2. Degree of necessity

Given the truth of *X is a cat*, assign a 'degree of necessity' (e.g. logically necessary, canonically necessary, expected, possible) to the following:

    (a) X likes classical music.
    (b) X has a tail.
    (c) X catches mice.
    (d) X divides by 2 without remainder.
    (e) X is visible (i.e. reflects light).
    (f) X is not a dog.
    (g) X is ginger and white.
    (h) X has whiskers.

3. What are the presuppositions of the following?

    (a) Lesley is a lesbian.
    (b) Lesley plays the clarinet brilliantly.
    (c) Lesley will graduate next year.
    (d) Lesley is sorry for all the trouble she has caused.
    (e) It was Lesley who wrote the letter.
    (f) When Lesley was ill, Jane deputized for her on the committee.

4. On what dimension of descriptive meaning do the following differ?

(a) (i) The prisoner was killed.
     (ii) The prisoner was murdered.
(b) (i) The prisoner was murdered.
     (ii) The prisoner was executed.
(c) (i) The shirt was not clean.
     (ii) The shirt was filthy.
(d) (i) Lesley is a young woman.
     (ii) Lesley is in her twenties.
(e) (i) We're coming up to the exams.
     (ii) The exams will soon be here.

5. On what dimension(s) of non-descriptive meaning do the following differ?

(a) (i) Are you leaving?
     (ii) You're not leaving, surely?
(b) (i) He's been dismissed.
     (ii) He's got the sack.
(c) (i) He has a fractured humerus.
     (ii) He has a broken arm.
(d) (i) Get lost!
     (ii) Please go away.

(The sentence pairs in question 3, Chapter 2, can also be examined from this point of view.)

Suggestions for further reading

For syntactic versus semantic anomaly, see Cruse (1986: ch. 1); for types and degrees of semantic anomaly, see Cruse (1986: ch. 4.12).

Lyons's categorization of meaning into descriptive and non-descriptive types can be found in Lyons (1977: ch. 2.4). Also worth looking at for classifications of meaning types are Halliday (1970) and Leech (1974). The account given here largely follows Cruse (1986: ch. 12.2) (this section describes allowable differences between propositional synonyms). Presupposition is just touched on in this chapter; Cruse (1992d) gives a fuller, but still introductory, survey of different theoretical approaches; a much more detailed account can be found in Levinson (1983: ch. 4).

Langacker (1991b: ch. 1) discusses a variety of dimensions along which meaning can vary; see also Cruse (2002c) for dimensions of descriptive meaning.

Compositionality

CHAPTER 4

Compositionality

4.1 The principle of compositionality

In this chapter, the focus is on the way meanings combine together to form more complex meanings. We begin by considering a basic principle governing the interpretation of complex linguistic expressions, the **principle of compositionality**. The strongest version of this principle runs as follows:

> (I) The meaning of a grammatically complex form is a compositional function of the meanings of its grammatical constituents.

This incorporates three separate claims:

> (i) The meaning of a complex expression is completely ***determined*** by the meanings of its constituents.
> (ii) The meaning of a complex expression is completely ***predictable*** by general rules from the meanings of its constituents.
> (iii) Every grammatical constituent has a meaning which contributes to the meaning of the whole.

(Claim (ii) incorporates claim (i), but claim (i) could be true without claim (ii) being true. Claim (iii) is presupposed by the other two, as they are formulated above.)

What is the rationale behind this principle? It derives mainly from two deeper presuppositions. The first is that a language has an infinite number of grammatical sentences; the second is that language has unlimited expressive power—that is, anything which can be conceived of can be expressed in language. There is no way that the meanings of an infinite number of sentences can be stored in a kind of sentence dictionary—there is not enough room in a finite brain for that. The infinite inventory of sentences arises from rule-governed combinations of elements from a finite list according to generative rules at least some of which are recursive; the only way such sentences could, in their entirety, be interpretable is if their meanings are composed in rule-governed ways out of the meanings of their parts.

To begin with we shall assume that there is nothing problematic about the principle of compositionality and consider only straightforward cases; later we shall deconstruct the notion to some extent (although, in one form or another, it is inescapable).

4.2 Modes of combination

The principle of compositionality, although basic, does not take us very far in understanding how meanings are combined. There is more than one way of combining two meanings to make a third (to take the simplest case). We may make a first division between **additive modes** of combination and **interactive modes**. A combination will be said to be additive if the meanings of the constituents are simply added together, and both survive without radical change in the combination. Typical of additive combinations are simple syntactic coordinations:

(1) [A man and a woman] [entered the room and sat down].
(2) Jane is [tall and fair].

In interactive types of combination, the meaning of at least one constituent is radically modified. We can distinguish two types of interactive modification: the **endocentric** type, where the resultant meaning is of the same basic type as one of the constituents, and the **exocentric** type, where the resultant meaning is of a different basic type from either of the constituents. Let us look first at endocentric interactive combinations.

4.2.1 Endocentric combinations

Even under the general heading of endocentric combinations there are different modes of interaction between meanings. The following are illustrative (but not necessarily exhaustive).

4.2.1.1 Boolean combinations

The **Boolean combination** is the most elementary type, and is illustrated by *red hats*. Extensionally, the class of red hats is constituted by the intersection of the class of hats and the class of red things; in other words, red hats are things that are simultaneously hats and red. Notice first that what *a red hat* denotes is of the same basic ontological type as what *a hat* denotes (i.e. a THING), and hence we are dealing with an endocentric combination; second, the effect of *red* is to restrict the applicability of *hat*, and hence we are dealing with an interactive combination.

4.2.1.2 Relative descriptors

The **relative descriptor** exemplifies a more complex interaction between meanings. It is illustrated by *a large mouse*. This cannot be glossed "something which is large and is a mouse", because all mice, even large ones, are small animals. *Large* must be interpreted relative to the norm of size for the class of mice, and means something more like "significantly larger than the average mouse". Here we have a two-way interaction, because *mouse* determines how *large* is to be interpreted, and *large* limits the application of *mouse*. It is nonetheless the case that what *a large mouse* denotes is of the same basic ontological type as what *a mouse* denotes, so we are still in the realm of endocentric combinations.

4.2.1.3 Negational descriptors

In **negational descriptors**, the effect of the modifier is to negate the head, while at the same time giving indications as to where to look for the intended referent. The following are examples of this type:

(3) a former President
an ex-lover
a fake Ming vase
an imitation fur coat
reproduction antiques

Notice that *an imitation fur coat* is not something that is simultaneously a fur coat and an imitation: it is an imitation, but it is not strictly a fur coat. On the other hand, there is no radical change in basic ontological type as a result of combining the meanings.

4.2.1.4 Indirect types

Indirect combinations require a more complex compositional process, but still can be held to be rule-governed. Consider the (often-discussed) case of *a beautiful dancer*. This phrase is ambiguous. One of the readings is of the standard Boolean type, denoting someone who is simultaneously beautiful and a dancer. The other reading, however, requires some semantic reconstruction of the phrase so that *beautiful* becomes an adverbial modifier of the verbal root *dance* and the phrase means "someone who dances beautifully".

4.2.2 Exocentric combinations

An exocentric combination is one where the resultant meaning is of a radically different ontological type from that of any of the constituent meanings; in other words, there has been some sort of transformation. An example of this would be the combination between a preposition such as *in*, which denotes a relation, and a noun phrase such as *the box*, which denotes a thing, producing a prepositional phrase *in the box*, which denotes a place. Another example would be the production of a proposition from the combination of, say, *John*, a person, and *laughed*, an action. These types, especially the latter one, are in some ways deeply mysterious, but we shall not dwell on them any further here.

4.3 Limits to compositionality I: idioms etc.

Some aspects of the combination of meanings seem to call into question the principle of compositionality; and while the abandonment of the principle would seem too drastic, it may be that it should be reconsidered and perhaps reformulated. We are not talking here about the existence of non-compositional expressions, which can be accommodated by a reformulation of the principle: what is being referred to here concerns the validity of the principle in cases where it is usually considered to be operative. We shall look at three types of case which might undermine one's faith in the principle. But first we must look at **non-compositional expressions**.

4.3.1 Non-compositional expressions

The principle of compositionality as set out above is not universally valid, although it must in some sense be a default assumption. That is, someone hearing a combination for the first time (i.e. one that has not been learned as a phrasal unit) will attempt to process it compositionally, and the speaker will expect this. The reason for the non-applicability of the principle is the existence of expressions not all of whose grammatical constituents contribute an identifiable component of its meaning. Think of phrases like *paint the town red* or *a white elephant*: knowing what *white* means and what *elephant* means is no help whatsoever in decoding the meaning of *white elephant*. It is possible to reformulate the principle to cover such cases:

> (II) The meaning of a complex expression is a compositional function of the meanings of its semantic constituents, that is, those constituents which exhaustively partition the complex, and whose meanings, when appropriately compounded, yield the (full) global meaning.

Notice that this version is tautologous unless the notion "semantic constituent" can be defined independently. If it can, then we will have a way of accurately characterizing expressions (at least some of) whose grammatical constituents are not semantic constituents (thereby abandoning assumption (iii) given earlier).

4.3.1.1 Semantic constituents

Semantic constituents can in general be recognized by the **recurrent contrast test**. Prototypically, semantic constituents have the following characteristics:

> (i) They can be substituted by something else (belonging to the same grammatical class), giving a different meaning.

This expresses the old principle "Meaning implies choice": that is, an expression cannot have meaning unless it was chosen from a set of possible alternatives. The corollary of this is that if an element is obligatory, it cannot be said to have meaning. So, for instance, *cat* in *The cat sat on the mat* satisfies this criterion because it can be substituted by *dog* giving the semantically different *The dog sat on the mat*; conversely, *to* in *I want to eat* does not satisfy this criterion because it is both grammatically obligatory and unique. As we shall see, this criterion is too strict and is probably best regarded as prototypically valid.

> (ii) At least some of the contrasts of meaning produced by substitution in one context should be reproducible using the same items in a (formally) different context.

This sounds clumsy and obscure. It attempts to state precisely the simple idea that a meaningful linguistic item should be capable of carrying a constant meaning from context to context. Let us now look at some examples of this test in operation:

(4) (mat/box) The cat sat on a —— = (mat/box) The —— is dirty.
     (The same contrast holds between *The cat sat on a mat* and *The cat sat on a box* as between *The mat is dirty* and *The box is dirty*.)

Here we have two items, *mat* and *box*, which produce the same semantic contrast in two different contexts. These two items therefore pass the recurrent contrast test for semantic constituency, and can be considered to be semantic constituents of the sentences which result when they are placed in the appropriate slots. Although this shows that, for example, *mat* is a semantic constituent of *The cat sat on the mat*, it does not prove that it is a **minimal semantic constituent**, that is, one that cannot be divided into yet smaller semantic constituents. For that we must test the parts of *mat*. Let us now apply the recurrent contrast test to the *-at* of *mat*:

(5) (-at/-oss) The cat sat on the m——. = (?) (-at/-oss) He has a new b   .

Notice first of all that the first part of the test is satisfied: substituting *-at* by *-oss* gives us *The cat sat on the moss*, whose meaning is different from that of *The cat sat on the mat*. The second part of the test is not satisfied, however, because no context can be found where putting *-oss* in place of *-at* produces the same contrast of meaning that it does in *The cat sat on the mat*. (Only one of the contexts where the substitution of forms is possible is illustrated in (5).) What is being claimed is that the contrast between *The cat sat on the mat* and *The cat sat on the moss* is not the same as that between *He has a new bat* and *He has a new boss*, and that an equivalent contrast can never be produced by switching between *-at* and *-oss*. Some people are uncertain what is meant by 'the same contrast'. It may be helpful to think in terms of a semantic proportionality like *stallion:mare::ram:ewe* ("*stallion* is to *mare* as *ram* is to *ewe*"), which can be verbalized as 'the contrast between *mare* and *stallion* is the same as that between *ewe* and *ram*'.

It is useful to run through a few of the results of this test. We find, for instance, that although the *dis-* of *disapprove* comes out as a semantic constituent (because the presence vs. absence of *dis-* has the same semantic effect in the context of *approve* as it has in the context of *like*), the *dis-* of *disappoint* is not a semantic constituent because the semantic effect of removing it does not recur with any other stem (intuitively, adding *dis-* does not create an opposite, as it does with both *approve* and *mount*). On the same basis, the *re-* of *re-count* ("count again") is a semantic constituent, but not the *re-* of *recount* ("narrate"), nor the *re-* of *report, receive, revolve*, etc. The reader should find that, on reflection, these results accord with intuition. Perhaps less in accord with intuition, at least initially, is the fact that neither the *straw-* nor the *-berry* of *strawberry*, and neither the *black-* nor the *-bird* of *blackbird*, pass the test for semantic constituency. Let us take the *blackbird* example (the same arguments apply to lots of similar cases). Surely a blackbird is not only a bird, but also black? Yes, of course. However the test says not only that the contrast between *A blackbird was singing* and *A bird was singing* is not matched by that between, say, *John was wearing a black suit* and *John was wearing a suit*, but that it cannot be matched at all. Think of it this way: adding together the meaning of *black* and the meaning of *bird* does not give us the meaning of *blackbird*, it gives us the meaning of *black bird*. To understand what *blackbird* means, we have to have learned to attach a meaning to the whole complex *blackbird* which is not derivable from *black* and *bird*. Some might wish to argue that *black-* in *blackbird* carries whatever meaning differentiates blackbirds from other kinds of bird. However, this is not intuitively appealing: can one give even an approximate paraphrase of this meaning? Furthermore, there is no evidence that elements like *black-* behave in any way like semantic constituents (for more detailed arguments, see Cruse 1986: ch. 2.4).

With this notion of semantic constituent we can make non-tautologous sense of the principle of compositionality as expressed in (II) above. We can also characterize a type of grammatically complex expression not all of whose grammatical constituents are semantic constituents. These we shall call **idioms**. By this definition, *blackbird* is an idiom, but the term is more usually applied to phrasal units, and we shall now consider some of these.

4.3.1.2 Idioms

Phrasal idioms are expressions like:

to pull (someone)'s leg
to paint the town red
to kick the bucket
to be round the twist
to be up the creek
to have a bee in (one)'s bonnet

It is important to realize that when one of these expressions is used in a sentence, it is rare that the whole sentence is idiomatic in the sense defined above. Take the case of *Jane pulled Martha's leg about her boyfriend*. By the recurrent contrast test, the following items come out as (minimal) semantic constituents: *Jane*, *-ed*, *Martha*, *about*, *her*, *boyfriend* (possibly *boy* and *friend*), *pull- -'s leg*. Strictly, it is only the last item which is an idiom; notice that it has the same semantic status as a single lexical item, such as *tease* or *congratulate*. All the items except those which form part of the idiom can be changed without destroying the idiomatic meaning; however, changing *pull*, or *leg*, causes the idiomatic meaning to be lost. Although it is not true of all idioms, it seems fruitless to ask what *pull* and *leg* mean in *to pull someone's leg*: they do not mean anything, just as the *m-* of *mat* does not mean anything—all the meaning of the phrasal unit attaches to the phrase, and none to its constituents.

Phrasal idioms have some peculiar grammatical properties, which can be attributed either to the fact that their constituents have no meaning or to the fact that such meaning is not independently active. The following are the main points:

(i) Elements are not separately modifiable without loss of idiomatic meaning:

(**6**) *She pulled her brother's legs.
(**7**) *She pulled her brother's left leg.
(**8**) *She pulled her brother's leg with a sharp tug.

Only the idiom as a whole is modifiable:

(**9**) She pulled her brother's leg mercilessly.

(ii) Elements do not coordinate with genuine semantic constituents:

(**10**) *She pulled and twisted her brother's leg.
(**11**) *She pulled her brother's leg and arm.

(Notice, however, the normality of *She pulled her brother's and her father's leg*, where only semantic constituents are coordinated.) The asterisks in (10) and (11) apply only to the idiomatic reading.

(iii) Elements cannot take contrastive stress, or be the focus of topicalizing transformations, and the like:

(**12**) *It was her brother's **leg** that she pulled.
    (cf. *It was her brother's **leg** that she pulled*, which is normal.)
(**13**) *What she did to her brother's leg was pull it.

(iv) Elements cannot be referred back to anaphorically:

(**14**) *Mary pulled her brother's leg; John pulled it, too.
    (cf. the normality of *Mary pulled her brother's leg; John did, too*, where the whole idiom is referred to anaphorically.)

(v) An idiom does not survive the substitution of any of its constituent elements by a synonym or near-synonym:

(15) *The poor old chap kicked the pail.
(16) *She tugged his leg about it.
(17) *She pulled his lower limb about it.

In all these respects the superficially anomalous behaviour of idioms is in fact a natural consequence of the fact that their constituents are, in a real sense, meaningless. For instance, the typical function of an adjective is to restrict or modify in some way the meaning of the noun it modifies. But if the noun has no meaning, it is scarcely surprising that appending an adjective to it should be anomalous. The same applies to processes which normally function to highlight or focus on the meaning of a particular element, as in (iii) above. Finally, since *pull* in *to pull someone's leg* does not have any meaning, no sense can be attached to the notion of replacing it with a synonymous item (any more than there is sense in the idea of replacing the *m-* in *mat* with a synonymous item).

(vi) Some aspects of grammar (e.g. voice) may or may not be part of an idiom:

(18) His leg was being pulled continually by the other boys.
(The idiomatic meaning is not destroyed here, so 'active voice' is not part of the idiom proper.)
(19) *The bucket was kicked by him.
(Here the idiomatic meaning is destroyed when voice is changed, and therefore can be considered part of the idiom proper.)

4.3.1.3 Frozen metaphors

We have been looking at expressions which are non-compositional in the sense that their apparent constituents are not real semantic constituents. There is, however, a class of idiom-like expressions which come out as non-compositional by the recurrent contrast test, and which may show some of the features of syntactic frozenness typical of idioms, such as resistance to modification, transformation, and so forth, but which differ from idioms in an important respect: the effect of synonym substitution is not a complete collapse of the non-literal reading. Compare the substitutions in (20) with those in (21):

(20) The ball's   in your court now.
                on your side of the net

A cat can look at a queen.
   mouse   archbishop

I can read her like an open book.
   decipher

He has one foot in the grave.
      both feet   tomb
      one leg   coffin

(21) I gave him a piece of my mind.
         part   conceptual system

He drives me up the wall.
    forces   room partition

He has a bee in his bonnet about it.
      hornet   helmet

In the examples in (20) one can hardly say that the substitution has no effect, but the non-literal meaning is still recoverable, or at least approximately so, and the change in meaning is commensurate with the closeness of the synonymy relation. This seems to indicate that the connection between the meanings which result from normal compositional processes in these expressions and their non-compositional readings is not an arbitrary one. What seems to happen on synonym substitution is that the original metaphorical process is revived, yielding a reading not far from the conventionalized reading. In the examples in (21), there is always an element of the global meaning of the complex expression (sometimes all of it) which is arbitrary with respect to the 'free' meanings of the constituents.

It has been implied in the preceding discussion that the literal meanings of the constituents of idioms are not always completely inactive or irrelevant to the idiomatic reading. The degree of relatedness between literal and non-literal meanings of idioms varies continuously from none at all to such a high degree that the expression falls into a shadowy border area between idiomaticity and full compositionality. If we look at noun compounds, *a red herring* represents one end of the scale, namely zero relatedness between literal and non-literal readings; *blackbird* is an intermediate case; *bread and butter* is in the borderline zone: what is not recoverable from a straightforward composition in this case is the fact that the bread is sliced and the butter spread on it (a loaf of bread and a pack of butter would qualify as *butter and bread*, but arguably not as *bread and butter*).

4.3.1.4 Collocations

We have so far been thinking of compositionality exclusively from the point of view of the hearer: given an expression consisting of more than one meaningful element, how do we work out what the global meaning of the expression is? There is, however, another side to compositionality, namely the point of view of the speaker: given that a speaker wishes to formulate a particular message, and no single element is available, how do they construct a complex expression to convey it? Corresponding to the speaker's viewpoint, there are idioms of encoding. Some of these are also idioms of decoding, but there are others which are not idioms of decoding. To these we shall give the name **colloca-tions**. Like the more familiar kind of idioms, they have to be individually learned. As examples of collocations take the intensifiers *great*, *heavy*, *high*, *utter*, *extreme*, and *severe*. Table 4.1 shows that they have definite preferences and dispreferences.

Table 4.1

	great	heavy	high	utter	extreme	deep	severe
frost	–	+	–	–	?	–	+
rain	–	+	–	–	–	–	–
wind	?	–	+	–	–	–	–
surprise	+	–	–	+	+	–	–
distress	+	–	–	–	+	+	+
temperature	?	–	+	–	+	–	–
speed	+	–	+	–	?	–	–

4.3.1.5 Clichés

Some expressions which are apparently fully compositional should arguably be included in the class of phrasal units; these are the so-called **clichés**. Let us take as an example the politician's *I've made my position absolutely clear* (when he's been slithering and swerving for five minutes in the course of a probing interview). In so far as its propositional meaning is concerned, this expression would have to be categorized as fully compositional. However, it does have global properties, as a whole phrase, although of a more subtle kind. It seems highly likely that such phrases are stored as complete units in the brains of both speaker and hearer; as such, they are easy to retrieve while speaking and easy to decode for the hearer. They also tend to slip past without making much of an impact, their truth or falsehood not seriously examined. They function as default encodings of certain meanings. The effect of using a non-default encoding of the same meaning is to call attention to the utterance: it becomes 'marked'. Being less frequently encountered, it takes more processing effort on the part of both encoder and decoder and, by the principle of relevance, the hearer looks for some modification of the message that would have been con-veyed by the default form. In the case of an alternative formulation of the same propositional content like *I've given an unambiguous exposition of my views*, the message might be harder to dismiss, but also the speaker might be taken to be stepping outside his conventional role as politician, which could on certain occasions not be desirable.

   The exact relation between minimal idioms like *bread and butter* and what we have called clichés is not clear. It may be that the latter should be con-sidered to lie on the same scale as the former, but are even more minimally idiomatic, since no propositional difference is involved.

4.4 Limits to compositionality II: non-compositional aspects of compositional expressions

4.4.1 Noun compounds

Many noun compounds can be considered to be idioms (see below) by our criteria. For instance, *tea towel* is clearly of the same general type as *blackbird*. But there are other examples which show recurrent semantic properties, which enable the constituents to satisfy the criteria for semantic constituents, but which display semantic properties that are not predictable in any way except perhaps on the basis of pragmatic world knowledge. For instance, consider the different relations between the first and second elements in the following:

pocket knife   ("knife that can be carried in the pocket")
                  (The same relationship appears in *pocket calculator* and *hand gun.*)

kitchen knife ("knife for use in the kitchen")
                  (The same relationship appears in *kitchen paper* and *garden knife.*)

meat knife   ("knife for cutting meat")
                  (The same relationship appears in *meat tenderizer* and *bread knife.*)

The relations fall into clear types (to a large extent), but there is no obvious way of predicting that for instance, a *tablecloth* is used to cover a table but a *dishcloth* is used to wipe dishes.

4.4.2 Active zones

Active zone is Langacker's term for the precise locus of interaction between two meanings in combination, typically an adjective and its head noun, or a verb and its complement. Some examples will make the notion clear. Take the case of a colour adjective and its head noun. Very often the colour does not apply globally to the object denoted by the head noun (although it may do), but only to a part:

a red hat	whole hat is red
a red book	outside covers are red
a red apple	a significant portion of outer skin is red
a yellow peach	inner flesh is yellow
a pink grapefruit	inner flesh is pink
a red traffic sign	symbols only are red
a red pencil (1)	red on outside
a red pencil (2)	writes red

red eyes   'white' of eyes is red
blue eyes   iris is blue

Is this idiom? Intuitively it is not, and the constituents of such expressions can easily be shown to pass the recurrent contrast test (it may of course be the case that the test is faulty, or insufficiently sensitive). These cases also seem to be different from the noun-compound cases: here, specification of the active zone in different ways does not radically change the mode of interaction: in all the above cases we know that the colour adjective indicates that the referent of the head noun is distinctive by virtue of its possession of an area with certain perceptual properties. But active zones need in some sense to be learned, and are not predictable by any sort of formal rule.

4.4.3 Complex categories

The point at issue in relation to complex categories is what happens when simple categories are merged to form a complex category. This is known in prototype theoretical circles as the **guppy effect**. Essentially, it is claimed that certain properties of a complex category cannot be predicted from the corresponding properties of the constituent categories. The example which gives its name to the 'effect' brings us back once again to noun compounds. When informants are asked to say what they consider to be the best or most representative example(s) of the category PET, they tend to go for cats and dogs; when asked to name the best examples of the category FISH, they choose trout, or salmon, or something of the sort. However, when asked for the best example of the category PET FISH, the answer is guppy, which is not regarded as central in either of the constituent categories. The effect is not confined to noun compounds: the same can be observed with an adjective–noun phrase such as *orange apple*. Items chosen by subjects as the best examples of the category ORANGE APPLE are different from those chosen as the best examples of the category APPLE, and their colour does not correspond to that chosen when asked which from a range of colours is the best example of the colour ORANGE. We shall return to the guppy effect and its significance in Chapter 7; for the moment we shall merely note its existence and the fact that it indicates a limitation on compositionality.

The guppy effect has given rise to much comment. Some have argued that the lack of compositionality reveals a weakness in prototype theory; simultaneously, prototype theorists have laboured to devise an algorithm which will enable the prototype of a complex category to be calculated from the individual prototypes of the component categories (with limited success). My own feeling is that the characteristics of a complex category *are* calculable from those of its component categories; the problem is that current descriptions of categories are so impoverished. Suppose we take a thoroughgoing holistic view of categories, in which the entirety of encyclopedic information about a category is a legitimate part of its characterization. So, for instance, the description of ORANGE would provide a complete range of hues falling under ORANGE, together with an index of centrality (or whatever); likewise, the description of APPLE would include, among other things, an indication of all the hues that apples can manifest. Given this information, the prototypical ORANGE APPLES are simply those APPLES whose hues approximate most closely to a prototypical ORANGE. There is obviously no requirement here either for the resultant apples to be prototypical apples or for them to have a proto-typical orange colour. Where is the mystery? The same argument applies to PET FISH: the prototypical pet fish are those fish which manifest the greatest proportion of the characteristics of prototypical pets: to work this out we need a detailed enough knowledge of the range of characteristics displayed by fish and by pets. (Notice that the grammar has some influence here: prototype pet fish are those fish nearest to prototype pets; this is not necessarily the same category as those pets which are nearest to prototype fish.)

4.5 Some reflections on compositionality

The debate about compositionality is by no means over. Let us conclude by distinguishing three positions vis-à-vis the principle of compositionality.

(i) The building-block model (alternatively, 'checklist theories'). This is intimately connected with strong componentialism: the meaning of an expression can be finitely described, and is totally accounted for by standard compositional processes acting on the equally determinate meanings of its component parts.

(ii) The scaffolding model (perhaps better, 'the semantic skeleton' model). According to this view, what compositionality provides is the bare bones of a semantic structure for a complex expression, which is fleshed out by less predictable pragmatic means, using encyclopedic knowledge, context, and so on. This can be viewed as a weaker version of the principle of compositionality.

(iii) The holistic model. This, too, is a strong version of compositionality. It requires that the meaning of every item is an indefinitely large entity which consists of its relations with all other items in the language. In a sense, all the effects of combination with other items are already pres-ent in the meaning: all that is needed is to extract the relevant portions. This radical view has its own problems, but it should be considered alongside the others.

Discussion questions and exercises

1. Identify the type of combination exhibited in the following phrases:

a forged passport	a dead cat	long eyelashes
a clever footballer	a high price	artificial cream
a former Miss World	a black hat	a brilliant pianist
a poor singer	a small planet	a striped dress

2. Each of the following sentences contains at least one conventional-ized expression of some sort. Attempt a classification of these under the following headings (using the definitions given in the chapter):

(a) true idioms; (b) frozen metaphors; (c) collocations; (d) clichés (fixed but more or less transparent expressions).

  (a) You have to hand it to him — he's got guts.
  (b) The ball's in your court now.
  (c) You're completely up the creek on this one.
  (d) Why don't you just wait and see?
  (e) She's got a bee in her bonnet about it.
  (f) The affair was blown up out of all proportion.
  (g) He took it in good part.
  (h) Use your loaf!
  (i) The situation went from bad to worse.
  (j) He swallowed it lock, stock and barrel.
  (k) They beat the living daylights out of him.
  (l) Well, you live and learn, don't you?

3. Make a study of English words carrying the prefix *dis-*. In how many of these is the prefix an independent semantic constituent? (See Cruse 1986: ch. 2.) Where *dis-* is a semantic constituent, how many distinct sense relations does *X: dis-X* represent? Discuss any difficulties.

4. Consider what the active zones are in the following:

  (a) The irate father spanked his son.
  (b) Mary filled the car up with petrol before driving on to the ferry.
  (c) Blue spectacles.
  (d) Tinted spectacles.
  (e) A red knife.
  (f) A sharp knife.
  (g) A fast computer program.
  (h) A quick cup of coffee.

Suggestions for further reading

The principle of compositionality is a key feature of any formal approach to semantics. Chapter 1 of Cann (1993) provides a good introduction; a more advanced treatment can be found in Partee (1984) and Bartsch (2002).

The account of idioms given here follows that of Cruse (1986: ch. 2). For a comprehensive survey of English idioms, see Makkai (1972). The syntactic behaviour of idioms is discussed in Fraser (1970), Katz (1973), and Newmeyer (1974). An interesting discussion of idioms from a psycholinguistic point of view is Gibbs (1990). (Gibbs's position on idioms is not as incompatible with Cruse 1986 as he seems to think.)

For collocations (defined more inclusively than here) see Mackin (1978). An up-to-date account of noun compounds from a cognitive linguistic viewpoint can be found in Coulson (2000). Langacker's notion of 'active zones' is expounded in Langacker (1991b: 189–201). For different types of adjective–noun combination, see Dillon (1979).

Part 2
Words and their Meanings

To the layman, words are par excellence the bearers of meaning in language. While it is in danger of understating the importance of other linguistic structures and phenomena in the elaboration of meaning, this view is not entirely unjustified: words do have a central role to play in the coding of meaning, and are responsible for much of the richness and subtlety of messages conveyed linguistically. Hence it is no accident that this part of the book is the most substantial. Here, after the introductory Chapter 5, we discuss how word meanings vary with context (Chapter 6), the relations between word meanings and concepts (Chapter 7), paradigmatic sense relations (Chapters 8 and 9), larger vocabulary structures (Chapter 10), how new meanings grow out of old ones (Chapter 11), how words affect the meanings of their syntagmatic neighbours (Chapter 12), theories of lexical decomposition (Chapter 13), and finally, a brief introduction to a new way of looking at word meanings (Chapter 14).

Introduction to lexical semantics

Introduction to lexical semantics

5.1 The nature of word meaning

In a descriptive introduction to meaning such as this, it is inevitable that the meanings of words should loom large, even though in more formally oriented accounts word meanings are left largely unanalysed, or reduced to mere skeletons of their true selves. There are, of course, more or less reputable justifications for such neglect. However, most (linguistically innocent) people have an intuition that meaning is intimately bound up with individual words; indeed, this is above all what words are for. While such an intuition seriously underestimates other aspects of meaning, it is not in itself wrong, and an adequate introduction to meaning should not shrink from the slipperiness and complexity of word meaning simply because it cannot be neatly corralled into a favoured formalization. Hence, the present and the following eight chapters will be devoted to various aspects of lexical semantics.

5.1.1 What is a word?

There has been a great deal of discussion of the nature of the word as a grammatical unit, too much even to summarize here. Most of it, anyway, is not relevant to our concerns. But it is as well to have some idea of what we are dealing with. The notion has notoriously resisted precise definition. Probably the best approach is a prototypical one: what is a prototypical word like? Well, for our purposes, the classical characterization as 'a minimal permutable element' will serve. This attributes two features to a prototypical word:

(i) It can be moved about in the sentence, or at least its position relative to other constituents can be altered by inserting new material.
(ii) It cannot be interrupted or its parts reordered.

In other words, in making changes to a sentence we are by and large obliged to treat its words as structurally inviolable wholes. Let's see briefly how this works. Take a sentence like (1):

(1) The government is strongly opposed to denationalization.

Reordering appears in such examples as (2)–(4):

(2) The government is opposed to denationalization—strongly.
(3) What the government is strongly opposed to is denationalization.
(4) It is denationalization that the government is opposed to.

And the possibilities for the insertion of new material are as follows:

(5) The (present) government, (apparently), is (very) strongly (and implac-ably) opposed (not only) to (creeping) denationalization, but . . . etc.

Notice that the only possible insertion points are between words. Words, of course, are separated by spaces in writing, although not usually by silences in speech. They also have a characteristic internal structure, in that they proto-typically have no more than one **lexical root**. (This notion will become clearer below, but, for instance, the lexical roots of the following words are shown in capitals:

GOVERNment reORDERing STRONGly deNATIONalization OPPOSed TYPically CLEAR er LEXical)

Some words, such as HEDGE-HOG, BUTTER-FLY, and BLACK-BOARD, seem to have more than one lexical root. These, however, are atypical, and for many of them it is possible to argue that the apparent roots are not fully autonomous, semantically, but form a fused root. Other words have no lexical roots at all: these are the so-called **grammatical words** like the, and, and of. There will be more on the 'lexical'/'non-lexical' distinction below.

At this point it is necessary to be somewhat more precise about what we mean by a word. In one sense, *obey*, *obeys*, *obeying*, and *obeyed* are different words (e.g. for crossword purposes); in another sense, they are merely different forms of the same word (and one would not, generally speaking, expect them to have separate entries in a dictionary). On the other hand, *obey* and *disobey* are different words in both senses, whereas *bank* (river) and *bank* (money) are the same word for crossword purposes, but we would expect them to have separate dictionary entries and they are therefore different words in the second sense. Finer distinctions are possible, but for our purposes it will be sufficient to distinguish **word forms** and **lexemes**. Word forms, as the name suggests, are individuated by their form, whether phonological or graphic (most of our examples will be both); lexemes can be regarded as groupings of one or more word forms, which are individuated by their roots and/or derivational affixes. So, *run*, *runs*, *running*, and *ran* are word forms belonging to the same lexeme **run**, while *walk*, *walks*, *walking*, and *walked* belong to a different lexeme, **walk**, distinguished from the former by its root; likewise, *obey*, *obeys*, *obeying*, and *obeyed* belong to a single lexeme, and *disobey*, *disobeys*, *disobeying*, and *dis-obeyed*, despite having the same root as the first set, belong to a different lexeme, distinguished this time by the possession of the derivational affix *dis-*.

A simple test for derivational affixes (the matter is in reality, however, complex and controversial) is that they are never grammatically obligatory. For instance, in *John is disobeying me*, *disobey* can be substituted by *watch*, without giving an ungrammatical sentence, which shows that *dis-* is not essential to the grammatical structure of the sentence. This is true of all occurrences of *dis-*. On the other hand, any verb which will fit grammatically into the frame *John is —— me* must bear the affix *-ing*, showing that it is not a **derivational** but an **inflectional affix**: word forms that differ only in respect of inflectional affixes belong to the same lexeme. It is the word-as-lexeme which is the significant unit for lexical semantics.

5.1.2 Lexical and grammatical meaning

A distinction is often made between lexical and grammatical meaning (some-times only the latter is allowed as being properly linguistic). There are dangers in all dichotomies; this one is harmless provided it is borne in mind that in reality there is a continuously varying scale of what might be termed lexicality and grammaticality. A convenient way of presenting the distinction is in terms of the sorts of element which carry the meaning in question. We can divide grammatical units into **closed-set items** and **open-set items** (another dichotomy which disguises a graded scale). Central examples of closed-set items have the following characteristics:

(i) They belong to small substitution sets (perhaps as small as one).
(ii) Their principal function is to articulate the grammatical structure of sentences.
(iii) They change at a relatively slow rate through time, so that a single speaker is unlikely to see loss or gain of items in their lifetime. (No new tense markers or determiners have appeared in English for a long time.) In other words, the inventory of items in a particular closed-set grammatical category is effectively fixed (i.e. 'closed', hence the name).

These may be contrasted with open-set items, which have the following characteristics:

(i) They belong to relatively large substitution sets (especially if semantic plausibility is ignored).
(ii) There is a relatively rapid turnover in membership of substitution classes, and a single speaker is likely to encounter many losses and gains in a single lifetime. (Think of the proliferation of words relating to space travel, or computing, in recent years.)
(iii) Their principal function is to carry the meaning of a sentence.

Both closed- and open-set items carry meaning, but their different functions mean that there are differences in the characteristics of the meanings that they typically carry.

A closed-set item, in order to be able to function properly as a grammatical element, has to be able to combine without anomaly with a wide range of roots; and for this to be possible it must have a meaning which is flexible, or broad enough, or sufficiently 'attenuated' not to generate clashes too easily, and it must signal contrasts which recur frequently. Hence, meanings such as "past", "present", and "future", which can co-occur with virtually any verbal notion, and "one" and "many", which can co-occur with vast numbers of nominal notions, are prototypical grammatical meanings.

In contrast, there is no limit to the particularity or richness of the meaning an open-set element may carry, as there are no requirements for recurrent meanings or wide co-occurrence possibilities. Hence, open-set items typically carry the burden of the semantic content of utterances. Because of the richness of their meanings and their unrestricted numbers, they participate in complex paradigmatic and syntagmatic structures.

What are called **content words** (basically nouns, verbs, adjectives, and adverbs) prototypically have one open-set morpheme (usually called the **root morpheme**) and may also have one or more closed-set items in the form of affixes. Lexical semantics is by and large the study of the meanings of content words, and is oriented principally to the contribution that open-set items make to these. Grammatical semantics concentrates on the meanings of closed-set items. However, a strict separation between grammatical and lexical semantics is not possible because the meanings of the two kinds of element interact in complex ways.

5.1.3 Word meaning and sentence meaning

In general, word meanings are not the sort of semantic units that one can communicate with on an individual basis, unless other meaning components are implicit. A word, on its own, does not actually say anything, does not convey 'a whole thought': for that purpose, more complex semantic entities are necessary, built out of word meanings, certainly, but having at least the complexity of propositions (argument+predicate). Words (and at a more basic level, morphemes) form the building blocks for these more complex structures.

5.1.4 The notion "possible word meaning"

It is worthwhile to pose the question of whether there are any restrictions on possible meanings for words. We may approach this in two stages. We can first ask whether there are any universal restrictions; and we can then enquire as to the existence of language-specific restrictions.

Let us take the first question first. Is there anything conceivable that could never be the meaning of a word? It will be as well to restrict ourselves to notions that can be expressed by a combination of words, otherwise we shall be in really deep water. One line of thinking can, I think, be disposed of relatively quickly. It may be thought that no language could possibly have a word meaning, for instance, "to face west on a sunny morning while doing something quickly". I confess that I would be astonished to find such a word. But the reason is not that it is theoretically impossible, but that it would be of such limited utility. Languages have words, at least partly, because in the cultures they serve, the meanings such words carry need to be communicated. (Of course, cultural evolution can leave words stranded, as it were, but this does not invalidate the basic point that words at some stage must be motivated in terms of possible use.) This means that if some culture had a use for the notion expressed, then it would not be surprising if there were a word for it. In the case in question, for instance, maybe the word could designate a specific sort of act of disrespect towards the Sun God, which carried specific penalties. If we take into account the possibility of outlandish (to us) religious beliefs, it is clear that the scope for improbable word meanings of this sort is (almost) unlimited.

Now let us look at a different sort of case. Take the sentence (6):

(6) The woman drank the wine slowly.

The notion "drank slowly" could easily be lexicalized (i.e. expressed by a single word): we have in English, after all, verbs such as *quaff* and *sip*, which combine the meaning of "drink" with some adverbial manner component. Similarly, a verb meaning "drink wine" is not at all implausible, as one of the senses of *drink* in English is specifically "drink alcoholic beverage" (as in *Mary doesn't drink, she'll just have an orange juice*). In contrast to these more or less plausible word meanings, consider next the possibility of having a word meaning "The woman drank" (*blisk*), or "the wine slowly" (*blenk*). On this system, *Blisk wine* would mean "The woman drank wine", and *Blisk blenk* would mean "The woman drank the wine slowly". It seems clear that here we are in the realms not of implausibility, but of impossibility.

As a further example, consider the phrase *very sweet coffee*. It is perfectly within the bounds of possibility that there should be a single word meaning "sweet coffee", or "very sweet", even "very sweet coffee", but it is not conceivable that there should be a word meaning "very —— coffee" (i.e. any adjective applied to *coffee* would be automatically intensified). What is the difference between the possible and the impossible cases? There seem to be two parts to the answer. First, a word meaning is not allowed to straddle the vital subject–predicate divide. Second, possible word meanings are constrained in a strange way by semantic dependencies. It is first necessary to distinguish **dependent** and **independent** components of a semantic combination. The independent component is the one which determines the semantic relations of the combination as a whole with external items. So, for instance, in *very large*, it is *large* which governs the combinability of the phrase *very large* with other items. Thus the oddness of, say, *?a very large wind* is attributable to a semantic incompatibility between *large* and *wind*—there is no inherent clash between *very* and *wind*, as the normality of *a very hot wind* demonstrates. By similar reasoning, the independent item in *warm milk* is *milk*, and in *drink warm milk* is *drink*. By following this line of reasoning, we can establish chains of semantic dependencies. For instance, the chain for *very young boy* is:

"very"→"young"→"boy"

and that for drink warm milk is:

"warm"→"milk"→"drink"

The constraint that we are looking at says that the elements that constitute the meaning of a word must form a continuous dependency chain. This means, first, that there must be a relation of dependency between elements. This rules out "wine slowly" as a possible word meaning, because there is no dependency between "wine" and "slowly" in "Drink wine slowly". Second, there must be no gaps in the chain which need to be filled by semantic elements from outside the word. This rules out cases like "very —— milk", where the dependency chain would have to be completed by an external item such as "hot".

Two further suggestions regarding possible word meanings are worth examining. The first is from the famous American linguist Noam Chomsky (1965: 201):

> ... there are no logical grounds for the apparent non-existence of words such as LIMB, similar to *limb* except that it designates the single object consisting of a dog's four legs so that *its LIMB is brown* would mean that the object consisting of its four legs is brown. Similarly, there is no a priori reason why a natural language could not contain a word HERD like the collective HERD except that it denotes a single scattered object with cows as parts, so that *a cow lost a leg* implies *the HERD lost a leg*, etc.

Chomsky's points were taken up by the British linguist Steven Pulman in his book *Word Meaning and Belief* (1983). First, he pointed out that some 'scattered objects' are nameable, such as fences, constellations, villages, and forests. To adapt Pulman slightly, we can say that nameable collections of otherwise independently nameable entities generally show one (or more) of the following features:

(i) The collection is relatively spatio-temporally contiguous (fence, forest, village).
(ii) It is the product of human agency (fence, village, artistic installation).
(iii) The members of the collection jointly fulfil a function not fulfilled by any of them separately (fence, bikini).

Notice that both Chomsky and Pulman insist on a distinction between singular scattered objects and collectives. But the criteria are not clear. Pulman describes collectives as 'things which are designated by singular count nouns or proper names but nevertheless regarded as plural: collective words like *herd*, *pile* and *flock*, and proper names like *the United States* or *the Commonwealth*'. (Notice that the possession of one of the features mentioned above seems to be necessary for these collective words.) But what is meant by 'regarded as plural'? A word like *committee* can take plural concord with a verb: *The committee have decided*, which could be taken as evidence that *committee* is regarded as plural, but this is not the case with, for instance, *pile*: **The pile of stones have to be removed*.

Chomsky is not much more explicit for LIMB, although he is for HERD. In the case of LIMB, he gives as the sort of sentence which would prove that there was a genuine word LIMB, something like *The* LIMB *of the dog is brown*, meaning that the dog's legs are brown. Actually, such cases do exist: *The foliage of this tree is light green* means simply that the leaves of the tree are light green. Chomsky's requirements for HERD are perhaps more strict. It seems that for HERD to be a bona fide example, a part of a cow must count as a part of a HERD (which it clearly does not for the 'normal' word *herd*). Notice that this criterion would rule out *foliage*: one would not say *The foliage of this tree has prominent veins*, but *The leaves of this tree have prominent veins*. (Similarly: **John's priceless library of first editions has lost several pages*.) But it is not clear that it holds for *fence*, either (and others discussed by Pulman as bona fide singular non-collectives). If the separate (and separated) posts which constituted a fence each had a hole in it, would one say *The fence has holes in it* or *The fence posts have holes in them*? I would be happier with the latter. On the other hand, I would be happy with *You can't wear this bikini because it has holes in it* (cf. also *This bikini has a reinforced gusset*). I suspect that there is, in fact, no sharp distinction between the HERD type of example and the *herd* type. I am inclined to agree with Chomsky, however, to the extent that the HERD type are somewhat rare.

The second suggestion concerns the putative 'impossible' words *benter* and *succeive*, suggested by the American linguist Ray Jackendoff, a follower of Chomsky with a strong interest in semantics (1990: 261). Let us consider *benter* first. This is proposed as a logically coherent converse of *enter* which cannot be lexically realized. Sentences such as (7) are fully normal:

(7) Mary entered the room.

The proposed converse of this would be (8):

(8) The room bentered Mary.

(On the pattern of: *Mary followed John* and its converse *John preceded Mary*.) Another example sometimes cited is *succeive*, which is intended to denote the converse of *receive*:

(9)   John received the parcel.
(10) The parcel succeived John.

Intuitively, there seems to be some resistance to words having such meanings, which goes beyond the mere fact that they do not exist in English. However, the prohibition is perhaps not absolute, as the following observations suggest.

First, the meaning of *benter* is not all that far removed from that of such words as *envelop*, *incorporate*, and *engulf*, which seem to have the right sort of meaning. In the case of *succeive*, the word *reach* appears capable of encoding, at least approximately, its supposed meaning:

(11) I sent John a parcel; he received it yesterday.
(12) I sent John a parcel; it reached him yesterday.

The constraints on word meaning discussed above would seem to be universal in nature. However, there also exist constraints of a more language-specific type. Some languages seem to proscribe the packaging together of certain sorts of meaning in a single word. A single example will suffice. Consider sentence (13):

(13) John ran up the stairs.

Here, the word *ran* encapsulates two notions, that of movement and that of manner. This is a common pattern in English:

(14) John   crawled across the road.
            staggered into the room.
            waltzed through the office.
            etc.

However, this pattern is not possible in many languages, including French. In French, such sentences must be rendered as in (15):

(15) Jean monta l'escalier en courant.

Here, the notions of motion and direction are jointly packaged into *monta*, but manner has to be expressed separately. Notice that the French pattern is not prohibited in English (*John mounted the stairs running*), but is markedly less natural.

5.2 The major problems of lexical semantics

Linguists with different theoretical commitments will give different accounts of what the core tasks of lexical semantics are; the following is an attempt at a relatively theoretically neutral summary.

5.2.1 Description of content

Describing content is in a sense the most obvious task: how do we say what a word means? Unfortunately, even at this level of generality it is impossible to escape the tentacles of theory, because there are scholars who maintain that the notion 'the meaning of a word' is not a coherent one; and for those who believe there is such a thing, the nature of the description of it will hang

crucially on what sort of thing it is believed to be. We shall look briefly below
at some of the options.

5.2.2 Contextual variation

However one characterizes the notion of the meaning of a word, one is forced
to confront the fact that the semantic import of a single word form can vary
greatly from one context to another. There are various theory-dependent
strategies for attacking this problem, but the facts will not go away: the variation must be accounted for. Variation is not random: part of a satisfactory
account will identify and explain patterns of variation.

5.2.3 Sense relations and structures in the lexicon

Regular patterns appear not only in the nature and distribution of the meanings of a single word in different contexts, but also between different words
in the same context. This results in structured groupings of words in the
vocabulary on the basis of recurrent meaning relations.

5.2.4 Word meaning and syntactic properties

An important question is whether and to what extent the syntactic properties
of words are independent of, or are controlled by, their meanings. There are
still many different views on this topic.

5.3 Approaches to lexical semantics

5.3.1 One-level vs. two-level approaches

A major dividing line which separates semanticists is the question of whether
a distinction can be made between semantics and encyclopedic knowledge.
Those who believe such a division can be made often draw an analogy with
phonetics and phonology. Human beings can make and learn to recognize an
almost infinite variety of speech sounds, but in any particular language, only a
handful of these function distinctively to convey meanings, or enter into systematic relations of any complexity. These are the true linguistic elements on
the 'sound' side of language. In a similar way, the variety of 'raw' meanings is
virtually infinite, but only a limited number of these are truly linguistic and
interact systematically with other aspects of the linguistic system. The vast
detailed knowledge of the world, which speakers undoubtedly possess is,
according to the dual-level view, a property, not of language elements, but of
concepts, which are strictly extralinguistic. Truly linguistic meaning elements
are of a much 'leaner' sort, and are (typically) thought of as (more) amenable
to formalization. One criterion suggested for recognizing 'linguistic' meaning
is involvement with syntax, whether by virtue of being the meaning carried by

some grammatical element, or because it correlates with such factors as agreement patterns or sub-categorization of major syntactic categories.

Partisans of the single-level view claim that no non-arbitrary basis for assigning aspects of meaning (or knowledge) to the 'semantic' or 'encyclo-pedic' side of a purported dichotomy has been put forward which survives even a cursory scrutiny. Most cognitive linguists would take the view that all meaning is conceptual, and that the 'extra' level of structure proposed by the two-level camp does not actually do any theoretical work. The distinction between grammatical and lexical/encyclopedic meaning is not necessarily denied, but it is likely to be seen as a continuum, rather than a dichotomy, and entirely conceptual in nature.

5.3.2 Monosemic vs. polysemic approaches

The point at issue in relation to the distinction between the monosemic and the polysemic approach is how many meanings ought to be attributed to a word. There is no dispute about clear-cut cases of homonymy, like that of *bank*, where there is no conceivable way of deriving one meaning from the other. The dispute centres on clusters of related senses characteristic of poly-semy. (For greater detail, see Chapter 6.) The monosemic view is that as few senses as possible should be given separate recognition in the (ideal) lexicon of a language, and as many as possible derived from these. The argument usually goes like this: if one reading of a word is in any way a motivated extension of another one, then only one should be recorded, and the other should be left to the operation of **lexical rules**, which in general apply to more than one instance and hence represent systematicity in the lexicon.

The polysemic approach rejects the assumption that a motivated extension of a word sense does not need to be recorded in the lexicon. The basic reason for this is that lexical rules only specify *potential* extensions of meaning, only some of which become conventionalized and incorporated in the lexicon: others are possible, and may appear as nonce forms, but there is nonetheless a clear distinction between these and those which are established (in principle, anyway: actually there is a continuous scale of establishment). Take the case of *drink*. In many contexts, it is clear what is being drunk, but obviously one would not wish to create a different lexical entry for *drink* corresponding to every possible drinkable liquid. To this extent, the monosemists and the polysemists would agree. However, it is possible for some particular drinkable items to be incorporated into a specific reading for *drink*. In principle, any class of beverage could be incorporated in this way, but in fact, in English, only "alcoholic beverages" can be encoded thus: *I'm afraid John has started drinking again.* Now in principle, this could have happened with fruit juice instead of alcohol, but it is a fact about the English lexicon that *drink* has one of these possibilities but not the other. The majority view nowadays is probably monosemic, but the position adopted in this book is polysemic.

5.3.3 The componential approach

One of the earliest and still most persistent and widespread ways of approaching word meaning is to think of the meaning of a word as being constructed out of smaller, more elementary, invariant units of meaning, somewhat on the analogy of the atomic structure of matter (although the immediate inspiration for the first proposals on these lines was not physics but phonology). These 'semantic atoms' are variously known as **semes, semantic features, semantic components, semantic markers, semantic primes** (to cite a few of the terms). Here, the merest outline of the approach is presented; componential semantics is treated in greater detail in Chapter 13.

Probably the first statement of a componential programme for semantics within modern linguistics was due to the Danish structural linguist Louis Hjelmslev. He believed as a matter of principle that the meaning side of the linguistic sign should show the same structuring principles as the sound side. For him the notion of **reduction** was of major importance. The phonological structure of hundreds of thousands of different signs in a language can be analysed as combinations of syllables drawn from a list of a few hundred, and these in turn can be shown to be built out of phonemes belonging to an inventory of fifty or so, thus arriving at the ultimate phonological building blocks, the distinctive features, whose number is of the order of a dozen. In the same way, the meaning side of signs should be reducible to combinations drawn from an inventory significantly less numerous than the stock of signs being analysed. Hjelmslev did not have any universalist pretensions, each language being unique and needing an analysis in its own terms, nor were his *figurae* (his term for the basic elements) in any way abstract (1961): they were the meanings of words in the language. What he seemed to have in mind, therefore, was the discovery of a set of basic words, out of whose meanings all other word meanings could be constructed. Hjelmslev was the first structural semanticist (1961): the approach was developed considerably by European linguists, with a German variety and a French variety.

A componential approach developed in America, seemingly independently (and largely in ignorance) of the movement in Europe. It first appeared amongst anthropological linguists, and scored a significant success in reducing the apparent impenetrable complexity of kinship systems to combinations from a limited set of features. A new version, proposed by Jerrold Katz and Jerry Fodor (1963), appeared in the context of early Chomskyan generative grammar. This was much more ambitious than anything which had appeared previously: first, it formed an integral part of a complete theory of language; second, it made claims of universality and psychological reality; and third, the features were not confined to the meanings of existing words, but were of an abstract nature. This approach did not take hold in mainstream generative linguistics, and among current generativists a thoroughgoing componential approach is found only in the work of Jackendoff (1983; 1990; 1996).

An extreme version of componential semantics is found in the work of the Polish-Australian linguist Anna Wierzbicka. This is a highly original approach, which is not an offshoot of any of the approaches described above, but takes its inspiration from much earlier philosophical work, notably by the philosopher Gottfried Leibniz. Wierzbicka's view is that there exists a very restricted set of universal semantic atoms in terms of which all conceivable meanings can be expressed. Her inventory of primes is astonishingly small (she started out with eleven, but the list has now grown to fifty or so); they are not abstract, and hence unverifiable by direct intuition like those of Katz and Fodor, but are concrete, and any analysis should satisfy the intuitions of native speakers.

5.3.4 'Holist' approaches

It is a belief of all componentialists that the meaning of a word can, in some useful sense, be finitely specified, in isolation from the meanings of other words in the language. Among philosophers of language, this is known as the localist view. For a localist, contextual variation can be accounted for by rules of interaction with contexts. The contrary position is the holistic view, according to which the meaning of a word cannot be known without taking into account the meanings of all the other words in a language. There are various versions of holism: two will be outlined here.

5.3.4.1 Haas

I first learnt semantics from William Haas at Manchester, whose highly idiosyncratic view of meaning derives from an aspect of the philosopher Ludwig Wittgenstein's work, namely, his 'use' theory of meaning, which is encapsulated in the dictum: 'Don't look for the meaning—look for the use.' In other words, the meaning of an expression is the use to which it is put. As it stands, this is not very helpful, merely suggestive. Haas gave it a personal twist, inspired by the dictum of J. R. Firth (the founder of the 'London' or 'Firthian' school of linguistics: 'Words shall be known by the company they keep.' This interprets 'use' as the contexts, actual and potential, in which the expression occurs normally (i.e. without anomaly). Haas went further than this. He said that the meaning of a word was a **semantic field** (not the usual semantic field) which had two dimensions: a **syntagmatic** dimension, in which all possible (grammatically well-formed) contexts of the word were arranged in order of normality; and a **paradigmatic** dimension, in which for each context, the possible paradigmatic substitutes for the word were arranged in order of normality. Relative normality was for Haas a primitive notion. In principle, 'context' includes extralinguistic context; but Haas argued that since every relevant aspect of extralinguistic context can be coded linguistically, nothing is lost by restricting attention to linguistic contexts. The word's semantic field, as understood by Haas, constitutes its meaning. Notice that every word therefore participates in the meaning of every other word (he was inspired here by Leibniz's monads); there is therefore no distinction between word meaning and encyclopedic knowledge. Haas's view was that the semantic field of a word (as he defined it) actually constituted the meaning of the word; here, the view will be taken that the semantic field of a word reflects its meaning.

5.3.4.2 Lyons

A second variety of holism is represented by Lyons (1977). The essence of this approach is the quintessentially Saussurean belief (the Swiss scholar Ferdinand de Saussure is often regarded as the 'father' of modern linguistics) that meanings are not substantive but relational, and are constituted by contrasts within the same system. Lyons states that the sense of a lexical item consists of the set of sense relations which the item contracts with other items which participate in the same field. Sense relations, he insists, are not relations between independently established senses; one should rather say that senses are constituted out of sense relations. So, for instance, the meaning of *horse* should be portrayed along the lines shown in Fig. 5.1.

In this system, the links are of specific sorts, such as "is a kind of" (e.g. *horse:animal*), "is not a kind of" (e.g. *horse:cow*), "is a part of" (e.g. *mane: horse*), "is a characteristic noise produced by" (e.g. *neigh:horse*), "is a dwelling place for" (e.g. *stable:horse*). Since the words illustrated also enter into relations with other words than *horse*, the full meaning of *horse* is a complex network of relations potentially encompassing the whole lexicon.

5.3.5 Conceptual approaches

Conceptual approaches (at least as the term is used here) are single-level approaches, and identify the meaning of a word with the concept or concepts it gives access to in the cognitive system. Among cognitive linguists, the prototype model of concept structure has occupied a prominent position.

Fig. 5.1

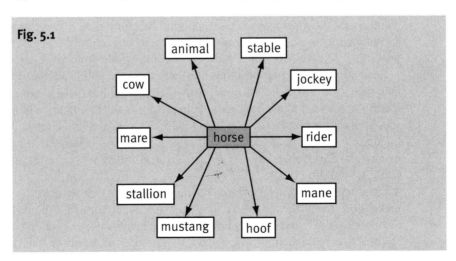

The origins of the prototype approach can be traced to Wittgenstein (1972) (who initiated more than one line of thinking that was to influence linguistics). He is usually credited with being the first to challenge the classical Aristotelian notion of natural categories as being definable in terms of necessary and sufficient criteria. He put forward the well-known example of GAME, challenging his readers to come up with the necessary and sufficient criteria for something being a game. None of the obvious suggestions is criterial:

involves physical activity
has winners and losers
is played for amusement
has rules, etc.

None of these is either exclusive to games or necessary for something to be a game. Wittgenstein proposed the notion of **family resemblance**: the members of a large family typically resemble one another in a variety of ways, but there are no features which they all have, and there may be members who share no features, but these will nonetheless be linked to the others by a chain of resemblance. Although important in breaking the stranglehold of Aristotelian theory, this notion is not very helpful for semantic analysis. Wittgenstein did not say what family resemblance consisted of, in particular how in-family resemblances differ from out-family resemblances. In other words, there was nothing other than arbitrary stipulation to stop everyone in the world from belonging to the same family. (However, a similar problem still bedevils modern descendants of Wittgenstein's family resemblance.)

The notion of non-Aristotelian categories was taken up and further refined by cognitive psychologists, especially the American cognitive psychologist Eleanor Rosch (1973; 1978) and her co-workers, who established what is now known as **prototype theory** as an account of natural categories. On this account, members of a category are not equal—they vary in how good they are, or how representative, of the category. The very best are the **prototypical** members, and the category is essentially built round these: other examples are assimilated to the category or not according to how closely they resemble the prototype. A fuller account of prototype theory will be found in Chapter 7.

Jackendoff (1983; 1990; 1996) is another linguist who locates word meaning in conceptual structure (his picture of conceptual structure bears strong resemblances to that of the cognitive linguists). Like the cognitive linguists, he sees no need for an intermediate 'linguistic semantics'. Unlike many cognitive linguists, however, he is strongly componentialist, and believes that intuitively perceived relationships should (must) be accounted for in terms of shared semantic building blocks. He also has a strong predilection for precisely formalized representations. Perhaps the most important characteristic separating Jackendoff from the cognitive linguists is his continued espousal of the Chomskyan precepts of strong innateness, the insufficiency of general cognitive abilities to explain all linguistic behaviour, and the autonomy of syntax.

5.3.6 Formal approaches

Formal approaches to semantics attempt to express the facts of meaning through a strict formalism, preferably closely related to one of the standard logics. The hoped-for pay-off from adopting this sort of approach includes greater explicitness, testability of hypotheses, easier link-up with syntax, and machine implementability. Those who are less sympathetic to this kind of approach point to the existence of significant aspects of semantics which are continuously variable, and to the somewhat meagre descriptive results so far achieved. Formalist approaches will not be given any prominence in the present work, which aims rather at a certain descriptive richness.

Suggestions for further reading

This chapter mostly serves as an introduction to topics which are treated in greater detail in later chapters, so most of the relevant reading is given later. For the same reason, no discussion questions are included.

On word and lexeme, see Lyons (1977: ch. 13). Pulman (1983) is a major reference for nameability; see also Jackendoff (1990), for *benter* and *succeive*. For the different ways of 'packaging' meaning in lexical items, see Talmy (1985).

For Lyons's notion of sense, see Lyons (1977: ch. 7.3); for Haas's contextual approach, see Haas (1962; 1964).

CHAPTER 6

Contextual variability of
word meaning

Contextual variability of word meaning

6.1 Preliminaries

Once we try to grapple with the notion 'the meaning of a word', we come up against a serious problem: the interpretation we give to a particular word form can vary so greatly from context to context. The observable variations range from very gross, with little or no perceptible connection between the readings, as in: *They moored the boat to the bank* and *He is the manager of a local bank*, through clearly different but intuitively related readings, as in *My father's firm built this school* (*school* here refers to the building) and *John's school won the Football Charity Shield last year* (in this case *school* refers to (a subset of) the human population of the school), to relatively subtle variations, as in the case of *path* in *He was coming down the path to meet me even before I reached the garden gate* and *We followed a winding path through the woods* (a different mental image of a path is conjured up in the two cases), or *walk* in *Alice can walk already and she's only 11 months old* and *I usually walk to work*, where not only is the manner of walking different, but so also are the implicit contrasts (in the first case, standing up unaided and talking and in the second case, driving or going by bus/train, etc.).

This type of variation, which is endemic in the vocabulary of any natural language, means that answers must be sought to questions like: Do words typically have multiple meanings? How do we decide what constitutes 'a meaning'? Is there a finite number of such meanings? How are the meanings related to one another? The present chapter attempts to address questions of this sort.

We shall begin by identifying two properties of variant readings of a word which are relevant to the problem of individuating and counting them. Suppose we find a perceptible difference in the readings of a word in two contexts. We can first of all ask whether (or to what extent) there is a sharp semantic boundary between the two readings (in our terms, how **discrete** are they?); a second question is whether they are mutually exclusive (in our terms, are they

antagonistic?). Both of these will be taken as aspects of the **distinctness** of two readings.

6.2 Aspects of distinctness

6.2.1 Discreteness

To begin with, only enough criteria will be given to establish the notion of discreteness; more subtle types of evidence, valid in particular contexts, will be brought into the discussion later. Four criteria will be considered here; three of them have often been regarded as **ambiguity tests** (and latterly dismissed as such). There are good reasons, however, for claiming that they are not tests for ambiguity (see later), but for discreteness.

6.2.1.1 The identity test

The first criterion goes under the name of the **identity test**. Consider the following sentence:

(1) Mary is wearing a light coat; so is Jane.

Intuitively, *light* means two different things: "light in colour" or "light in weight". Bearing in mind these two interpretations, there are four different situations with regard to the properties of Mary's and Jane's coats: (i) they are both lightweight, (ii) they are both light-coloured, (iii) Mary's coat is light-weight and Jane's is light-coloured, (iv) Jane's coat is lightweight and Mary's is light-coloured. Notice, however, that sentence (1) is capable of designating only two of these situations, namely (i) and (ii). In other words, once one has decided on a reading for *light* one must stick with it, at least through sub-sequent anaphoric back-references. This is known as the **identity constraint**. The constraint applies equally to speaker and hearer. A speaker can be held to account for the use of the above construction if they intended two different readings of *light*; in the case of the hearer, there is a processing constraint which makes it difficult to attach both readings simultaneously to one occur-rence of the word. Notice that the pressure for identity of reading is much reduced (although perhaps not completely absent) if *light* is mentioned twice; (2) is not anomalous:

(2) Mary is wearing a light coat; Jane is wearing a light coat, too, as a matter of fact. However, whereas Mary's coat is light in colour but heavy, Jane's is dark in colour, but lightweight.

The identity constraint observed in (1) should be contrasted with its absence in (3):

(3) Mary has adopted a child; so has Jane.

The child must obviously be either a boy or a girl, but there are no constraints on the possible readings: the child adopted by Jane does not have to be of the same sex as Mary's, hence there is no support here for any suggestion that "boy" and "girl" correspond to distinct readings of *child*.

6.2.1.2 Independent truth conditions

The second criterion for the discreteness of two readings is that they have independent truth-conditional properties. A good test of this is whether a context can be imagined in which a *Yes/No* question containing the relevant word can be answered truthfully with both *Yes* and *No*. Consider the case where Mary is wearing a light-coloured, heavyweight coat. If someone asks *Were you wearing a light coat?*, Mary can truthfully answer either in the positive or the negative: *Yes, I was wearing my pale green winter coat/No, I was wearing my thick winter coat*. On the other hand, if one were to ask the Mary in (3) *Is it true that you have adopted a child?*, there are no conceivable circumstances in which she could truthfully answer both *Yes* and *No*.

6.2.1.3 Independent sense relations

The third indicator of discreteness is the possession by two readings of genuinely independent sets of sense relations (these are treated in detail in Chapters 8 and 9). Care must be taken here in the definition of 'independent'; here, however, we shall confine ourselves to clear cases. For instance, the two readings of *light* have distinct opposites, *dark* and *heavy*. The fact that these two are completely unrelated strengthens the case for discreteness. The two obvious readings of *bank* also have quite independent sense relations. The (river) *bank* is a meronym (i.e. designates a part) of *river*, and has *mouth*, *source*, and *bed* among its co-meronyms (i.e. sister part-names). The (money) *bank* is not a part of anything but is a sub-type of *financial institution*, and has, for instance, *building society* as one of its sisters.

6.2.1.4 Autonomy

The fourth indicator of discreteness is what we shall call **autonomy**. Basically this refers to the usability of the word form in one of the senses when the other is explicitly denied, or ruled out by reason of anomaly, or some such. Consider the two readings of the word *dog*, "canine species" and "male of canine species". In the sentence *I prefer dogs to bitches*, the general sense is ruled out on the grounds of semantic anomaly (compare *?I prefer fruit to apples*), but the sentence is fully normal. This shows that the specific sense has autonomy. Compare this with the sex-specific interpretation of *child*, as in *This child seems to have lost his parents*. Although *I prefer boys to girls* is normal, *?I prefer children to girls* is not, showing that the sex-specific interpretation of *child* is not autonomous and hence, in the absence of other indications, not discrete.

6.2.2 Antagonism

The readings of an indisputably ambiguous word such as *bank* display another property besides discreteness, which we shall regard as criterial for ambiguity. This is **antagonism**. Consider a sentence which admits both readings, such as *We finally reached the bank*. It is impossible to focus one's attention on both readings at once: they compete with one another, and the best one can do is to switch rapidly from one to the other. In any normal use of this sentence, the speaker will have one reading in mind, and the hearer will be expected to recover that reading on the basis of contextual clues: the choice cannot normally be left open. If the hearer finds it impossible to choose between the readings, the utterance will be judged unsatisfactory, and further clarification will be sought.

A sentence which calls for two discrete and antagonistic readings to be activated at the same time will give rise to the phenomenon of **zeugma**, or punning, as in *?John and his driving licence expired last Thursday* (*John* calls for the "die" reading of *expire*, while *his driving licence* calls for the "come to the end of a period of validity" reading); another example of punning is *When the Chair in the Philosophy Department became vacant, the Appointments Committee sat on it for six months* (this plays on multiple meanings of both *chair* and *sit on*).

It may be presumed that antagonistic readings are *ipso facto* also discrete, and therefore that antagonism represents the highest degree of distinctness.

6.3 Senses

We shall take antagonism between readings as a defining criterion for the **ambiguity** of a linguistic expression. Where the ambiguous expression is a word, like *bank* or *light*, we shall say that it has more than one **sense**. (Later on, degrees of distinctness that fall short of full sensehood will be introduced.)

6.3.1 Establishment

It is almost certainly the case that all words are potentially usable with meanings other than their default readings (i.e. the meanings which would come to mind in the absence of any contextual information). Examples such as the following can be multiplied indefinitely:

(4) (a) John ordered a pizza.
   (b) The pizza doesn't look too happy with what he's been given.
(5) (a) Some of the guests are wearing roses, some carnations.
   (b) The carnations are to sit on the left.
(6) (a) 'I'm off to lunch,' said John.
   (b) 'This is my lunch,' said John, waving a five-pound note.

However, although one has no trouble working out what is meant, no one would dream of registering the (b) readings above in a dictionary, nor is there any reason to suppose that they are permanently stored in the mental lexicon. In the following cases, however, it is fairly safe to assume that both readings are permanently laid down in some internal store:

(7) (a) John planted five roses.
    (b) John picked five roses.
(8) (a) That must be an uncomfortable position to sleep in.
    (b) What is your position on capital punishment?

These may be described as **established**, and the former set as **non-established**. For a word to be described as ambiguous, it must have at least two established senses.

6.3.2 Motivation: homonymy and polysemy

Given that a word is ambiguous, it may be the case that there is an intelligible connection of some sort between the readings, or it may be seemingly arbitrary. For instance, few people can intuit any relationship between *bank* (money) and *bank* (river), although a connection between *bank* (money) and, say, *blood bank* is not difficult to construe (both are used for the safe keeping of something valuable), or between *river bank* and *cloud bank*. In the case of *bank* (river) and *bank* (money), we say that *bank* displays **homonymy**, or is **homonymous**, and the two readings are **homonyms**. It is normal to say in such circumstances that there are two different words which happen to have the same formal properties (phonological and graphic). A lexicographer would normally give two main entries, *bank*[1] and *bank*[2]. Where there is a connection between the senses, as in *position* in (8a) and (8b), we say that the word is **polysemous**, or manifests **polysemy**. In this book the less common practice will be adopted of referring to the related readings of a polysemous word as **polysemes**.

Of course, the degree to which two readings can be related forms a continuous scale, and there is no sharp dividing line between relatedness and unrelatedness; furthermore, individual speakers differ in their judgements of relatedness. However, this does not render the distinction between polysemy and homonymy useless, because there are many clear cases. Notice that homonymy is possible only with established readings. It is probably wise to reserve the term 'polysemy', too, for established senses like those of *position*, and to designate cases like *pizza* in (4a) and (4b) by the expression 'coerced polysemy'.

6.3.3 Non-lexical sources of ambiguity

Ambiguity has been presented here as a lexical phenomenon; it is important to emphasize, however, that there are other sources of ambiguity. One of these, of course, is syntax, as in *Mary saw the man with the telescope*. Many syntactic ambiguities arise from the possibility of alternative constituent structures, as here: *with the telescope* is either a manner adverbial modifying *saw*, or a prepositional phrase modifying *the man*. In neither case is there any other syntactic difference. An identity constraint operates here, too, in that coordinated items must have parallel constituent structures. Hence, (9) has only two readings (rather than four):

(9) Mary saw the girl with the telescope and the man with the dog.

A syntactic ambiguity may involve functional alternation in one or more items, as in Hockett's classic telegram: *Ship sails today*, where *ship* and *sails* both change their syntactic categories in the two readings.

A word should be said about cases like *The man entered the room*. In any specific context of use, *the man* and *the room* will designate a particular man and a particular room, and in a different context, a different man and a different room. Is this ambiguity? It is not usually recognized as such, since there is no evidence that multiple entries will be necessary, either in the mental lexicon, or in any ideal language description. However, there seems no great harm in calling this phenomenon **pragmatic ambiguity** or **open ambiguity** (because the number of readings is potentially infinite).

6.4 Varieties of polysemy

There is, by definition, a motivated relationship between polysemous senses. There are various ways of classifying the sorts of relation that can hold between polysemous senses. We shall begin by distinguishing linear and non-linear relations.

6.4.1 Linear relations between polysemes

Senses have a **linear** relation if one is a specialization of (i.e. a hyponym or meronym—see Chapter 8, section 2.1) the other (which of course entails that the latter is a generalization of the former). We can distinguish specialization from generalization if we recognize one of the senses as more basic than the other: if A is more basic than B, and B is more specialized than A, then B is a specialization of A (*mutatis mutandis* for generalization).

6.4.1.1 Autohyponymy

Autohyponymy occurs when a word has a default general sense, and a contextually restricted sense which is more specific in that it denotes a subvariety of the general sense. An example of this is *dog*, which has two senses, a general sense, "member of canine race", as in *Dog and cat owners must register their pets*, and a more specific reading, as in *That's not a dog, it's a bitch*. Notice that the specific reading demonstrates autonomy, since the second clause contradicts the general reading of *dog*: if the animal is a bitch, then it *is* a dog. Another example is *drink*, whose general reading occurs in *You must not drink anything on the day of the operation* and whose specific reading is exemplified in *John doesn't drink—he'll have an orange juice*, which also exhibits autonomy, because presumably John is going to drink (general reading) the orange juice.

6.4.1.2 Automeronymy

Automeronymy occurs in a parallel way to autohyponymy, except that the more specific reading denotes sub-part rather than a sub-type, although it is by no means always easy to determine whether we should be talking about automeronymy or autoholonymy—that is to say, it is not easy to see which is the more basic use. An example of this may be *door*, which can refer either to the whole set-up, with jambs, lintel, threshold, hinges, and the leaf panel itself, as in *Go through that door*, or just to the leaf, as in *Take the door off its hinges*. Notice the zeugma in the following, which confirms the discreteness of the specific reading: *?We took the door off its hinges and walked through it*.

6.4.1.3 Autosuperordination

An example of autosuperordination is the use of *man* to refer to the human race (or indeed any use of masculine terms to embrace the feminine). There is no doubt that these are contextually restricted. (This fact may lend some force to the feminist argument that such uses should be suppressed; if the "male" reading is the default one, then the notion that the sentence applies mainly to males could arise by a kind of inertia.) Another example, but involving the generalization of a feminine term, is the use of *cow* to refer to bovines of both sexes, especially when there is a mixed group (as in *a field full of cows*, which does not exclude the possibility of the odd bull); the normal reference of the term is the female animal.

6.4.1.4 Autoholonymy

As was mentioned above, discriminating automeronymy from autoholonymy is not easy, because there seem often to be different default readings in different contexts; that is to say, different contexts, which in themselves appear to exert no particular selective pressure, nonetheless induce different readings. Consider the case of *body*, as in *Jane loves to show off her body*. This surely denotes the whole body, not just the trunk (even though a lot of what Jane presumably enjoys displaying is actually part of the trunk!). But consider *She received some serious injuries/blows to the body*. Here, just the trunk is indicated. Another similar example is *arm: a scratch on the arm* is definitely on the non-hand part of the arm, but in *He lost an arm in the accident* or *She was waving her arms about*, the whole arm is indicated. We shall tentatively consider these to be cases of autoholonymy, on the grounds that the inclusion of the hand in the latter cases is pragmatically entailed in those contexts, whereas the exclusion of the hand in the former case is totally unmotivated (admittedly, the case of *body* is not quite so clear). There are clearer cases in other languages, for instance, the well-known *Have you eaten rice?* in, for instance, Malay, as a way of enquiring whether someone has had a meal (which would prototypically include rice as a part).

6.4.2 Non-linear polysemy

6.4.2.1 Metaphor

Many polysemous senses are clearly related metaphorically. A detailed consideration of metaphor will be postponed until Chapter 11: here we will simply characterize metaphor as figurative usage based on resemblance. A good example of a set of readings related metaphorically is provided by *position*:

That is an uncomfortable *position* to sleep in.
This is a good *position* to see the procession.
Mary has an excellent *position* in ICI.
What is your *position* on EU membership?
You've put me in an awkward *position*.

6.4.2.2 Metonymy

Another rich source of polysemous variation is metonymy, which is also dealt with in greater detail later, but may be characterized for the moment as figurative use based on association:

There are too many *mouths* to feed.
(Don't talk with your *mouth* full.)
That's a nice bit of *skirt*.
(She wore a red *skirt*.)
John has his own *wheels*.
(One of the *wheels* fell off.)
Jane married a large *bank account*.
(Jane has a *bank account*.)
He is the *voice* of the people.
(He has a loud *voice*.)

6.4.2.3 Miscellaneous

For some polysemous senses, although they are obviously related, it does not seem very illuminating to describe their relationship in terms of either metaphor or metonymy. An example is the calendric and non-calendric readings of words denoting periods of time, such as *week*, *month*, *year*. The clearest example is probably *month*, because the two readings do not even indicate the same length of time. A calendric month begins on the first day of the said month, and ends on the day before the first of the following month; a non-calendric month starts on any day, and ends four weeks later.

6.4.3 Systematic polysemy

Some cases of polysemy are systematic in the sense that the relationship between the readings recurs over a range of lexical items that is at least partly predictable on semantic grounds. Probably the least systematic is metaphor. There seems to be little pressure for systematicity in metaphor. For instance, in metaphors derived from the human body, one cannot assume that if *foot* is used for the lowest part of something, then *head* will be used for the upper part (or vice versa):

foot of mountain   *head/top of mountain
foot of tree   *head/crown of tree
head of a pin   *foot/point of a pin

We do speak of the *head* and the *foot* of a bed, but this is arguably a case of metonymy, that is to say, it indicates which part of the body is normally in that position.

The most systematic metaphors are probably the most basic ones, many of which are so naturalized that they hardly feel like metaphors any more. I am referring to cases like UP IS MORE/DOWN IS LESS. That is to say, if one can refer to something as *rising* (prices, popularity, hopes, etc.), the chances are pretty good that they are also capable of *falling*.

Metonymy can be highly systematic. Some examples are the following:

"tree species"/"type of wood"   beech, walnut, oak
"fruit"/"tree species"   apple, pear, cherry
"flower"/"plant"   rose, daffodil, azalea
"animal"/"meat"   rabbit, chicken, armadillo
"composer"/"music by same"   Beethoven was deaf.
                                  Do you like Beethoven?
"food"/"person ordering same"   The omelette is overcooked.
                                  The omelette complained.

There is some systematicity, too, in linear polysemy. Take the case of *dog*. The story is that in a situation where a category has a binary subdivision, and only one of the subdivisions has a name, then the superordinate term will develop a more specific reading to fill the gap. So, for instance, in the case of *dog*, of the subcategories of male and female animals, only the female has a distinct name, namely *bitch*, so the superordinate term moves down to fill the gap. In the case of *duck*, it is the female sub-category which is unnamed, so *duck* functions as partner for *drake* as well as denoting the kind of bird. In other cases one can argue that the development has proceeded in the other direction, in that the name of one of the sub-categories (typically the most significant and familiar one, if there is a difference) moves up to function as a superordinate. This is perhaps what has happened in the case of *cow*, and presumably, too, in the case of *rice* mentioned earlier.

6.5 Between polysemy and monosemy

In most accounts of contextual variation in the meaning of a word, a sharp distinction is drawn between 'one meaning' and 'many meanings', between monosemy and polysemy. But this is too crude: there are many degrees of distinctness which fall short of full sensehood, but which are nonetheless to be distinguished from contextual modulation (see below).

6.5.1 Facets

We have taken antagonism as a criterion for ambiguity, and hence for full sensehood; however, by no means all discrete readings of a word are mutually antagonistic. A clear example of this is provided by certain readings of the word book. Sentences (10) and (11) below exemplify two such readings:

(10) Please put this book back on the shelf.
(11) I find this book unreadable.

In the first case it is the physical object which is referred to, in the second case the text which the physical object embodies. However, this is not ordinary ambiguity: the two readings coordinate quite happily, without producing a sense of punning:

(12) Put this book back on the shelf: it's quite unreadable.

Such readings are called **facets**, and we may refer, to the [TEXT] facet and the [TOME] facet. There is considerable evidence of the discreteness of facets.

6.5.1.1 Identity constraint

Consider the following sentence: *John thinks this is the most remarkable book of the century; so does Mary.* If it is known that John is speaking of the text, there is a strong presumption that that is what Mary admires, too; likewise if John is impressed by the physical presentation.

6.5.1.2 Independent truth conditions

Consider the following exchange:

(13) A: Do you like the book?
    B: (i) No, it's terribly badly written.
        (ii) Yes, it's beautifully produced.

It is possible to conceive of a situation in which both of B's replies are true simultaneously. In reply (i), book is being interpreted as if only the [TEXT] facet was relevant, and in (ii), as if only the [TOME] facet was relevant. This independence of the facets is an indication of their distinctness.

6.5.1.3 Independent sense relations

The subvarieties of *book* [TEXT] are such things as *novel, biography, dictionary*, and so on. These do not correspond to the subvarieties of *book* [TOME], like *paperback, hardback*, and so on; that is to say, it is not the case that novels are typically hardbacks and biographies paperbacks, or whatever. Similarly, the parts of a text: *chapter, paragraph, sentence*, and so on, do not regularly correspond to the parts of a physical book, such as *cover, page*, or *spine*.

6.5.1.4 Ambiguity in containing constructions

The phrase *a new book* has two readings: "a new text" and "a new tome". This is genuine ambiguity: the two interpretations are fully antagonistic. But there is neither lexical nor syntactic ambiguity present. What happens is that the modifying adjective *new* is required to attach itself to one facet or another (this is the origin of the antagonism). However, two different adjectives, say *interesting* and *heavy*, may attach themselves to two different facets without tension, as in Fig. 6.1.

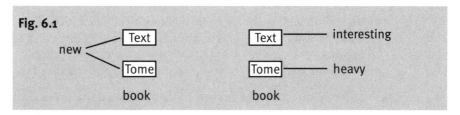

Fig. 6.1

new ⟨ Text / Tome ⟩ book   Text —— interesting / Tome —— heavy   book

6.5.1.5 Independent metaphorical extension

In the phrase *a book of matches*, the metaphor relates only to the [TOME] facet; the [TEXT] facet is completely irrelevant.

6.5.1.6 Independent proper noun

David Copperfield can be loosely described as the name of a book; but strictly speaking it is the name of a [TEXT], not of a [TOME].

Facets are not merely discrete, they are also autonomous. Consider the following:

(**14**) I'm not interested in the cover design, layout, printing, and so on, I'm interested in the book itself.

(**15**) I'm not interested in the plot, characters, or the quality of the writing, I'm interested in the book itself.

In (14) there are no problems about interpreting *book* as [TEXT], and in (15), as [TOME]. This use of *the X itself* is a particularly strict test for autonomy. A further indication of autonomy is that *book* can refer to only a text, or only a tome, that is, a text that has been composed but is not yet embodied, or a book which has as yet no text in it (*I've bought a book to write the minutes of the meeting in*).

Facets can be described as fully discrete but non-antagonistic readings of a word. Another important characteristic is that they are characteristically of distinct ontological types. However, in spite of their discreteness and onto-logical distinctness it would not be correct to say that they represented distinct concepts: they are somehow fused into a single conceptual unit. Amongst the evidence for this claim the following may be cited:

(i) Ordinary speakers are not normally aware of the dual nature of *book*: it has to be pointed out to them (however, once pointed out, it becomes obvious). The facets form a single, unified 'gestalt'. The default reading of *book* is the combined one.

(ii) As we have seen, predicates selecting different facets can coordinate without zeugma, and there is no normal requirement for speakers to intend, or hearers to identify, only one of the facets, as is the case with true ambiguity.

(iii) The combined reading functions as a basic-level item.

(iv) Some predicates require both facets to be present: *publish a book*, *Mary is reading a book*.

(v) The combined meaning can be metaphorically extended: *John's mind is a closed book to me*. This cannot be construed unless one takes into account both facets.

(vi) The combination may bear a proper name (e.g. *Britain* (see below)).

These points, although perhaps none of them is conclusive on its own, add up to an impressive case for the conceptual unity of the meaning of *book*.

It is not at present clear quite how widespread in the vocabulary the facet phenomenon is. It is certainly not unique to *book*; in fact anything that can be thought of as having both concrete form and semantic (in the widest sense) content seems to display facets. So, for instance, *Mary's speech was inaudible* and *Mary's speech was very interesting* manifest different facets of *speech*. Likewise, *a beautiful CD* and *a flexible CD* (and the ambiguity of *a new CD*) point to the dual nature of the meaning of *CD*.

An example of another large group of faceted words is *bank*:

(16) The bank in the High Street was blown up last night.
(17) That used to be the friendliest bank in town.
(18) This bank was founded in 1575.

These sentences involve facets which can be designated, respectively, as [PREM-ISES], [PERSONNEL], and [INSTITUTION]. These can coordinate together without zeugma:

(19) The friendly bank in the High Street that was founded in 1575 was blown up last night by terrorists.

A parallel set of facets will be found in *school*, and in *university*. A third group is represented by *Britain* in the following:

(20) Britain lies under one metre of snow.
(21) Britain mourns the death of the Queen's corgi.
(22) Britain has declared war on San Marino.

In (20) *Britain* designates a concrete geographic entity, in (21) the population, a human entity, and in (22) an abstract political entity. According to my intuitions, although they are discrete, they all coordinate together fairly happily without zeugma, as in (23):

(23) Britain, despite the fact that it is lying under one metre of snow and is mourning the death of the Queen's corgi, has declared war on San Marino.

6.5.2 Perspectives

There is another type of difference between readings which displays a certain level of discreteness without antagonism, but not as much as facets do, and without autonomy. These will be referred to as **perspectives**. A simple way of explaining these would be by analogy with looking at an everyday object from in front, from the sides, from behind, from on top, etc. All these different views are perceptually distinct, but the mind unifies them into a single conceptual unity. Something similar happens with meaning. Consider the case of *house*. A house can be thought of as an example of a particular architectural style, as a dwelling, as a piece of property, or as a piece of construction work. Each of these points of view causes a transformation in the accessibility profile of knowledge associated with the lexical item *house*. Some of these profiles may be sufficiently distinct to give rise to discontinuity phenomena, such as ambiguous phrases without ambiguous lexical items. An example might be *a delightful house*, which could be delightful from the point of view of its architectural qualities, or because of its qualities as a place to live in. (It could, of course, be both, but my intuition is that one would mean either one thing or the other.) Think also of *John began the book*. This is ambiguous, and two of its possible readings are that John began reading the book and that he began writing it. Notice that in both cases it is the [TEXT] facet which is involved, so the ambiguity here cannot be explained by appeal to facets.

How many different perspectives are there? One might suppose there to be an indefinitely large number; but if we apply the constraint that different ways of seeing must give some evidence of discreteness, such as the possibility of ambiguous phrases, there seem not to be so very many. On one account, there are only four, which we shall illustrate in connection with the word *horse*. (What follows is a reinterpretation of the so-called **qualia roles**, introduced by James Pustejovsky, an American linguist working in the Chomskyan tradition (Pustejovsky 1995).

6.5.2.1 Seeing something as a whole consisting of parts

Consider the viewpoint of a veterinarian, acting in a professional capacity. Such a person is primarily concerned with the proper functioning of the horse's body and its parts. Their approach has parallels with that of a garage mechanic to a car. (This corresponds to Pustejovsky's **constitutive role**.)

6.5.2.2 Seeing something as a kind, in contrast with other kinds

For this perspective, think of the way a taxonomic zoologist would view a horse. This would involve the way horses differ from other species, such as deer, or zebras, and also how the various sub-species and varieties of horse differ from one another. Ordinary speakers, too, have a 'mindset' for classification; most 'folk taxonomies' depend heavily on perceptual features such as size, shape, and colour, so these will figure largely in this perspective. (Some of the classificatory features will inevitably involve parts, but the point of view is different.) (This corresponds to Pustejovsky's **formal role**.)

6.5.2.3 Seeing something as having a certain function

A characteristic way of looking at things is in terms of their function: think of the way a jockey, or a Kazakh tribesman, will view his horse. Some things, of course, have many different uses, and each use will cause a different highlighting and backgrounding of conceptual material. But it is implicit in the fourfold division we are adopting here that within-perspective differences will be markedly less distinct (by various measures) than between-perspective differences. This is an empirical matter which has not been properly explored. As an example of between-perspective distinctness, think of a veterinarian's and a jockey's/racehorse trainer's differing interpretations of *This horse is in excellent condition*: health and race-fitness are not the same thing. (This corresponds to Pustejovsky's **telic role**.)

6.5.2.4 Seeing something from the point of view of its origins

Adopting this perspective means thinking of something in terms of how it came into being. For a living thing like a horse, this would involve the life cycle, conception and birth, and so on. It would also include the poet's view of his/her poem, a builder's view of a house, a farmer's view of farm products, and so on. Mention has already been made of the ambiguity of *John began the book*, which is ambiguous even when *book* is interpreted exclusively as [TEXT]: the ambiguity can be explained by saying that on the interpretation "John began reading the book", a functional perspective is being taken, since the purpose of a book is to be read, whereas on the interpretation "John began writing a book", a 'life cycle' perspective (in the broadest sense) is being taken. (There is a third possible interpretation: that John began binding or putting together a book physically. This, too, would be to take a 'life cycle' perspective, but would apply to a different facet. (This corresponds to Pustejovsky's **agentive role**.))

6.5.3 Micro-senses

Antagonism should probably be regarded as a scalar property, which the truly ambiguous items (i.e. fully fledged independent senses) presented above display to a high degree. However, there are also readings with a lower level of both discreteness and antagonism than full senses, and we shall call these micro-senses. A good example of this is afforded by the word *knife*. Although there is a superordinate sense of *knife*, according to which a penknife, a table knife, and a pruning knife are all knives, in certain contexts the default reading of *knife* is a specific one appropriate to the context. Consider a mealtime context. Johnny is tearing pieces of meat with his fingers. He has a penknife in his pocket, but not a knife of the appropriate kind:

Mother: Johnny, use your knife.
Johnny: I haven't got one.

Johnny's response is perfectly appropriate: he does not need to be more specific. In this context, *knife* means "knife of the sort used at table". The independence of this reading is further confirmed by the fact that it forms part of a lexical hierarchy, with *cutlery* as an inclusive term, and *fork* and *spoon* as sister cutlery items. The inclusive reading is backgrounded in the above example, and probably only ever appears under contextual pressure; it is also relatively vague, whereas the specific readings are relatively rich and clearly defined. Other readings of *knife* have different sense relations. For instance, a pruning knife is a *tool*, a commando's knife is a *weapon*, and a surgeon's knife is a *surgical instrument*. There is reason to believe that the mental representation of a word like *knife* is a collection of specific readings loosely held together under a sketchy superordinate umbrella, rather than as a schematic specification which is enriched in various ways in particular contexts. That is to say, the specific readings of *knife* are selected from an established set, and are not the result of contextual enrichment of the inclusive reading (i.e. they are not the result of contextual modulation (see below)).

6.5.4 Sense spectra

Micro-senses function like senses within their home domain, but they are less accessible from other domains. Another similar phenomenon is that of **local senses**. These, too, are domain-specific; they differ from micro-senses, however, in that (i) they are points on a semantic continuum (called in Cruse 1986 a **sense spectrum**); (ii) the degree of antagonism between readings depends on how far apart they are on the spectrum (in other words, superordination is also local); (iii) literal and figurative readings can be intuited; and (iv) there is no inclusive reading. The example of a sense spectrum given in Cruse (1986) was that of *mouth*. We may presume that the core (literal) meaning of *mouth* is the mouth of an animal or human, and that the other readings are metaphorical extensions of this. One of the most 'distant' extensions (in the sense of being farthest away from the literal meaning) is *mouth of river*. If we try to coordinate this with the literal reading, zeugma results: *?The poisoned chocolate slipped into the Contessa's mouth just as her yacht entered that of the river.* However, coordination of readings closer together on the spectrum produces no zeugma: *The mouth of the cave resembles that of a bottle.*

Points on the spectrum that are close together in the sense that they coordinate without zeugma are nonetheless fairly insulated from one another in actual use, as they typically belong to different domains. Within their home domains they are quite like normal senses, with their own sense relations and so on. Thus *mouth* in the river domain is a meronym (designates a part) of *river*, with *source, bank*, and *bed* as sister parts; *mouth* in the bottle domain also designates a part, and has *neck* and *base* among its sister parts. Notice that there is no overall category of mouths which covers all the metaphorical extensions. Semantic spectra seem to be characteristic of situations where a core sense has a variety of relatively minor metaphorical extensions, and seem particularly prevalent when the basis of the metaphor is physical shape (as with *tongue, foot, head, arm*, or *pin*).

6.6 Sense modulation

The effects of context on the meaning of a word can be summarized under the three headings **selection, coercion,** and **modulation.** All the examples of contextual variation in word meaning that we have examined so far have involved, as it were, ready-made bundles of meaning, selectively activated by contexts. This selection operates largely through the suppression of readings which give rise to some sort of semantic clash with the context (see Chapter 12 for more detailed discussion of this). If all the readings are suppressed except one, then this one will be 'selected', and generally in such a situation the alternatives do not even enter the consciousness of either speaker or hearer. It sometimes happens that none of the established readings of a word is compatible with the context. Because of a tacit assumption that speakers are usually trying to convey an intelligible message, this typically triggers off a search through possible meaning extensions, such as metaphor or metonymy, for a reading which is compatible with the context. If one is found, this will be taken to be the intended reading, and we can say that context has **coerced** a new reading. However, selection and coercion do not exhaust the possibilities of contextual variation: a lot of variation arises as a result of contextual effects which do not go beyond the bounds of a single sense. This is called here **contextual modulation.** There are two main varieties, **enrichment** and **impoverishment,** according to whether the effect is to add or remove meaning.

6.6.1 Enrichment

The most obvious effect of context is to add semantic content, that is, to enrich a meaning or make it more specific. The enrichments arise as a result of processes of inference which are in principle no different from those operating more generally in language understanding (for instance, those which generate conversational implicatures: see Chapter 18). There are two main ways of being more specific: by narrowing down to a sub-class (i.e. hyponymic specialization) and by narrowing down to a sub-part (i.e. meronymic specialization). Both may, of course, operate at the same time.

6.6.1.1 Hyponymic enrichment

The context may simply add features of meaning to a word which are not made explicit by the lexical item itself. For instance, gender may be determined:

(**24**) Our maths *teacher* is on maternity leave.

or height:

(**25**) My *brother* always bumps his head when he goes through the door.

or temperature:

(**26**) The *coffee* burnt my tongue.

or legality:

(**27**) Our house was burgled while we were away. They only *took* the video, though.

Contextual determination may be to a specific kind of the class normally denoted by the lexical item employed, rather than adding a feature:

(**28**) I wish that *animal* would stop barking/miaowing.
(**29**) John is *going* well in the 1500-metres freestyle.

In some cases, the specialization is to a prototypical example:

(**30**) I wish I could fly like a bird.

Notice that prototypical and non-prototypical interpretations coordinate without zeugma:

(**31**) An ostrich is a bird, but it can't fly like one.

The first occurrence of bird designates the whole class, but the second (via anaphora) must receive a prototypical interpretation. The normality of (31) shows that we are not dealing with separate senses.

6.6.1.2 Meronymic enrichment

Specification may also be to part of what the lexical item used normally refers to. This may be a definite identifiable part:

(32) The car has a puncture.

The only part of a car that this can refer to is one of the tyres. The specification may, on the other hand, be less definite:

(33) The car was damaged when John drove it into a tree.

Here the damage can be located at the front end of the car rather than the rear end, but there is still a range of possibilities, and the damaged area may not constitute a definite part. This kind of narrowing down to a part is widespread in language use and not usually noticed. For instance, a *red book* has red covers, not red letters, whereas a *red warning sign* most likely has red letters. A number of similar examples were mentioned in Chapter 4 (section 4.4.2).

6.6.2 Impoverishment

The effect of context is not always to enrich: it may also impoverish, if it makes clear that a lexical item is being used in a vague sense. Compare the following:

(34) The draughtsman carefully drew a circle.
(35) The children formed a circle round the teacher.

It is clear that the use of *circle* in (34) is in some sense the core one: the occurrence in (35) represents a kind of relaxation of the central, prototypical meaning, in that no one would expect the children to form a geometrically exact circle, and the description is vague in the sense (a) that it covers a range of possible dispositions of the children and (b) that it is not clear what arrangements are excluded. The vague use of words is widespread and normal.

It may be useful to distinguish cases like (35), where context demands a vague use, but there is no explicit signal of vagueness, from cases like (36), where it is arguable that the word *turban* is not being used vaguely:

(36) He was wearing a sort of turban.

Here, of course, the phrase *a sort of turban* is vague. It is also worth pointing out that although all words in principle are to some extent susceptible to vague use, some words are more susceptible than others. Just to give one example, although strictly speaking *twelve* and *a dozen* are synonymous, the latter lends itself more readily to approximate use.

Discussion questions and exercises

1. How would you characterize the differences between the (i), (ii), and (iii) readings of the italicized items in the following?

   (a) (i) A *volume* of verse.
        (ii) A *volume* of 20 litres.
   (b) (i) Mary ordered an *omelette*.
        (ii) The *omelette* wants his coffee now.
   (c) (i) John is a *complete* soldier.
        (ii) Have you got a *complete* soldier? (No, the right leg is missing.)
   (d) (i) The *school* in George Street is going to be closed down.
        (ii) The whole *school* joined the protest march.
        (iii) That *school* is always being vandalized.
   (e) (i) The drawer contained a collection of *knives* of various sorts.
        (ii) When you set the table, make sure that the *knives* are clean.
   (f) (i) They *led* the prisoner away.
        (ii) They *led* him to believe that he would be freed.
   (g) (i) She was told not to eat or *drink* after 8 a.m.
        (ii) It was after her husband left her that she began to *drink*.
   (h) (i) My *cousin* married an actress.
        (ii) My *cousin* married a policeman.
   (i) (i) Put that *encyclopedia* down!
        (ii) I can't understand this *encyclopedia*.
   (j) (i) He has a *light* workload this semester.
        (ii) There will be some *light* rain in the evening.

2. Consider how many distinct meanings of *collect* are represented in the following. How would you organize them in a dictionary entry? Compare your results with the treatment given in one or more standard dictionaries.

   (a) The books collected dust.
   (b) He collects stamps.
   (c) The postman collects the mail every day.
   (d) She collected her things and left.
   (e) She sat down to collect her thoughts.
   (f) She collects the children from school at 4 o'clock.
   (g) Dust collects on the books.
   (h) The students collected in front of the notice board.
   (i) They are collecting for Oxfam.
   (j) He collects his pension on Thursdays.
   (k) The dustmen collect the garbage on Wednesdays.
   (l) She collected two gold medals in Tokyo.
   (m) They collected rainwater in a bucket.
   (n) They collect the rent once a fortnight.
   (o) He will collect quite a lot on his accident insurance.

Suggestions for further reading

For a useful discussion of a range of approaches to polysemy see Geeraerts (1993). Chapter 3 of Cruse (1986) deals with context variants, but the present account differs from this in certain important respects, and is closer to Cruse (1995). For a more detailed account of facets see Cruse (2000a) and Croft and Cruse (forthcoming); for micro-senses see Cruse (2000a), (2000b), (2002e) and Croft and Cruse (forthcoming).

Most linguists take a more monosemic view than the one presented here. For an extreme monosemic position, see Ruhl (1989) (Cruse 1992b is a critical review of this). Among those accepting a high degree of polysemy is Langacker (e.g. 1991b: ch. 10); the elaboration of Langacker's account in Tuggy (1993) is of particular interest. For a discussion of vagueness in language see Channell (1994).

CHAPTER 7

Word meanings and concepts

Word meanings and concepts

7.1 Introduction

The view taken in this book is that the most fruitful approach to meaning is to regard it as conceptual in nature. This is not to deny that there are (presumably important) relations between linguistic forms and extralinguistic reality. Our approach is, however, based on the assumption that the most direct connections of linguistic forms (phonological and syntactic) are with conceptual structures, and that until these are sorted out there is little hope of making progress with the more indirect links with the outside world. The consequences of this view for lexical semantics are spelled out in more detail in this chapter.

7.1.1 The importance of concepts

Concepts are vital to the efficient functioning of human cognition. They are organized bundles of stored knowledge which represent an articulation of events, entities, situations, and so on in our experience. If we were not able to assign aspects of our experience to stable categories, it would remain disorganized chaos. We would not be able to learn from it because each experience would be unique. It is only because we can put similar (but not identical) elements of experience into categories that we can recognize them as having happened before, and we can access stored knowledge about them. Furthermore, shared categories are a prerequisite to communication.

7.1.2 Word–concept mapping

We shall assume a fairly simplistic model both of the structure of the conceptual system and of the relations between linguistic forms and concepts. In this model, concepts are linked together in a complex multi-dimensional network (see Fig. 7.1). The links are of specific types (e.g. *is a kind of, is a part of, is used for*, etc.), and are of variable strength. These links correspond to concepts of a more schematic kind than the concepts which they serve to connect, which are typically richer and more complex. Linguistic forms map onto

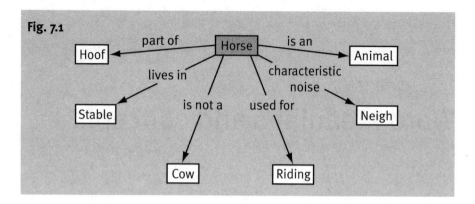

Fig. 7.1

conceptual structures of comparable complexity. Here we shall confine our attention to individual words. Each full lexical item directly activates a concept and indirectly activates linked concepts according to the strength of the link. There is no direct link between, for instance, the word *horse* and the concept ANIMAL: the word *horse* has a direct link only with the concept HORSE.

7.1.3 Conceptual structure

Before we go on to a detailed look at the nature of concepts, it will be useful to stand back and take a look at conceptual structure in a wider perspective. The view outlined here is quite close to what Jackendoff has developed over the last decade or so.

It is usually taken for granted that the expressive possibilities of language are infinite: not only is there an infinite number of possible grammatical constructions in a language, but there is no area of semantic space that cannot be designated linguistically, and semantic space is considered also to be in principle infinite. Since the brain is a finite physical object, it cannot store an infinite number of linguistic forms mapped onto an infinite number of concepts. Hence, just as the formal side of language solves the problem of infinity by providing a set of units with recursive rules for combination, in a similar way there must be primitive entities and formation rules, which specify well-formed complex conceptual structures.

Three independent levels of structure are proposed by Jackendoff: phonological, syntactic, and conceptual, the latter constituting the level of meaning. A complete description of a language must incorporate a specification of primitives and formation rules for each level, together with correspondence rules, which indicate the relationships between structures on the three levels.

It is a general requirement of any account of conceptual structure that it be rich enough to account for every last nuance expressible in language. Conceptual structure could in principle be richer than expressible linguistic meanings, but it cannot be less rich. Jackendoff calls this the **expressive constraint**. (He also has a **grammatical constraint**, which amounts to a bias in favour of conceptual structures that can be put into transparent correspondence with surface syntactic structures, and against 'deep structures' of a radically different form to the corresponding surface forms.)

In many linguistic theories, a level of semantic structure is postulated, in addition to conceptual structure. Only the former is 'truly linguistic', the latter being part of general cognition. The arguments on this topic are complex and controversial. However, the view taken in this book is that there is only one level; that is to say, syntactic structures map directly onto conceptual structures. The basis for this view is that there is no work for a distinct semantic level to do: everything needed to motivate grammatical structure is present in conceptual structure. The simplest arrangement should be adopted until there is overwhelming evidence that only a more complex system can handle the facts: such evidence, in our view, is at present lacking.

7.2 The nature of concepts

Concepts serve to categorize experience and give access to knowledge concerning entities which fall into the categories. In this section we shall consider how conceptual categories can best be characterized.

7.2.1 The classical approach

The classical approach to categorization, which goes back at least to Aristotle but is still often taken for granted, defines a category in terms of a set of **necessary and sufficient criteria** (or conditions, or features) for membership. So, for instance, the criteria for some X to qualify for inclusion in the category GIRL are:

X is human
X is female
X is young

If any of these criteria are not satisfied, then X is not a girl (i.e. the criteria are individually necessary); if all the criteria are satisfied, then X is a girl (i.e. the criteria are jointly sufficient). (The above set of criteria can be taken as a definition of the meaning of *girl*.)

7.2.2 Some problems of the classical approach

There is a certain undeniable obviousness about this way of defining categories. However, it has a number of shortcomings.

7.2.2.1 Lack of plausible analyses

The superficial plausibility of the Aristotelian analysis of *girl* (and similar words) is misleading. Words like *girl*, which apparently can be satisfactorily defined by means of a set of necessary and sufficient features, constitute a relatively small proportion of the vocabulary at large and are confined to certain semantic areas, such as kinship, and specialized terms for animals specifying age and sex, and so on. There are many everyday words whose meanings cannot be captured by means of a set of necessary and sufficient features. Wittgenstein's famous example is *game*. He argued that it was impossible to draw up a list of features possessed by all games which jointly distinguish games from non-games. One might suggest the following as possible criteria:

(i) involves winning and losing
(ii) involves more than one person
(iii) has arbitrary rules
(iv) done purely for enjoyment

However, for each of these criteria there are activities that we call games which do not satisfy them. Thus, there are many games which do not involve winning and losing: party games, such as charades, Matthew, Mark, Luke, and John, kissing games; children's games such as leapfrog, hallalevo, and hopscotch; solitaire is a game for one person; many children's games, such as dressing-up games and ducks and drakes, have no statable rules; and finally, many games are played professionally, and not simply for enjoyment. However, in spite of the lack of compliance with the above criteria, we communicate using the word *game* perfectly successfully, and without any sense of linguistic imperfection. Such examples can be multiplied almost indefinitely: *apple, dog, table, water, house, flower, dance, violin,* etc.

7.2.2.2 Fuzzy boundaries

An Aristotelian definition of a category implies a sharp, fixed boundary. However, much empirical research on category structure has been taken to demonstrate that the boundaries of natural categories are fuzzy and contextually flexible. For instance, the American scholars Brent Berlin and Paul Kay (1969), who studied colour categories from a psycholinguistic and anthropological linguistic perspective, found that while judgements of central examples of colours were relatively constant across subjects and reliable within subjects on different occasions, judgements of borderline instances, for instance between red and orange, or between blue and purple, showed neither agreement amongst subjects nor reliability with a single subject on different occasions. William Labov, an American sociolinguist, studied subjects' naming of line drawings illustrating cups, mugs, vases, bowls, and the like which systematically varied parameters such as ratio of height to width, curved or straight sides, presence or absence of a handle (Labov 1973). Again, the finding was that certain items received reliable assignation to a particular category, while others were uncertain. He also found that contextual conditions could alter subjects' responses, so that, for instance, an instruction to imagine all the items as containing rice extended the boundaries of the BOWL category, while a similar instruction to imagine coffee as contents extended the CUP category. Such results receive no natural explanation within the classical (Aristotelian) picture.

7.2.2.3 Internal structure of categories

As far as the classical conception of categories goes, everything that satisfies the criteria has the same status—that is to say, something is either in the category or not in it, and that is all there is to say about the matter. However, language users have clear intuitions about differences of status of items within a category: some members are felt to be 'better' examples of the category than others. For instance, an apple is a better example of a fruit than is a date, or an olive. In other words, categories have internal structure: there are central members, less central members, and borderline cases. No account of these facts can be given using the classical approach.

7.2.3 The standard prototype approach

We shall first of all describe what might be called the 'standard' approach to prototype theory, deriving from the work of Eleanor Rosch (1973; 1978) and her co-workers (Rosch and Mervis 1975). The main thrust of Rosch's work has been to argue that natural conceptual categories are structured around the 'best' examples or prototypes of the categories, and that other items are assimilated to a category according to whether they sufficiently resemble the prototype or not.

7.2.3.1 GEO and family resemblance

Rosch's most basic experimental technique is the elicitation of subjects' **Goodness-of-Exemplar** (GOE) ratings. Subjects are asked to give a numerical value to their estimate of how good an example something is of a given category. The rating scale typically goes something like this:

1: very good example
2: good example
3: fairly good example
4: moderately good example
5: fairly poor example
6: bad example
7: very bad example/not an example at all

So, for instance, if the category was VEGETABLE, the ratings of various items might be as follows:

POTATO, CARROT	1
TURNIP, CABBAGE	2
CELERY, BEETROOT	3

AUBERGINE, COURGETTE	4
PARSLEY, BASIL	5
RHUBARB	6
LEMON	7

Significantly, subjects do not find this to be a totally meaningless task. While there is of course a great deal of variation between subjects, statistically the results within a culturally and linguistically homogeneous population cluster strongly round particular values. The prototypes of categories are determined by selecting the item with the lowest average numerical score.

Ratings of GOE may be strongly culture dependent. (Familiarity is undoubtedly a factor influencing GOE scores, but the scores cannot be reduced to familiarity.) For instance, in a British context (say, a typical class of undergraduates), DATE typically receives a GOE score of 3–5 relative to the category of FRUIT, but an audience of Jordanians accorded it an almost unanimous 1.

Wittgenstein described the instances of the category GAME as manifesting a relationship of **family resemblance**: the members of a human family typically resemble one another, but there may well not be any set of features that they all possess, and it may be possible to find two members who have no features in common. However, they will be linked by a chain of intermediate members with whom they do share features. So, for example, A may have no features in common with C, but has the same nose as B, who in turn has the same eyes as C. Prototype theory embraces Wittgenstein's notion that family resemblance unites the members of a category, but adds to it the vital idea of central and peripheral members.

7.2.3.2 Prototype effects

Taken in isolation, the existence of stable GOE scores might be thought to be of minor cognitive significance. However, there is abundant evidence that prototypicality, as measured by GOE scores, correlates strongly with important aspects of cognitive behaviour. Such correlations are usually referred to as **prototype effects**. The principal prototype effects are as follows:

Order of mention. When subjects are asked to list the members of a category, and especially if they are put under time pressure, the order of listing correlates with GOE ratings, with the prototypical member showing a strong tendency to appear early in the list.

Overall frequency. The overall frequency of mention in such lists also correlates with GOE score.

Order of acquisition. Prototypical members of categories tend to be acquired first, and order of acquisition correlates with GOE rating.

Vocabulary learning. Children at later stages of language acquisition, when vocabulary enlargement can be greatly influenced by explicit teaching, learn new words more readily if they are provided with definitions that focus on prototypical instantiations than if they are given an abstract definition that more accurately reflects the total range of the word's meaning.

Speed of verification. In psycholinguistic experiments in which subjects are required to respond as quickly as they can to a categorization task, subjects produce faster responses if the tasks involve a prototypical member. In a typical set-up, subjects see a pair of words, say FRUIT:BANANA, flashed up on a screen, and they are to respond as quickly as possible by pressing one of two buttons, the one labelled *Yes* if the second named item belongs to the category indicated by the first item and *No* otherwise. Results show that responses to, for instance, FRUIT:APPLE, where the second item is a prototypical member of the class denoted by the first, are faster than, say, FRUIT:DATE (for average British subjects).

Priming. Another psycholinguistic technique involves the phenomenon of **priming**. In a typical set-up, subjects see strings of letters flashed on to a screen and their task is to respond *Yes* (by pressing the appropriate button) if the string of letters makes a word of (say) English, and *No* if it does not. Responses are timed electronically. It is a well-established experimental fact that if a word is preceded by a semantically related word, response to it will be speeded up. So, for instance, a *Yes* response to DOCTOR will be faster if NURSE has been just previously presented. It is found that the presentation of a category name has the greatest speeding-up effect on the prototype of a category, and the effect is proportionately less as we move away from the centre of the category to the periphery (as measured by GOE scores).

7.2.3.3 Intuitive unity, definitional polyvalence

Most of the work on prototypes has been carried out by psychologists, and the nature of the experiments reflects this. A purely linguistic characterization of categories with a prototypic organization (it is not necessary to assume that all categories have this sort of structure) is that they show intuitive unity, but are definitionally polyvalent. That is to say, they cannot be captured by means of a single definition, but require a set of definitions. For instance, the semantic field covered by the term *game* can be quite well described by means of a restricted set of definitions, but no satisfactory unitary definition exists.

7.2.3.4 Fuzzy boundaries

A common position is to maintain that only the prototype has 100 per cent membership of a category, the degree of membership of other items being dependent on their degree of resemblance to the prototype, this in turn being reflected by their GOE score. (It has sometimes been claimed—wrongly, in my opinion—that when subjects give GOE ratings, they are actually judging degree of membership.) From this one would have to conclude that a natural category has no real boundaries, and indeed this has been explicitly claimed by, for instance, Langacker (1991b: 266):

> There is no fixed limit on how far something can depart from the prototype and still be assimilated to the class, if the categorizer is perceptive or clever enough to find some point of resemblance to typical instances.

Not all scholars belonging to the cognitive linguistics fraternity agree that GOE and DOM (degree of membership) should be equated. However, there is general agreement that category boundaries are typically fuzzy. (Arguments against the GOE=DOM claim will be detailed below.)

7.2.3.5 The mental representation of categories

The earliest hypotheses regarding the mental representation of categories suggested that there was some sort of portrait of the prototypical member, against which the similarity of other items could be computed and their status in the category determined. This idea fell out of favour when it was realized that many 'portraits' would have to be three-dimensional and would have to incorporate characteristic behaviour (although Jackendoff still envisages all these possibilities for his 3-D representation of conceptual categories). Many prototype theorists (following the American cognitive linguist George Lakoff) speak only of 'prototype effects', and remain uncommitted on the subject of the form of mental representations.

More recently, feature-based treatments of prototype structure have appeared. With these, categories with a prototype structure are represented by a set of features. Unlike the classical features, however, these do not constitute a set of necessary and sufficient criteria, except perhaps for the prototype itself. Rather, the features are such that the more of them that are manifested in some particular instantiation, the higher the GOE score the item in question will obtain (note that in GOE terms a score of 1 is high and 7 low). In such systems, features may be differentially weighted, that is to say, some features will have a greater effect on determining centrality in the category than others (there is nothing in principle to prevent some features being necessary). The general idea can be illustrated using the category VEHICLE. The features listed in (1) would seem to be plausible (note that these have not been subjected to empirical testing, and are based on my intuitions: the list is illustrative, not necessarily exhaustive):

(1) (a) Designed to go on roads.
   (b) Has its own propulsive power.
   (c) Can go faster than an unaided human.
   (d) Can carry persons/goods in addition to driver.
   (e) Has four wheels.
   (f) Metallic construction.
   (g) Persons/goods enclosed.
   (h) Manœuvrable.

Clearly a central example of the category of vehicle, such as CAR, will have all these features. If they are correct, it ought to be possible, for items judged not to be central, to pinpoint features they do not possess. For instance, a typical class of students will mark the following items as non-prototypical in the class of VEHICLE. For each of them, there are features from the above list which are missing:

TRAIN: Not designed to go on roads.
          Not manœuvrable.
TRACTOR: Not designed to go on roads.
          Driver not always enclosed
BICYCLE   Doesn't have own propulsive power.
          Does not carry persons/goods in addition to driver.

(The category VEHICLE, like GAME, is one for which it is not possible to draw up an adequate set of necessary and sufficient features; notice, however, that there may be features—[CONCRETE] is a possible example—which are necessary.)

7.2.3.6 Basic-level categories

Categories occur at different levels of inclusiveness, as shown in (2):

(2) (a) vehicle—**car**—hatchback.
    (b) fruit—**apple**—Granny Smith.
    (c) living thing—creature—animal—**cat**—Manx cat.
    (d) object—implement—cutlery—**spoon**—teaspoon.

One level of specificity in each set has a special status (shown in bold in (2)); it is called the **basic** or **generic** level of specificity. The characteristics of the basic level are as follows.

(i) It is the most inclusive level at which there are characteristic patterns of behavioural interaction: imagine being asked to mime how one would behave with an animal. This is rather difficult without knowing whether the animal in question is a crocodile or a hamster. Likewise with, say, an item of furniture. However, the assignment is relatively easy if it involves a cat, horse, mouse, or chair.

(ii) It is the most inclusive level for which a clear visual image can be formed: this is similar in principle to the previous characteristic: try to visualize an item of cutlery or a vehicle, without its being any specific type. A fork or a lorry, however, are easy to visualize.

(iii) Basic-level items are used for neutral, everyday reference. They are often felt by speakers to be the 'real' name of the referent: suppose A and B are sitting at home; A hears a noise outside and says *What's that?* B looks out of the window and sees an alsatian in the garden. How does B reply? Out of the following choices, normally (b) will be chosen:

(a) It's an animal.
(b) It's a dog.
(c) It's an alsatian.

The other two responses would require special contextual conditions.

(iv) The basic level is the level at which the 'best' categories can be created. Good categories are those which maximize the following characteristics:

(a) distinctness from neighbouring categories;
(b) within-category resemblance;
(c) informativeness: that is to say, the amount of information we gain access to if we know that something belongs to the category.

Consider a division of the class ANIMAL into MALE and FEMALE. This would yield two clear categories which might have utility in certain circumstances. But they would not be good categories by the above criteria because (a) distinctness from neighbouring categories is restricted to one feature, (b) internal homogeneity is likewise restricted: as a result, a female mouse resembles a male mouse far more than it resembles a female elephant (and the same is true for all animals), even though it falls into a different category. The best subdivisions of the class of animals (by these criteria) are such categories as CAT, DOG, COW, LION, or GIRAFFE.

(v) The names of basic-level categories tend to be morphologically simple, and 'original', in the sense of not being metaphorical extensions from other categories: take the case of *spoon*, which is a basic-level term; all the more specific categories have more complex names: *teaspoon, tablespoon, soup spoon, coffee spoon*, etc.

7.2.3.7 Non-basic level categories

Besides basic-level categories, we also find categories which are more inclusive (**superordinate** categories), and categories which are subdivisions of basic-level categories (**subordinate** categories). Superordinate categories, like ANIMAL, FURNITURE, CUTLERY, CLOTHES, are typically distinct, but have fewer common properties than basic-level categories. Subordinate categories such as SPANIEL, COLLIE, DACHSHUND, ALSATIAN have a high level of within-category resemblance, but a relatively low level of distinctness from neighbouring categories.

7.2.4 Problematic aspects of the prototype model

While the standard prototype-theoretical approach undoubtedly sheds light on the nature of natural conceptual categories, it is not without its problematic aspects.

7.2.4.1 The bases of GOE ratings

The first point is that although subjects readily enough make GOE judgements on the basis of two words (category name and item name), this is surely rather unnatural: it would presumably be more revealing to produce GOE ratings for actual objects or events, etc. Furthermore, this would be likely to highlight the fact that the GOE scale is a conflation of several more basic scales. One of these is undoubtedly familiarity, although it can be shown that GOE ratings cannot be reduced to familiarity ratings. Another is well-formedness: APPLE may well receive a high rating in the category FRUIT if only the words are presented, but what if an actual apple were presented, and it happened to be rotten? Well-formedness does not necessarily correlate with familiarity. Most mushrooms are at least slightly deformed in one way or another. Yet there seems little doubt that a perfectly formed specimen would receive the highest GOE rating (other things being equal). Another factor is important, which in Cruse (1990) is called 'quality'. Think of an emerald. Most emeralds are pale in colour and have faults in the form of tiny cracks etc. The best emeralds are deep in colour, but these are rare, and are even more susceptible to faults. An emerald with a deep glowing green colour would be voted the prototype on the basis of its 'quality', which is distinct from frequency and well-formedness. Here, then, we have at least three independent strands potentially making up a GOE score, and there may be more.

7.2.4.2 Category boundaries and boundary effects

One of the most serious shortcomings of the 'standard' prototype view is that no category boundary is recognized (see the quotation from Langacker at section 7.2.3.4). The few scholars who do admit that a boundary exists evince little interest in it (e.g. Lakoff). Yet a category without a boundary is virtually useless: a primary function of a category is to discriminate between things which are in it and things which are not in it. The classical view of categories, with necessary and sufficient features, set a boundary (albeit an unnaturally sharp one) but allowed no internal structure. In throwing this out, prototype theory has thrown out one of the baby twins with the proverbial bath water. The view taken here is that a fully satisfactory description of a category must specify both internal structure and location of boundary area. It is accepted that category boundaries are to a greater or lesser extent fuzzy (so classical definitions are not adequate); but even fuzzy boundaries have locations, which are in principle specifiable. Both category centres and category boundaries have both linguistic and behavioural correlates, and should be given equal status in accounts of category structure.

7.2.4.3 Degrees of membership

As we have seen, the standard prototype view is that only the prototype of a category has 100 per cent membership of the category, other items having a degree of membership dependent on their resemblance to the prototype. Such a view is possible only if categories are not assigned boundaries. Once boundaries are assigned, then an item must be a full member of the category, not a member at all, or a borderline example. Even a non-central member of a category, like OSTRICH in the category of BIRD, is a full member. On this view, the notion of degree of membership of a category applies only to borderline cases. For instance, most people would probably judge BICYCLE and SKATEBOARD to be borderline instances of the category VEHICLE. Here, the notion of degree of membership becomes operational, and I myself, for instance, would judge BICYCLE to have a higher degree of membership than SKATEBOARD.

7.2.4.4 Complex categories

The categories which result from the combination of two (or more) basic categories are often regarded as presenting particular problems for prototype theory. The most famous example is PET FISH, which was discussed in Chapter 4, section 4.4.3. To recapitulate briefly, the item which emerges as prototypical in studies of this category (at least in an American setting) is GUPPY. This is held to be a problem because a guppy is not judged, in separate tests, either to be a prototypical fish (e.g. TROUT is rated more highly), or a prototypical pet (e.g. CAT and DOG are rated more highly). As we argued earlier, it is probably unreasonable to expect that the prototype of a complex category X × Y should be prototypical in X and Y separately. However, it might be reasonably demanded of a prototype approach that the prototype of a complex category should be predictable from the representations of the component categories. Some attempts have been made to do this, but they are inconclusive.

7.2.5 Types of conceptual category

It is worthwhile considering briefly the characteristics of the category NATURAL CONCEPTUAL CATEGORY. In particular, we might speculate on what the features of a good example of such a category might be. First, it seems clear that a good category will distinguish clearly between things that are in it and things that are not in it; in other words, it will have a relatively well-defined boundary. Second, bearing in mind that a major function of conceptual categories is to provide headings under which information/knowledge can be economically stored, it is reasonable to expect a good category to be richly informative, in the sense that knowing that some entity belongs to a particular category gives access to a substantial body of knowledge about the entity. This, in turn, would seem to correlate with a well-developed and richly articulated internal structure.

It is almost certainly a mistake to imagine that all categories are built to the same pattern. There is, for instance, variation in the relative importance of the internal structure and the boundary. An extreme case would be a category with boundaries but no internal structure at all. This would be the case for a category defined purely by means of a list of members (it is not clear that any natural categories are so constituted, or at least not any of the more permanent type that get associated with lexical items: nonce categories can be like this, e.g. dividing people into groups on the basis of the alphabetical position of their names). The balance of salience between boundary and internal structure can vary. For instance, GAME has very fuzzy boundaries, but a rich internal structure, whereas ODD NUMBER has clear boundaries, but a relatively weak internal structure (people do make differential GOE judgements on odd numbers: 3, 5, and 7 are judged to be the 'best', and such numbers as 319,947 come low down on the list, but the basis for such judgements seems to be relatively 'thin').

7.3 Beyond individual concepts

It is generally recognized nowadays that concepts cannot be treated in isolation. Every concept is embedded in a larger body of knowledge of some sort, and an understanding of any concept requires account to be taken of one or more wider domains. This was a key tenet of Fillmore's 'frame semantics'. This was originally put forward as a more satisfactory alternative to feature theories of word meaning (called by Fillmore 'check-list theories'), which he saw as failing to account for important aspects of the way words are understood. A few examples will make the notion clearer. Take example (3):

(3) John asked to see the menu.

This evokes a scene in a restaurant or café, with John as a customer, most likely seated at a table and contemplating ordering a meal. The person from whom John requests a menu is most likely to be a waiter (there may be significance in the fact that the menu was not presented automatically). The menu is no more than a printed list of food items, but a full understanding of the sentence requires a complex body of background knowledge to be activated. As a further example, consider the word *weekend*. This just means Saturday and the immediately following Sunday, but its significance can only be appreciated against the background of a stereotypic working week. The word *lap* refers to a part of the body, but it cannot be understood except in the light of its function of supporting an object such as a handbag, or a child or small pet. Some words which seem at first sight to be explicable by a feature analysis turn out on closer examination to require appropriate frames to be activated. For instance, the contrast between *boy* and *girl* may seem to be fully accountable for by the features [MALE] and [FEMALE]. But this does not explain the fact that the age range for girls is typically much greater than for boys. This has its roots in societal attitudes to males and females, which are part of the frames evoked by the two words.

A notion similar to that of 'frame' was adopted by Langacker. He pointed out that concepts only make sense when viewed against the background of certain domains, which are usually themselves concepts of a more general or inclusive nature. To take an obvious example, an autonomous, free-standing specification of the concept FINGER is well-nigh unthinkable; it is an essential feature of this notion that it is a spotlighted portion of a HAND. Separated from a hand, a finger is a sausage-shaped piece of bone and flesh. Notice that HAND and FINGER are dependent on one another: HAND cannot be properly characterized without making any reference to FINGER. As another example, consider the wheel of a bicycle. In isolation from a bicycle (or other wheeled device), a wheel is just a circular structure; but the concept WHEEL is more than this, and can only be characterized by reference to a more inclusive domain of some kind such as BICYCLE or WHEELBARROW. Langacker refers to the region or aspect of a domain highlighted by a concept as the **profile**, and the domain of which a part is rendered salient in this way is called the **base**; thus, WHEEL profiles a region of the base BICYCLE. According to Langacker, the profile cannot be apprehended on its own.

It is important to note that profile and base are relational terms, not absolute ones. Take the case of WHEEL. This profiles a region of its base BICYCLE. But it in turn functions as the base domain for more specific profilings, such as HUB, RIM, and SPOKE. And FINGER functions as a base for more specific profilings such as (FINGER)NAIL and KNUCKLE. In other words, the base–profile relation forms chains of elements (the term 'domain' is usually reserved for concepts which function as a base for at least one profile). However, the chains are not endless: in the direction of specificity, NAIL, for instance, is probably the end of the chain involving HAND for most of us. There is also a limit to the degree of inclusiveness, in that there are some domains which are not profiles of anything more inclusive; these are called basic domains and include such elementary notions as SPACE, TIME, MATTER, QUANTITY, and CHANGE (these bear some resemblance to Jackendoff's basic ontological categories, but they are not identical).

To complete this elementary sketch of the relation between concepts and domains, one further elaboration is necessary. This is that a concept is typically profiled, not against a single base domain, but against several, the whole complex going under the name of **domain matrix**. As a relatively simple example, take the notion of TENNIS BALL. This is obviously profiled against BALL along with sister categories such as CRICKET BALL and FOOTBALL. BALL in turn is profiled against SPHERE (then SHAPE and ultimately SPACE, as well as (at least) THING, SIZE, WEIGHT, and ELASTICITY). At some stage, TENNIS BALL presupposes TENNIS, but the relationship is perhaps not immediate: we perhaps have TENNIS EQUIPMENT as an intermediate domain, which will also include RACKET, COURT, and NET, and TENNIS ACTIONS (for want of a better name) such as SERVICE, RETURN and LOB, which will be immediate base domains for BALL, and probably also TENNIS JUDGEMENTS such as IN, OUT, FAULT, LET, and SCORING, all of which crucially involve BALL, and must be considered additional base domains. A lot of this is speculative and arguable, but it is clear that from the cognitive linguistic perspective a full comprehension of the meaning of tennis ball is going to involve all these things.

Discussion questions and exercises

1. Suggest a set of prototype features for one or more of the following conceptual categories (or select your own example(s)):

CLOTHES   FRUIT   MUSICAL INSTRUMENT   HOBBY   BUILDING   HOUSEHOLD APPLIANCE

For each category, draw up a list of possible members, including some marginal cases, and ask another person to assign GOE ratings. Consider to what extent the ratings can be accounted for in terms of your suggested features.

2. Which of the following would you consider to be basic-level categories?

BIRO   TEASPOON   SANDAL   UNDERWEAR   SEAGULL   DAISY   GRASS   BULLDOZER   BUS
MOUNTAIN BIKE   SELF-RAISING FLOUR   WALNUT   SUGAR   ARMCHAIR   DELICATESSEN
SUPERMARKET   PETROL STATION   TOWN HALL   PARK   MOTORWAY   ROAD   CANAL
POLICE STATION   BUILDING   GROCERIES   WINE   CHAMPAGNE   BEVERAGE   MILK

Suggestions for further reading

That meaning is essentially conceptual in nature is one of the central tenets of cognitive linguistics. For elementary introductions to cognitive linguistics see Ungerer and Schmid (1996) and Lee (2002). Croft and Cruse (forthcoming) provides a more advanced introduction. Ultimately, a reader interested in this approach will want to tackle the foundational text. The 'bible' of the cognitive approach is Langacker's two-volume *Foundations of Cognitive Grammar* (1987 and 1991a). However, this is not an easy read; fortunately, many of the basic topics are expounded in a much more accessible form in Langacker (1991b). The interested reader will also find articles on a wide range of cognitive linguistic topics in the journal *Cognitive Linguistics*.

An alternative 'conceptual' approach to meaning can be found in the works of Jackendoff; Jackendoff (1983) provides a good introduction; his latest position is expounded in Jackendoff (2002). An interesting comparison between Jackendoff's approach and the cognitive linguistic approach (including a contribution from Jackendoff himself) can be found in vol. 7(1) of *Cognitive Linguistics*, which also gives a fairly full bibliography of Jackendoff's later work.

Cruse (1990) provides an introduction to prototype theory as applied to lexical semantics. (The volume which includes this article also contains many other articles on prototype theory in linguistics.) A fuller account is to be found in Taylor (1989); Cruse (1992c) is a critical review of this. Ungerer and Schmid (1996) has an interesting chapter on categorization. Cruse (1995) attempts to apply prototype theory to lexical relations. Prototype theory is not the only theory of conceptual structure. A discussion of various alternatives (from a psychological viewpoint) can be found in the articles in Lamberts and Shanks (1997). Croft and Cruse (forthcoming: ch. 4) proposes an alternative approach within a cognitive linguistics framework.

Paradigmatic sense relations of inclusion and identity

Paradigmatic sense relations of inclusion and identity

8.1 The nature of sense relations

This chapter is mainly about a particular type of sense relation, that is, a semantic relation between units of meaning. But before discussing this in detail, we must look at the idea of a sense relation from a broader perspective.

8.1.1 What makes a significant sense relation?

Taking the most general view, there is a unique sense relation of some sort holding between any two words chosen at random, say, *dog* and *banana*. We could even give this relation a name, say, dogbananonymy. However, it would not be a very interesting or significant relation. We need, therefore, to consider what makes a sense relation significant.

8.1.1.1 Recurrence

Probably the first point to make is that one of the main ways that sense relations can be significant is in structuring the vocabulary of a language. Natural vocabularies are not random assemblages of points in semantic space: there are quite strong regularizing and structuring tendencies, and one type of these manifests itself through sense relations. Now it is obvious that a sense relation which holds between only two vocabulary items cannot play much of a role in structuring a vocabulary. So sense relations which recur frequently across the vocabulary are at a premium. For instance, the relation between *dog* and *animal* and between *banana* and *fruit* is much more 'interesting', from this point of view, than that between *dog* and *banana*.

8.1.1.2 Discrimination

Conversely, a relation which holds between **all** pairs in the language, or even the majority, is for that reason less interesting as a relation. In other words, to be interesting a sense relation must not only include a significant number of lexical pairs but also exclude a significant number. An example of a non-discriminating relation is 'can occur in the same English sentence as . . .'. The relation between *dog* and *animal* is discriminating in this sense, because it does not hold between, for instance, *dog* and *banana*, or between *dog* and *fruit*.

8.1.1.3 Lexicalizability

The significance of a relation is enhanced if it corresponds to an easily intuited concept, especially if the concept has been lexicalized or is readily expressible in verbal form. (This betrays the cognitive bias of the author, and no apology is offered.) A sense relation which ordinary speakers find hard to grasp is probably not worth recognizing (or, at least, it will have to earn its status in some other way). On this basis, too, the relation between *dog* and *animal* comes out as significant, since it is easily verbalizable as *A dog is a kind of animal*; likewise, the relation between *long* and *short* is captured by the ordinary everyday word *opposite*.

8.1.1.4 Abstract vs. concrete relations

Sense relations may be relatively abstract or relatively concrete. This distinction can best be explained by example. Suppose we are told that lexical items X and Y manifest the same relation as *dog:animal* and *apple:fruit*. What can we say about the semantic area to which X and Y belong, or about the nature of the meaning which differentiates X from Y? The answer is: nothing at all. All we know is that X is more specific than Y, and that, prototypically, all the features of Y are contained in the meaning of X. Suppose, now, that we are told that the lexical items A and B are related in the same way that *mare* and *stallion*, and *ewe* and *ram*, are related. In this case we can say much more about the meanings of A and B, and what differentiates them. We know, for example, that A and B refer to members of one species of animal, and that what differentiates A from B is that A refers to the female of the species and B to the male. The (relevant) relation between X and Y is, by our terminology, an abstract one, whereas that between A and B is (semantically) concrete. Lexical semanticists have mostly been concerned with abstract relations, and it is with these that we shall begin. This does not mean, however, that more concrete relations are without interest; examples will crop up in later discussions.

8.1.1.5 Multiple simultaneous relations

It is perfectly possible for a number of relations to hold simultaneously between a pair of lexical items, even without taking account of polysemy. This is because relations, like word meanings, come in varying degrees of specificity. For instance, taking the pair *true* and *false* as an illustration, the following relations hold between them:

   (i) *True* has a different meaning from *false* (a relation which can be given the label **heteronymy**).

(ii) *True* and *false* cannot both be true when applied to the same proposition.

(iii) *True* and *false* are opposites.

(iv) *True* and *false* cannot both be false when applied to the same proposition.

These relations are progressively more specific, and later relations presuppose relations occurring earlier in the list. Thus, relation (i) holds between *father: architect, red:green, long:short*, as well as *true:false*. Relation (ii) presupposes relation (i) but is more specific, as it holds between *red:blue, long:short*, and *true:false*, but not *father:architect*; relation (iii) presupposes relation (ii), and holds between *long:short* and *true:false*, but not *red:blue*; relation (iv) presupposes relation (iii) and holds between *true:false* but not *long:short*. All of these relations are abstract, and each of them has some significance in lexical semantics, as we shall see.

8.1.2 What sort of entities do sense relations relate?

Sense relations are uncontroversially relations *of* sense, but what are they relations **between**? The obvious answer might appear to be that they are relations between senses. However, we saw in Chapter 6 that sense units that do not have the status of full senses can contract sense relations (for instance, the [TEXT] facet of *book* has the same relation to *novel* that *animal* has to *dog*). A more satisfactory answer is therefore that sense relations are relations between discrete units of sense. (For Lyons, sense relations are relations of sense between lexemes: they cannot be relations between senses, because for him sense relations are constitutive of sense. The position adopted in this book, however, is that meanings are conceptual in nature; in the last analysis, therefore, sense relations are relations between concepts.)

8.1.3 Varieties of sense relation

Sense relations situate themselves on one of three major axes: **paradigmatic, syntagmatic,** or **derivational**. The significance of each of these three types of relation is different.

8.1.3.1 Paradigmatic relations

Paradigmatic relations reflect the semantic choices available at a particular structure point in a sentence. For instance:

I'll have a glass of ——.

> beer
> wine
> water
> lemonade
> etc.

Typically, paradigmatic relations involve words belonging to the same syntactic category, although not infrequently there are minor differences:

We bought some ——.

       knives

       forks

       spoons

       cutlery

Here, *cutlery* is a mass noun, whereas all the others in the list are count nouns. In principle, paradigmatic relations may hold between members of any of the major syntactic categories. The following are examples involving verbs and adjectives respectively:

John —— across the field.

    ran

    walked

    crawled

I'd like a glass of —— sherry.

        dry

        sweet

Notice that the pairs *knives/forks*, *knives/cutlery*, and *dry/sweet* exemplify different paradigmatic sense relations. These will be dealt with in greater detail below.

8.1.3.2 Syntagmatic relations

Syntagmatic relations hold between items which occur in the same sentence, particularly those which stand in an intimate syntactic relationship. For instance, it is by virtue of syntagmatic sense relations, in this case between adjective and head noun, that *I'd like a glass of dry sherry* is normal, whereas *I'd like a glass of striped sherry* is odd. For similar reasons,

(1) The girl ran across the field.

is normal, but

(2) The girl sat across the field.

and

(3) The smell ran across the field.

are odd. Notice that in (2) it is the combination of verb and prepositional phrase (i.e. *sat* and *across the field*) which causes the oddness, whereas in (3), it is the combination of subject and verb (i.e. the *smell* and *ran*).

Any well-formed sentence of a natural language can be thought of as a string of elements, each one chosen from a set of possibilities provided by the language (at least, each one which is not uniquely determined by the syntax, like the *to* of *I want to leave now*). In each case, the set of possibilities from which the choice was made is not completely free, but is constrained by the other elements in the sentence, in the sense that a choice from outside a certain range will result in semantic incoherence. Thus, if we do not choose something from the realm of liquids for the completion of *John drank a glass of* ——, the result will not be coherent. Syntagmatic sense relations, therefore, are an expression of coherence constraints. Paradigmatic sense relations, on the other hand, operate within the sets of choices. Each such set represents the way the language articulates, or divides up, some conceptual area, and each displays a greater or lesser degree of systematic structuring. Paradigmatic relations are an expression of such structuring. For instance, in the conceptual area of drinkable things, English provides a cover term, *liquid*, and a range of more specific terms such as *milk*, *beer*, *lemonade*, *brandy*; the more specific terms all stand in a particular semantic relation with the cover term, and in a different relation with each other, and some of them, for example *wine*, function as cover terms for yet more specific ones, thus extending the structuring of the field. (Relations such as these are discussed in some detail below.) It can be seen, therefore, that paradigmatic and syntagmatic relations function in tandem, syntagmatic relations delimiting the space within which paradigmatic relations operate.

8.1.3.3 Derivational sense relations

Derivational sense relations are only accidentally found between words forming part of a set of paradigmatic choices, and only accidentally contribute to cohesion. They do, however, participate in one type of structuring of the vocabulary of a language, since they manifest themselves between items in what are called **word families** (i.e. words derived from a single root). Consider the following set of words:

(i)	*cook* (v.tr.)	*Mary is cooking supper tonight.*
(ii)	*cook* (v.intr.)	*Can John cook?*
(iii)	*cook* (v.intr.)	*The chicken is cooking.*
(iv)	*cook* (n.)	*Lesley is a good cook.*
(v)	*cook* (n.)	*Lesley is a cook.*
(vi)	*cooker*	*We've bought a new cooker.*
(vii)	*cooking* (n.)	*John's in love with Mary's cooking.*
(viii)	*cookery*	*John is taking cookery lessons.*

The semantic relations between these words are partly systematic, partly idiosyncratic. Take the relation between *cook* (iii) and *cooker*. There is an obvious sense in which the *-er* of *cooker* has an instrumental meaning: a cooker is something that is used for cooking. But if John cooks the chicken over a fire, the fire does not thereby become a cooker. There is therefore some specialization of sense in the derivation of *cooker* from *cook* (iii) (if indeed that is the true source). However, it does not appear that there is any specialization in the

meaning of the morpheme COOK, nor, indeed, in the meaning of the instrumental affix. The specialization seems to operate at the level of the whole word
cooker. It is not sufficient to say, either, that a cooker must be an apparatus
designed to be used for cooking (this is not true of fires generally), since a
barbecue is not a cooker, nor is a microwave oven. Consider, now, the relationship between *cook* (iii) and *cook* (i) and (ii) (which are closely related). *Cook*
(iii) refers only to the fact that the chicken is undergoing heat treatment so as
to render it more acceptable as food. Sentence (ii), however, is not simply
asking whether John is able to cause foodstuffs to undergo heat treatment
(anyone can drop a chicken into a fire): it enquires whether John has certain
complex and valuable skills. In this case, *cook* (ii) seems to carry a greater
semantic load than *cook* (iii).

8.2 Paradigmatic relations of identity and inclusion

For convenience of exposition, we shall divide paradigmatic sense relations
into two broad classes, those which express identity and inclusion between
word meanings and those expressing opposition and exclusion. We shall begin
with the former.

8.2.1 Hyponymy

One of the most important structuring relations in the vocabulary of a language is **hyponymy**. This is the relation between *apple* and *fruit*, *car* and *vehicle*,
slap and *hit*, and so on. We say that *apple* is a **hyponym** of *fruit*, and conversely,
that *fruit* is a **superordinate** (occasionally **hyperonym**) of *apple*. This relation is
often portrayed as one of inclusion. However, what includes what depends on
whether we look at meanings extensionally or intensionally. From the extensional point of view, the class denoted by the superordinate term includes the
class denoted by the hyponym as a sub-class; thus, the class of fruit includes
the class of apples as one of its subclasses. If we are dealing with verbs, we
have to say that, for instance, the class of acts of hitting includes as a sub-class
the class of acts of slapping. Looking at the meanings intensionally, we may
say that the meaning (sense) of *apple* is richer than that of *fruit* and includes,
or contains within it, the meaning of *fruit*. This can be seen more clearly in the
case of words which have obvious definitions. For instance, from the definition
of *stallion* as "male horse" we can see that the meaning of *stallion* includes
within it the meaning of *horse* plus something else. Similarly, if we define
murder as "kill with intent and illegally", we can see that *murder* both has more
meaning than *kill* and includes the meaning of *kill*.

Although hyponymy is a paradigmatic relation, it has syntagmatic consequences. There are expressions which prototypically require items related
hyponymously:

apples and other fruit
?fruit and other apples
?apples and other pears
Apples are my favourite fruit.
?Apples are my favourite pears.
?Fruit are my favourite apples.

8.2.1.1 Hyponymy and entailment

Hyponymy is often defined in terms of entailment between sentences which differ only in respect of the lexical items being tested: *It's an apple* entails but is not entailed by *It's a fruit*, *Mary slapped John* entails but is not entailed by *Mary hit John*. There are two sorts of difficulty with defining hyponymy in this way. One is that a sentence containing a hyponym does not invariably entail the corresponding sentence with the superordinate. For instance, although *It's a tulip* entails *It's a flower*, *It's not a tulip* does not entail *It's not a flower*, nor does *John became a Roman Catholic* entail *John became a Christian* (it depends what he was before his conversion). Ideally, it ought to be possible to specify the sorts of sentence within which entailment holds; however, this turns out to be no easy task (see Cruse 1986: ch. 4.4 for some discussion). The second difficulty is that entailment between test sentences is not invariably diagnostic of hyponymy (*The bullet was embedded in John's thigh* entails *The bullet was embedded in John's leg*, but *thigh* is not a hyponym of *leg*).

8.2.1.2 Hyponymy and transitivity

Understood as a purely logical notion, hyponymy is a transitive relation: if A is a hyponym of B, and B a hyponym of C, then A is necessarily a hyponym of C (consider A = *spaniel*, B = *dog*, C = *animal*). However, several cases where transitivity seems to break down have been pointed out:

A hang-glider is a type of glider.
A glider is a type of aeroplane.
*A hang-glider is a type of aeroplane.

A car seat is a type of seat.
A seat is a type of furniture.
*A car seat is a type of furniture.

One suggested resolution of this apparent anomaly is to say that for informants to assent to statements like *A is a type of B*, it is sufficient that a prototypical A is a type of B: it is not necessary that all As should be Bs. Transitivity breaks down in the above examples because a hang-glider is not a prototypical glider, and a car seat is not a prototypical seat. (A slightly different account will be offered in Chapter 14.)

8.2.1.3 Taxonymy

Many hyponyms and superordinates collocate normally in sentences formed on the pattern of *A horse is an animal* and *A horse is a type/kind/sort of animal*. However, a significant number of cases are normal in the first of these patterns, but not the second:

A kitten is a cat. /?A kitten is a sort of cat.
A stallion is a horse./ ?A stallion is a type of horse.
A queen is a woman. /?A queen is a kind of woman.

In Cruse (1986) the relation exemplified by *horse:animal* but not *stallion:horse* was labelled **taxonymy**, because of its relevance to classificatory systems. Taxonymy is thus a sub-type of hyponymy. The question of what distinguishes taxonyms from other hyponyms is not an easy one to answer. It appears that a taxonym must engage with the meaning of its superordinate in a particular way, by further specifying what is distinctive about it. Take the case of *A strawberry blonde is a type of blonde*. The key distinctive characteristic of a blonde is the possession of fair hair, and *strawberry blonde* makes this more precise. Contrast this with *?A blonde is a type of woman*. The key distinctive characteristic of a woman in the class of human beings is her sex; however, *blonde* does not serve to specify this any further, hence it cannot represent a 'type'. A similar contrast can be seen between *A mustang is a type of horse* and *?A stallion is a type of horse: stallion* specifies sex, but this is not a specification of what distinguishes horses from other animals.

8.2.2 Meronymy

Another relation of inclusion is **meronymy**, which is the lexical reflex of the part–whole relation. Examples of meronymy are: *hand:finger, teapot:spout, wheel:spoke, car:engine, telescope:lens, tree:branch*. In the case of *finger:hand, finger* is said to be the **meronym** (the term **partonym** is also sometimes found) and *hand* the **holonym**. Meronymy shows interesting parallels with hyponymy. (They must not, of course, be confused: a dog is not a part of an animal, and a finger is not a kind of hand.) In both cases there is inclusion in different directions according to whether one takes an extensional or an intensional view. A hand physically includes the fingers (notice that we are not dealing with classes here, but individuals); but the meaning of *finger* somehow incorporates the sense of *hand*.

There is no simple logical definition of meronymy in terms of entailment between sentences, as there is with hyponymy. But the relation does nonetheless have logical properties, which are particularly manifest in connection with locative predicates. For instance, if X is a meronym of Y, then for an entity A, *A is in X* entails but is not entailed by *A is in Y*. For instance, a cockpit is part of an aeroplane, hence *John is in the cockpit* entails *John is in the aeroplane*. For similar reasons, *John has a boil on his elbow* unilaterally entails *John has a boil on his arm*. However, there are too many exceptions for it to be possible to frame a straightforward definition on this basis: for instance, even though a steering wheel is part of a car, *The wasp is on the steering-wheel* does not entail *The wasp is on the car*, but rather, *The wasp is IN the car*. Meronymy can also be characterized in terms of normality in diagnostic frames, such as *An X is a part of a Y, A Y has an X/Xes*:

A finger is a part of a hand.
A hand has fingers.

8.2.2.1 Prototype features of meronymy

In comparison with hyponymy, meronymy is a much less sharply delimited relation. There are many borderline cases where informants are either unsure or in are disagreement. Judgements are also affected by contextual factors. For instance, people are unsure as to whether a pan lid is or is not part of a pan, but they are more likely to say that it is if it is necessary to the proper functioning of the pan, if it is sold together with the pan, or if it is attached to the pan in any way. As a lexical relation, meronymy has a typical prototypic structure, with a clear core and a somewhat hazy boundary. A number of features appear to contribute to 'goodness of exemplar':

Necessity. Some parts are necessary to their wholes, whereas others are optional. For instance, although a beard is part of a face, beards are not necessary to faces. On the other hand, fingers are necessary to hands. (We are not talking here of **logical** necessity, of course. This is what in Cruse (1986) was called **canonical necessity**: that is, a **well-formed** hand must have fingers.) Necessity also operates in the reverse direction: some parts are non-canonical if they are not parts of appropriate wholes (e.g. a finger), whereas some parts are capable of constituting satisfactory wholes on their own, and are only optionally parts of something else. Consider the case of a concert hall as part of a leisure centre. Presumably, other things being equal, necessity points towards centrality.

Integrality. Some parts are more integral to their wholes than others. One way of diagnosing integrality is by judging how easy it is to describe the part as being attached to its whole. For instance, both *The handle is a part of the door* and *The handle is attached to the door* are normal, as are *The hand is a part of the arm* and *The hand is attached to the arm*. On the other hand, *The fingers are attached to the hand* and *The handle is attached to the spoon* are both odd, and the difference seems to lie in the degree of integration of part into whole. Here again there seems to be a positive correlation between integrality and the centrality of a pair as manifestations of meronymy.

Discreteness. Some parts are more clearly divided from their sister parts than others (within a properly assembled whole). Obviously if they can be detached without harm, the division is clear. Likewise, if the part moves independently of the whole, like an arm with respect to the body, the division is clear. But some parts, such as the tip of the tongue, or the lobe of the ear, are less clearly separated. Other things being equal, we may presume that the more discrete a part is, the more prototypical the relation is.

Motivation. Generally speaking, 'good' parts have an identifiable function of some sort with respect to their wholes. For example, the handle of a door is for grasping and opening and shutting the door; the wheels of a car enable it to move smoothly over the ground; the blade of a knife is what enables the knife to fulfil its characteristic function of cutting. Functional motivation is especially important for a part which is not physically distinct, or is so only vaguely, like the tip of the tongue.

Congruence. The features of congruence are **range**, **phase**, and **type**.

   (i) Range: In many (perhaps in most) cases, the range of generality of the meronym is not the same as that of the holonym. The most frequent non-congruent cases are first, when the meronym is the more general in that it stands in that relation to more than one holonym, in which case we may speak of a **supermeronym**. Examples of this are: *handle:knife/ umbrella, spout:teapot/watering can, wheel:car/train, leg:chair/table, switch:radio/lamp,* and *lens:telescope/microscope.* Another common non-congruent case is when the ranges of generality of meronym and holonym overlap, giving rise to a **semi-meronym/holonym**. As an example of this consider *handle:door*: there are doors without handles, and handles not attached to doors, so neither range includes the other. Intuitively, the 'best' examples of meronymy are those, like *hand:finger*, which show range congruence. (There is an alternative way of looking at 'supermeronyms' like *handle, wheel,* and *spout,* which recruits the notion of micro-sense. It is arguable that there is a separate micro-sense for every different holonym. Take the case of *wheel.* In everyday life we have very little use for an undifferentiated notion of wheel: on the vast majority of occasions of use of the word, we have in mind a specific type of wheel. Think of two people, A and B, working on a bicycle. A says to B *Have you got a spare wheel?.* Suppose B does not have a spare bicycle wheel, but has a spare car wheel. He can quite correctly answer *No*.)

   (ii) Phase: Parts and wholes are phase-congruent when, as in prototypical cases, they exist at the same time. But take the case of grape juice:wine or flour:bread. It does not seem wholly wrong to say that grape juice is part of wine, or that flour is part of bread, but it does not seem quite right either. It is more correct in these cases to speak of **ingredients**, which go toward the making of something but may not exist as such in the final product.

   (iii) Type: Prototypical parts and wholes are of the same ontological type. I will not try to define this, but merely illustrate it. For instance, ideally, if a part is designated as a mass noun, then the whole should be likewise (*?A grain is a part of sand, ?Wood is part of a table*). Think, too, of *vein:hand* and *nerve:leg* (as opposed to *palm:hand* and *calf:leg*, on the one hand, and *vein:vascular system* and *nerve:nervous system*, on the other). The consistent type pairs are somehow 'better'. (Cruse (1986) refers in such cases to **segmental parts** (leg, arm, finger) and **systemic parts** (nerve, vein, bone, etc.).)

8.2.2.2 Parts and pieces

The relation 'piece of' is significantly different from the relation 'part of':

The floor of the garage was cluttered with parts of the car.
After the explosion, pieces of the car littered the ground over a wide area.

The main differences are as follows:

(i)   Pieces are exclusively concrete, whereas parts may not be: one can have, say, a part of a concert, but hardly a piece of a concert.
(ii) A piece must have once belonged to an undamaged whole, hence an exact replica of a piece does not qualify as a piece; a part (think of a 'spare part') is only required to have the potential to belong to a whole, so an exact replica of a part may qualify as a part.
(iii) Parts prototypically have motivated boundaries which can often be discerned in the assembled whole; pieces have arbitrary boundaries which cannot be seen in the undamaged whole.
(iv) Parts typically have a determinate function with respect to their wholes; pieces have no statable relation to their wholes.
(v)   Pieces do not fall into stable categories that can be designated by common nouns.

8.2.2.3 Transitivity of meronymy

As with hyponymy, we would expect a logical conception of meronymy to be transitive: if A is wholly located within the confines of B, and B is wholly located within the confines of C, then A is necessarily wholly located within the confines of C. (Notice that the 'piece of' relation is transitive in this way.) However, speakers' judgements of meronymy do not always point to transitivity:

Fingers are parts of the hand.
The hand is a part of the arm.
?Fingers are parts of the arm.

Cruse (1986) suggests that this failure of transitivity is connected with the distinction between **attachments** (i.e. parts about which it can normally be said that they are attached to their immediate wholes) and **integral parts** (i.e. parts that cannot be described in the above way). It seems that transitivity does not hold across the boundary of an attachment. However, it must be said that this correlation, even if valid, does not constitute an explanation.

8.2.3 Synonymy

If we interpret synonymy simply as sameness of meaning, then it would appear to be a rather uninteresting relation; if, however, we say that synonyms are words whose semantic similarities are more salient than their differences, then a potential area of interest opens up. What sorts of difference do not destroy an intuition of sameness? Why are such synonyms so frequent? (Absolute sameness of meaning would seem to be functionally unmotivated.) Do they proliferate in particular areas of the vocabulary? Some of these questions are insufficiently researched, and will not be answered here.

Let us first distinguish three degrees of synonymy: absolute synonymy, propositional synonymy, and near-synonymy.

8.2.3.1 Absolute synonymy

Absolute synonymy refers to complete identity of meaning, and so for the notion to have any content we must specify what is to count as meaning. Here a contextual approach will be adopted, according to which meaning is anything which affects the contextual normality of lexical items in grammatically well-formed sentential contexts. Against this background, absolute synonyms can be defined as items which are equally normal in all contexts: that is to say, for two lexical items X and Y, if they are to be recognized as absolute synonyms, in any context in which X is fully normal, Y is, too; in any context in which X is slightly odd, Y is also slightly odd, and in any context in which X is totally anomalous, the same is true of Y. This is a very severe requirement, and few pairs, if any, qualify. The following will illustrate the difficulty of finding uncontroversial pairs of absolute synonyms (+ indicates 'relatively more normal' and – indicates 'relatively less normal'):

(i) *brave:courageous*
Little Billy was so brave at the dentist's this morning. (+)
Little Billy was so courageous at the dentist's this morning. (–)

(ii) *calm:placid*
She was quite calm just a few minutes ago. (+)
She was quite placid just a few minutes ago. (–)

(iii) *big:large*
He's a big baby, isn't he? (+)
He's a large baby, isn't he? (–)

(iv) *almost:nearly*
She looks almost Chinese. (+)
She looks nearly Chinese. (–)

(v) *die:kick the bucket*
Apparently he died in considerable pain. (+)
Apparently he kicked the bucket in considerable pain. (−)

Among the items sometimes suggested as candidates for absolute synonymy, and for which differentiating contexts are hard to find, are *sofa:settee*, and *pullover:sweater*. However, even for these items, in a typical class of students a sizeable minority will find contexts which for them are discriminatory. One thing is clear, and that is that under this description absolute synonyms are vanishingly rare, and do not form a significant feature of natural vocabularies. The usefulness of the notion lies uniquely in its status as a reference point on a putative scale of synonymity.

Notice that by the definition given above, only one differentiating context is needed to disqualify a pair of words as absolute synonyms. However, only one such context would be a suspicious circumstance: unless there were at least one class of such contexts, one might legitimately doubt whether the effect was a genuine semantic one. Notice, too, that there is a problem, not taken up here, of ensuring that the same unit of meaning is involved in all the contexts used in the argument.

8.2.3.2 Propositional synonymy

Propositional synonymy can be defined, as its name suggests, in terms of entailment. If two lexical items are propositional synonyms, they can be substituted in any expression with truth-conditional properties without effect on those properties. Put in another way, two sentences which differ only in that one has one member of a pair of propositional synonyms where the other has the other member of the pair are mutually entailing: *John bought a violin* entails and is entailed by *John bought a fiddle*; *I heard him tuning his fiddle* entails and is entailed by *I heard him tuning his violin*; *She is going to play a violin concerto* entails and is entailed by *She is going to play a fiddle concerto*. Notice that *fiddle* is less normal in the last example, while leaving truth conditions intact, which shows that *fiddle* and *violin* are not absolute synonyms.

Differences in the meanings of propositional synonyms, by definition, necessarily involve one or more aspects of non-propositional meaning, the most important being (i) differences in expressive meaning, (ii) differences of stylistic level (on the colloquial–formal dimension), and (iii) differences of presupposed field of discourse. Most usually, more than one of these comes into play at any one time. Take the case of *violin:fiddle*. Here the difference depends on certain characteristics of the speaker. If the speaker is an 'outsider' to violinistic culture, *fiddle* is more colloquial, and possibly also jocular compared with *violin*. However, if the speaker is a professional violinist talking to another professional violinist, *fiddle* is the neutral term, with no jocularity, disrespect, or colloquiality, whereas *violin* is used mainly to outsiders. In the case of *shin:fibula*, the difference is almost purely one of field of discourse: *shin* is the everyday term, with no special expressive or stylistic loading, whereas *fibula* is used by medical specialists acting in that role (again neutrally). As a final set of examples consider:

This was the first time they had had intercourse.
This was the first time they had made love.
This was the first time they had fucked.

The first version would be more likely than the others in a court of law, the second is probably the most neutral, while the third would be more likely in a typical 'bonkbuster' novel.

Propositional synonyms seem to be commonest in areas of special emotive significance, especially taboo areas, where a finely graded set of terms is often available occupying different points on the euphemism–dysphemism scale. They also seem to be prevalent in connection with concepts which are applicable in distinct contexts, with differing significance and implications in those contexts.

8.2.3.3 Near-synonymy

The borderline between propositional synonymy and near-synonymy is at least in principle clear, even if decisions may be difficult in particular cases. The borderline between near-synonymy and non-synonymy, however, is much less straightforward, and it is not obvious what principle underlies the distinction. Two points should be made at the outset. The first is that language users do have intuitions as to which pairs of words are synonyms and which are not. No one is puzzled by the contents of a dictionary of synonyms, or by what lexicographers in standard dictionaries offer by way of synonyms, even though the great majority of these qualify neither as absolute nor as propositional synonyms. The second point is that it is not adequate to say simply that there is a scale of semantic distance, and that synonyms are words whose meanings are relatively close. (This would explain the somewhat uncertain lower boundary of near-synonymy: people are typically vague as to what constitutes, say, an old woman or a tall man.) The reason this is not adequate is that there is no simple correlation between semantic closeness and degree of synonymy. The items in the following are semantically closer as we go down the list, but they do not become more synonymous:

entity   process
living thing   object
animal   plant
animal   bird
dog   cat
spaniel   poodle
etc.

In principle this list could continue indefinitely without ever producing synonyms. The point is that these words function primarily to contrast with other words at the same hierarchic level (see Chapter 10). In other words, a major function of *dog* is to indicate "not cat/mouse/camel/(etc.)", that is, to signal a contrast. Synonyms, on the other hand, do not function primarily to contrast with one another (this is what was meant by saying earlier that in the case of synonyms, their common features were more salient than their differences). In certain contexts, of course, they may contrast, and this is especially true of near-synonyms: *He was killed, but I can assure you he was NOT murdered, madam.*

Characterizing the sorts of difference which do not destroy synonymy is no easy matter. As a rough and ready, but not very explicit, generalization it may be said that permissible differences between near-synonyms must be either minor, or backgrounded, or both. Among 'minor' differences may be counted the following:

(i) adjacent position on scale of 'degree': *fog:mist, laugh:chuckle, hot: scorching, big:huge, disaster:catastrophe, pull:heave, weep:sob*;

(ii) certain adverbial specializations of verbs: *amble:stroll, chuckle:giggle, drink:quaff*;

(iii) aspectual distinctions: *calm:placid* (state vs. disposition);

(iv) difference of prototype centre: *brave* (prototypically physical):*courageous* (prototypically involves intellectual and moral factors).

An example of a backgrounded major distinction would be *pretty* ("female" presupposed) vs. *handsome* ("male" presupposed), the propositional meaning of both of which may be glossed as "good-looking". When the gender distinction is foregrounded, as in *man:woman*, the resulting terms are not synonymous. Saying why we get near-synonyms in a particular instance, rather than fully contrastive terms, is also difficult. A possibility is that contrastive terms appear when the conceptual differences involved have concrete behavioural consequences. Much research remains to be done in the field of synonymy.

Discussion questions and exercises

1. Which of the following hyponym–superordinate pairs represent taxonymy (assume most usual 'default' readings)?

sow:pig   poodle:dog   sheepdog:dog   mother:woman   cottage:house   hailstone: precipitation   ice:water   teenager:person   boot:footwear   icing sugar:sugar

2. Classify (the most relevant readings of) the following pairs of words using the following categories:

  (a) Central/prototypic examples of meronymy.
  (b) Examples of meronymy, but non-central.
  (c) Borderline cases.
  (d) Not examples of meronymy.

Attempt to explain the degrees of centrality that you find in terms of a set of prototypic features:

belt:buckle	shoe:lace
jacket:lapel	building:façade
hand:vein	bottle:cap
beard:hair	bread:crumb
hot-water bottle:water	omelette:egg
colander:hole	fork:prong
finger:tip	bed:sheet
cassette player:cassette	candle:wick
potato:peelings	door:hinge

3. Consider the following set of words:

brave   courageous   gallant   valiant   intrepid   heroic   plucky   bold   daring

  (a) What types of synonymy are represented?
  (b) Look the words up in a typical learner's dictionary, such as the *Oxford Advanced Learner's Dictionary* or the *Collins Cobuild Dictionary*, and consider how adequately they are differentiated.

Suggestions for further reading

The pioneering work on sense relations is Lyons (1963); see also Lyons (1968, 1977).

The topics of this chapter are discussed in greater detail in Cruse (1986), especially chapters 4–8. A prototype-theoretical treatment of sense relations is presented in Cruse (1994b; 2002a). An initial attempt at a formal semantic approach can be found in Cann (1993), and a more developed treatment in Cann (2002). For a psychologist's view of sense relations, see Chaffin (1992). Green et al. (2002) is a collection of articles on sense relations from various theoretical perspectives. A new approach to sense relations is sketched in Chapter 14 below, a fuller account will be found in Croft and Cruse (forthcoming).

For hyponymy, see Cruse (2002f) and Brown (2002a); for a cross-linguistic (anthropological) treatment of meronymy, see Anderson (1978) and Brown (1976; 2002b).

For synonymy, see Cruse (2002d).

Paradigmatic relations of exclusion and opposition

Paradigmatic relations of exclusion and opposition

9.1 Incompatibility

Very often a superordinate has more than one immediate hyponym, and among these there is typically a set of terms each of which is related to all the others by the relation of incompatibility. An example of this is the set of terms denoting kinds of animal (under the superordinate *animal*):

superordinate   *animal*
incompatible hyponyms   *dog, cat, mouse, lion, sheep*, etc.

superordinate   *horse*
incompatible hyponyms   *stallion, mare*

The relation between these hyponyms is an important and rather special one. It is not simply a difference of meaning. Whereas hyponymy can be thought of as a relation of inclusion, incompatibility is a relation of exclusion. This is easiest to grasp in its extensional manifestation: incompatibles are terms which denote classes which are disjunct, i.e. they have no members in common. Hence, if something is a mouse, then it is not a dog, horse, or elephant: nothing in the world can belong simultaneously to the class of mice and the class of dogs. (It is more difficult to give an intensional characterization of incompatibility: most accounts simply stipulate that certain meanings cannot co-occur.)

It is important to understand that co-hyponyms are not necessarily incompatible in the above sense. For instance, *queen* and *mother* are both hyponyms of *woman*, but there is nothing to prevent someone who is a queen from at the same time being a mother. (In some cases the compatibility of co-hyponyms is only apparent. For instance, *novel* and *paperback* at first sight seem to be compatible co-hyponyms of *book*. However, a closer study reveals that they are hyponyms of different sense units within the meaning of *book* (i.e. they are facets—see Chapter 6).) The co-hyponyms of each of the subunits are incompatibles in the orthodox way:

superordinate	*book* (TOME)
incompatible hyponyms	*paperback, hardback*
superordinate	*book* (TEXT)
Incompatible hyponyms	*novel, biography, textbook*

9.1.1 Co-taxonymy

In Chapter 8 a special variety of hyponymy was distinguished, taxonymy. In parallel fashion, a subvariety of incompatibility holds between sister taxonyms of a superordinate, which may be termed **co-taxonymy**. This can be diagnosed by means of the diagnostic frame *A is a kind of X; B is a different kind of X*. Taxonymy in combination with co-taxonymy corresponds to a fundamental and vital mode of categorization of experience: successive subdivision into (prototypically) mutually exclusive subcategories.

9.1.2 Co-meronymy

A relation of exclusion parallel to that which holds between co-taxonyms holds also between co-meronyms. If A and B are sister meronyms of X, then no portion of X can belong simultaneously to A and B; that is to say, sister parts do not overlap. This logical relation holds also between sister pieces.

We have seen a number of parallelisms between, on the one hand, taxonyms and co-taxonyms and, on the other, meronyms and co-meronyms. Further such parallels will be explored in Chapter 10.

9.2 Opposites

Everyone, even quite young children, can answer questions like *What's the opposite of big/long/heavy/up/out?* Oppositeness is perhaps the only sense relation to receive direct lexical recognition in everyday language. It is presumably, therefore, in some way cognitively primitive. However, it is quite hard to pin down exactly what oppositeness consists of. The following points seem to be relevant (a full account will not be attempted here; see Cruse 1986 for a fuller treatment):

(i) *Binarity*: opposites are, of course, incompatibles by the definition given above: *X is long* entails *X is not short*. But they are not ***just*** incompatibles. There is nothing in the notion of incompatibility itself which limits the number of terms in a set of incompatibles; but there can only be two members of a 'set' of opposites. Hence, binarity is a prerequisite.

(ii) *Inherentness*: we must, however, distinguish between accidental and inherent binarity. There are, for instance, only two classes of buses on the '-decker' dimension, namely single-deckers and double-deckers.

There may well be reasons, to do with stability and the height of bridges and so forth, for the absence of triple-deckers, but there is no *logical* reason. Likewise, there are only two sources of heat for cooking in the average suburban kitchen, namely gas and electricity; and only two sorts of hot drink served after lunch in the Senior Common Room at Manchester University, tea and coffee. But there is no more than the feeblest hint of oppositeness about *single-decker:double-decker*, *gas: electricity*, or *tea:coffee*. That is because the binarity is accidental and pragmatic, rather than inherent. By contrast, the possibilities of movement along a linear axis are logically limited to two: the binarity of the pair *up:down* is thus ineluctable, and they form a satisfactory pair of opposites. Inherent binarity can thus be considered a prototypical feature for oppositeness.

(iii) *Patency*: inherent binarity is necessary for a prototypical pair of opposites, but is not sufficient. Take the case of *Monday:Wednesday*. The time dimension is linear, and *Monday* and *Wednesday* are situated in opposite directions from *Tuesday*. Yet they do not feel at all like opposites. What is the difference between these and *yesterday* and *tomorrow*, which display a much more marked opposite character? It seems that in the case of *Monday* and *Wednesday*, their location in opposite directions along the time axis relative to *Tuesday* (and hence the binarity of their relationship) is not encoded in their meanings, but has to be inferred, whereas the directionality of *yesterday* and *tomorrow* relative to *today* is a salient part of their meaning. In Cruse (1986) this difference was referred to as **latent** as opposed to **patent** binarity. The patency of the binary relation can thus be added to the list of prototypical features of opposites.

Lexical opposites fall into a number of different fairly clearly distinguishable types, of which only the four principal ones will be described here.

9.2.1 Complementaries

The following pairs represent typical complementaries: *dead:alive*, *true:false*, *obey:disobey*, *inside:outside*, *continue* (V-ing):*stop* (V-ing), *possible:impossible*, *stationary:moving*, *male:female*. Complementaries constitute a very basic form of oppositeness and display inherent binarity in perhaps its purest form. Some definite conceptual area is partitioned by the terms of the opposition into two mutually exclusive compartments, with no possibility of 'sitting on the fence'. Hence, if anything (within the appropriate area) falls into one of the compartments, it cannot fall into the other, and if something does not fall into one of the compartments, it must fall into the other (this last criterion distinguishes complementaries from mere incompatibles). Thus if we consider the conceptual domain of possible responses to a felicitous command (i.e. one where the issuer has authority over the recipient, the action required is both possible and not already carried out, the recipient can hear and understand the command, and so on), it is clear that responses must fall into either the category of obedience or that of disobedience. Likewise, an entity belonging to the realm of living things must either be alive or dead, and a concrete object must be either stationary or moving.

Complementarity can be given a strict logical definition:

F(X) entails and is entailed by not-F(Y)

From this it follows that *X or Y* is logically equivalent to *X or not-X*, which is a tautology; and *neither X nor Y* is equivalent to *neither X nor not-Y*, which is a contradiction. Thus, *This proposition is either true or false* is a tautology, and *This proposition is neither true nor false* is a contradiction.

It is important to emphasize that the relation of complementarity holds only within some specific domain which is frequently implicit. For instance, the relation between *dead* and *alive* presupposes the domain of animate things, and implicitly excludes anomalous entities such as vampires and zombies; the relation between *male* and *female* presupposes that the terms are predicated of a species which has genders, and again excludes various developmental or genetic abnormalities; the relation between *open* and *shut* applied to a door presupposes that the door has not been removed from its hinges.

9.2.2 Antonymy

The most extensively studied opposites are undoubtedly **antonyms**. (Note that *antonym* is frequently used as a synonym for *opposite*; it is here used in the narrower sense introduced by Lyons 1963.) Antonyms fall into several relatively well-defined groups. One of these has a fair claim to be the central variety, so this group will be described in some detail, and the others will be sketched in more briefly.

9.2.2.1 Polar antonyms

The following are examples of **polar antonyms**:

long:short	heavy:light	thick:thin
fast:slow	strong:weak	high:low
wide:narrow	large:small	deep:shallow

The main diagnostic features of polar antonyms are as follows:

(i) Both terms are fully gradable, that is to say, they occur normally with a wide range of degree modifiers: *very/slightly/rather/quite/a bit/too/long*. (Complementaries characteristically show some reluctance to be graded: *?very/slightly/a bit/too dead*.)

(ii) They occur normally in the comparative and superlative degrees: *long, longer, longest*; *light, lighter, lightest*. But even when used in the positive degree, they typically need to be interpreted comparatively in relation to some reference value. This is often contextually determined, but in the default case is usually some kind of average value for the class of entities denoted by the head noun. So, for instance, *a long poem* would, out of context, be taken to refer to a poem that was longer than the average poem. *My goodness! Isn't Tom tall?* would in all probability need a reference point drawn from the context, for example, "tall for his age", "tall since the last time I saw him".

(iii) They indicate degrees of some objective, unidimensional physical property, prototypically one which can be measured in conventional units such as centimetres, kilograms, miles per hour One of the terms, when intensified, denotes a progressively higher value of the property (*very long* indicates more units of length than *long*), while the other term when intensified denotes a lower value of the property (*very short* denotes fewer units of length than *short*).

(iv) They are incompatibles, but not complementaries. *It's neither long nor short* is not a contradiction (it might be of average length), nor is *It's either long or short* a tautology.

(v) Comparative forms stand in a converse relationship (see below for further information on this relation): specifically, if X and Y are (polar) antonyms, and A and B are nouns, then *A is X-er than B* entails and is entailed by *B is Y-er than A*. (*A is heavier than B* entails and is entailed by *B is lighter than A*.)

(vi) The comparative forms of both terms are **impartial**; that is to say, use in the comparative does not presuppose that the term in the positive degree is applicable. Thus, *X is longer than Y* does not presuppose that X is long, similarly with *shorter*. Compare this with *hotter*, which is **committed,** in that *X is hotter than Y* presupposes that X is hot.

(vii) One of the terms yields an impartial question in the frame *How X is it?* and an impartial nominalization, whereas its partner term is committed in both uses. Compare *How long is it?*, which merely enquires about length without any presuppositions, and *How short is it?* Similarly, *Its length worries me* tells us nothing about whether 'it' is long or short, but *Its shortness worries me* indicates that 'it' is short. Notice that it is the term that indicates more of the relevant property that yields the impartial question: *How long/strong/big/thick/wide/fast is it?*

9.2.2.2 Equipollent antonyms

The two other main types of antonym can most easily be diagnosed by the impartiality or committedness of their comparatives. In the case of **equipollent antonyms**, neither term is impartial (i.e. both are committed); for instance, *hotter* presupposes "hot", and *colder* presupposes "cold". For this reason, both the following are odd:

?This coffee is cold, but it's hotter than that one.
?This coffee is hot, but it's colder than that one.

(It would be more normal to say *warmer* and *cooler*, respectively, in these situations.) Neither term yields a neutral *how*-question. Equipollent antonym pairs typically denote sensations (*hot:cold, bitter:sweet, painful:pleasurable*), or emotions (*happy:sad, proud of:ashamed of*).

9.2.2.3 Overlapping antonyms

With **overlapping antonyms**, for instance *good:bad*, one member yields an impartial comparative and the other a committed comparative:

?John is an excellent tennis player, but he's worse than Tom.
John's a pretty useless tennis player, but he's better than Tom.

In this case, *good* yields a neutral *how*-question (*How good was the film?*), whereas *bad* gives a committed question (*How bad were the exam results?*). All overlapping antonym pairs have an evaluative polarity as part of their meaning: *good:bad kind:cruel clever:dull pretty:plain polite:rude*. It is invariably the positively evaluative term which is associated with impartial use. A property of overlapping antonyms that is worth pointing out is that of **inherentness**. Take the case of *bad:good*. If two bad things differ in degree of badness one may, without oddness, describe one as *worse than* the other: *The weather last year was bad, but this year it was worse; This year's drought is worse than last year's*. However, of two bad things, it is not always possible to describe one as *better than* the other: *The weather is bad this year, but it is better than last year* is acceptable, but *?This year's famine is bad, but it's better than last year's* is odd. The general principle is that only things that are not inherently bad (i.e. where good examples are possible) can be described using *better*: inherently bad things can only be described as *worse*, or *not as bad*. A parallel restriction is that the position of inherently bad things on the good-bad scale cannot be questioned with *How good . . .?* (**How good is Mary's toothache?*).

9.2.3 Reversives

Reversives belong to a broader category of **directional opposites** which include straightforward directions such as *up:down, forwards:backwards, into:out of, north:south*, and extremes along some axis, *top:bottom* (called **antipodals** in Cruse 1986). Reversives have the peculiarity of denoting movement (or, more generally, change) in opposite directions, between two terminal states. They are all verbs. The most elementary exemplars denote literal movement, or relative movement, in opposite directions: *rise:fall, advance:retreat, enter: leave*. (Notice, however, that even in these cases it is the overall effective direction of movement from origin to goal which counts, not the details of the path traversed in between). The reversivity of more abstract examples resides in a change (transitive or intransitive) in opposite directions between two states: *tie:untie, dress:undress, roll:unroll, mount:dismount*.

Interestingly, the manner of the process or action seems to have little significance; at least it does not have to be the same for the two processes or actions. For instance, the action of tying a bow in a ribbon is likely to be rather different from the action of untying the same bow. What counts here is the fact that in one case the ribbon starts out untied and ends up tied (for *tie*) and that in the other case it starts out tied and ends up untied (for *untie*).

9.2.4 Converses

Converses are also often considered to be a subtype of directional opposite. They are also, paradoxically, sometimes considered to be a type of synonym. There are valid reasons for both views. Take the pair *above:below*, and three objects oriented as follows:

A

B

C

We can express the relation between A and B in two ways: we can say either *A is above B*, or *B is below A*. The logical equivalence between these two expressions is what defines *above* and *below* as converses. But since both are capable of describing the same arrangement, a unique situation among opposites, there is some point in thinking of them as synonyms conditioned by the order of their arguments. Consider now, however, A and C in relation to B: clearly A is above B and C is below B, hence *above* and *below* denote orientations in opposite directions, and are therefore directional opposites.

Other converse pairs with a salient directional character are: *precede:follow, in front of:behind, lend:borrow* (the thing borrowed/lent moves away from or towards the person denoted by the subject of the verb), *bequeath:inherit, buy:sell* (a double movement here, of money and merchandise). The directional nature of some converse pairs, however, is pretty hard to discern (*husband:wife, parent:offspring, predator:prey*), although it is perhaps not completely absent.

Converses may be described as **two-place** if the relational predicate they denote has two arguments (e.g. *above:below*) and **three-place** if it has three (e.g. *lend:borrow: A borrowed B from C/C lent B to A*); *buy:sell* are arguably four-place converses: *John sold the car to Bill for £5,000/Bill bought the car from John for £5,000.*

The members of a converse pair may not be congruent in respect of range. This is the case, for instance, with *doctor:patient*, since dentists, physiotherapists, and suchlike also have patients, and this destroys the strict logical relation, although it does not disqualify such pairs from being converses. A similar lack of congruence can be observed in *lecturer:student* and *rapist:victim*. However, it might be more satisfactory to deal with this apparent lack of range congruence in terms of micro-senses (cf. the treatment in Chapter 8 of lack of range congruence between meronym and holonym). We rarely deal with, for instance, victims or patients as a unitary class, but almost always as some contextually determined sub-type, and the sub-types (dental patients, victims of bullying) display the characteristics of micro-senses.

9.2.5 Markedness

The notion of **markedness** is often applied to pairs of opposites: one term is designated as the **marked** term and the other as the **unmarked** term of the opposition. Unfortunately, this concept is used in a variety of different ways by different linguists, so it is necessary to be more specific. Lyons (1977) distinguishes three major conceptions of markedness, which may or may not coincide in a particular instance or type of instances. The first is **morphological markedness**, where one member of the opposition carries a morphological 'mark' that the other lacks. This mark, in the case of opposites, is invariably a negative prefix:

possible:impossible   happy:unhappy
kind:unkind   true:untrue

The second notion of markedness is **distributional markedness**: the unmarked term according to this conception is the one which occurs in the widest variety of contexts or context types. By this criterion it could be argued that long is unmarked with respect to short because it occurs in a variety of expressions from which short is excluded:

This one is ten metres long.
What is its length?
How long is it? (neutral question)

The third notion of markedness is the most interesting in the present connection. Lyons gives it the name **semantic markedness**. According to this conception, the unmarked term is the one which is used in contexts where the normal opposition between the terms is **neutralized**, or non-operational. In such contexts, the meaning of the term is what is common to the two terms of the opposition. Take the case of *lion:lioness*. In *The lion and the lioness were lying together*, there is a sex contrast between the terms. But in *We saw a group of lions in the distance*, the sex contrast is neutralized, and the group may well contain both males and females. This notion can be applied to, for instance, antonyms, too. Thus, in the neutral question *How long is it?*, we can say that the normal contrast between *long* and *short* has been neutralized, and *long* refers to what is common to *long* and *short*, namely, the scale of length. (Notice that in some oppositions—those known as 'equipollent'—both terms are marked.)

The notion of markedness is sometimes applied to the terms of the opposition, and sometimes to uses of those terms. Hence, while *How **long** is it?* (with the intonation nucleus on *long*) represents an unmarked use of the unmarked term *long*, ***How** long is it?* (with the intonation nucleus on *How*) represents a marked use of the same term, as it presupposes that the referent is long rather than short. Notice that our use of the term '*impartial*' cannot always be translated as 'unmarked'. For instance, in the case of a comparative such as *shorter*, although it is impartial, because it does not presuppose the applicability of the default sense of *short*, it is not unmarked, because the contrast between *shorter* and *longer* is not neutralized.

9.2.6 Polarity

Another notion that is often applied to opposites is **polarity**, whereby terms are designated as **positive** and **negative**. This notion is used in an even greater variety of ways than markedness. The following are the main ones:

(i) **Morphological polarity**: one term bears a negative affix, the other does not.

(ii) **Logical polarity**: The determination of logical polarity depends on the fact that one negative cancels out another: if John is not not tall, then John is tall. The prototypical example of this is *true:false*. Is *true* to be analysed as equivalent to "not false", or is *false* to be glossed "not true"? Which is the negative term and which the positive? The criteria for logical polarity give an immediate answer:

It's true that it's true. = It's true.
It's false that it's false. = It's true.

False suffers the reversal when applied to itself, and is thus the negative term. The following are further examples of the same phenomenon:

She succeeded in succeeding.
She failed to fail. (reversal)

A large measure of largeness.
A small measure of smallness. (reversal)

This is a good example of a good book.
This is a bad example of a bad book. (reversal)

In each of these cases, the item which produces reversal is the negative member of the pair.

(iii) **Privative polarity**: One term is associated with the presence of something salient, and the other with its absence. On this criterion, *alive* is positive and *dead* negative, because something that is alive possesses salient properties such as movement, responsiveness, consciousness, which a dead thing lacks; *married* is positive and *single* negative, because a married person has a spouse and a single person does not (notice that we have *unmarried*, but not **unsingle*—negative terms rarely take a negative prefix); *dress* is positive and *undress* negative, because the end result of dressing involves the presence of clothes, whereas the end result of undressing involves the absence of clothes. This notion can be generalized to include "relative abundance" and "relative lack" (of some salient property). This move allows us to categorize *long, heavy, thick, wide, strong, fast*, and so on, as positive in this sense, because they denote a relative abundance of salient properties such as extension, weight, speed, and so on, compared with their partners *short, light, narrow*, etc.

(iv) **Evaluative polarity**: One term is evaluatively positive, or commendatory, and the other is negative. The obvious key example of this is *good:bad*. Other examples are: *kind:cruel, pretty:plain, clean:dirty, safe:dangerous, brave:cowardly*.

There is a relation between polarity and partiality: in the most general terms, positively evaluative members of a pair of opposites have the greater potential for impartial use. However, there are relations of dominance among the different types of polarity. For instance, evaluative polarity generally dominates privative polarity. Take the case of *clean:dirty*. The most natural analysis in terms of privativeness is that *clean* denotes the 'absence' term (*Cleanness is the absence of dirt*) and *dirty* the 'presence' term (*?Dirtiness is the absence of cleanness*). Yet it is *clean* that yields, for instance, a neutral question: *How clean is it?* This, however, is in accordance with the fact that *clean* is evaluatively positive. Similarly, privative polarity dominates logical polarity. Consider *far:near*; it seems that *far* is logically negative:

A is far from everything far from B. = A is near to B.
A is near to everything near to B. = A is near to B.

But *far* is privatively positive as it denotes the greater amount of the most salient property, namely distance. The neutral question *How far is it?* thus complies with privative rather than logical polarity. The exact details of these relationships remain to be worked out.

Discussion questions and exercises

1. Identify the types of opposition/exclusion relation exemplified by (the relevant readings of) the following pairs:

    (a) moving:stationary
    (b) aunt:uncle
    (c) engine:chassis (of car)
    (d) possible:impossible

(e) fall ill:recover
(f) black:white
(g) probable:improbable
(h) bequeath:inherit
(i) cricket:football
(j) approve:disapprove

2. Classify the following antonym pairs (as polar, equipollent, overlapping, privative, or implicit superlatives). Note any alternative classifications for different readings:

far:near   happy:unhappy
beneficial:harmful   satisfied:unsatisfied
happy:sad   comfortable:uncomfortable
brilliant:stupid   polite:rude
deep:shallow   easy:difficult
advantageous:disadvantageous   thick:thin
fat:thin   rough:calm (of sea)

Suggestions for further reading

Incompatibility is discussed in Cruse (1986: ch. 4.1); see also Cruse (1994b), and (2002a) for a prototype account.

All aspects of oppositeness are discussed in Cruse (1986: chs. 9–11); see also Lehrer (1985). For later developments within this approach, particularly on antonymy, see Cruse (1992a), Cruse and Togia (1995) and Croft and Cruse (forthcoming); for reversives, see Cruse (2002b).

Alternative approaches to antonymy can be found in Lehrer and Lehrer (1982) (a formal account) and Mettinger (1994) (a structuralist approach).

CHAPTER 10

Word fields

Word fields

10.1 Introduction

The vocabulary of a language is not just a collection of words scattered at random throughout the mental landscape. It is at least partly structured, and at various levels. In this chapter we look at some of those structures. There are various modes of structuring. It is useful, at the outset, to distinguish two major types of structure, the linguistic and the psycholinguistic. No one with a cognitive linguistic bias would be willing to concede that these might be independent; however, the connection might well be indirect. Linguistic structures in the lexicon are defined linguistically—those which we shall be concerned with here are defined semantically, in terms of meaning relations; psycholinguistic structures are defined in terms of such properties as associative links, priming characteristics, and patterns of speech error. Obviously a semantic structure will be reflected in some way in patterns of language use, and in that sense is necessarily 'psychologically real'. But the specific and characteristic psycholinguistic techniques of investigation may not reveal it as a coherent structure. The position taken here is that the two approaches are complementary; the rest of this chapter will concentrate on aspects of linguistic structuring in the lexicon.

Linguistic structures in the lexicon may have a phonological, grammatical, or semantic basis. Obvious examples of grammatical structuring are word classes (grouping of words according to their syntactic properties) and word families (sets of words derived from a common root). Here we shall be concerned with semantically defined structures, particularly those generated by sense relations, or sets of sense relations. We begin with those based on paradigmatic sense relations.

10.2 Hierarchies

One of the most important types of paradigmatic structure in the lexicon is the **branching hierarchy**, which prototypically has the form shown in Fig. 10.1.

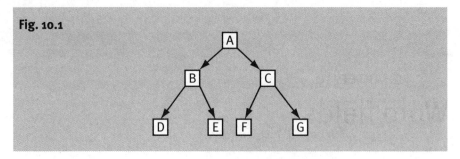

Fig. 10.1

A given type of hierarchy can be characterized in terms of two relations, a **relation of dominance** and a **relation of differentiation**. The relation of dominance is the one which holds between A and B, A and C, B and D, B and E, C and F, and C and G in Fig. 10.1, and is symbolized by the lines joining the nodes (branching points). The relation of difference is the one which holds between B and C, D and E, and F and G. In a well-formed hierarchy, the relations of dominance and differentiation are constant throughout the structure.

A further characteristic of a well-formed hierarchy is that the branches never come together again as one descends the hierarchy; to put it in another way (the so-called **unique mother constraint**), for any element in the hierarchy except the highest (A in Fig. 10.1, sometimes called the **beginner**), there is one and only one element which immediately dominates it. Only certain types of relation guarantee this state of affairs.

In a lexical hierarchy, which is the sort that concerns us here, A, B, ... G correspond to lexical items (or more accurately, units of sense). There are two main sorts of lexical hierarchy: (i) taxonomic (or classificatory) hierarchies, in which the relation of dominance is taxonymy (or, more accurately, its converse, for which there is no special name) and the relation of differentiation is co-taxonymy; and (ii) meronomic (or part–whole) hierarchies, in which the relation of dominance is meronymy (or more accurately, holonymy) and the relation of differentiation is co-meronymy. We shall consider each of these in turn.

10.2.1 Taxonomic hierarchies

Taxonomic hierarchies are essentially classificatory systems, and they reflect the way speakers of a language categorize the world of experience. A well-formed taxonomy offers an orderly and efficient set of categories at different levels of specificity. An example of (part of) a taxonymy is given in Fig. 10.2.

10.2.1.1 Levels

A characteristic of taxonomic hierarchies is that they have well-developed levels. These can be clearly seen in Fig. 10.2. As illustrated, *tableware* is at level 1, *cutlery* etc. at level 2, *fork* . . . *tablecloth* at level 3, and so on. Only four levels

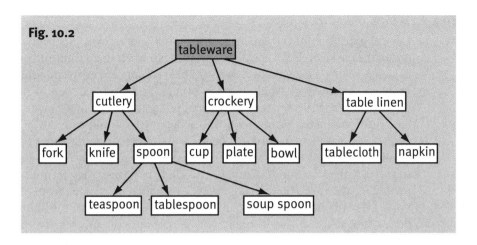

Fig. 10.2

have been shown, but it is arguable that this is only a fragment of a larger hierarchy of something like *household goods*, in which the sister nodes to *tableware* would be occupied by such items as *appliances, furniture*, and *soft furnishings*. Levels can be established in two ways, which in a prototypical hierarchy give the same answer but in real-life hierarchies sometimes diverge. To determine the level of an element by the first method one simply counts the nodes to the top of the hierarchy (the unique item which dominates all the others in the hierarchy, the **beginner**) including the element in question. By this method, one can easily determine that *tablespoon* is at level 4. Levels established by counting nodes are called **technical levels** in Cruse (1986). The other approach to levels consists in looking for distinctive characteristics of the items at different levels. This approach yields **substantive levels**. The substantive level displaying the richest set of characteristic properties is undoubtedly what psychologists call the **basic level**, and anthropological linguists the **generic level**. The basic level in the hierarchy illustrated in Fig. 10.2 is level 3.

The main characteristics of the basic level were described in 7.2.3.6. Vocabulary items at levels below the basic level are more likely to be compound words than those at the basic level (think of *teaspoon, tablespoon, soup spoon, coffee spoon, butter knife, steak knife, cake fork*, etc.). In hierarchies where the basic-level items are count nouns, the items at higher levels are frequently mass nouns. This is particularly the case for taxonomies of artefacts (or more generally, words in whose meaning functional rather than perceptual features are dominant): *cutlery, crockery, furniture, stationery, underwear, hosiery, poultry*.

Research by anthropological linguists has shown that taxonomic hierarchies which appear in everyday language rarely have more than five or six levels, and even this number is uncommon: they mostly occur in small fragments. Our example has four levels, five if we include *household goods*. The number limitation does not apply to expert, technical vocabularies.

10.2.1.2 Gaps and autotaxonymy

Lexical gaps are not infrequent in taxonomic hierarchies, especially in levels above the basic level. We speak of a lexical gap when there is intuitive or other evidence of the existence of a well-established concept corresponding to the point in the structure where the gap occurs. For instance, there is no super-ordinate (in English) for the set of verbs of "going under one's own steam on land" (for an animal or human), whose hyponyms would be *crawl, walk, run, hop*, etc. Nor is there a word for the general notion of "going under one's own steam", whose hyponyms would include the (missing) word just mentioned, together with *swim* and *fly*, and so on. There is no everyday term for devices for telling the time (*timepiece* belongs to a different register from *clock* and *watch*). There is no everyday term in English for members of the animal king-dom (equivalent to *bête* in French or *beastie* in Scottish): *creature* is from a more formal register, and *animal* in this sense (as in *the animal kingdom*) only occurs in technical registers.

Sometimes (what would otherwise be) a gap in a hierarchy is filled by an extended sense of an item immediately above or below it, thus creating an example of autotaxonymy: one reading of a lexical item functioning as a taxo-nym/superordinate of another (it is not always easy to tell which is the original sense and which the extended sense). The following are examples of this (the readings marked with a [1]) are superordinates of those marked [2]):

(1a) A: Haven't you got any trousers[1] to wear?
       B: Yes, I've got my new jeans.

(1b) A: Are you going to wear your jeans?
       B: No, I think I'll wear my trousers.[2]

(2a) Potatoes are one of the most nutritious of all vegetables[1].
(2b) Do you want any vegetables[2], or just potatoes?

(3a) A: I hear they've bought a house[1]?
       B: Yes, a lovely cottage near Netherfield.

(3b) A: Do they live in a cottage?
       B: No, in a house[2].

10.2.1.3 Real-life taxonomies

We have so far been discussing what in some ways are ideal taxonomies. How-ever, real-life taxonomies are often not so straightforward: branches seem to converge and the position in the hierarchy of common lexical items may seem obscure. One of the complicating factors is the existence of terms with a restricted perspective alongside the purely or predominantly speciating ('kind-forming', i.e. taxonymic) terms. The field of clothing will be used to illustrate these points. We shall take *clothing* as the beginner of the clothing taxonomy (notice that there is arguably a more inclusive taxonomy of "things you can wear", which would include, for instance, *watches* and *perfume*). The first true taxonyms we encounter as we go down the hierarchy are those at the basic level: *trousers, jacket, dress, skirt, shoe, bra, knickers*. There seems to be no intermediate level corresponding to *cutlery* and *crockery* in the tableware hierarchy. However, the picture is complicated by the existence of various sorts of restricted perspective-terms, which look at first as though they were the counterparts of *cutlery* and so on. Some of the perspectives are:

where worn relative to body:	*underwear, footwear*
when worn:	*evening wear, nightwear*
who wears it/only visible to intimates:	*lingerie*
worn while doing what:	*sportswear, slumberwear*

There is no term for everyday, publicly observable, not-for-special-purpose clothing; this type functions as a kind of unnamed default category, only deviations from which are lexically distinguished. Notice the following points. A further specification of *lingerie* would need to mention *vest, knickers, nightie, pyjamas*. But the first two are *underwear*, and the latter are *night/ slumberwear*. However, men's vests and men's pyjamas are not lingerie. If we call the default clothing *neutralwear*, then a reading of *dress*, let's call it *dress^1*, will appear amongst its taxonyms/hyponyms. But this is a hyponym of a more general reading of *dress, dress^2*, which includes both *dress^1* and *evening dress*. *Tennis shoe* is a hyponym of *sportswear*, but *shoe* is also hyponymic to *evening wear* and *footwear*. All this makes it virtually impossible to construct a well-formed hierarchy from clothing terms. The appearance of chaos can be mitigated if we bear in mind the following points:

(i) Neat hierarchies appear only if the perspective is kept constant; if this is not the case, cross-classification can occur.
(ii) Each perspective potentially yields a separate hierarchy.
(iii) Different hierarchies can intersect in various ways
(iv) With the possible exception of hierarchies with unmarked perspective, the elements in taxonomic hierarchies are not full lexical senses, but contextually circumscribed microsenses.

We might thus expect to be able to establish well-formed, but partial, hierarchies under specific perspectives. An example might be the WHERE WORN perspective, whose beginner would not be lexicalized, but which would have as hyponyms: *underwear, footwear, headwear*. These all seem to be mutually exclusive, with no common descendants/convergent branches. Another perspective might be OCCASION/FUNCTION, again with a non-lexicalized beginner, whose hyponyms would include:

evening wear   sportswear   leisurewear   slumberwear   outdoor wear.

These are less obviously distinct, in that some items could arguably fall under more than one heading (e.g. *anorak*). But if we say that the nodes of the hierarchy are occupied by micro-senses (that is to say, for example, that a leisurewear anorak is different from a sportswear anorak), then the well-formedness of the hierarchy can be preserved.

10.2.1.4 Contrastive aspects

The taxonomies of different languages can differ not only in the names of the categories but also in which categories are recognized. A few examples of this will suffice. Take first the term *animal* in English, in its everyday sense which contrasts with *bird, fish*, and so on. Strange as it may seem to English speakers, there is no such category in French, and it is difficult to explain to speakers of French exactly what the category comprises. The French word *animal* designates all members of the 'animal kingdom', including birds, fish, insects, etc. The nearest equivalent to this in English, although it does not belong to the same register as the French word, is *creature*. There is thus no single word French translation of *animal* as it occurs in, for instance, *The Observer's Book of British Wild Animals*; it has to be rendered as something like *Les mammifères, reptiles et amphibiens sauvages de la Grande Bretagne*. Another similar case is *nut* in English, which again has no equivalent in French (nor in German). For English speakers, *walnuts, hazelnuts*, and *almonds* belong to a single category, namely that of *nuts*; there is no such category for a French speaker (or thinker!). (There is a **botanical** category of 'dry fruit', but most French speakers do not know it.) Other examples: in French, *une tarte aux pommes* is a kind of *gâteau*, but *an apple tart* is not a kind of *cake*; in French, *la marmelade* belongs firmly in the category of *confiture*, but *marmalade* is felt by many English speakers not to be a kind of *jam*; in German, an *Obstgarten* is a kind of *Garten*, but an *orchard* is not a kind of *garden* for an English speaker. These sorts of examples could be multiplied indefinitely.

10.2.2 Meronymic hierarchies

The second major type of lexical hierarchy is the **meronomy**, in which the relation of dominance is (the converse of) meronymy, and the relation of differentiation is co-meronymy. Probably the most familiar of the extensive meronomies is the segmental version of the human body as seen from the outside, as shown in Fig. 10.3.

Some of the details of this hierarchy are disputable; for instance, whether shoulders are parts of arms, as shown, or parts of the trunk. Commonly encountered machines also have well-developed meronomies associated with them, but few people who are not experts could give a full account of the parts of a car, washing machine, or computer. Most of our knowledge is in the form of fragments of meronomies.

10.2.2.1 Levels

The major formal difference between a taxonomy and a meronomy is the lack of clear generalized levels in the latter. In a sense, the body meronomy

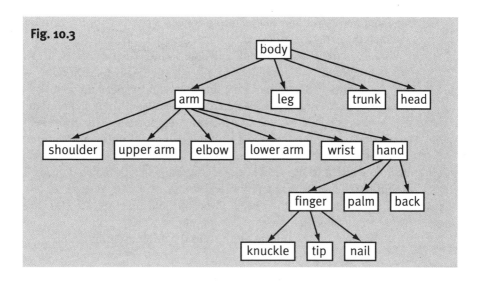

Fig. 10.3

illustrated is uncharacteristic because of the homologies between the arm and the leg: *knee* corresponds to *elbow, sole of foot* to *palm of hand, toes* to *fingers,* etc. But this does not extend to other parts of the body. Speakers have no intuitions as to whether, for instance, the *fingernail* is or is not at the same level as the *anus*, or, in a different domain, the *hub-cap* to the *seat cushions* or the *carburettor jets* in a car. For this reason, there seems to be no equivalent to the basic level of a taxonomy, no unmarked level of specificity independent of context. Of course there are unmarked levels of specificity in particular contexts, but these appear to be governed by something like Gricean principles (see Chapter 18). For instance, one would be more likely to say *Mary felt someone touching her arm* than *Mary felt someone touching her upper arm*: the latter would require special contextual conditions. (Even though the arm is part of the body, *Mary felt someone touching her body* would be interpreted differently.) On the other hand, *Ahmad came into view, the falcon chained to his wrist* would be more likely than *Ahmad came into view, the falcon chained to his arm* (it is not immediately clear why this is so).

10.2.2.2 Lexical gaps

In a taxonomic hierarchy, the beginner is frequently not lexicalized. This is never the case in a meronomy. Gaps do occur, however, and most often in a characteristic position: not infrequently, the main functional part has no name, and speakers are embarrassed if they are asked to supply it. For instance, what do we call the part of a *teapot* to which the *spout, handle*, and *lid* are attached? Some people reply: *But that IS the teapot*; other responses are *bowl* and *body*. But there seems to be no fully established term. Another example: a *spoon* has two main parts, the *handle* and the ——? Again the response is usually hesitation and embarrassment, with some again suggesting *bowl* and *body*. Yet another example concerns the part of a pair of spectacles to which the arms are attached.

Some apparently 'accidental' gaps are found, such as the part of a *fork* to which the *prongs* are attached (or, indeed, the part of the *hand* to which the *fingers* are attached, and of which the *palm* and the *back* are parts). These are, however, relatively rare. In some cases we find automeronymy, that is, when part and immediate whole have the same name (but distinct senses, cf. auto-hyponymy). A good example of this is to be found in the human body meronomy. The term *body* is used both (i) for the whole ensemble and (ii) as a close equivalent to *trunk* (it is, in fact, perhaps the more usual term). It is *body* in sense (ii) which is the metaphorical source of the suggestions of *body* for the main parts of *teapot* and *spoon*. Other possible examples of this are *arm*, in two senses, one which includes *hand* and one which excludes *hand*, and *wheel*, which has two senses, one including and the other excluding *tyre*.

10.2.2.3 Contrastive aspects

Languages typically show differences in respect of the way wholes are divided into lexically distinguished parts, although there are reasons to believe that the underlying principles are more or less universal. This means that differences are mostly confined to (i) different groupings of the same smaller units and (ii) differences in how far subdivision is carried. Radically non-congruent divisions are rare. An example of (i) is provided by English and Modern Greek in respect of divisions of the arm. In English, *hand* extends to the wrist and no further; in Modern Greek (which is not unique in this respect), *xeri* goes up to the elbow. There is a parallel relation between *foot* and *podi*: the latter extends to the knee. Notice that both systems respect the joints as natural boundaries for parts. Which part of *xeri* is being referred to in a particular instance is left to context to determine (there is rarely any ambiguity). But since the part of *xeri* which corresponds to *hand* is the most salient part, and overwhelmingly the most frequently involved in activities and so on, in the vast majority of contexts, little is lost by translating, or otherwise equating *hand* and *xeri*.

The other type of difference appears when one language provides finer divisions than another. One might say, for instance, that *pommette* in French is a subdivision of the part denoted in English by *cheek* (and French *joue*). The *pommette* is the rounded part of the cheek over the cheekbone; *cheekbone* will not do as an equivalent, because one cannot say *She has red cheekbones*, whereas in French one can say *Elle a les pommettes rouges* (this would go into English as *red cheeks*). Another example is the Turkish word *ense*, which means "back of the neck". It is worth asking whether the absence of an English equivalent for *pommette* or *ense* represents a **lexical gap** or a **conceptual gap**. This distinction is by no means always easy to make, although there are clear cases. For instance, for French speakers there is no natural category to which *peanuts, almonds*, and *walnuts* belong (English *nuts*), nor one which includes *rabbits* and *frogs* and *crocodiles* but excludes *birds* and *fish*

(English *animals*). Here we have a conceptual gap. On the other hand, English speakers would probably agree that there was a useful concept of "animal locomotion", which would include *walk, gallop, hop, crawl*, and so forth. But since we have no verb denoting just that, we can speak of a lexical gap. In the case of *pommette*, there is probably a conceptual gap: English speakers feel no need to single out this area of the cheek. The case of *ense* (cf. French *nuque*) is less clear. The concept is easy enough to grasp for English speakers, but then so are concepts like "the right side of the head" and "the underside of the tongue", which English speakers can construe when necessary, but which would not be felt to be salient enough to merit lexical recognition. It might also be relevant to ask whether there is any sign of (incipient) lexification of *back of the neck*, such as non-compositional specificity of meaning (as in the case of *blackbird*), or morphological evidence such as the existence of *fingertip*, but not *nosetip alongside *tip of the finger* and *tip of the nose*: these would point to the emergence of a lexifiable concept. All things considered, my intuition is that *ense*, like *pommette*, does not designate a viable concept (i.e. a concept waiting for a name) for an English speaker.

Meronomic systems of different languages also differ in the way analogous parts of different wholes are grouped for naming purposes. In French, for instance, the handle of a door, the handle of a suitcase, and the handle of a pump would be given different names (for a door, *bouton* (if round, otherwise *poignée*); for a suitcase, *poignée*; for a pump, *manivelle*). They may also differ in the way similar parts of the same whole are grouped for naming purposes. For instance, in English, we distinguish one of the digits of the hand from all the others by means of the term *thumb*; there is a sense of *finger* which excludes *thumb: The hand has four fingers and a thumb* (as well as one which includes *thumb: five-finger exercises*). In Turkish, no such distinction is made among the digits of the hand, although the thumb, like the other digits, can be distinguished, in this case, by the expression büyük parmağı ("big finger"—cf. English *big toe*).

One further point deserves mention. Many languages designate the digits of the hand and those of the foot by unrelated terms (*finger, toe*); many others, however, call the digits of the foot by a name equivalent to '*foot-fingers*' (e.g. *doigts de pied* in French). It is claimed that the reverse process, naming the fingers *hand-toes*, never occurs, and that this is motivated by the cognitive salience of the hand as opposed to the foot. This may well be the case, but perhaps the claim should not be made too strongly. I would not find it unnatural to refer to the *heel* of the hand.

10.3 Linear structures

10.3.1 Bipoles

The simplest kind of linear structure is a pair of opposites. But there is per-haps not a great deal to say about these as structures, other than what has been said under the heading of opposites in Chapter 9.

10.3.2 Bipolar chains

However, the scale on which a pair of opposites operates is often host to a number of terms which denote different degrees of the property. The most frequent pattern is for **implicit superlative** terms of opposite polarity at each end of the scale (there is a polarity switch between the basic antonym pair):

> minuscule   tiny   small   large   **huge   gigantic**

Further examples of such chains are:

> spotless   clean   dirty   filthy
> fantastic   excellent   good   bad   awful   abysmal
> beautiful   pretty   plain   ugly
> adore   love   like   dislike   hate   abominate

Implicit superlatives in English can be recognized by a number of features:

(i) They are resistant to verbal grading compared with normal antonyms: *very huge, huger, extremely tiny, very minuscule*, etc. are all to some degree odd (some more than others) although the comparatives of these words are usually happier with *even* (*The first one was huge, the second one was even huger*).

(ii) They can be prosodically graded, by varying the pitch range of an intonational fall carried by the adjective—the greater the fall, the higher the degree of the underlying property; normal antonyms sound odd with this intonation.

(iii) They can be modified by a low-pitch unstressed *absolutely*: *absolutely huge! absolutely tiny! ?absolutely large!*

(iv) They resist affixation of -*ish*: *largish, smallish, *hugish, *minusculish*

The temperature terms in English illustrate two much less frequent phe-nomena in bipolar scales: **attenuative** terms as well as implicit superlatives (i.e. *warm* and *cool*), which occupy a position on the scale between the basic ant-onyms, and a term which covers the mid-point between the basic pair of opposites (*lukewarm*), which has no polarity (does *more lukewarm* indicate a higher or lower temperature than *lukewarm*?):

> freezing   cold   cool   lukewarm   warm   hot   scorching

10.3.3 Monopolar chains

In **monopolar chains**, there is no sense that terms at the ends of the chains are oriented in opposite directions. There are various different types of monopolar linear lexical structure. There are also various possible ways of describing and classifying them. The following system largely follows Cruse (1986).

10.3.3.1 Degrees

Degrees incorporate as part of their meaning different degrees of some continuously scaled property such as size or intensity, but there is no relation of inclusion. Their boundaries are typically vague, and they have intuitively not lost all their gradability. We can distinguish cases where the terms actually designate values of the underlying property from those which do not, but encapsulate values of a gradable property. Examples of the former type are:

fail   pass   distinction

An example of the second type is:

mound   hillock   hill   mountain

Notice that these encapsulate some notion of size, but that they do not actually refer to sizes, but to types of earth protuberance. Other examples are:

Haze   mist   fog   pea-souper
chuckle   laugh   guffaw
glance   look   stare
puddle   pond   lake   sea   ocean
breeze   wind   gale   hurricane

10.3.3.2 Stages

Stages are points in a lifecycle (taken in a broad sense) of something and normally involve the notion of progression:

primary   secondary   undergraduate   postgraduate
infancy   childhood   adulthood   old   age
egg   larva   pupa   butterfly

10.3.3.3 Measures

Measures are based on a part–whole relationship, with each whole divided into a number of identic parts; there is typically a geometric relationship between values of the scaled property designated by adjacent terms:

second   minute   hour   day   week   month   (etc.)
inch   foot   yard   (etc.)   mile
ounce   pound   stone   (etc.)   ton

10.3.3.4 Ranks

In **ranks** the underlying property does not vary continuously, but in discrete jumps; there is none the less something that a term has more or less of than its neighbours:

> lecturer   senior lecturer   reader   professor
> private   corporal   sergeant

In the above cases, the underlying property can be considered to be something like "seniority". But notice that this does not vary gradually: one sergeant cannot outrank another.

The cardinal integers can be considered to fall under this heading, the variable property being "numerosity" (which again, does not vary continuously: no group of twelve items can outnumber another group of twelve items). The levels of a taxonomic hierarchy are also ranks:

> variety   species   genus   family

10.3.3.5 Sequences

In all the above cases, there is some property which an item has more of than items which precede it in the sequence, and less of than items which follow it. However, there are also ordered terms for which this does not seem to be the case; these are called **sequences**. There is nothing that *Tuesday* has more of than *Monday*:

> Monday   Tuesday   Wednesday   Thursday
> January   February   March   April
> Spring   Summer   Autumn   Winter
> morning   afternoon   evening   night

These categories should not be taken too seriously: it will be noticed that several sets could be considered under more than one heading. There may be a satisfactory taxonomy, but it has not been found yet: it may be better to think in terms of features which cross-classify.

10.4 Grids

Grids are generated by recurrent concrete sense relations, or—which comes to much the same thing—by recurrent (and therefore independent) semantic components. The unit of a grid is the **cell**, which consists of four lexical items, any one of which must be uniquely predictable from the remaining three. The following are examples of cells:

> (i) man   woman   (ii) hand   finger
>   ram   ewe   foot   toe
> (iii) dog   puppy   (iv) take   steal
>   cat   kitten   kill   murder

These can be given componential analyses as follows:

(i) [x] [MALE]   [x] [FEMALE]
     [Y] [MALE]   [Y] [FEMALE]
(ii) [x]   [x] [DIGIT]
     [Y]   [Y] [DIGIT]
(iii) [x]   [x] [YOUNG]
     [Y]   [Y][YOUNG]
(iv) [v.(1)]   [v.(1)] [ILLEGALLY]
     [v.(2)]   [v.(2)][ILLEGALLY]

Notice that the following is not a well-formed cell:

flower   tulip
animal   cat

In a sense, the relation of taxonymy recurs, here. But the criterion of full predictability of any item from the other three is not met. Prediction is possible in one direction:

flower   tulip
?   cat

But in the other direction prediction is not possible:

flower   tulip
animal   ?

A word needs to be said about the relations involved in these structures. In many cases, these are simply concrete versions of already familiar relations. Consider (ii). The relation between *hand* and *finger* is (a concretely specified version of) the familiar one of meronymy, and that between *hand* and *foot* is (a concretely specified version of) co-meronymy. But what of the relation between *finger* and *toe*? They are not co-meronyms, because they are not parts of the same (immediate) whole. This is a new relation, which appears only in connection with recurrent concrete relations: in Cruse (1986) terms related as *finger* is to *toe* are termed **analogues** (the relation may be called **analogicity**). Another example of analogicity is:

captain   team
headmaster   school
vice-chancellor university
boss   business
governor   prison

The terms on the left are analogues (of one another).

It is clear that the introduction of concrete relations has brought with it whole new dimensions of structuring in the lexicon. An important and interesting question is whether there is a finite number of such structures, or whether the number is indefinitely large. Even if the number turns out to be indefinitely large, there is still a question of whether the number of distinct relations is finite (indefinitely large structures could in principle be generated from a finite number of relations). No firm position will be taken on this point here; but it bears mention that some linguists believe the number to be limited (one suggestion is fifty-three!).

All the grids illustrated above have been paradigmatically consistent. But there is nothing in the notion of a grid which imposes paradigmatic constraints. The following are well-formed grid cells:

pen   write   bird   fly   dog   bark
spade   dig   fish   swim   cat   miaow

However, there must be a paradigmatic relation between analogues; for instance, anything which bears the same relation to something else as *pen* does to *write*, or *spade* to *dig*, must be a noun.

10.5 Clusters

Clusters are essentially groups of synonyms. The name is intended to indicate that the sharpness and complexity of structuring is much less than in other types of field: they are somewhat informal groups. There are two main types of cluster, the **centred cluster** and the **non-centred cluster**.

10.5.1 Centred clusters

A centred cluster has a more or less clear core of one or two items, and a penumbra of more peripheral items. Among the characteristics of the core items are:

(i)   They are expressively neutral.
(ii) They are stylistically unmarked, that is, they occur in a wider range of registers than any of the other terms.
(iii) They are propositionally superordinate.

In the set: *die, pass away, pop off, decease, breathe one's last, kick the bucket, die* is clearly the core member: it is expressively neutral, and stylistically unmarked. Feature (iii) is not applicable, since the members of the set are all propositional synonyms.

In the set: *walk, amble, stroll, stride, saunter, walk* is the core item: there is no marked expressive variation in this set, but *walk* is stylistically unmarked, and is a superordinate of all the others. Although *amble, stroll*, and so on are hyponyms of *walk*, they do not form a satisfactory hierarchy, because the relation of difference is too weak: there is considerable overlap between, say, *amble* and *stroll*, which can be differentiated only by examining their prototype centres.

In the set: *brave, courageous, intrepid, gallant, fearless, valorous, heroic, plucky*, there are two candidates for the core, *brave* and *courageous*. The criteria do not favour either one of these—they are both relatively unrestricted contextually compared with their fellows—so we must recognize a two-member core.

10.5.2 Non-centred clusters

In **non-centred clusters**, the items spread over a spectrum of sense, but there is no superordinate item. Typically they display very slight propositional differences, which do not destroy synonymy as long as the items are reasonably close together on the spectrum, but may not be felt to be synonyms if they are widely separated. Typical examples are (taken as referring to sounds):

rap tap knock slap thwack crack bang thump bump pop tick
click ring tinkle clink clank jingle jangle ping . . .

Clusters may overlap: this is unusual and non-canonical in taxonomic and meronomic hierarchies. For instance, the following two clusters overlap:

(i) unusual, rare, uncommon, infrequent (etc.)
(ii) odd, queer, strange, weird, peculiar, extraordinary, alien (etc.)

Group (i) consists of words denoting low frequency of occurrence, whereas the words in group (ii) denote unfamiliarity (of course, these notions are not unconnected). Although the groups are in a sense distinct, intuitively, *unusual, odd*, and *strange* (at least) are felt to be synonyms.

10.6 Miscellaneous types

We have now dealt, albeit briefly, with the major types of word field that can be treated in terms of characteristic structures. There are other important groupings of words, for which the notion of structure seems less appropriate. Two examples will be mentioned. First, there are the so-called **word families**. These are words derived from a common root, like *cook* (v.), *cook* (n.), *cookery, cooker, cooking* (n.), etc. Of course there are semantic processes at work here which recur with other roots, but there does not seem much to say about this group of words (or other similar ones) *as a group*. Second, there are groupings of words by, for instance, register, as in colloquial or formal use, or by field of discourse, such as the vocabulary appropriate for (and possibly restricted to) a religious sermon, a legal document, or a medical textbook. Again, as structures these have no particularly striking properties.

Discussion questions and exercises

1. Construct the best lexical hierarchies you can from the following sets of words, noting any difficulties. For Set (a) you will need to supply a number of superordinates.

    (a) tablecloth   wine glass   table mat   salt
         napkin   teaspoon   breadknife   coaster
         tumbler   vinegar   water jug   fork
         cake dish   saucer   napkin ring knife
         butter knife corkscrew   cake slice   pepper
         breadboard   butter dish   soup spoon   teaspoon
         serving spoon soup bowl   dessert spoon mug

    (b) jacket   knickers   sportswear   T-shirt
         shirt   blouse   underpants   trousers
         jeans   cardigan   coat   pyjamas
         sweater   suit   evening wear vest
         overcoat   waistcoat   clothes   underwear
         skirt   anorak   nightwear   tracksuit
         shoes   slippers   sandals   boots
         socks   stockings   tights   top
         bodysuit   kilt   dress   knitwear
         nightdress   jeanswear   leggings   dressing gown
         blouson   blazer   trenchcoat   briefs
         bra   stole   gloves   sporran

    (c) book   novel   headline   section
         booklet   paperback   textbook   review
         programme   volume   thesis   title
         preface   catalogue   hardback   periodical
         pamphlet   footnote   biography   encyclopedia
         index   brochure   questionnaire memorandum
         journal   circular   manifesto   magazine
         handbook   article   tract   page
         newspaper   dictionary   thesaurus   editorial
         leader   paragraph   leaflet   letter
         note   chapter   leader   monograph
         paper   sentence   advertisement glossary

Suggestions for further reading

The topics covered in this chapter are covered in greater detail in Cruse (1986: chs. 5–8).

For discussion of 'folk taxonomies' by anthropological linguists see Berlin et al. (1973), Brown et al. (1976), Berlin (1992), Hunn (1983), Brown (1995) and Brown (2002a). Lehrer (1974) contains a detailed study of the field of cooking terms in English.

Meronomies are discussed in Brown (1976) and Brown (2002b). Brown (2002a) and (2002b) are especially interesting on the general principles of naming.

CHAPTER 11

Extensions of meaning

Extensions of meaning

11.1 Literal and non-literal meaning

Most people are aware that if someone says *Jane's eyes nearly popped out of her head*, a **literal** truth has not been expressed: Jane's eyes were not, as a matter of fact, on the point of being projected from her head; the message is rather that Jane was very surprised. At the everyday level, the contrast between literal and figurative use does not seem problematic. It is not so easy, however, to be more precise about what 'literal meaning' really is. Let us look at some possible ways of pinning down the essence of literalness.

11.1.1 The reading of a word with the earliest recorded use

Dictionaries often organize their entries historically, with the earliest first. It would be a reasonable requirement of a dictionary that it should indicate which meanings are literal and which figurative: most users would probably assume that the literal meaning would be given first. However, this is not really a satisfactory explanation of what literalness is. The most obvious objection is that while we might reasonably expect an intelligible path of change from past meanings to present meanings, most speakers are ignorant of the history of their language, so history cannot be the (direct) cause of current intuitions.

11.1.2 The most frequently occurring reading of a word

Frequency is another common principle for organizing dictionary entries. At first sight this seems more promising as a rationale for intuitions of literalness. However, this turns out not to be so. An example is the verb *see*. Two of the readings of this verb are "have a visual experience" and "understand" (as in *Do you see what I mean?*). There can be little doubt that it is the first of these readings which intuition points to as the literal reading. Yet it appears that the second reading has a greater text frequency. Clearly, we must look elsewhere for an account of literalness.

11.1.3 The default reading of a word

The **default** reading of a word is the one which first comes to mind when the word is encountered out of context, or the reading which one would assume to be operative in the absence of contextual indications to the contrary. This criterion would seem to give the right answer for *see*: it is the first meaning to come to mind, and if, say, a foreigner were to ask the meaning, one would hardly begin by saying that it meant to "understand". However, even if the literal meaning coincides with the default reading, we are still none the wiser as regards the underlying reason: it should be possible to come up with a genuinely semantic characterization.

11.1.4 The reading from which the most plausible path of change begins

Consider the following three readings of the noun *position*:

(1) Mary has been offered an excellent position with a firm of solicitors.
(2) What is your position on the single currency?
(3) This is an excellent position from which to watch the parade.

It seems implausible that one could begin with either (1) or (2) and derive the remaining two readings by metaphorical extension. On the other hand, starting from (3), involving location in physical space, the extension to mental space in (2) and a place in an institutional hierarchy in (1) seems relatively natural. This criterion also gives a plausible account of *see*: it is easy to derive the "understand" reading of *see* metaphorically from the "have a visual experience" reading, but not vice versa. In both these cases, the most plausible starting point is also intuitively the literal reading. But what about *expire*, with its two readings "die" and "come to the end of a period of validity"? In this case, either reading can be convincingly derived from the other. Which, then, is the literal reading? According to my intuitions the expiring of driving licences is the extended reading, but to my undergraduate students it is the other way round. It is not clear what the basis for the differing intuitions is.

11.1.5 The reading most closely related to basic human experience

The criterion of the reading most closely related to human experience follows from a claim that not only much of language but also many conceptual categories are metaphorical in nature, and are extensions from basic experience, especially, but not exclusively, spatial experience. On this basis, the "location in physical space" reading of *position*, the "have visual experience" reading of *see*, and the "die" reading of *expire* would be literal, and their other readings figurative/extended. However, on its own this factor cannot explain why my students feel that the "driving licence" reading of *expire* is the literal one.

Perhaps a distinction ought to be made between diachronic and synchronic processes of extension. It seems that for diachrony, the 'plausible path' criterion and the 'basic experience' criterion give the right answer. Let us suppose that if there is only one plausible path, then the diachronic literal/ figurative relationship persists in the face of later frequency changes. When there are alternative metaphorical extensions, however, while these criteria give the right answer for historical development, synchronically, an individual will take the most frequent/familiar reading (which will probably, incidentally, also be the one which is learned first) as literal, and the least familiar as extended. (Notice that the two directions of derivation for *expire* produce two distinct metaphors, not the same metaphor from different angles, or whatever.) For this explanation to be correct, it would have to be the case that when I first encountered the word *expire*, the "die" reading was much more frequent than it is now.

11.2 Naturalized, established, and nonce extensions

11.2.1 Naturalized extensions

What is historically no doubt an extended meaning may be so entrenched and familiar a part of a language that its speakers no longer feel that a figure of speech is involved at all: such readings of a word (or expression) will be said to be **naturalized**:

(4) He's *in love*.
(5) It's hard to *put into words*.
(6) The *kettle's boiling*.

11.2.2 Established extensions

There are also readings which are well established, and presumably have entries in the mental lexicon, but are nonetheless felt to be figures of speech:

(7) John's *a parasite/a lounge lizard/a couch potato*.
(8) She *swallowed* the story.
(9) There are too many *mouths* to feed.

11.2.3 Nonce readings

Nonce readings are ones for which there are no entries in the mental lexicon; they therefore cannot be 'looked up', but have to be generated and interpreted using strategies of meaning extension such as metaphor and metonymy. The following are selected (almost) at random from Patricia Cornwell's best-seller *Hornet's Nest*:

(10) West gave him a look that was heat-seeking, like a missile.
(11) He had never told her his fantasies about being overpowered by her,

cuffed, pinned, held, yoked, and hauled away in the paddy wagon of erotic captivity.

(12) His heart rolled forward at such a pitch, he could not catch up with it.

11.3 Metaphor

A typical dictionary definition of **metaphor** is: "The use of a word or phrase to mean something different from the literal meaning" (*Oxford Advanced Learner's Dictionary*). This is not very enlightening: since it does not even hint at any rationale for such a curious practice, it makes metaphor seem, at best, carelessness, and, at worst, perversity. However, as Lakoff (and others) have persuasively argued, metaphor is all-pervasive in language, and is for the most part effortlessly interpreted, so it deserves more constructive consideration.

11.3.1 Approaches to metaphor

There have been many more or less suggestive commentaries on metaphor, most, however, leaving much to be explained. The Greek word from which the term metaphor originated literally meant "transfer". For Aristotle, what was transferred was the meaning of one expression to another expression: for him, a metaphorical meaning was always the literal meaning of another expression. (This is the so-called **substitution** view of metaphor.) Although Aristotle recognized the crucial role of resemblance in metaphor, in the classical tradition metaphor was regarded essentially as a decorative device.

Another aspect of metaphor—the usually incongruous nature of the expression on a literal interpretation—was pointed out by Dr Johnson, who defined it as "heterogeneous ideas yoked by violence together". There is still a degree of disagreement (and confusion?) over the exact role of 'deviance' or 'semantic clash' in metaphor; we return to this topic below.

In modern times, the literary scholar I. A. Richards (1965) is usually credited with giving an impetus to metaphor studies. He made a distinction between three aspects of metaphor: **vehicle**, the item(s) used metaphorically, **tenor**, the metaphorical meaning of the vehicle, and **ground**, the basis for the metaphorical extension, essentially the common elements of meaning, which license the metaphor. For example, in *the foot of the mountain*, the word *foot* is the vehicle, the tenor is something like "lower portion", that is, the intended meaning of the vehicle, and the ground (never properly spelled out by Richards) is (presumably) the spatial parallel between the canonical position of the foot relative to the rest of the (human) body, and the lower parts of a mountain relative to the rest of the mountain.

This account at least focused attention on the fact that there must be some essential connection between tenor and vehicle—a word cannot be used to mean just anything—but the nature of the connection, the 'how' of metaphor, was not really elucidated. Richards also rejected the notion that metaphors can in general be translated into literal language, pointing out that there was a species of interaction between meanings ("the interanimation of words") that cannot be reproduced in literal language.

11.3.1.1 Haas: the interaction of semantic fields

A more thoroughgoing interaction theory, and more solidly grounded in language, was that of Haas (see 'Suggestions for further reading' at the end of this chapter). For Haas, the meaning of a word constituted a 'semantic field'. This consisted of all the possible contexts of the word organized in terms of normality, the most normal contexts forming the 'core' region of the field, and the least normal forming the periphery. Essentially, the semantic field of every word encompassed the whole vocabulary, but each word imposed a different 'core–periphery' organization on it. When two words were brought into interaction, a new semantic field was created, whose core was formed by the contexts with the highest joint degree of normality for both words. This new semantic field defined a new meaning, the metaphorical one. For instance, referring to the metaphor *leg of the table*, Haas has the following to say:

> . . . a word e.g. *leg*, is transferred to new contexts: from its normal *of the* ——— contexts (*of the man/woman/child/horse*, etc.) to the given new context of the *table*; and we select from the more or less normal contexts of the displaced *legs* just those that fit. Though the legs of a table do not *move* or *stretch* or *hurt*, are neither *quick* nor *slow*, not *muscular* or *energetic* or *tired*, they are still found to be *long* or *short, strong* or *weak, thick* or *slim, beautiful* or *ugly*, they *stand (on)* and *support*, may be *broken* or *cut*, etc.

Although Haas would have no truck with feature theories of meaning, his account of metaphor is similar in spirit to analyses in terms of semantic features, in which semantic anomalies are resolved by eliminating incompatible features from a composite expression, and allowing only compatible features to form part of the resultant meaning of the expression.

11.3.1.2 Black: analogue models

One of the virtues Haas claimed for his account of metaphor was that it avoided reference to 'pure ideas', 'private thoughts', and 'hidden intentions', and referred exclusively to 'public occurrences of words—occurrences in the contexts, present or remembered, of other words and of situations'. Most modern accounts, on the other hand, unashamedly embrace 'pure ideas' (in their modern guise of concepts, domains, and so on).

The ideas of the American philosopher Max Black have been influential in the development of modern theories of metaphor. First of all, Black rejected both the substitution view of metaphor (see above) and what he regarded as a special version of it, the **comparison** view, according to which the 'literal' equivalent of a metaphor is the corresponding simile, so that, for instance, the literal equivalent of *the leg of the table* would be *the part of the table which is like a leg* (Haas used to maintain that no distinction could be drawn in principle between metaphor and simile).

Black's picture of the mechanism of metaphor involved the projection of a set of 'associative implications' derived from one entity (the 'secondary subject') onto another entity ('the primary subject'). In Black's own example:

(13) Marriage is a zero-sum game.

the primary subject is *marriage* and the secondary subject is *zero-sum game* (Black makes it clear that the relevant entities ('subjects') are notions in the minds of speakers and hearers). The relevant associated implications of the secondary subject might be as follows (after Black 1979: 29–30):

(i) A game is a contest
(ii) between two opponents
(iii) in which one player can win only at the expense of the other.

The metaphor works by imposing the same implications (or similar/analogous ones) on to the primary subject, as follows:

(iv) A marriage is a sustained struggle
(v) between two contestants
(vi) in which the rewards (power–money–satisfaction) of one contestant are gained only at the other's expense.

The notion that the implications are not necessarily identical for the two subjects is important: Black sees the 'implicative complex' of the secondary subject as an 'analogue model' of the implicative complex intended to be inferred for the primary subject. It is hard to see a Haasian selection of normal contexts achieving this. On the other hand, Black's view of the workings of metaphor is remarkably similar to the more recent Lakoffian picture of the projection of the structure of a 'source domain' onto a 'target domain' (see below).

11.3.1.3 Relevance theory and metaphor

In relevance theory (Sperber and Wilson 1986), a distinction is made between 'representative' and 'interpretive' uses of language, which for our present purposes we can take as parallel to the 'literal/figurative' distinction (for a fuller account of relevance theory, see Chapter 18). This account of metaphor incorporates two significant claims. The first is that metaphor is nothing special or deviant, and is simply an extreme case of 'loose talk'. Take the case of *The children stood in a circle round the teacher*. Do we imagine the children forming a geometrically exact circle? No, only a shape which has a sufficient resemblance to a circle. We do not feel this to be metaphorical, but this is perhaps merely a function of the degree of resemblance: for instance, some people probably find *electronic pet* slightly metaphorical; a greater proportion will feel the presence of metaphor in *emotional blackmail*, and so on. But the mechanism of interpretation is the same for all these: look for relevant resemblances (this does not explicitly include, but nor does it explicitly exclude, wider-ranging structural parallels).

The second point highlighted by the relevance-theoretical treatment is that the interpretation of an utterance used interpretively is very much a function of context: interpreters look to maximize contextual relevance with the least expenditure of effort (this notion is explained in greater detail in Chapter 18). This point is also well made by Black, but it is given less prominence by cognitive linguists.

11.3.1.4 Lakoff

According to Lakoff, metaphors are not merely decorative features of certain styles, but are an essential component of human cognition. Nor are they purely linguistic, but are conceptual in nature. They are 'a means whereby ever more abstract and intangible areas of experience can be conceptualised in terms of the familiar and concrete'.

Metaphors involve (i) a source domain, usually concrete and familiar, (ii) a target domain, usually abstract or at least less well-structured, and (iii) a set of mapping relations, or correspondences. For example, the ARGUMENT IS WAR metaphor uses notions drawn from the domain of war, such as winning and losing, attacking and defending, destroying, and undermining, to depict what happens during an argument. Likewise, the LIFE IS A JOURNEY metaphor borrows structuring ideas from the domain of a journey and applies them to life: *We've come a long way together, but we have decided to take our separate paths*; *He has come to a crossroads in his life*; *This young man will go far*.

The correspondences involved in metaphor are of two kinds, (i) ontological, involving entities in the two domains, and (ii) epistemic, involving relations of knowledge about the entities. This can be illustrated using Lakoff's example of the metaphor which he expresses as ANGER IS HEAT OF FLUID IN CONTAINER (Lakoff (1987: book ii, ch. 1)):

(i) Ontological correspondences

source: HEAT OF FLUID	target: ANGER
container	body
heat of fluid	anger
heat scale	anger scale
pressure in container	experienced pressure
agitation of boiling fluid	experienced agitation
limit of container's resistance	limit of person's ability to suppress anger
explosion	loss of control

(ii) Epistemic correspondences

When fluid in a container is heated beyond a certain limit, pressure increases to point at which container explodes.

When anger increases beyond a certain limit, 'pressure' increases to point at which person loses control.

An explosion is damaging to container and dangerous to bystanders.

Loss of control is damaging to person and dangerous to others.

Explosion can be prevented by applying sufficient force and counter-pressure.

Anger can be suppressed by force of will.

Controlled release of pressure may occur, which reduces danger of explosion.

Anger can be released in a controlled way, or vented harmlessly, thus reducing level.

An important feature of metaphor is that the mapping from source to target domain is partial: for instance, in the ARGUMENT IS WAR metaphor, there are ARGUMENT correspondences for:

winning and losing
taking up positions
defending one's position against attack
attacking and demolishing opponent's position
probing opponent's weaknesses
using weapons
shooting down opponent's aircraft, etc.

but no correspondences for:

taking hostages/prisoners
field hospital
anti-personnel mines
parachutes, etc.

Similarly, in the ANGER IS HEAT OF FLUID IN CONTAINER metaphor, the 'cooking' aspect of, for instance, *boiling* and *simmering* has no correspondence in the ANGER domain.

Lakoff emphasizes that metaphors are conceptual, not merely linguistic. Speaking of another metaphor, LOVE IS A JOURNEY (which underlies such expressions as *We've come a long way together* and *We've decided to go our separate ways*), Lakoff has the following to say:

What constitutes the LOVE IS A JOURNEY metaphor is not any particular word or expression. It is the ontological mapping across conceptual domains, from the source domain of journeys to the target domain of love. The metaphor is not just a matter of language, but of thought and reason. The language is secondary. The mapping is primary, in that it sanctions the use of source domain language and inference patterns for target domain concepts. The mapping is conventional; that is, it is a fixed part of our conceptual system, one of our conventional ways of conceptualising love relationships. (Lakoff 1993: 208)

Sometimes the strong claim is made that without metaphor, certain conceptual domains would have no structure at all. For instance, speaking of the LOVE IS A JOURNEY metaphor, Kövecses, a follower of Lakoff, says (2002: 7):

Constituent elements of conceptual domain A are in systematic correspondence with conceptual elements of domain B. From this discussion, it might seem that the elements in the target domain have been there all along and that people came up with this metaphor because there were pre-existing similarities between the elements in the two domains. This is not so. The domain of love did not have these elements before it was structured by the domain of journey.

In support of this claim, he points to the difficulty of thinking of the salient aspects of a love relationship without using the metaphor:

Try to imagine the goal, choice, difficulty, progress, etc. aspects of love without making use of the journey domain. Can you think of the goal of a love relationship without at the same time thinking of trying to reach a destination at the end of a journey?

Furthermore, he points to the frequent difficulty in naming the elements of the target domain without using the language of the source. For instance, the notions of "progress" and "goal" used in the previous quote are also metaphoric extensions from literal meanings which are spatial in nature. That is to say, there is no way of escaping the metaphor: the CONCEPT of "love" is fundamentally a metaphorical one.

One consequence of the conceptual nature of metaphor is that often a range of different linguistic expressions can tap the same metaphor, and this can be done flexibly and productively. For instance, the lexical resources of the source domain can be exploited in the target domain (this means that a conceptual metaphor cannot be reduced to a finite set of expressions). What Lakoff calls **elaborations** involve more specific versions of the basic metaphor, whose characteristics in the source domain carry over to the target domain. For instance, the difference in intensity between *boil* and *simmer* in reference to a heated liquid carries over to indicate corresponding differences in degree of anger in *to boil with anger* and *to simmer with anger*.

Another consequence of the conceptual nature of metaphor is that certain patterns of reasoning may carry over from the source domain to the target domain. Lakoff calls these **metaphorical entailments**. For instance, if you destroy all your enemy's weapons, you win the war; similarly, if you demolish all your opponent's points in an argument, you win the argument.

The existence of a conceptual metaphor also explains why new and imaginative extensions of the mapping can be understood instantly. Lakoff (1990) illustrates this using a line from a song:

We're driving in the fast lane on the freeway of love.

This exploits the LOVE IS A JOURNEY metaphor mentioned above (lovers = travellers; relationship = vehicle; shared experiences = journey). When you drive in the fast lane you go a long way (have a lot of shared experiences) in a short time, and it can be exciting (sexually) and dangerous (relationship may not last/lovers may be hurt emotionally).

It is not only complex and intangible concepts like emotions which are understood metaphorically. According to Lakoff, basic semantic notions such as time, quantity, state, change, cause, and category membership are also metaphorically understood as extensions of basic conceptual elements which he calls **image-schemas**, involving space, motion, and force.

(i) Categories: categories are understood in terms of containers/bounded regions of space. Something can be in or out of a category, and can be put into or removed from a category, just as with a container. The logic of categories is the same as (may even be ultimately derived from) the logic of containers. If X is inside container A and container A is inside container B, then X is inside container B: this transitivity carries over into category membership.

(ii) Quantity: two metaphors are involved in the conceptualization of quantity:

(a) MORE IS UP; LESS IS DOWN. This metaphor is exemplified in the following:

(14) Output rose dramatically.
(15) Fatal accidents are well down on last year.
(16) Efficiency savings have plateaued.
(17) Our pass rate is much higher than theirs.

(b) LINEAR SCALES ARE PATHS. This metaphor appears in the following:

(18) John is by far the best in the class.
(19) Bill has been catching up fast, and he's now about level with John in ability.
(20) John is streets ahead of Bill in academic ability.

(The logic of paths carries over into the logic of linear scales. For instance, if C is ahead of B on a path, and B is ahead of A, then C is also ahead of A; similarly, if C is ahead of B in ability, and B is ahead of A, then C is ahead of A (i.e. has more ability than A).)

(iii) Time: time is understood in terms of things, locations, distances, and motion. Times are things; the passing of time is motion; time intervals are distances; future times are in front of the observer, past times behind. The passage of time can be construed in two ways, according to whether the speaker/observer is stationary or moving (it is always the case that one thing is moving, and the other is stationary):

(a) Events stationary, observer moving:

> (**21**) We're coming up to exam time.
>
> (**22**) I don't know how I'm going to get through next week.
>
> (**23**) We have left all that behind us.

(b) Events moving; observer stationary:

> (**24**) The exams will be upon us soon.
>
> (**25**) The day just rushed past.
>
> (**26**) Doomsday is edging closer.
>
> (**27**) The holidays passed peacefully enough.

(iv) Causation: causation may be seen as a force which produces movement (i.e. change) towards a location, which may be an action (as in (28)), or a state (as in (29)):

> (**28**) Frustration drove Jane to murder.
>
> (**29**) John's words sent Jane into a state of panic.

Lakoff's arguments that metaphor has (or, at least, has had) an essential constructive role in our mental life are persuasive. But a number of questions remain. One of these concerns the status of metaphorical processes in adult cognition. Obviously, they come into play in the interpretation of fresh metaphors (nonce readings); but many of the metaphors Lakoff discusses are fully naturalized in the language, others are at least established; for both types it seems necessary to assume that they are permanently laid down (entrenched) in the mental lexicon. Interpreting these would seem therefore to be a matter of selection of existing readings, rather than generation using metaphorical strategies (although we still need to explain the intuitive distinction between naturalized and merely established metaphors—perhaps this is due to a subliminal activation of the metaphorical process in the latter case). However, it is possible that metaphor is vitally operative either at earlier stages of the development of a language (or, indeed, at earlier stages in the evolution of language), or at earlier stages in the acquisition of language, for every individual.

In spite of Lakoff's insistence on the constructive role of metaphor, and his criticism of earlier views of metaphor as merely decorative, some of the metaphors that he discusses are arguably decorative in function. One of these is the following, a translation of an Indian poem:

Slowly slowly rivers in autumn show
sand banks
bashful in first love woman
showing thighs. (Lakoff 1990)

Lakoff calls such metaphors **image metaphors**: they are characterized by the fact that both source and target domains are well structured in their own right. What is the function of the metaphor here? It seems to be merely to invest the natural features of a landscape with an erotic aura—surely a species of 'decoration'? Lakoff (1990: 67) argues that the success of such a metaphor is a function of the richness of the image-schematic correspondences between the two domains ('We suggest that conventional mental images are structured by image-schemas and that image metaphors preserve image-schematic structure, mapping parts onto parts, wholes onto wholes, containers onto containers, paths onto paths, and so on'). There are certainly many correspondences in the above metaphor between the colour, shape, and untouched smoothness of the sand banks revealed by the slowly falling water level in the river and the thighs of a shy young woman divesting herself for her first lover. But while the richness of the correspondences may be necessary for a successful metaphor, they surely are not sufficient—just as important is the appropriate selection of domains in the first place.

11.3.1.5 Metaphor and blending

Lakoff's model of metaphor has been highly influential, but it is not without its critics. Two lines of criticism may be singled out. The first concerns the degree of interaction between the source and target domains. In Lakoff's model this is limited to the projection of structure from the source domain to the target domain by means of determinate correspondences; otherwise, the domains remain distinct. Other scholars, however, have pointed to a much more intimate fusion between the domains, and a richer, more open-ended range of correspondences. This property of metaphor can be highlighted by comparing metaphors with their corresponding similes. For some writers, metaphors are implicit similes; for some, similes are implicit metaphors. However, it is arguable that at least prototypical similes and prototypical metaphors are distinct, and a major difference lies in the fact that in metaphor there is a fusion of domains, whereas in similes there is no fusion. Consider the following metaphors from Patricia Cornwell's *Black Notice*, and their simile equivalents:

(30) Icicles bared long teeth from the eaves.
    (cf. Icicles were like long teeth being bared)
(31) The elevator has a mind of its own.
    (cf. The elevator behaves like a being with a mind of its own.)

An even more dramatic example is (32), (which is not easy to transform into a simile) where notions of "thoughts" and "unpleasant small creatures with claws" fuse into something quite sinister:

(32) A myriad of ugly, dark thoughts clung to my reason and dug in with their claws.

In this example, not only is there fusion, but the total effect cannot be accounted for in terms of a determinate set of correspondences.

The second shortcoming of Lakoff's model is that it cannot account for the emergence of features in the metaphor which are not present in either the source domain or the target domain. Take the case of the metaphor *That surgeon is a butcher*. This clearly imputes incompetence to the surgeon, although incompetence is not stereotypically attributed to either profession.

A model of metaphor which attempts to accommodate these aspects of metaphor is blending theory. Whereas Lakoff's model operates with two conceptual domains and correspondences between them, blending theory sets up a separate representation of the metaphor which draws selected conceptual features from source and target domains and combines these to form a new structure, the **blend**. This material is then elaborated on the basis of encyclopedic knowledge. In the case of the metaphor *That surgeon is a butcher*, the blend contains a representation of someone in charge of an operation, but using the techniques of a butcher. It is the basic incompatibility between the goal and the means which leads to the inference of the surgeon's incompetence.

11.3.2 Close relatives of metaphor

11.3.2.1 Personifications

Death is frequently personified as a coachman, footman, reaper, devourer, destroyer, etc. but never as a university lecturer or supermarket manager. Why? In most personifications events (like death or natural disasters) are understood in terms of actions by some agent (like reaping, carrying away, or destroying), and it is the agent of such actions that is personified. The success of a personification thus depends (at least in part) on significant correspondences between the event and the implied actions of the agent indicated by the personification.

11.3.2.2 Proverbs

A proverb describes a specific event or state of affairs which is applicable metaphorically to a range of different events or states of affairs provided they have the same or sufficiently similar image-schematic structure.

11.3.3 Metaphor and deviance

There has been much discussion—and disagreement, not to say confusion—about the relationship between metaphor and deviance, between those who maintain that the ubiquity and utter naturalness of metaphor make it perverse to qualify it as 'deviance', and those who claim that deviance is an essential clue to the fact that an expression is metaphorical (or at least, not literal). The reader will probably already have spotted the fact that these two supposedly opposed views do not really address the same issue, and we must first clarify a source of confusion (which is surprisingly prevalent in current discussions).

There can surely be no disagreement about the claim that metaphor is a natural and vital expression of the human cognitive-linguistic endowment. However, the question remains of how we recognize that an expression is not being used literally. This is where the notion of deviance, or at least anomaly, comes legitimately into the picture. It is perfectly compatible with the idea of the naturalness of metaphor to claim that figurative expressions are recognized by the fact that they are anomalous on a literal reading, and that this triggers off a search for a relevant non-literal interpretation derivable from the literal reading. Haas says:

If there is to be general agreement amongst us about the meaning of a new and metaphorical utterance, then that agreement can only be due to the fact that the utterance consists of familiar words and that its sense is DERIVABLE from the familiar meanings of those words. Although some part of the utterance (a word or phrase) or even the whole of it strikes us as displaced in the context in which it occurs, the abnormal contribution it makes to the sense of the utterance must be derivable from the knowledge we share of its normal occurrences.

A word of caution is necessary at this point. There are current claims that there is no evidence that metaphorical meanings are computed by first computing the literal meanings. However, experiments claiming to demonstrate this do not clearly separate conventionalized metaphors from fresh metaphors: obviously, if a metaphor is conventionalized, its activation is merely a matter of the selection of an appropriate meaning, no different from the selection of the appropriate reading of *bank* in *She works in a bank*. The mechanism suggested above applies only to freshly coined metaphors.

Even with this proviso, however, the thesis that anomaly is an essential clue to non-literalness is not universally accepted. Black (1979) gives the following example:

Suppose I counter the conversational remark, 'As we know, man is a wolf . . .' by saying, 'Oh, no, man is not a wolf but an ostrich'. In context, 'Man is not a wolf' is as metaphorical as its opposite, yet it clearly fails the controversion [= anomaly] test.

However, Black's point is considerably weakened by the observation that the literal reading of *Man is not a wolf* would sit very oddly in the context he provides. And in fact he concedes this point later in the same article:

The decisive reason for the choice of interpretation may be, as it often is, the patent falsity or incoherence of the literal reading—but it might equally be the banality of that reading's truth, its pointlessness, or its lack of congruence with the surrounding text and non-verbal setting.

This is very close to an admission of the central role of deviance in the interpretation of metaphor. However, it is possible to argue that actual deviance of the literal reading is not strictly necessary, as long as there is a clear superiority of the figurative reading in terms of relevance, appositeness, or aesthetic richness. This argument is most convincing for poetic language. But for everyday language use it is less plausible: it has the disadvantage that it seems to require us to explore the possible figurative readings for everything we hear or read.

11.4 Metonymy

The second major strategy for extending word meanings is metonymy. Metonymy is responsible for a great proportion of the cases of so-called **regular polysemy**, where a parallel alternation of meaning applies over a class of instances, such as the TREE–WOOD readings of *oak, ash, beech, pine, cherry*, etc.

11.4.1 Metonymy and metaphor

Metonymy and metaphor are quite distinct processes of extension, in spite of the fact that there may exist extensions that cannot be classified, because the end-point could have been reached by either route. Claimed examples of this phenomenon are *head of the bed* and *back of the chair*: is the reason we label them as we do because a person's head normally rests at that part of the bed, or a person's back rests on that part of a chair? Or is it because of some resemblance between a bed and a supine person, or between a chair and a standing person? We may never know. A typical formulation of the difference between the two tropes states that metaphor is based on resemblance, whereas metonymy is based on association.

This captures some of the difference between metaphor and metonymy, but leaves an important point unhighlighted. Metaphor involves the use of one domain as an analogical model (in Black's terms) to structure our conception of another domain; in other words the process crucially involves two (in the simplest cases) distinct conceptual domains. Metonymy, on the other hand, relies on an (actual, literal) association between two components within a single domain (and no restructuring is involved). Take the famous *ham sandwich* case:

(33) The ham sandwich wants his coffee now.

This is, of course, 'café language', but is perfectly intelligible to all. The domain invoked is a café, or similar establishment, where a customer is (perhaps momentarily) distinguished by the fact that he has ordered a ham sandwich. This fact associated with the customer serves as a convenient identifying device. There is no question of drawing any structural parallels between the person referred to and a ham sandwich. Suppose, however, that the customer were heavy-jowled and of lugubrious mien, and the waitress had said:

(34) The abandoned bloodhound wants his coffee now.

Here the hearer is invited to see the characteristic lineaments of a bloodhound's face in the customer's visage; no literal association between the customer and any actual bloodhound is imputed or evoked.

While it is necessary to maintain the distinction between metonymy and metaphor as *processes*, it is important to emphasize that a clear distinction between metonymic and metaphorical *expressions* is not always possible, because of the fact that the two processes may both contribute to a figurative reading. Lakoff points out that metonymy lies at the core of some conventional metaphors. For instance, underlying the ANGER IS HEAT metaphor is the physiological fact that an angry person subjectively feels hot. Another type of interaction between metonymy and metaphor occurs in what has been called **metaphtonymy** (Goóssens 1990). An example of this is *My lips are sealed*. If no metaphor were present, this could be taken metonymically to indicate that one was physically unable to speak. However, a literal sealing of the lips is not normally indicated, but a metaphorical sealing, meaning that one is under some sort of constraint preventing one from commenting on some topic. In this case both metaphor and metonymy contribute to the figurative meaning.

11.4.2 Patterns of metonymy

There are certain highly recurrent types of metonymy. The following may be signalled:

(i) CONTAINER for CONTAINED

(35) The kettle's boiling.
(36) Room 44 wants a bottle of champagne.
(37) The car in front decided to turn right.

(ii) POSSESSOR for POSSESSED/ATTRIBUTE

(38) Why is John not in *Who's Who*?
(39) A: John Smith.
    B: That's me!
(40) Where are you parked?
(41) Shares fall 10 per cent after Budget.

(iii) REPRESENTED ENTITY for REPRESENTATIVE

(42) England won the World Cup in 1966.
(43) The government will announce new targets next week.

(iv) WHOLE for PART

(44) I'm going to wash the car/fill up the car with petrol.
(45) Do you need to use the bathroom?

(v) PART for WHOLE

(46) There are too many mouths to feed.
(47) What we want are more bums on seats.
(48) I noticed several new faces tonight.

(vi) PLACE for INSTITUTION

(49) The White House denies the allegations.
(50) The Palace defends the sackings.

The above list is by no means exhaustive. An interesting and only partially understood question is why some relationships are metonymically viable, but others are not, or are considerably less so. Take, for instance, the part–part relation, which, since it involves items clearly associated within a single domain, might be expected to yield lots of metonymy. But it is relatively rare. (It is, however, easy to come up with odd instances:

(51) I'm having my wheels serviced. (wheels → car; car → engine)
(52) I was obliged to spank one of the new faces.)

11.4.3 What is metonymy for?

There are many cases where an indirect metonymic strategy of reference appears to be preferred to a more direct mode of reference. (In some instances the metonymic mode may be considered to be conventionalized, but the question still arises of why it should be so.) The following are examples (some repeated for convenience):

(53) Where are you parked?
(54) The kettle's boiling.
(55) Room 44 wants a bottle of champagne.
(56) Why is John not in *Who's Who*?
(57) John stroked the dog.

An important question is thus why metonymy should 'feel' more natural in these instances. What is the advantage of metonymy here? One possible motivation is that the expression is rendered shorter, hence more economical of effort. The full versions of the above would be:

(58) Where is your car parked?
(59) The water in the kettle is boiling.
(60) The person in Room 44 wants a bottle of champagne.
(61) Why is John's name not in *Who's Who*?
(62) John's hand stroked the dog.

However, this cannot be the full story, because many parallel cases can be invented which do not seem nearly as natural:

(63) ?Where are you being serviced/repaired? (Where is your car being serviced/your watch being repaired?)
(64) ?The oven is burning. (Something/the cake in the oven is burning.)
(65) ?The office is typing. (The person/the secretary in the office is typing.)

(66) A: Where is your briefcase?
     ?B: I'm in the bedroom. (My briefcase is in the bedroom.)

Another possibility is that the target entity is more easily accessible via the metonymic vehicle than directly. However, this notion is not so easy to pin down in a satisfactory way.

It is also the case that often, even though an indirect metonymic reference is not necessarily the preferred or default strategy, some metonyms are acceptable whereas others, ostensibly following the same general principle, are not. The following are examples of this:

(67) I see you've got yourself some wheels/* a clutch pedal.
(68) *We've bought some new legs. (="a new table".)
(69) Room 23 is not answering.
(70) ?Room 23 is asleep/out/in the bar.
(71) She's in the phone book.
(72) *She's on the back of my hand. (="Her phone number is on the back of my hand".)
(73) The car in front decided to turn right/*smoke a cigarette.

Clearly, more work needs to be done before it can be claimed that metonymy is well understood. However, it seems that the motivation for using metonymy will turn out to be one or more of the following:

   (i) economy;
  (ii) ease of access to referent;
 (iii) highlighting of associative relation.

11.5 Semantic change

One can hardly read a chapter of, say, a novel by Jane Austen (to go no further back in time) without becoming aware of the fact that words change their meaning through time. In the case of Austen, the changes are relatively uncommon, and relatively subtle. For instance, *interfere* has not yet developed its negative aspect: its meaning is closer to modern *intervene*; *handsome* is applied indifferently to men and women (and girls); *amiable* was a much more positive recommendation of a person's character than now; *direction* no longer refers to the indicated destination of a letter. Historical processes of semantic change are of course intimately linked to synchronic processes of meaning extension. One possible scenario might run as follows.

  (i) Word W has established a literal sense, S^1.
  (ii) Some creative person uses W in a new figurative sense, S^2 (according to the rules of synchronic extension).

(iii) S^2 'catches on', and becomes established (i.e. laid down as an entry in the mental lexicons of members of the speech community), so that W becomes polysemous between S^1 and S^2. S^1 is still perceived as literal, and S^2 as figurative.

(iv) S^1 begins to become obsolescent. S^2 begins to be perceived as literal, and S^1 as figurative.

(v) S^1 is lost, at which point the meaning of W has changed from S^1 to S^2.

This can be illustrated with English *expire*. First, before there were such things as tickets and licences with limited periods of validity, this just meant "die". Then, it was metaphorically extended to mean "come to the end of a period of validity", which existed as a clear figurative use alongside the literal use. Nowadays, the "die" sense is quite uncommon, and classes of students will declare that for them it is a metaphorical extension of the "cease to be valid" sense. Stage (5) is perhaps yet to occur, but there is no doubt that the default reading has changed.

This example illustrates one way in which synchronic meaning extension forms an essential part of diachronic change (there are, of course, other scenarios). In principle, the meaning of a word may change along any of the semantic dimensions identified in Chapter 3; however, no attempt will be made here to give a full account of historical change in word meaning.

Discussion questions and exercises

1. Using Lakoff's study of anger as a model, investigate the metaphorical representation of other emotional states such as fear and depression.

2. How many examples of non-literal language use can you find in the following sentences (from Grafton 1994)? Classify each example as metaphor, metonymy or hyperbole.

(a) Occasionally I went over to the shallow end of the pool and got my feet wet. If I lowered myself into the depths by as much as six inches, I suffered shortness of breath and a nearly overwhelming desire to shriek.

(b) I had a quick bowl of soup with Henry and then downed half a pot of coffee, managing in the process to offset my lethargy and kick into high gear again. It was time to make contact with some of the principals in the cast.

(c) The hotel's air-conditioning, which was fitful at best, seemed to drone off and on in a fruitless attempt to cut into the heat.

(d) I'm sorry sir, room 323 is not answering.

(e) I went out on to my balcony and leaned my elbows on the railing, staring out at the night.

(f) I was aware of the yawning three-storey drop, and I could feel my basic dislike of heights kick in.

(g) His name was being withheld from the local papers because of his age.

(h)   I could practically hear Mac squinting through the telephone lines.
(i)   July in Santa Teresa is an unsettling affair.
(j)   I rolled out of bed, pulled on my sweats, brushed my teeth and combed my hair, avoiding the sight of my sleep-smudged face.
(k)   A: 'Can you get me an address?'
      B: 'Shouldn't be too hard. She's probably in the book.'
(l)   He was mortgaged to the eyeballs, so his house wasn't worth a cent.
(m)   The day seemed interminable, all heat and bugs, kids shrieking in the pool with ear-splitting regularity.
(n)   'I want to talk to Lieutenant Whiteside first. Can you have me switched over to his extension?'
(o)   Steep hills, pleated with erosion, rose up on my left, while to the right, the heaving gray Pacific was pounding against the shore.

Suggestions for further reading

On metaphor, an excellent source of readings is Ortony (1979); the present account has drawn heavily on the paper by Max Black in that volume, but many of the other papers are well worth reading, and will give an idea of a variety of approaches. Haas's account of metaphor has not been published, but can be accessed at the Manchester University Linguistic Department's website: http://lings.ln.man.ac.uk/Html/wh. Lakoff's views appear in several publications: a popular introduction is Lakoff and Johnson (1980); a later account with a literary focus is Lakoff and Turner (1989). The fullest exposition of Lakoff's approach, applied particularly to ANGER, is to be found in Lakoff (1987: book ii, ch. 1), to which may be added Lakoff (1990). A more recent introduction to metaphor on Lakoffian lines is Kövecses (2002). An analysis of LOVE on Lakoffian lines is Kövecses (1988). See also Dirven (2002). For blending theory, see Grady et al. (1999) and Coulson (2000).

For post-Lakoff treatments of metaphor see Glucksberg (2001) (strongly critical of Lakoff) and Stern (2000). Croft and Cruse (forthcoming) has a discussion of the relationship between metaphor and simile.

On metonymy, see Croft (1993), Kövecses and Radden (1998), and Croft and Cruse (forthcoming).

CHAPTER 12

Syntagmatic relations

Syntagmatic relations

12.1 Normal and abnormal co-occurrence

It is an obvious fact that some combinations of words 'go together' naturally, and it is easy to imagine a situation in which they could function as part of a discourse. Other sets of words do not go together in this way: it is impossible, or at least very difficult, to imagine a situation in which they could be used (although we must not underestimate the flexibility and ingenuity of the human mind in this respect). This chapter is about the semantic relations between lexical units in the same discourse, string, sentence, or other syntactic structure, which govern their well-formedness. (There are, of course, important relations between larger discourse elements such as clauses, sentences, and larger units which are important for discourse cohesion and coherence. Here, however, we are concerned only with the lexical level.) All meanings co-present in a discourse affect one another to some degree and in one way or another. The interactions are complex and not yet fully understood; here only a sketchy outline can be offered. Before any details can be examined, it is necessary to make a distinction between two types of interaction between meaningful elements in a discourse: **discourse interaction** and **syntagmatic interaction**. We shall be eventually concerned mainly with the latter type.

Consider the following sentence:

(1) John and Mary will be joined in holy matrimony next week: who's going to get the spuds?

There are two sorts of oddness here. The first is the register clash between *holy matrimony* and *spuds*. This can easily be cured:

(2) John and Mary will be joined in holy matrimony next week: who is going to get the potatoes?

But we are still left with the difficulty of finding the relevance of potatoes to John and Mary's marriage. (There would be no problem if *potatoes* was replaced by *confetti*, or even *rice*.) These are both aspects of discourse interaction, as in each case the clash, as we may call it, is not between one item and

its most intimate syntactic neighbour. The register clash is relatively superficial. Certain lexical items—they may have any syntactic function—serve
as markers of degree of formality. Obviously contradictory markers are going
to clash. The irreconcilability of *marriage* and *potatoes* has a much deeper origin—to do with the construction of plausible scenarios involving the two
concepts, and drawing on cultural knowledge which we cannot go into
here—but is not obviously syntactically governed. The second type of interaction, syntagmatic interaction, occurs between items that are part of the
same syntagma, or grammatical construction, such as an adjective and the
noun it modifies, a verb and its direct object, or a verb phrase and its subject.

Another distinction needs to be made (it has already been adumbrated
above) before the discussion can be advanced. There are two potential focuses
of interest in studying syntagmatic semantic relations: one is whether, or to
what extent, a particular combination makes sense, the other is whether, or
to what extent, a combination is normal or abnormal. Although these two
characteristics often coincide, they are by no means the same thing. For
instance, *My geraniums kicked the bucket in the hot weather* is perfectly under-
standable, but is nonetheless somewhat odd; conversely, a difficult article on a
topic in, say, formal semantics, may have no odd sentences in it. In this chapter
we shall be concentrating mainly on whether syntagmatic combinations are
normal or abnormal.

It is undeniable that the normality of a particular string of words (even one
which is close-knit syntactically) can be affected by the wider context in which
they are set. This means that we must be careful what we mean when we say
that a particular string is abnormal. Take a case like *heavy on air*. This might
strike the ear as odd, if no context is given. But suppose the conversation is
about space travel and the need to develop ways of recycling vital materials
like water and air. In this context it is not difficult to make sense of a statement
to the effect that a particular device is heavy on air. The reason the original
presentation was odd was that the default readings of the constituent items do
not go together; the effect of the context was to enable a relevant selection of
interpretations to be made. Similarly, Chomsky's *colourless green ideas* might
not be so anomalous if used to describe a boring lecture on environmental
issues. The moral of this is that we are not concerned with strings of words,
but with strings of readings. Very often, a potential anomaly is a clue to the
fact that either a different reading of some item in the string must be selected
or a new reading must be created.

12.2 Types of abnormality

Two basic types of abnormality resulting from the combination of two senses
can be distinguished. The first is where meanings simply do not 'go together';
the second is when one meaning adds nothing new to another one with which

it is combined and thus appears unnecessary, or redundant. We shall call these **semantic clash** and **pleonasm**, respectively.

12.2.1 Semantic clash

The sorts of clash we are interested in here are those which resist contextual manipulation and can reasonably be considered to be lexical in nature. It is a feature of units of meaning that they impose semantic conditions of some sort on their syntagmatic partners: if these conditions are satisfied, the result is semantically well formed, and the combination is readily interpretable; if the conditions are not satisfied, some sort of clash results, which may trigger off a semantic transformation of some kind, which produces a reading that *does* satisfy the conditions. (For this reason, virtually no combination of *words* can be ruled out as anomalous.) We shall call the conditions **co-occurrence preferences** (rather than, as they are often designated, **co-occurrence restrictions**, which suggests a more yes/no, law-like condition than we actually find); they can also be thought of as presuppositions of the unit which imposes the conditions. Clashes come in varying degrees of severity. Presumably this property varies continuously, but as a first approximation, we can distinguish a number of degrees of clash.

The first distinction is between clashes which result from the non-satisfaction of **collocational preferences**, and those which result from the non-satisfaction of **selectional preferences**. This latter distinction—between collocational and selectional preferences—depends on whether the preferences in question are an inherent consequence of propositional content or not. Take the case of *My geraniums have kicked the bucket*. There is here a semantic clash between *geraniums* and *kicked the bucket*: for full normality, *kick the bucket* requires a human subject. But the propositional content of *kick the bucket* is the same as that of *die*: it would not be honest to answer the question *Did my geraniums kick the bucket while I was away?* in the negative, if the geraniums in question had died, on the grounds that only humans can kick the bucket. The point is that kicking the bucket is not a special way of dying that only humans can suffer; it is more correct to say that the expression *kick the bucket* can only be used without oddness to refer to dying if certain contextual conditions are satisfied, one of them being that the 'patient' should be human, another being that the situation should be informal. The conditions (preferences) do not arise ineluctably from the propositional meaning, but are, as it were, tagged on independently and somewhat arbitrarily. Contrast this case with the oddness of *My letter to Mary kicked the bucket*. Here the clash is not just, or even principally, between *letter* and the 'tagged on' meaning present in *kicked the bucket*, since the oddness is not significantly improved by putting *died* in place of *kicked the bucket*. There is a much more radical clash between the propositional meaning of *kick the bucket* and *my letter*, in that the concept of dying is only applicable to things/entities that at some time were alive. "Living subject" can be thought of as a logical presupposition of the default meaning of *die*; "human subject" is merely a stylistic presupposition of *kick the bucket*. If a collocational preference is contravened, we may say that **inappropriateness** results: inappropriateness is then the lowest degree of clash.

If what is here called a selectional preference is contravened, the clash is more serious. Two degrees of clash can just about be distinguished here. Consider *The cat barked*, or *a tiny giant*. Bark means "to make a noise" and is characteristic of dogs. But notice the difference between this case and *kick the bucket* in relation to humans. Whereas humans do not have a special way of dying (at least, this is not what *kick the bucket* denotes), dogs do have a special way of making a noise. So *bark* is not adequately glossed as "make a noise" (applied to dogs): it must be "make the characteristically canine noise". And it would not be misleading to answer the question *Did I hear the cat bark?* in the negative, if the cat had, in fact, miaowed (or, indeed, if it had been the dog which had made the noise). On the other hand, *bark* and *miaow* are in a sense the same kind of thing, both animal noises, so the clash is at an intermediate level. In Cruse (1986) this was called **paradox**. Paradox is also involved when the 'wrong' value on a dimension is indicated: *It's too small to fit into this box*; *Rain falls upwards, usually*; *If you walk any faster, you'll be standing still*. Paradoxes are typically 'correctable'.

The most serious degree of clash is **incongruity**. This is when the ontological discrepancy is so large that no sense can be extracted at all, without radical reinterpretation. Since there is not even an inkling of sense, in the worst cases, there is no feeling that the utterance could be corrected. Examples are:

purple gestures of rat milk
the sky's nipple is a dictionary
crystalline miasmas of safety-pins
in phonemic toe-buckets

This is reminiscent of the worst sort of avant-garde poetry. A way of firming up these distinctions will be offered below, but it must be re-emphasized that degree of clash varies continuously, and the divisions are only first approximations.

12.2.2 Pleonasm

A pleonastic relation between two elements occurs when one of them seems redundant, and appears not to add any semantic information not already given by the other element. So, for instance:

(3) John kicked the ball with his foot.

Here *with his foot* adds nothing, since we know from *kick* what the instrument of striking was. Pleonasm can be avoided either by omitting *with his foot*:

(4) John kicked the ball.

or by replacing *kick* with *strike*:

(5) John struck the ball with his foot.

Notice, however, that (6) is not pleonastic:

(6) John kicked the ball with his left foot.

This is because the phrase *with his left foot* now contains new information: the repetition involved in *foot* is unavoidable as otherwise *left* could not be incorporated. Similarly (7) is pleonastic, because *male* gives no information that is not already conveyed by *uncle*:

(7) One of my male uncles told me.

On the other hand, *my gay uncle* is not pleonastic, although *gay* (on one interpretation) incorporates the notion "male", since *gay* also brings new information not present in *uncle*.

  It is important to realize that repetition does not automatically bring about pleonasm. In some cases it is required by the grammar. For instance, in the phrase *two books*, one might argue that plurality is signalled twice, once by the numeral *two* and then by the *-s* of *books*. In some languages, such as Turkish, although a plural affix exists, the noun would have no plural marker in such circumstances: *kitaplar* ("books", *-lar* is the plural affix); *iki kitap* ("two books"). In some cases, the repeated item simply applies twice, sometimes with dramatic effects:

(8) I don't not want it.

Here the negative acts on itself, cancelling itself out. (In many languages there is obligatory duplication of negative marking, without the above semantic effect.) In some cases, repetition has an intensifying, rather than a pleonastic effect:

(9) That is very, very good.
(10) Mary rushed quickly to the window.

Notice that the idea of "quickly" is part of the meaning of rush, which is why we get a paradox if we qualify an act of rushing with the opposite term:

(11) ?Mary rushed slowly to the window.

Sometimes the interpretation is not clear, as in *Will you repeat it again, please?*, which some speakers will interpret simply as an intensification, while others require a previous repetition for well-formedness. The underlying rules are not clear, but it seems that repetition causes intensification most frequently when a graded property is involved.

12.3 Syntagmatic sense relations

If we try to set up syntagmatic sense relations on the pattern of paradigmatic relations we find right at the outset that there are certain differences. The main one is that there are no relations of a syntagmatic nature that have the generality and context-independence of paradigmatic relations such as hyponymy and meronymy. All relations are tied to particular grammatical constructions, or at least to families of constructions. To take a simple example, the following exemplifies a clash between *chair* and *saw*:

(12) The chair saw John.

But these two words do not necessarily clash:

(13) John saw the chair.

The clash only occurs when the words are in a particular grammatical relationship. Bearing this fact in mind, we can set up three basic relations, according to whether the words in question go together normally, clash, or yield pleonasm:

philonyms: go together normally
                  SAW the CHAIR
xenonyms: clash
                  HEARTFELT INSOMNIA
tautonyms: produce pleonasm
                  an ACADEMIC UNIVERSITY

Remember that in each case the grammatical relation between the terms must be specified, and that we are assuming the combinations to be fully grammatical. The grammatical relations can be specified in a semantically neutral way: for instance, *chair* and *see* are subject–verb xenonyms, and *heartfelt* and *thanks* are modifier–head philonyms; or they can be specified in a semantically more concrete way: for instance, *man* and *see* are experiencer–verb philonyms, *snap* and *pleasure* are verb–patient xenonyms.

12.4 The directionality of syntagmatic constraints

Constraints on co-occurrence between lexical items usually have directional properties. Two aspects of this are of particular interest. The first concerns which item does the selecting (the **selector**) and which gets selected (the **selectee**). It is necessary to separate two notions of selection here. If we are thinking of the selection from a set of polysemous or homonymous readings, then in a sense the process is obviously at least potentially bi-directional and there is no clear distinction between selector and selectee. In the combination *a hard match*, for example, *hard* rules out the reading "device for producing a flame" for *match*, and *match* rules out the reading "not soft" for *hard*, and we are left with the interpretation "difficult contest". Here we have a combination of two words, each having more than one reading, but there is only one philonymous combination of readings, and this emerges as the preferred interpretation. However, if we look closely at the relations between the meanings of items in a grammatical construction, we usually find another species of directionality, in that it is much easier to specify the restrictions imposed by one of the items than the other. Suppose we set ourselves the task of specifying the semantic nature of the adjectives which form philonymous modifier–head pairs with a noun such as *match* ("contest"). Think of the range of possibilities:

(14) home, ill-tempered, exciting, hard-fought, postponed, three-day, all-ticket, important, decisive, qualifying

There is no cover term, or superordinate notion which encompasses all these, even approximately. The only thing they have in common is that they go normally with *match*. But look now at *hard* ("difficult") and perform the same exercise:

(15) game, exercise, problem, journey, climb, job, crossword, exam

In this case we can roughly define the qualifying head nouns as falling under the general heading of "human activity requiring effort". The same can be done with the other readings of both *hard* and *match*: in each case, the philonym partners of the *hard* readings can be given a general specification, but those of the *match* readings cannot. In fact it becomes clear that the mechanism of selection for *match* readings is as follows: *match* readings select those adjectives whose co-occurrence preferences they satisfy. In other words, the apparent bi-directional selection has a unidirectional basis.

The direction in which selection operates, is correlated with grammar. The relevant generalization is that adjectives select their head nouns and verbs select their complements; nouns, in general, are always selectees. This can be made into a more satisfying generalization in logical terms: predicates select, and arguments are selected. Why this should be so is an interesting question.

The second aspect of directionality concerns the phenomenon of pleonasm. Generally speaking, if a combination of words is to be normal (i.e. non-pleonastic), the combination must yield more information (in a broad sense) than either of the combined items on its own. This is fairly obvious. What is slightly less obvious is that the burden of providing extra information falls asymmetrically on the combined items. The categories used above, of predicate and argument, are of no help in formulating a regularity here. What we need instead are the categories of **(semantic) head** and **(semantic) dependant**.

Roughly speaking, the semantic head of a combination (construction) is the element which governs the semantic relations of the combination, viewed as a unit, with other elements or combinations. Take the case of an adjective–noun combination: this combination may in turn combine with a verb, but it is only the semantic properties of the noun which determine whether the combination is normal or philonymic. Take the combination *The small table sneezed*, which we can all agree is odd. Suppose we hold *sneezed* constant and ask ourselves what is the minimal change which will restore normality. The answer is that we must change *table* (*The small boy sneezed*); no fiddling about with the adjective will produce any effect. Of course, *small* semantically interacts with *table* (**the small phoneme/meaning*), but once the combination is effected, *small* has no further combinatory role to play. Similar arguments show that it is the verb which governs the combinatorial properties of a verb phrase.

Now that we have a notion of semantic head and its dependants, we are in a position to state a generalization regarding pleonasm: it is the duty of a non-head to bring information not available in the head; the head is under no such compulsion. This conforms with the observation of pleonasm in:

(16)   a female aunt
      a new innovation
      Please repeat it for me again.
      He kicked it with his foot.
      She chewed it in her mouth.
      I heard it by listening.
      (etc.)

(The reader may consider me pedantic on some of these examples.)

12.5   Syntagmatic and paradigmatic relations

There are certain systematic connections between syntagmatic and paradigmatic sense relations which are worth signalling.

12.5.1   Pleonasm

In cases of pleonasm, the oddness can in general be 'cured' by substituting one of the tautonyms by a hyponym or hyponymous expression, or the other by a superordinate. This gives us a way of identifying the head and dependent elements: the head is the item whose substitution by a superordinate cures the pleonasm. What the successful substitutions do, of course, is to restore the situation where the dependent item contributes new information. Some examples follow:

(17) male uncle (pleonastic)
     gay/macho uncle (normal: *gay* and *macho* are hyponyms of *male*)
     male relation (normal: *relation* is a superordinate of *uncle*)
(18) He kicked it with his foot. (pleonastic)
     He kicked it with his left foot. (normal: *left foot* is hyponymous to *foot*)
     He struck it with his foot. (normal: *struck* is superordinate to *kick*)

12.5.2 Clash

The severity of a clash can be roughly estimated by examining the minimal change required to cure it. This enables us to put a little more flesh on the notions of *inappropriateness, paradox*, and *incongruity*.

Inappropriateness is a type of clash which can be cured by substitution of one of the xenonyms by a propositional synonym:

(19) The geranium passed away. (inappropriateness)
     The geranium died. (normal: *died* is a propositional synonym of *pass away*)

Paradox is a more serious type of clash which can be cured by substituting one of the xenonyms by an incompatible or immediate superordinate:

(20) The cat barked. (paradox)
     The dog barked. (normal: *dog* is an incompatible of *cat*)
     The animal barked. (normal: *animal* is a superordinate of *cat*)
     The cat emitted a noise. (normal: *emit a noise* is superordinate to *bark*)

Incongruity is an incurable clash:

(21) powdered thrills (?finely divided thrills; ?powdered experiences)

12.5.3 Normality/philonyms

It is not generally the case that if X is a philonym of Y, then any superordinate of X is also a philonym. (One can easily think of cases where the result is normal: *The dog/animal barked*, to look no further.) This is because the result may be pleonastic: *He kicked it with his left foot/?foot*. Nor is it the case that if X is a philonym of Y, then any hyponym of X is also a philonym. Again drawing on the above examples, *The dog barked/The collie barked* is fine, but *The animal barked/?The cat barked* is not. However, it might be surmised that if X is a philonym of Y, no superordinate of X can be a xenonym of Y. Thinking of a hyponym as having 'more meaning' than its superordinate, and assuming that any clash must be attributable to some bit of the meaning of X, how can taking away a bit of meaning produce a clash? Well, what about *a homeopathic doctor/?a homeopathic human being*? The explanation for this seems to run as follows. If the meaning of X can be represented as [A] + [B], then an adjective modifying X may attach itself uniquely to [B]. Suppose, now, that Y contains only the component [A]; the adjective is then forced to attach itself to [A], with which it may clash. This is a plausible explanation of what happens with *homeopathic doctor*: if we analyse "doctor" into [HUMAN] + [PRACTISES MEDICINE], then *homeopathic* will modify only the second component, and when that is removed, it will be forced to modify [HUMAN], with which it clashes. Whether this can happen also with natural kinds is an interesting question.

12.6 Some puzzles

The effect of putting words together is not always what might be predicted on general grounds. A particular example of this is the failure of pleonasm to appear in certain circumstances. Consider the following examples:

(22) Mary rushed quickly to the door.
(23) John murmured softly in Bertha's ear.
(24) Some children were shouting loudly in the street.
(25) During last summer's scorching heat-wave . . .
(26) Jack gasped—a huge giant stood at the door.

Somehow, these are not as bad as they should be: after all, surely quickness is of the essence of rushing, softness of murmuring, loudness of shouting, and so on. Also, substituting antonyms for these epithets results in paradox:

(27) ?Mary rushed slowly to the door.
(28) ?John murmured loudly in Mary's ear.
(29) ?Some children were shouting softly in the street.
(30) ?Jack gasped—a small giant stood at the door.

In examples like (22)–(26), instead of pleonasm, we seem to get either reinforcement or something like semantic agreement. It is difficult to say under what circumstances pleonasm does not appear. All the examples mentioned here involve some gradable (adverbial) property which is incorporated into the meaning of a verb: expressing the same idea with a separate adverb has the effect of reinforcing the notion. The same effect appears with *Johnny was very, very, very naughty*, where every extra *very* adds intensity; on the other hand, in *Johnny was extremely, extremely, extremely naughty*, the extra *extremely*s come across (to me at least) as merely redundant.

Another type of situation where pleonasm fails to appear occurs with certain verbs of bodily motion. Consider the following:

(31) Mary shrugged her shoulders.
(32) Mary stamped her foot in annoyance.
(33) Mary pouted her lips.

Why are these not pleonastic? What else can one shrug with except one's shoulders, or pout with, except one's lips? Also, *What Mary pouted were her lips* and *What Mary shrugged were her shoulders* are pleonastic, and, of course, *What Mary shrugged were her thighs* and *What Mary pouted were her ears* are paradoxical. The generalization here seems to be that these verbs denote actions which can serve as signals. If the body part is not explicitly mentioned, then the signalling function of the action is highlighted (*Mary shrugged, Mary pouted*); if the body part is mentioned, the action itself is highlighted, and this may or may not be intended also to carry the conventional message (cf. *John shrugged his shoulders to dislodge the parrot* and *?John shrugged to dislodge the parrot*). The impossibility of **Mary smiled her lips* or **Mary frowned her forehead* is presumably due to the fact that these are basically intransitive verbs.

12.7 Specifying co-occurrence preferences

In this section some of the problems of stating the co-occurrence regularities of words will be discussed, without, perhaps, all of them being resolved.

Classically, selectional restrictions were stated in the form of semantic categories to which lexical partners had to belong (recall that most selectees are nouns). Furthermore, these categories were of the classical variety, with sharp boundaries and necessary and sufficient criteria for membership. So, for instance, in the case of *X drank Y* and *X poured Y into Z*, the selectional restrictions of both *drink* and *pour* require that Y denote a liquid. Violation of the restriction leads to anomaly. Hence, the following are normal:

(34) John drank the milk.
(35) John poured the milk into the cup.
(36) Mary drank the beer.
(37) Mary poured the petrol into the can.

while the following are not:

(38) ?John drank the bread.
(39) ?John poured the cabbage into the pan.
(40) ?Mary drank her wedding ring.
(41) ?Mary poured the cup into the milk.

In some cases (but probably not any of the above), the anomaly can be resolved by reinterpreting the sentence as a metaphor:

(42) Mary drank in John's words.

If the patient (i.e. the thing affected) of either of these verbs is not specified, then the feature [LIQUID] will be transferred to them; thus, in each of the following, a normal interpretation would be that the patient is in liquid form:

(43) Mary drank the medicine.

(44) John poured the butter over the meat.
(45) The aliens were drinking a purplish substance.

This is all very well, so far as it goes. However, consider, first, the following:

(46) Mary poured the sugar into the bowl.
(47) The lorry poured the bricks onto the road.

By no stretch of the imagination can the sugar and bricks be considered to belong to the category of liquids, yet these sentences are not as anomalous (are they at all?) as they ought to be. One possibility is that we have misidentified the selectional restriction: perhaps the restriction for pour, at least, should require that the patient is capable of flowing. This would seem reasonable for sugar, but is it plausible for bricks? Do they flow? Here we seem to be stretching the meaning of *flow* somewhat.

Second, consider the following:

(48) Mary drank the petrol.
(49) John drank the sulphuric acid.

Are these normal? The patients are certainly liquids. If not, is this a sign that the selectional restrictions as specified are inadequate? If we think of drinking as a purely physical activity—the ingestion of liquids—then these are not odd. If Mary took in some petrol in the way that people normally take in water, then we would have to describe her action as drinking. However, there are other aspects to drinking: people usually drink to satisfy a thirst, for nourishment, or for enjoyment. Drinking harmful liquids is definitely eccentric.

A way of accommodating both these types of case is to take a view akin to the prototype view of categories. There are no hard and fast rules for combining words: combinations are not either normal or anomalous, they are more or less normal. We can therefore say, for instance, that *pour* has a preference for liquid patients; that is, the more the patient behaves like a liquid, the more normal the result will be (or, the better an example of the use of *pour* we will have). In a sense, bricks in large enough numbers falling out of a lorry, and from a distance, have some of the characteristics of "flowing", and to that extent resemble a liquid. In the case of drinking, there are prototypical and less prototypical instances of drinking. To characterize prototypical instances, we need to bring in more than just the physical nature of what is drunk. For these reasons, it is better to speak of selectional preferences. And yet there is still a problem here. In some sense, liquidness is more essential to drinking than harmlessness. It is necessary, for drinking (or pouring) to occur, that the patient should be sufficiently liquid-like; it is not necessary that the liquid should be nourishing, therapeutic, or thirst quenching. So we haven't completely got rid of necessity.

In some cases it is difficult to pin down exactly what the co-occurrence constraints are. Take the case of the adjective *avid*. Dictionaries typically mention interest, enthusiasm:

Someone who is avid has an extreme interest in something so that they do it with enthusiasm. (*Collins Cobuild Dictionary*)

strongly interested, enthusiastic. (*Longman Dictionary of the English Language*)

These definitions seem to capture the sense of *avid* in, for example: *an avid reader, an avid television viewer, an avid stamp collector*. But this sense does not rule out the following less normal collocations, which seem to fall under the definitions given: *?an avid footballer, ?an avid gambler, ?an avid musician* (although *an avid concert-goer* is OK), *?an avid botanist*. Some sense of consumption or acquisition seems to be necessary: compare *?an avid computer hacker*, which has no orientation towards reception, and *an avid net-surfer*, which has. Even this is not quite right, because *an avid womanizer* and *an avid drinker* do not feel good either (although the latter case might be explained by the necessity for "interest"): it seems that satisfaction of the basic appetites does not count. It is not clear what sort of account of selectional preferences is called for in such cases. It may be that we could build up a picture of a prototypical avid person in terms of which an account of preference grading could be framed. (The picture is complicated by the slightly different but nonetheless related requirements of *avid for*: This is satisfactory in combination with: *praise, affection, knowledge, recognition*; but less so with: *sex*(?), *food, exercise, music, money*.)

12.8 Co-occurrence patterns between words

It is a commonplace observation that words prefer some partners to others. And some dictionaries take it upon themselves to impart what they call 'collocational information' to their readers. In this section we shall look at the different factors (not excluding the semantic factors discussed above) which govern the relative frequency of association of two (or more) words, and in the process we shall hope to provide a rationale for a useful lexicographic practice.

The question we shall attempt to answer will be formulated comparatively: Why does A have a greater affinity for X than for Y? This will be helpful in isolating the different factors. The notion of (collocational) affinity refers to the ratio between the actual co-occurrence of two words, and their predicted co-occurrence on the basis of their individual frequencies in the language. The first distinction to be made is between those cases where the reason for A's preference for X over Y is due to a semantic clash between A and Y, and the absence of such a clash between A and X, and those cases where there is no such clash between A and Y, and yet A has a greater affinity for X. We shall begin with the latter type of case.

12.8.1 Extralinguistic factors

Some of the possible reasons for the greater affinity of A for X rather than Y are not located in the language at all, but in the extralinguistic world. For instance, one reason why *Jane fried the egg* is more frequent than *Jane fried the lettuce* is simply that people in the world are more likely to fry eggs than lettuce. It is not that there is anything about lettuce that prevents it being fried: on the contrary, fried lettuce is delicious. Similarly, the reason *old* has a greater affinity for *clothes* than for *newspapers* is simply that people tend to throw newspapers away when their day is past, but hang on to clothes a bit longer, so that there are more old examples around. However, frequency in the extra-linguistic world is not the only consideration, since something may be very frequent, but not often noticed or realized, and is therefore not often talked about. So, for instance, there are probably more old pebbles in the world than old men; but first, old pebbles do not enter our consciousness very often, that is to say, they have low salience, and second, it is much less easy to gauge the age of a pebble than that of a man, that is to say, this is knowledge that we are less likely to have. A further governing factor is significance, i.e. to what extent it matters whether something is old or not. It may be presumed that the more significance something has, the more it gets talked about. Again, there are probably as many old trees as old men, but it matters little, generally speaking, whether a tree is old or young. But it makes a great deal of difference (gener-ally) whether a man is old or young. This is the probable explanation of why the most frequent collocation of *old* in present-day English is *man*.

12.8.2 Stereotypic combinations

A factor leading to collocational affinity which lies on the border between the linguistic and the non-linguistic is the existence of stereotypic combinations, such as the co-occurrence of *beautiful* with *flower(s)*, or *dear* with *friend*. This is to be distinguished from what will be called clichés below: there, it is a matter of there being a standardized way of saying something (although there are alternatives); here, it is a matter of there being a standardized thing to say, or perhaps more revealingly, a standardized thing to think. This seems more a matter of the culture than of the language as such.

12.8.3 Default patterns (clichés)

A number of factors leading to collocational affinity are, of course, part of the language. We shall make a distinction between patterns of co-occurrence, divergence from which leads to anomaly of some kind, and those where there is not necessarily any anomaly, merely a degree of markedness or heightened salience. An example of the latter type is *barefaced lie*, where *shameless, bra-zen, unabashed, insolent*, or *blatant* would be semantically compatible, but the choice of one of these would be less 'automatic'. Another example is:

(50) X was last night under intense pressure to resign.

Here, the meaning of *intense* would be equally well conveyed by *strong* or *extreme*, but *intense* is significantly more likely. Similarly, *fresh allegations* (cf. *new allegations*), *gross negligence* (cf. *great negligence*), etc.

12.8.4 'Arbitrary' collocational restrictions

It is obvious enough that the meanings of words have an effect on their collocational affinity. A foreigner who knew the meanings of the words would not need to be told that *The farmer killed the rabbit* is more likely to occur in English than *The farmer killed the gate*. It is not that occasions of gate killing are rare in English-speaking countries (but a national pastime elsewhere); it is rather that they are inconceivable anywhere. This is because things have to be alive before they can be killed, and gates are just not living things. Here it is a matter of the satisfaction, or otherwise, of inherent selectional preferences. A person who consistently got this sort of thing wrong would be suspected either of a deficient knowledge of the meanings of the words or of insanity. However, as we saw above, there are also selectional preferences which are arbitrary in the sense of not being predictable from general knowledge. For instance, we say *a high wind* but *heavy rain*. In each case the adjective indicates the degree to which the relevant phenomenon is manifesting itself, and the degree is the same in both cases. But we cannot say *?a heavy wind* or *?high rain*. There is no inherent semantic incompatibility between "high degree" and "wind": the incompatibility is between the word *heavy* and the word *wind*. This is information that even a sane foreign learner cannot be expected to have, and should be presented in any dictionary that aims at comprehensiveness.

(Notice that it is not entirely clear that the collocational affinities proposed between *kill* and *rabbit*, and between *high* and *wind*, will show up as enhanced collocational frequency. In the case of *kill* and *rabbit*, the effect might be masked by the infrequency with which people kill rabbits, or the lack of newsworthiness of such events. In the case of *high* and *wind*, it could well be that the frequency of *high wind* is less than what would be predicted from the separate frequencies of *high* and *wind*. The problem here is what should be counted. If we count word forms, then it is not clear that affinity will be reflected in frequency. If, on the other hand, we look at occurrences of the notion "high wind", then we would expect the form *high wind* to be the most frequent. Or perhaps we should be more specific still, and ask ourselves, given that we wish to express the notion "high wind", and given that we wish to use the word *wind*, what would be its most likely partner.)

12.8.5 Non-compositional affinities

A special type of affinity holds between lexical items which occur in a non-compositional (e.g. idiomatic) combination such as *pull someone's leg*. Expressions of this sort were discussed in Chapter 4.

Discussion questions and exercises

1. None of the following sentences is ambiguous, although each one contains at least one ambiguous word. Explain carefully how the selection of appropriate senses operates:

   (a)   A: Are you going to the club tonight?
         B: I'll have to go to the bank first.
   (b)   Have you booked the right turn?
   (c)   She had gained several pounds since she had worn this ensemble last.

2. Identify the degree of clash in the following (i.e. inappropriateness, paradox, incongruity):

   (a)   She's more than just a pretty countenance.
   (b)   The president is said to be unconvinced by the locomotion.
   (c)   Mum, it's so nice to be back in my place of domicile again!
   (d)   The whole thing was over in an age.
   (e)   I don't know if he acted from motives of despair or crockery.

3. Consider the selectional restrictions governing the X-position in the following (give a prototype account where appropriate):

   a record X   X is sad   a leisurely X   Can you lend me an X? (consider why *tree* is odd in this position)

Suggestions for further reading

This chapter is mostly a development of ideas which first appeared in Cruse (1986), especially chs. 4.12 and 12.2. Cruse (2002a) takes a prototype-theoretical approach to syntagmatic sense relations. The notion of 'semantic head' presented here is quite closely parallelled by Langacker's 'profile determinant' (see Langacker 1991b). For a structuralist account of selectional restrictions, see Kastovsky (1980). Katz and Fodor (1963) give the first generative version. Jackendoff's 'preference rules' (see e.g. Jackendoff 1983) yield a prototype-like account of co-occurrence restrictions/preferences.

CHAPTER 13

Lexical decomposition

Lexical decomposition

13.1 Introduction

The search for semantic atoms, or 'the alphabet of thought'—the smallest units of meaning out of which all other meanings are built—has a long history, and is very much alive today still. It has survived intense opposition, even ridicule. In fact, it is probably true to say that virtually every attempt to explicate a rich word meaning ends up by giving some sort of breakdown into simpler semantic components. There seems no other way to do it, or at least nothing that is not merely a 'notational variant'. Some prototype theorists (see Chapter 7) valiantly stand out against the general trend, hoping to develop a more 'analogical' way of approaching meaning (as opposed to the 'digital' nature of componential theory). But it is nonetheless striking how easily even prototype theorists can slip into using feature representations. However, even within a broad acceptance of the validity of the feature approach, there is scope for quite radical disagreements on such topics as the nature of semantic features, how they are to be discovered and verified, how they combine, whether all aspects of word meaning are susceptible to a feature analysis, and so on.

13.2 The prima facie motivation for lexical decomposition

It is sometimes proposed that the semantic atoms of a natural language are the meanings of its lexical items. On this view, complex meanings are certainly built up out of combinations of simpler ones, but there is no need to break up the meanings of individual words (or at least, morphemes): they are considered to be unanalysable. It would therefore be useful for us to look first of all at the sorts of reason that have been put forward for lexical decomposition, and which give the componential enterprise a prima facie plausibility.

13.2.1 Partial similarities

One such reason is the intuition that a pair of words may be partially similar in meaning and partially different. There is a certain plausibility in construing this situation in terms of components of meaning some of which are common to the two words in question and some of which are not shared. As an obvious example of such a case, take *mare* and *stallion*. The similarity between these can be expressed by saying that they are both horses, that is, they share the component [HORSE], and that they differ in that *mare* has a component [FEMALE] not shared by *stallion*, and *stallion* has [MALE], which is not present in the meaning of *mare*. Or take the case of *heavy* and *light*: these share the component of [WEIGHT], and differ in that *heavy* has a component [MORE THAN AVERAGE], where *light* has [LESS THAN AVERAGE].

A concrete analogy for this might be a mixture of sand and salt, on the one hand, and a mixture of sand and sugar on the other. Both preparations share a property of grittiness, which can be attributed to the presence of sand in each; but they differ in taste, which can be attributed to the fact that one contains sugar and the other, salt. The concrete analogy of a mixture was chosen deliberately, because in a mixture, the properties of the individual constituents are still in evidence in the mixture. Many systems of lexical decomposition seem to aim at something of this sort. It is worth noticing, however, that if chemical compounding were thought to be a more appropriate analogy, the nature of semantic composition would change radically, and we would be looking for quite different sorts of components. Take the case of salt, which is a compound of sodium and chlorine: very few if any of the properties of either sodium or chlorine are observable in salt.

13.2.2 Correlations

The examples of partial similarity which provide the most convincing evidence for lexical decomposition are **correlations**, where the proposed components can be seen to be distributed independently of one another. The following are examples:

(1)

	[MALE]	[FEMALE]
[SHEEP]	ram	ewe
[HORSE]	stallion	mare

The components [MALE] and [FEMALE] are widely distributed in the language; [FEMALE], for instance, occurs in: *mother, daughter, wife, girl, woman, aunt, sow, cow, doe, filly, vixen, hen,* and many others; [HORSE] occurs in *horse, mustang, foal, gelding,* and probably also forms part of the definition of *stable, jockey, neigh, fetlock,* etc.

Further illustrative examples are given in (2) and (3):

(2)   [ADULT]   [YOUNG]
  [HUMAN] adult   child
  [SHEEP] sheep   lamb

Notice that when a polysemous word appears in a correlation, only one of its senses (see Chapter 6) is intended to be operative. For example, there is a sense in which a lamb is a sheep, but there is nothing odd about saying *Make sure that the lambs do not get separated from the sheep*. It is the latter sense which is intended in (2). (*Adult* is likewise polysemous.)

(3)   [ADULT]   [YOUNG]
  [MALE]   man   boy
  [FEMALE] woman   girl

A two-dimensional correlation does not necessarily give a full analysis of the meaning of a word. In (2), [YOUNG] [SHEEP] seems a satisfactory analysis of *lamb*, but [YOUNG] [FEMALE] is not a satisfactory analysis of *girl*: the [HUMAN] factor is missing.

13.2.3 Discontinuities

In some cases there is more direct evidence of the functional discreteness of a portion of meaning, in the form of a discontinuity of some sort in the semantic structure of a sense. Some examples will make this point clearer.

(i) The ambiguity of *I almost killed her* ((a) "I was on the point of carrying out an action (e.g. pulling the trigger of a gun) which would have caused her to die", (b) "I acted in such a way as to cause her to be almost dead" (e.g. by squeezing her windpipe)) suggests a functional autonomy for components [CAUSE] and [DIE] within the meaning of *kill*. The two meanings can be represented as follows:

(a) $_{almost}([CAUSE][DIE])$
(b) $[CAUSE] (_{almost}[DIE])$

(ii) The fact that *The astronaut re-entered the atmosphere* is appropriate even on the astronaut's first trip into space, indicates that we must analyse "re-enter" into (at least) MOVE and IN, since in the case mentioned, the recurrence signalled by re- applies only to IN, that is, the astronaut must on some previous occasion have been located inside the earth's atmosphere. (According to my intuitions—but this is a matter for argument—the sentence is not ambiguous: it does not matter whether the astronaut has had a previous experience of entering the atmosphere or not. However, we do need to be able to represent the difference between (a) *The astronaut entered the **atmosphere** again* (with unstressed *again*) and (b) *The astronaut entered the atmosphere **again*** (with stressed ***again***):

(a) ([MOVE] [IN])_{again}
(b) [MOVE] ([IN]_{again})

(iii) The fact that the default reading of *That's not a stallion* is that the animal indicated is a mare, that is to say, the negative applies only to the [MALE] component, leaving the [HORSE] component untouched (although complete negation is of course also possible in appropriate contexts) is evidence of the separability of [MALE]. (Notice also the potential ambiguity of *an overworked stallion* ("too much pulling of heavy carts"/"required to perform stud duties with too many mares"), which testifies further to the functional independence of [MALE].)

13.2.4 Simplex: complex parallels

In many cases, grammatically simple forms have semantic properties either very similar to, or closely parallel to, complex forms. Consider the case of *false* and *untrue*. In the case of *untrue*, the notions [NOT] and [VERACIOUS] (let's say) are expressed by different morphemes, so the meaning of *untrue* must be analysed as complex. But what about *false*? There is no morphological evidence for complexity, but in view of the close meaning relationship to *untrue*, it would seem almost perverse not to give *false* the same semantic analysis. There are countless similar cases. Synonymy is not necessary. Compare *rise/fall* with *lengthen/shorten* (in their intransitive senses). *Lengthen* and *shorten* are clearly related morphologically to *long* and *short*, and can be analysed semantically as [BECOME] [MORE] [LONG] and [BECOME] [MORE] [SHORT]. Now, given that the contrast between *lengthen* and *shorten* is the same as that between *rise* and *fall*, and given that the semantic relation between *lengthen* and *long* is the same as that between *rise* and *high* (and *fall* and *low*), surely this justifies a componential analysis of *rise* and *fall* as [BECOME] [MORE] [HIGH] and [BECOME] [MORE] [LOW], respectively?

13.3 The aims of lexical decomposition

In this section we look in greater detail at the sorts of ideal end-results that various semanticists have aspired to in embarking on a componential analysis of general vocabulary. It is worth pointing out that most have been content to work on small groups of words that it was hoped were representative of the lexicon as a whole.

13.3.1 Reduction (cf. dictionaries)

An important aim of many componentialists (although not necessarily all) has been to achieve a genuinely reductive analysis of the realm of meaning. As an illustration of this 'mindset', we may take the example of the Danish linguist Louis Hjelmslev.

Hjelmslev was a representative of early European structuralism in linguistics; his was the first definite proposal for a componential semantics, following up a suggestion of Saussure's. He started from Saussure's well-known conception of the linguistic sign, illustrated in Fig. 13.1. Saussure imagined a realm of all possible meanings, which he called the 'content plane' of language (originally, 'le plan du contenu') and a realm of all possible human linguistic sounds, which he called the 'expression plane' (le plan de l'expression'). He then characterized the linguistic sign as a slice through the two planes, which created an arbitrary (in the semiotic sense) association between a specific sound and a specific meaning.

Now, a study of the sound aspect of the signs in any natural language shows that they lend themselves to a genuine reductive analysis, that is, they can be progressively analysed into combinations of ever simpler units belonging to smaller and smaller inventories. Take the case of English. We may take it that the vocabulary of English comprises several hundreds of thousands of items. However, the sound structures of these items are not like the pebbles on a beach, each one idiosyncratically individual and not systematically related to any others: all the words of English (in their sound aspect) can be shown to be built up out of combinations of smaller units drawn from a much more restricted list of 200–300 syllables; these in turn can be shown to be made up of phonemes drawn from an even smaller list (20–80), themselves analysable as combinations of distinctive features numbering no more than a dozen or so. In this way, the initial bewildering variety is reduced to systematic order. Hjelmslev believed in the symmetry of the two planes of language, and

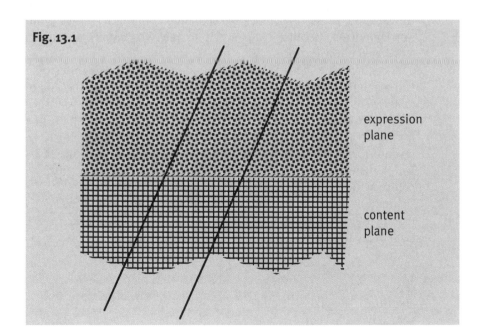

Fig. 13.1

expression plane

content plane

concluded that it ought to be possible to perform a parallel analysis of the content plane of signs which would achieve a similar reduction of bewildering variety to system and order.

For Hjelmslev, the simpler meaning units in question were essentially the meanings of other words. He thus hoped to arrive at a restricted basic vocabulary in terms of which all other meanings could be expressed. It is worth noting that this aspiration is still very much alive in the world of lexicography: many modern dictionaries, especially those targeted at foreign learners, such as the *COBUILD* dictionary and the *OALD*, deliberately aim to define all words using a restricted defining vocabulary.

The method of analysis was based on commutation, originally used to justify phonemic analysis. A phonemic difference was said to exist between two distinct elements of the expression plane when substitution of one for the other entails a change in the content plane. So, for instance, [p] can be shown to be a different phoneme from [b] in English, because [pin] is associated with a different meaning from [bin]. However, the aspirated bilabial stop [pʰ] is not a different phoneme from the unaspirated form [p], because a change of meaning is never associated with the choice of one rather than the other.

By the principle of symmetry, the same procedure is valid in the reverse direction—that is, we have isolated a semantic element when changing a bit of meaning entails a parallel change in the expression plane. For instance, an analysis of the meaning of *mare* into [HORSE] [FEMALE] is justified by the fact that changing [FEMALE] into [MALE] (by a kind of thought experiment) entails a change of the expression side of the sign to *stallion*, and changing [HORSE] into [SHEEP] entails a change of the expression to *ram*. However, if we postulate that the meaning of *horse* includes the semantic component [BLACK], then this is not supported, because changing it to [BROWN] entails no change in the associated phonetic form.

A distinction was made between components belonging to restricted inventories and those belonging to unrestricted inventories. Take the case of stallion analysed as [HORSE] [MALE], once again; the substitution possibilities of [MALE] are very restricted indeed, the only possibility being [FEMALE]; the possibilities for [HORSE], however, are much wider. Components belonging to restricted inventories are the more significant for reductive purposes, since they have the widest distribution, in the sense of occurring with the greatest variety of other components.

Mention has been made above of the importance to Hjelmslev of a reductive analysis. Let us see how this works out in practice. Take a set of words such as the following:

rise	raise	high
fall	lower	low
lengthen[1]	lengthen[2]	long
shorten[1]	shorten[2]	short

(*Lengthen*[1] and *shorten*[1] are intransitive, like *rise* and *fall; lengthen*[2] and *shorten*[2] are transitive/causative like *raise* and *lower*.)

This is a highly structured set, with many sets of correlated contrasts. If we take the lexical items to be the minimal semantic atoms, then this set needs twelve semantic units for its description. Such a description will not give an account of the parallelisms: these would have to be stated separately. Now suppose we perform the following analysis:

```
rise       = [BECOME] [MORE] [HIGH]
fall       = [BECOME] [MORE] [LOW]
raise      = [CAUSE] [BECOME] [MORE] [HIGH]
lower      = [CAUSE] [BECOME] [MORE] [LOW]
lengthen¹  = [BECOME] [MORE] [LONG]
shorten¹   = [BECOME] [MORE] [SHORT]
lengthen²  = [CAUSE] [BECOME] [MORE] [LONG]
shorten²   = [CAUSE] [BECOME] [MORE] [SHORT]
```

This new analysis shows that the contrast between, for instance, *rise* and *fall* is the same as that between *raise* and *lower*, since both are attributable to the contrast between [HIGH] and [LOW]. Also, the contrast between *high* and *raise* is the same as that between *long* and *lengthen*[2], and so on. Notice that this is achieved with the use of only seven components, as opposed to twelve without lexical decomposition. The economy becomes more striking if other items are added to the set:

```
wide     widen¹       widen²
narrow   narrow¹      narrow²
thick    thicken¹     thicken²
thin                  thin²
strong   strengthen¹  strengthen²
weak     weaken¹      weaken²
```

Without lexical decomposition these would add eighteen more semantic atoms, giving thirty in total; with decomposition along the above lines, only six new semantic elements are necessary, giving a total of thirteen for the set.

However, there are correlations in our set of words that cannot be expressed by our analysis as it stands, for instance:

rise:fall::lengthen[1]: shorten[1]

Accounting for this should lead to even greater economy in the inventory of components. Consider the following:

```
raise      = [CAUSE] [BECOME] [MORE] [HIGH]
lower      = [CAUSE] [BECOME] [MORE] [LOW]
lengthen²  = [CAUSE] [BECOME] [MORE] [LONG]
shorten²   = [CAUSE] [BECOME] [MORE] [SHORT]
```

The parallelism here can be captured if we analyse as follows:

raise   = [CAUSE] [BECOME] [MORE] [HIGH]
lower   = [CAUSE] [BECOME] [LESS] [HIGH]
lengthen^2 = [CAUSE] [BECOME] [MORE] [LONG]
shorten^2 = [CAUSE] [BECOME] [LESS] [LONG]

This seems on the right lines, but, as it stands, it loses the parallelism *raise:lower::high:low*. It appears that a more radical analysis is required:

raise   = [CAUSE] [BECOME] [MORE] [HEIGHT] [REF: X]
lower   = [CAUSE] [BECOME] [LESS] [HEIGHT] [REF: X]

Here we introduce the notion of a reference point: to raise something is to cause it to be at a greater height than some reference point, normally the height it was before the act of raising took place. This notion of reference point can be used also in the analysis of *high* and *low* (and mutatis mutandis, *long* and *short*) since something which is high is at a greater height (and something low is at a lesser height) than some reference point, often an average of some sort (see discussion of antonyms in Chapter 9):

high   = [MORE] [HEIGHT] [REF: Average]
low   = [LESS] [HEIGHT] [REF: Average]
long   = [MORE] [LENGTH] [REF: Average]
short = [LESS] [LENGTH] [REF: Average]

At first sight this does not seem to reduce the number of components. However, the pay-off comes when we extend the analysis to larger sets, because the addition merely of a single new dimension, for example, [SPEED], [WEIGHT], [HARDNESS], or whatever, allows us to account for the meanings and relationships of six new words.

The discussion so far has sought to illustrate the effects of allowing componential analysis to be motivated by the existence of correlations and the need to be reductive. It is as well, however, to bear in mind the limitations of such an analysis. Two are worth emphasizing at this point. The first is that the proportion of the vocabulary which lends itself to this sort of analysis is relatively restricted: the majority of words remain unanalysed. Areas which have proved amenable to componential analysis are, for example, kinship terms, terms referring to male/female/young/adult animals and humans, and binary oppositions like those discussed above. The second point is that even when a word can be analysed, like *stallion*, the analysis leaves much semantic knowledge unaccounted for.

A radical, relatively recent proposal for reductive analysis of word meaning is that of Anna Wierzbicka (1996), who is probably the most original of contemporary componentialists and certainly the most thoroughgoing. She takes her inspiration not from the structuralists but from much further back in the past: her source is Leibniz, who was the first to attempt to discover an 'alphabet of thought' by reducing complex meanings to combinations of simpler ones. Leibniz followed a Hjelmslev-like procedure of beginning with complex meanings (like "stallion") and reducing them to simpler ones, guided by the meanings of other words. When reduction could go no further, Leibniz thought, one would have arrived at the fundamental units of thought. Wierzbicka does things the other way round: she starts with a small list of what appear to be indispensable notions (her original list had exactly eleven members), and tries to express as many meanings as possible with these, only adding items to the list of primitives when forced to do so. Her current list (not held to be definitive) runs as follows:

"substantives"	[I], [YOU], [SOMEONE], [SOMETHING], [PEOPLE]
"determiners"	[THIS], [THE SAME], [OTHER], [SOME]
"augmentor"	[MORE]
"quantifiers"	[ONE], [TWO], [MANY/MUCH], [ALL]
"mental predicates"	[THINK], [KNOW], [WANT], [FEEL], [SEE], [HEAR]
"non-mental predicates"	[MOVE], [THERE IS], [(BE) alive]
"speech"	[SAY]
"actions and events"	[DO], [HAPPEN]
"evaluators"	[GOOD], [BAD]
"descriptors"	[BIG], [SMALL]
"time"	[WHEN], [BEFORE], [AFTER], [A LONG TIME], [A SHORT TIME], [NOW]
"space"	[WHERE], [UNDER], [ABOVE], [FAR], [NEAR], [SIDE], [INSIDE], [HERE]
"partonomy"	[PART (OF)]
"taxonomy"	[KIND]
"metapredicates"	[NO], [CAN], [VERY]
"interclausal linkers"	[IF], [BECAUSE], [LIKE]
"imagination and possibility"	[IF . . . WOULD], [MAYBE]
"words"	[WORD]

To qualify as a member of this list, a suggested primitive must be universal (this is of course hard to check, but it must be expressible in all known languages). Wierzbicka argues that since all humans are born with the same innate capacities, if the primitives are a reflection of innate semantic capacities, then an apparent primitive that appears in some languages but not others must be expressible in terms of primitives that appear in all languages. Primitives must also not be abstract, they must be accessible to direct intuition, and any proposed analyses should pass the test of native speaker judgements of plausibility. She dismisses analyses of the Katz and Fodor variety as not so much genuine analyses of meaning as translations into an artificial language (sometimes referred to in derogatory fashion as "markerese") for which no one has any intuitions. The following will give the flavour of a typical Wierzbickan analysis:

X punished Y for Z:
(a) Y did Z.
(b) X thought something like this:
(c)   Y did something bad (Z).
(d)   I want Y to feel something bad because of this.
(e)   It will be good if Y feels something bad because of this.
(f)   It will be good if I do something to Y because of this.
(g) X did something to Y because of this.

This analysis is intended to capture in maximally simple terms the fact that punishment is objectively justifiable causation of suffering for an offence. Notice that *it will be good* must be taken to indicate an objective evaluation; substitution of a subjective evaluation such as *I will feel good* in (e) and (f) would yield a definition of *take revenge on*.

The analyses are couched in the form of sentences. This means that there must also be a set of semantically interpretable syntactic primitives. This aspect of the system is under investigation, but is currently less well developed.

13.3.2 Lexical contrasts and similarities

A somewhat different approach to componential analysis takes as its primary aim the explication of lexical contrasts and similarities within the lexicon of a language. On this view, a minimal semantic component is the smallest possible difference between the meanings of two words; all components have to be justified by actual lexical contrasts; furthermore, the closer two word meanings are, the more components they should have in common. Let us see how this works out in practice, using in the first place a familiar example (in the literature). We shall attempt a componential analysis of the word *chair*, in the manner of Bernard Potier, a leading exponent of the French variety of componential analysis. Bear in mind that the aim is to distinguish *chair* from every other word in English, and also to indicate its semantic distance from other items. We shall begin with the most distant words and move steadily closer; this is not theoretically necessary, but it is convenient and makes it easier to be systematic. From each of the following contrasts, we can extract a feature, and the full set adds up to a specification of the meaning of *chair*:

chair vs. *thought* [CONCRETE]
    vs. *cat* [INANIMATE]
    vs. *trumpet* [FURNITURE]
    vs. *table* [FOR SITTING]
    vs. *sofa* [FOR ONE]
    vs. *stool* [WITH BACK]

Ideally, the components should be necessary, and should therefore be justifiable by entailment (for instance, *It's a chair* entails *It's inanimate, It's an item of furniture*, etc.). According to the above analysis, *chair* and *thought* represents the most distant pair, whereas *chair*'s nearest neighbours are *stool* and *sofa*, with each of which it shares five out of six components. If the above analysis is correct and complete, then there is nothing designated by a term in English which is not a *chair* and which shares all six features. (This does not mean that *chair* cannot be further subdivided: for instance, *armchair* would possess all the features of *chair*, plus [WITH ARMS]. But this is not a true contrast, since an armchair is a kind of chair.)

An analysis of this type clearly covers the whole vocabulary, and provides a great deal more information than the previous type. All the same, it is worth noting that there are things we know about chairs which are not represented, for instance, that a chair 3 inches wide would be no use, or one whose 'flat' portion was tilted at an angle of 60 degrees, or one made of cardboard. (Information of this type would typically be found in a prototype representation; for more details of this, see Chapter 7.)

As a second example, let us see if we can analyse the verb *walk*:

walk vs. *sleep* [ACTION]
      vs. *bite* [LOCOMOTION]
      vs. *drive* [USING BODY ONLY]
      vs. *fly* [ON GROUND]
      vs. *crawl* [BIPEDAL]
      vs. *hop* (like frog) [USING LIMBS ALTERNATELY]
      vs. *run* [ONE FOOT ALWAYS ON GROUND]

In this case it is not quite so clear what should be in the analysis. Should we, for instance, make a distinction between mental acts like thinking and physical acts like walking? Should we distinguish locomotion using mechanical energy from an external source, like driving a car, from, for instance, skiing, where only one's own energy is used? Have we adequately distinguished *walk* from, say, *dance*? However, the broad lines of the analysis are clear enough.

Notice that this approach does not guarantee a reductive analysis: we shall almost inevitably end up with as many components as words we are analysing. This is because so many features appear in the analysis of a single word: they are not independently distributed. The names of the animals provide a clear illustration of this. In order to distinguish cats, dogs, sheep, cows, wolves, seals, elephants, and so on from one another, each one must be allotted a distinguishing feature such as [CANINE], [FELINE], [BOVINE], [OVINE], [VULPINE], [PHOCINE], [ELEPHANTINE]. Hence, an analysis of the set of animal terms requires more features than there are animals, since each one will contain, in addition to the unique distinguishing feature, others such as [CONCRETE], [ANIMATE], [MAMMAL].

13.3.3 Lexical relations and entailments

A componential analysis can formalize, at least to some extent, certain recurrent meaning relations between lexical items. Sense relations are treated in greater detail in Chapters 8–10; here we shall concentrate on just two, for the purposes of illustration: the relation of inclusion which holds between *dog* and *animal, tulip* and *flower*, and so on (known as hyponymy), and the relation of exclusion that holds between *dog* and *cat*, and between *tulip* and *rose* (incompatibility). The first relation is the easier: we can say that word $W(1)$ is a hyponym of word $W(2)$ iff all the components of $W(2)$ are included in the componential specification of $W(1)$. By this definition (which is too simple, but we shall ignore the complications here) the following hyponymous relationships can be explicated:

stallion   [ANIMAL] [EQUINE] [MALE] is a hyponym of
horse   [ANIMAL] [EQUINE]
kitten   [ANIMAL] [FELINE] [YOUNG] is a hyponym of
cat   [ANIMAL] [FELINE]
chair   [CONCRETE] [INANIMATE] [FURNITURE]
             [FOR SITTING] [FOR ONE] [WITH BACK] is a hyponym of
furniture [CONCRETE] [INANIMATE] [FURNITURE]
and so on.

The examples considered so far are very straightforward, but there are some complications. For instance, we need some way of filtering out cases like *kill* ([CAUSE] [BECOME] [NOT] [ALIVE]) and *die* ([BECOME] [NOT] [ALIVE]), because although the specification of *kill* includes that of *die, kill* is not a hyponym of *die*, and *John killed* does not entail *John died*. (We also need to ensure that *dead* ([NOT] [ALIVE]) does not come out as a hyponym of *alive* ([ALIVE].) The moral is that a satisfactory system of lexical decomposition must take account of the different ways in which semantic components combine together (see section 4.5 below).

Explaining incompatibility is a little more complicated. This is because there is nothing in the specification of, say, *horse* ([ANIMAL] [EQUINE]) and *cat* ([ANIMAL] [FELINE]) which enables us to conclude that it is not possible for something to be both at the same time. Since we can conclude this, if our descriptive apparatus does not allow us to represent it, then it can be said to be to that extent deficient. The usual way round this is to include, as part of the semantic theory within which the proposed features operate, a specification of those sets of features whose members are mutually exclusive (sometimes called **antonymous n-tuples**). The following are examples:

[MALE]/[FEMALE]
[RED]/[GREEN]/[BLUE], etc.
[CANINE]/[FELINE]/[OVINE]/[BOVINE], etc.
[CIRCULAR]/[SQUARE]/[TRIANGULAR], etc.

Notice that grouping the features in this way means that we do not have to make special statements for every pair of lexical items. For instance, it is not only *dog* and *cat* that are incompatibles, but also any pair of words such that one contains one feature belonging to an antonymous n-tuple and the other contains another feature from the same antonymous n-tuple. Thus *puppy, bitch, spaniel, alsatian*, etc., all of which contain [CANINE], are each incompatible with words such as *kitten, tom, moggy* (which contain [FELINE]), *cow, calf, bull, heifer*, (which contain [BOVINE]), *horse, colt, filly, mare, mustang* (which contain [EQUINE]), and so on.

This approach can be extended (with some reservations) to cover certain entailments and the distinction between analytic and synthetic propositions. For instance, it was pointed out that hyponymy between two lexical items in parallel positions in two propositions may be reflected in a relation of entailment from the proposition containing the hyponym to that containing the superordinate, as in the case of *It's a dog* and *It's an animal*, and *A dog passed by* and *An animal passed by*. To the extent that this is valid for hyponyms, it can easily be expressed in componential terms. But equally, the same reservations apply: that propositions differing only in the specificity of lexical items in a particular position do not invariably show entailment. Sometimes the entailment is in the wrong direction, as in *All animals need food* and *All dogs need food*, or *That's not an animal* and *That's not a dog*. Sometimes there is no entailment at all, as in *John began to sprint* and *John began to run* (even though *John sprinted across the quad* entails *John ran across the quad*). Sometimes there is entailment without hyponymy, as in *Mary's birthmark is on her thigh* and *Mary's birthmark is on her leg*. The fact that native speakers can easily assess the presence or absence of entailment presumably means that there is some systematic relationship between hyponymy and entailment, which then can be translated into componential terms; but this will be possible only when the factors governing the different entailment-related effects are fully understood. To the best of my knowledge, this is not currently the case.

13.3.4 Anomaly

The task of predicting whether a combination of words is anomalous or normal is usually handled within componential systems by specifying selectional restrictions, that is, features which accompanying words must possess for a normal sentence to result. These also help to account for contextual disambiguation. So, for example, we can explain why in *John expired, expired* means "died", while in *My driving licence has expired*, it means "has become invalid". The solution is to specify the relevant selectional restrictions (adopting the convention that these appear in angled brackets):

expire = [BECOME] [NOT] [ALIVE]<[HUMAN]>
        = [BECOME] [NOT] [VALID]<[DOCUMENT]>

Of course, some way is needed of showing that the restrictions apply to the subject of the verb; we could, for instance, put the restrictions in initial position:

expire = <[HUMAN]>[BECOME] [NOT] [ALIVE]
expire = <[DOCUMENT]>[BECOME] [NOT] [VALID]

This formulation predicts that if the subject of *expire* is *the man*, then the reading "become invalid" will be anomalous, since the specification of the meaning of *the man* will not contain the feature [DOCUMENT], but the reading "die" will be normal, since the specification of *the man* will contain the feature [HUMAN]; hence the sentence *The man expired* will be normal, and because only one reading is normal, it will be unambiguous; similarly, mutatis mutandis, for *The driving licence expired*. It also predicts that if the subject of *expire* contains neither [HUMAN] nor [DOCUMENT] in its specification, then the sentence will be anomalous, as in *?The cup expired*.

As a second example, consider the word *pregnant*. At first sight, this seems straightforward:

pregnant = [WITH CHILD IN WOMB]<[ANIMAL] [FEMALE]>

This would correctly predict that *My sister is pregnant* is normal, and *The chair is pregnant* anomalous. However, it would also predict that *My neighbour is pregnant* would be anomalous, since although a full specification of the meaning of *neighbour* would presumably include [ANIMAL] and [HUMAN], it would not contain [FEMALE]. How, then, do we account for the difference between *The chair is pregnant* and *My neighbour is pregnant*? Notice that in the latter sentence, *pregnant* projects the feature [FEMALE] onto *neighbour*; what we need, therefore, is something in the specification of *neighbour* which licenses this projection, but blocks it in the case of *chair*. Basically, we need to indicate that although *neighbour* is unspecified for sex, it is nonetheless specifiable. For instance, something like the following would do the job:

neighbour [ANIMAL] [HUMAN] [MALE/FEMALE]
            [LIVING IN ADJACENT DWELLING]

The case of *pregnant* illustrates another problematic point: expressing a co-occurrence restriction, in the form adopted here, seems to make the restrictions relatively extrinsic to the meaning of the item, whereas in some cases they may intuitively be felt to be more essential. In the case of *pregnant*, is it not the case that [FEMALE] is central to the meaning? Take another example, the verb *drink*. Obviously, this requires its direct object to have the feature [LIQUID]; but should the analysis be as in (a) or as in (b)?

(a) *drink* [INCORPORATE] [BY MOUTH],<[LIQUID]>
(b) *drink* [INCORPORATE LIQUID] [BY MOUTH]

There are good reasons for distinguishing relatively extrinsic co-occurrence restrictions like [HUMAN] for *pass away* and *expire*, and the more inherent restrictions like those for *drink* and *pregnant* (see discussion in Chapter 12, section 12.8).

13.3.5 Discontinuities

It was suggested in section 13.2 above that a componential analysis provided a natural explanation for the apparent discrete nature of the variable scope of operators such as *again, almost,* and *not* within the meanings of lexical items, as in *John opened the door and immediately closed it again* vs. *John opened the door and immediately closed it AGAIN,* and the ambiguity of *When I saw who it was, I almost closed the door.* Two points are worth making in this connection. The first is that some examples of the phenomenon are more convincing than others. The case of *again* is convincing, because the possibilities are strictly limited. For instance, although *eat* and *drink* both (presumably) involve some such feature as [INCORPORATE], the repetition of this feature in *I drank, then ate again* does not license a 'first-time' interpretation of *ate;* that is, *again* cannot take [INCORPORATE] as its scope. The case is much less convincing with negation, however. It is true that *That's not a stallion* normally carries some sort of presumption that a horse is being referred to, and therefore that the referent is a mare. However, the next step in the argument, that this is because only [MALE] is within the scope of the negative, is more shaky. The reason is that negatives typically have the pragmatic function of correcting some previous or imagined incorrect statement; hence, one says *That's not a stallion* when someone has suggested, or seems to think, that it is a stallion. But this means that what features are denied and what are left intact depends on plausible confusions or errors on someone's part. For instance, (a) and (b) are both plausible, but (c) is not:

(4) That's not a horse, it's a deer.
(5) That's not a mouse, it's a shrew.
(6) ?That's not a horse, it's a mouse.

To explain this, we would need to say that both *horse* and *deer* contained a feature [LARGE], which was missing from *mouse* and *shrew*, which, in turn, have [SMALL], and that these features were outside the scope of the negative in (a) and (b), respectively. The problem here is that this seems to open the door to an unlimited number of features, based on the parameters of possible resemblance/confusion. For instance, the most natural interpretation of (d) is that there was a confusion in the identification of a sound:

(7) That wasn't a horse, it was a car.

Presumably there is some property of the sound which the speaker is not denying, and which led to the wrong identification. Does this justify yet another feature?

It will be recalled from Chapter 6 that the facets [TEXT] and [TOME] formed discrete entities within the meaning of *book*. The question then arises of whether we need to make a distinction between [TEXT] and [TOME] within the meaning of *book* and, for instance, [MALE] and [EQUINE] within the meaning of *stallion*; and if so, what is the difference? Intuitively, there does seem to be a difference. Both types would seem to be necessary; in fact, we would expect both [TEXT] and [TOME] to receive an analysis in terms of the other type of component. This is a difficult question, but perhaps the notion of autonomy is relevant: both [TEXT] and [TOME] can function as readings of *book*; on the other hand, neither [MALE] nor [EQUINE] can function as autonomous readings of *stallion*. Another way of looking at the difference is to say that [TEXT] and [TOME] retain their individual properties within the meaning of *book*, relatively unaffected by the presence of the other, somewhat like the components of a chemical mixture; [MALE] and [EQUINE], on the other hand, interact strongly, in that the way maleness manifests itself perceptually in the context of [EQUINE] is different from the way it manifests itself in the context of, say, [CANINE] (for instance, a horse's penis is not the same as a dog's penis).

13.4 Problematic aspects of lexical decomposition

13.4.1 Too hasty analyses: the abstractness of features

Some superficially plausible componential analyses have been attacked on the grounds that they are too crude and ignore nuances of meaning. For instance, Lyons questions the legitimacy of the following:

boy = [HUMAN] [MALE] [YOUNG]
girl = [HUMAN] [FEMALE] [YOUNG]

on the grounds that the parallelism *man:boy::woman:girl*, which is presupposed by the analysis, is only an approximate one. He points out that the transition from boyhood to manhood in ordinary everyday reference occurs at an earlier age than the corresponding transition from girlhood to womanhood (things are perhaps changing, but it is still the case that *the girls in the Lower Sixth* slides down more easily than *the boys in the Lower Sixth*, although lads seems unobjectionable).

   Another well-known example is the analysis of *kill* as [CAUSE] [DIE], which has been criticized on the grounds that *cause to die* is not synonymous with *kill*. There are events which count as instantiations of *cause to die* but not of *kill*. For instance:

(8) John caused Bill to die on Saturday by poisoning his cornflakes on Friday.
(9) ?John killed Bill on Saturday by poisoning his cornflakes on Friday.
(10) The lightning caused John to die when it struck the power cable supplying his life-support machine.

(11) ?The lightning killed John when it struck the power cable supplying his life-support machine.

One response to this sort of criticism is to say that semantic components are abstract elements in a semantic theory, with specific roles to play in modelling certain semantic phenomena. They are therefore not to be equated with the meanings of particular words, or indeed with any 'surface' meanings. A consequence of this is that their presence or absence cannot be directly intuited: the correctness of an analysis can only be verified by its success in modelling the relevant phenomena. Wierzbicka strongly criticizes this approach, and insists that semantic primitives must not be abstract: they must be accessible to direct intuition, and any proposed analyses should pass the test of native speaker judgements of plausibility. She dismisses analyses of the abstract variety as not so much genuine analyses of meaning as translations into an artificial language (sometimes referred to in derogatory fashion as "markerese") for which no one has any intuitions.

13.4.2 Bogus analyses

It has already been mentioned (in Chapter 8) that some pairs of words, like *stallion:horse*, wear, as it were, their hyponymous relationship on their sleeve, since one is readily definable in terms of the other (*A stallion is a male horse*), whereas for other hyponymous pairs, like *horse:animal* (true taxonyms), no such definition is available. This fact casts some doubt on analyses such as:

horse = [ANIMAL] [EQUINE]

and merits a closer look.

One objection to an analysis of this kind runs as follows. Consider, first, a specification of *stallion* as [HORSE] [MALE] (leaving *horse* unanalysed for the moment). Suppose we remove the feature [MALE], what are we left with? Well, this is an intelligible question, and obviously we are left with [HORSE]. Likewise, if we remove the feature [HORSE], we are left with the feature [MALE]. In each case what remains is an intelligible portion of meaning. But look now at *horse* = [ANIMAL] [EQUINE]. Removing [EQUINE] is no problem: we are left with [ANIMAL]. But what happens if we remove [ANIMAL]? What is left? In what sense does [EQUINE] represent an intelligible portion of meaning in the absence of [ANIMAL]? In fact, the only way of explaining what [EQUINE] means is to relate it to *horse*: [EQUINE] = "pertaining to horses". Hence, saying that *horse* = [ANIMAL] [EQUINE] is equivalent to saying "a horse is a horsey animal". If this is an analysis at all, it clearly is of a different type from "a stallion is a male horse".

13.4.3 Universal vs. language-specific components

Many systems of componential analysis aim at universality (for instance, Wierzbicka's), that is, the set of semantic components in terms of which

meanings are to be expressed are part of our innate cognitive/linguistic capacity, and should therefore be adequate for the description of any natural
human language. It is worth pointing out, however, that the analytic methods
of such as Hjelmslev and Pottier do not guarantee universality, since they are
based on reduction and/or contrasts within a single language. Universality
would have to be checked out separately, and that is no simple matter. (Wierzbicka always checks her components against as many languages as possible,
but they are always, in principle, provisional.)

13.4.4 Finiteness and exhaustiveness

There is a basic incompatibility between the aims of finiteness and exhaustive-
ness in a componential analysis, and different theorists attempt to resolve the
conflict in different ways. A favourite strategy is to have limited aims. For
instance, one could say that the function of semantic components is not to
account for lexical meaning in all its richness, but only to explicate the syntactic properties of words.

The system devised by Katz and Fodor (1963) illustrates this sort of
approach. First, what they set out to account for was limited to ambiguity,
anomaly, and logical properties such as entailment and analyticity. Second, a
distinction was proposed between those aspects of a word's meaning which
participated in systematic relations with other words, and an idiosyncratic,
unanalysable, unsystematic residue which fell outside the scope of the analysis
(some scholars consign this to a 'pragmatic' component of word meaning).
The systematic aspects were to be exhaustively accounted for by a finite set of
semantic markers drawn from a finite pool. For instance, one of the readings
of the word *bachelor* had the following analysis:

bachelor = (animal) (male) [young seal without a mate during the breeding
season]

(In Katz and Fodor's system, semantic markers were indicated by round
brackets and semantic distinguishers by square brackets.) The distinction
between markers and distinguishers was severely criticized because of unclear
criteria, but one of the motives was to preserve finiteness. However, the aim of
finiteness is compromised even with the specified limitations. Take the case of
the colour terms. According to Katz and Fodor, these all possessed the marker
(colour) and were distinguished from one another by distinguishers:

red   = (colour) [red]
green= (colour) [green]
and so on.

It was pointed out, however, that this failed to predict anomalies such as *This
red paint is green*. This could be averted by promoting the features distinguishing different colours to marker status:

red   = (colour) (red)
green= (colour) (green)
and so on.

However, this would have the unfortunate consequence that every perceptually discriminable shade of colour would have to be assigned a marker, since they are all incompatible with one another, and all are potentially designated by lexical items. Extending this to all areas of the vocabulary would surely multiply unacceptably the number of markers.

Limiting the role of components to the formalization of lexical contrasts, as in Pottier's system, would seem to guarantee a finite inventory. However, if we think that the lexemes of a language at any particular moment are just a selection from a vastly greater pool of potential words (is this finite?), any of which might enter the language at some point, then the notion of finiteness becomes less secure.

It is as well, too, to bear in mind an important distinction between a set of features which are sufficient to identify a lexeme (i.e. to distinguish it from all others) and a set of features which provide an exhaustive description of the meaning of a lexeme. An illuminating analogy is with identification keys for, say, wild flowers. Typically one is asked a series of questions, each one of which narrows down the choice until only one possibility remains. Let us suppose that questions asked establish that the plant has a prostrate habit, the leaves are grouped in threes on the stem, the flowers are red, and the petals have a triple notch at the end. Let us further suppose that only one species shows this particular set of characteristics. It is clear that this set of features, although adequate to identify our plant, does not in any way amount to a full description of the plant. The same is true of features of meaning: what is good enough for distinguishing from all other meanings does not *ipso facto* provide a specification of the meaning. Once the notion of 'full description' is raised, the notion of finiteness again begins to look shaky.

It is possible that some aspects of meaning are inherently not amenable to specification by means of a finite set of components. Plausible candidates for this status are properties which are continuously graded. Take the property of anomaly. It varies continuously from very slight, as in *The baby is sad* (N.B. *The baby looks sad* is normal) to extreme, as in *Zebra-green gravity evaporates against tunnels of truth*; it does not vary in discrete jumps. Katz and Fodor's system gives us a simple dichotomous characterization of sentences as anomalous or not; but this is not how things are in reality. There is no way a finite set of components can model a continuously varying property. Similarly, the Katz and Fodor system gives a yes/no answer to the question of whether one sentence entails another, rather than a point on a continuous scale of degree of necessity (see Chapter 3). Another important graded property is prototypicality, or centrality in a category (see Chapter 7).

13.4.5 Binarism

Some systems of componential analysis insist on the binary nature of semantic components, that is to say, components have one of two values, + or −. On this system, features are associated together in pairs. Take the case of "stallion" and "mare", which we analysed earlier as [HORSE] [MALE], and [HORSE] [FEMALE], respectively. The features [MALE] and [FEMALE] form an obvious binary pair, and in the binary system we would need only one component which could have one of two values. However, we must decide whether it should be [+/−MALE] or [+/−FEMALE]. One most commonly sees [+/−MALE] in such circumstances. However, the convention in phonology is for the **marked** term of a binary contrast to carry the positive sign and the **unmarked** term to bear the negative sign. There are various reasons for claiming that the meaning "female" is the marked term of the "male"/"female" opposition. One is the fact that in a great many cases a word referring to a female is formed from the word referring to the corresponding male by the addition of a morphological mark in the form of an affix: *prince/princess*; *lion/lioness*; *poet/poetess*; *usher/usherette*; *waiter/waitress*; *conductor/conductress*, etc. Cases where the word referring to a male is derived from the word referring to a female are extremely rare in English: *widow/widower*. A further indication of the marked nature of [FEMALE] is the fact that in general only the term referring to males can also have a generic use. So, for instance, *actors* can designate a group of males and females; *actresses* has no such use. This also applies where the terms are morphologically unrelated: *dogs* can be a mixed set, but not *bitches*; the *man-* of *mankind* embraces males and females. (Ducks and cows go against this tendency, but such cases are in the minority.) If, therefore, we follow the phonological convention, then *stallion* should be analysed as [HORSE] [−female].

A strict adherence to binarist principles leads to a number of problems. Two will be mentioned here. First, how do we distinguish between for example *horse*, which is neither male nor female (it is commonly said in such cases that the contrast is neutralized), and for example *table*, which is also neither male nor female, but differs from *horse* in that the contrast is not even applicable? One solution is to allow something like a 'zero' value of the feature, which indicates a neutralization of the contrast. Adopting this possibility, we would simply not specify the feature at all for *table*—the feature is absent—whereas for *horse* we would include the feature in our analysis, but give the zero value (Φ), as in [HORSE] [Φ FEMALE]. Notice, however, that in pure binarist terms this is cheating, as it involves a third value of the component.

A second problem arises when features apparently form a set consisting of more than two. Take the example of *chair*, where one of the features was [FOR SITTING]. What are the implicit contrasts here? Well, we need at least [FOR SLEEPING] (to account for *bed*), [FOR STORING] (to account for *cupboard*), and [FOR EATING AT] (not really satisfactory, but let it pass), for *table*. A binarist solution would be to divide these into two groups of two each, then further divide into two. But there does not appear to be a non-arbitrary way of doing this. A (not very plausible) suggestion might be to divide furniture into "human-supporters" (chairs and beds) and "thing-supporters" (cupboards and tables). An even more difficult case would be to give a binary analysis of colour terms. It seems altogether more plausible to recognize that there are binary features and non-binary features, without trying to force everything into the same mould.

Even if a binarist system is not adopted, antonymous n-tuples containing only two members, like [MALE]/[FEMALE], need to be specially signalled, since words differentiated by only these features have special properties. For instance, they are likely to be not only incompatibles, but also complementaries, like *man* and *woman*. (It is worth pointing out that defining lexical complementaries on the basis of differentiation by features drawn from a two-member set of antonymous n-tuples results in a much larger class of complementaries than that defined in Chapter 9. For instance, *brother* and *sister* would be complementaries by the feature definition, but *That's not my sister* does not entail *That's my brother*, so they would not qualify as complementaries by the earlier definition. Generally speaking, the detailed properties of the different sorts of opposite are very hard to model adequately in terms of features.)

13.4.6 How do components combine?

Most systems of lexical decomposition are very inexplicit about how the components combine to form larger units of meaning. Uriel Weinreich, an American semanticist who put forward constructive criticism of Katz and Fodor's system, advanced thinking somewhat by suggesting that the modes of composition for features were identical to those for words in sentences; and he introduced two basic modes of composition, according to whether the features in a compound formed clusters or configurations. In clusters, features combined in a Boolean fashion. This is, for instance, the way in which [HORSE] and [MALE] combine in "stallion": anything which is both male and a horse is a stallion. Some features, however, combine more in the way in which a verb and its direct object combine: the meaning of *drink wine*, for instance, is not formed in this way. Weinreich suggested that the features [FURNITURE] and [FOR SITTING] combine in this way in the meaning of *chair*. Wierzbicka also has recognized this problem and, adopting a broadly similar approach, has begun to elaborate a basic universal semantic grammar which governs the processes of composition. It must be said, though, that, while equating the composition of components to that of words in sentences may well be a step forward, the latter remain deeply mysterious, and are still mostly taken for granted.

13.5 What are the alternatives to lexical decomposition?

The question must be asked at some point whether there are any alternatives to semantic components: can we do without them in semantic analysis? There is no simple answer to this question. For some phenomena, there does seem to be an alternative. Take the case of entailment. Instead of saying that *It's a dog* entails *It's an animal* because all the components defining the meaning of *dog* are included in the set defining *animal*, why do we not simply state that the entailment holds? The description of the meaning of a word would then consist (at least partly) of a statement of the entailments it gave rise to in various sentential contexts. Not all entailments would have to be explicitly stated: for instance, the fact that *It's an alsatian* entails *It's an animal* would follow automatically from the fact that *It's an alsatian* entails *It's a dog*, and the latter entails *It's an animal*; also, there could presumably be some schematization of sentential contexts, so that the entailments below would not have to be stated separately:

I saw a dog	*I saw an animal*
I bought a dog	*I bought an animal*
I heard a dog	*I heard an animal*
etc.	

(I do not wish to minimize the difficulties of this, but it ought to be possible in principle.) One advantage of this approach would be that the description of word meaning could easily be opened up to include relationships with a lower degree of necessity than full logical entailment (componential analyses normally require full logical necessity). The result would then be little different from one type of prototype representation of word meaning (see Chapter 7). This is, essentially, the method of **meaning postulates**. Notice that meaning postulates presuppose nothing about atomicity, or the distinctness of bits of meaning, or, indeed, finiteness. Most things that can be said about word meaning in componential terms (in addition to entailment) can also be said using meaning postulates. For instance, instead of saying that *drink* requires its direct object to possess the component [LIQUID], we simply say that it must entail *liquid* (in suitable contexts). Antonymous n-tuples are automatically covered in the statements of entailments (e.g. *It's red* entails *It's not green*), instead of requiring a 'special' statement, as with a componential analysis.

Does this mean that componential analysis is completely dispensable? Well, not exactly. The prima-facie reasons for believing in semantic components given at the beginning of this chapter still stand, and a meaning postulate analysis gives no account of them. A meaning postulate analysis gives the same description of [MALE] as a component of *stallion* as of [EQUINE] as a component of *horse*; the fact that the former is intuitively satisfying and well supported, whereas the latter is 'bogus' receives no recognition. (A way of retaining the interesting properties of 'componentiality' without attributing them to words as inherent properties—in other words, to get the advantages of components without the disadvantages—will be suggested in Chapter 14.)

Discussion questions and exercises

Suggest a componential analysis of the following words along the lines of Pottier's analysis of chair (remember that each feature should be motivated by a possible contrast within the field):

skirt   book   cottage   teaspoon   violin   dream (v.)   kiss (v.)

Suggestions for further reading

The earliest proposals for a componential approach to semantics can be found in Hjelmslev (1961). European structuralism subsequently developed a French version and a German variety. The main French exponent was Pottier (see Pottier 1974, and Tuţescu 1975; Baldinger 1980 has a summary in English). For an account of the German variety of structuralism, see Coseriu (1975) and Geckeler (1971). Nida (1975), although purportedly a contribution to generative grammar, is very much in the spirit of European structuralism.

The earliest proposals for a componential semantics within the generative school were from Katz and Fodor (1963), which were further developed in Weinreich (1966) and Katz (1972). Current exponents are Jackendoff (e.g. 1983) and Pustejovsky (1995) (both of these are fairly technical, especially the latter).

The most recent account of Wierzbicka's views on semantic primes is Wierzbicka (1996). For sceptical views of the componential approach, see Bolinger (1965) and Sampson (1979); see also Taylor (1996) and Deane (1996) (whose target is Jackendoff's system).

New directions in lexical semantics: a dynamic construal approach

New directions in lexical semantics: a dynamic construal approach

14.1 Assumptions of traditional approach to word meaning

In this chapter we shall take a brief look at a recent approach to questions of word meaning which differs in certain key respects from more traditional approaches (including those described in previous chapters), and which aims to offer a more natural account, particularly of contextual variability in the semantic behaviour of words.

There are many different approaches to the study of the semantic properties of words, but most of them take it for granted that each word has a stable, inherent attribute called a 'meaning', which it is the job of a lexical semanticist to describe. When we encounter an utterance, we first retrieve from our mental lexicon the stored meanings of the different words, then we combine these together to arrive at a meaning for the utterance. Of course, each theory pictures word meanings in a different way; but there is general agreement that word meanings exist, and that logical and structural aspects of meaning, such as sense relations, and certain logical properties of utterances, are either directly represented in the lexical entry or can be inferred from the lexical entry.

Of course, there is also general agreement that meaning is highly context-dependent and that a major requirement of a satisfactory account of the relation between words and meanings is to integrate in a coherent picture both the appearance of determinate structural properties in the lexicon, and the apparently infinite flexibility of meaning in context. A fairly standard way of attempting this is to locate stable and determinate aspects of meaning in the lexicon (or at least infer it from lexical entries) and account for variability by means of pragmatic rules and principles.

However, it has proved extremely difficult to achieve a satisfactory picture using these assumptions, and some linguists have begun to explore the consequences of abandoning the assumption of stable word meanings. At first sight, this proposal is almost shocking: how can we communicate successfully if words have no stable, conventional meanings? Well, the proposal is not that words have no stable semantic properties, but rather that these properties are not meanings.

14.2 Basic features of the 'dynamic construal' approach

In the **dynamic construal** approach, words do not have meanings permanently assigned to them; rather, meanings emerge in actual use as a result of various processes of **construal** (mental processes of meaning construction). What every word does have as a permanent property is a mapping onto a body of conceptual content (here called **purport**) which is an essential part of the raw material for the construal processes, but which under-determines any specific meanings. The processes of construal which result in contextualized meanings are subject to a battery of **constraints** of various kinds and of different strengths, which make some readings more likely than others.

14.2.1 Meanings

The notion of 'meaning' is used here in a special sense. It is what we are conscious of when we grasp the import of an utterance. There is a moment of 'crystallization' of understanding. Meaning is produced by a series of processes of construal which are largely unconscious. There is a striking phenomenological difference between experienced meaning-in-use and what a dictionary seems to provide. Meaning in this sense is highly context-dependent.

14.2.2 Purport

Each lexical item (word form) is associated with a body of conceptual content which is here given the name **purport**. Purport is part of the raw material contributed by the word to processes of construal of meaning (the other part being a set of constraints); it does not correspond to any specific meaning. Purport is some function of memories of previous experiences of the contextualized use of the word. As such, it is continually developing: every experience of the use of a word modifies the word's purport to some degree.

14.2.3 Construal

Construal, as it is understood here, is the process of constructing a meaning, using purport as raw material, subject to a battery of constraints. There are many types of construal, and the full process may well comprise several distinct stages. A full account of construal types is not possible here, but some idea of the processes involved can be gleaned from a consideration of the following example:

(1) The ball struck John full on the face, and he suffered a broken nose and some bruising.

First of all, the word *ball* maps onto what can be considered to be two distinct regions of purport, corresponding roughly to "round object" and "social function". It is extremely difficult to construe these as a single unity (due to cognitive, 'reality', and conventional constraints), and therefore one of them will normally be selected as being relevant: that is to say, a certain region of the purport of *ball* will be selected, and other parts will play no further part in the construal process. The occurrence of *struck John in the face* in the linguistic context of *ball* will probably be sufficient to select the "round object" reading of *ball*, but this will almost certainly be reinforced by features of the situational context of the utterance. However, this is not the end of the process, because there are many different types of ball, and the consequences of being struck on the face differ greatly according to the type involved (think of a child's rubber ball and a cricket ball). Hence a more restrictive construal of *ball* is needed; this, too, will depend on a combination of contextual and conventional constraints.

On the basis of this information, some representation of an individual ball must then be construed. How detailed this representation is will depend largely on contextual factors: for instance, if the hearer did not actually witness the event, the representation may well be very sketchy. Context will also influence the highlighting of certain features of the ball at the expense of others: in the case of being struck on the face, the ball's weight, velocity, and hardness are likely to figure prominently (but not, for instance, its colour or price). Some aspects of the final construal will also depend (assuming that some game was in progress at the time of the incident) on whether John was a player, a spectator, or a passer-by. Notice that a similar type of meaning construction will be necessary for *struck* (the picture of being struck is very different for a tennis player striking a ball, say and a car striking a lamp post), and for *broken* (a broken nose is different in many respects from a broken windowpane).

14.2.4 Constraints

Of course, we are not free to construe an utterance in whatever way our fancy dictates (otherwise communication would be virtually impossible): there are pressures, of various strengths and types, to interpret in particular ways. Some constraints are very basic—for instance, the way the world is, and the ways in which our minds work. Besides these, two types of constraint which have particular relevance to language may be singled out: **conventional constraints contextual constraints**.

14.2.4.1 Conventional constraints

Conventional constraints—how the society in which we live habitually uses words, construes situations, and so on—are absolutely crucial to the functioning of language as a communicative system. There are two aspects of convention: one is the mapping between word forms and purports; the other is how the mapped-onto purport is construed. Certain construals because they are so frequent and so stable across contexts, become subject to very strong constraints and will acquire a special default status; and extra cognitive effort, or a strong countervailing constraint, will be required to impose a different interpretation.

14.2.4.2 Context

Conventional constraints are a major source of semantic stability, but this exists alongside a high degree of contextual variability. This variability affects all aspects of meaning, from basic structural and logical properties to the subtlest nuances. Many features of context can affect construal:

(i) linguistic context:
This includes previous discourse, i.e. what has been said immediately prior to a given utterance, and a word's immediate linguistic environment (i.e. the phrase or sentence in which it appears).

(ii) physical context:
What the participants can see, hear, and so on in their immediate situation.

(iii) cognitive context:
Speakers have an enormous store of knowledge and remembered experiences which forms a background against which utterances are processed (some of this will be presumed to be shared with the hearer), and which can affect how a word is construed.

(iv) type of discourse:
For instance, a word may well be construed differently according to whether it occurs in a poem, a medical consultation, a casual conversation or a police interrogation. The construal will also be sensitive to whether the situation is formal or informal, and what the field of discourse is (for instance, whether it is legal, political, medical or sporting, etc.).

(v) relations between communicants:
Construal may well depend on what the social and power relations are between utterer and addressee, and on what they think and feel about one another.

14.3 Some applications of the dynamic construal approach

In principle, the dynamic construal approach applies to all aspects of word meaning. It will be illustrated here in connection with the construal of sense boundaries, the construal of category boundaries and sense relations of inclusion and exclusion, and the construal of oppositeness.

14.3.1 Lexical ambiguity and the construal of sense boundaries

The possession of more than one sense is traditionally regarded as an inherent property of particular words, to be represented in the mental lexicon (and in any satisfactory dictionary). In the dynamic construal approach, sense boundaries are construed in context on particular occasions of use, subject to a range of constraints. Of course, with some words conventional constraints will be so strong that the same boundary will be construed on the vast majority of occasions of use. There may be some justification in regarding these as 'default' construals. Obviously, the less scope there is for context to influence construal in particular instances, the less difference there will be between the dynamic construal approach and the traditional approach. However, two important points should be made: first, probably no conventional constraint is so strong that it can never be overruled; second, the strength of conventional constraints is a significant variable, and many sense boundary effects are clearly dependent on context. This overall picture is more satisfactorily captured by a notion of dynamic construal with conventional constraints of varying strength: confining the study of word meaning to cases where there is a clear default reading seriously distorts the resulting picture.

A typical case of traditional lexical ambiguity is *bank*, with the two meanings "financial institution" and "margin of river". These two readings are so strongly supported by conventional constraints that it is extremely difficult to find contexts in which they are not distinct. However, it is not impossible. Take example (2):

(2) Not all banks are money banks.

To achieve a normal construal of (2) we have to interpret it as something like "Not all entities designated by the phonological form /bank/ are financial institutions"; in other words it requires a conceptual shift to a metalinguistic perspective. Examples like this have been used to argue that the zeugma test for ambiguity is not valid. But this objection rests on the assumption that a word found to be ambiguous in one context must be ambiguous in all contexts. No such assumption is made in the dynamic construal approach; indeed, from our point of view, the absence of zeugma correctly indicates that *banks* in 1 is not ambiguous. However, the fact that a unified reading for *bank* is possible in only a very restricted range of contexts is a sign that there are very strong constraints favouring a 'split' reading.

Variable construals of sense boundaries are well illustrated by facets and microsenses (discussed in Chapter 6). Taking facets first, it will be recalled that there are two facets of *book*, namely [TOME] and [TEXT], illustrated by *a green book* and *a difficult book*, respectively. There are uses of *book* in which a sense boundary is clearly detectable; see, for instance, the ambiguity of (3a) and (3b):

(3) a. two books
     b. a new book

(3a) can designate either two copies of the same text (i.e. *two* applies only to 'tomes') or two texts (which may, in fact, be contained within a single 'tome', as in *two books in one*); *a new book* may be a new copy of a very ancient text, or a copy (whether in pristine condition or not) of a recently published text. In an appropriate context, a question containing (3b) can be truthfully answered both in the affirmative and the negative, that is to say, responses can be relative to one facet to the exclusion of the other. Consider (4):

(4) Is that a new book?

It is not difficult to imagine a context where this question has two contradict-ory answers, both of them true. As a final example, in both (5) and (6) one of the facets (a different one in each case) is isolated from the other by a con-strued sense boundary:

(5) Don't tell me about the plot or the writing, tell me about the book itself. ([TEXT] excluded)
(6) Don't tell me about the cover design or the illustrations, etc., tell me about the book itself. ([TOME] excluded)

It may seem that nothing is lost by saying that *book* 'has' two facets as part of its inherent semantic nature. However, there are also contexts where there is apparently no trace of a boundary between the facets of *book*, although their 'content' is present:

(7) books and other publications
(8) They are planning to publish a book on the subject.

This is difficult to explain if the boundary is an inherent part of the meaning of *book*, but receives a natural account if the boundary is construed in some contexts but not others.

A similar picture emerges in the case of microsenses. For instance, for Tom's first answer in (9) to be logically well-formed (which it is), a sense boundary has to be construed separating tennis balls and footballs:

(9) Tom (who has a football under his arm):
    Hey, let's play tennis.
    Billy: You got a ball?
    Tom: (i) No.
         (ii) Yeah, but not a tennis ball.

But his second answer (also perfectly well-formed) requires no boundary to be construed. The crucial part of the context affecting boundary construal here is whether Tom prefaces his reply with *Yes* or *No*. Notice that the awkward question of whether *book* and *ball* are ambiguous or not does not arise if we adopt the dynamic construal approach, where sense boundaries are the result of particular construals in context.

The notion of contextually construed sense boundaries can also be applied to semantic features like the [MALE] of "stallion". Instead of saying that the meaning of the word *stallion* 'consists of' the feature [MALE] plus the feature [EQUINE] (or whatever), we can say that in certain contexts (for instance *That's not a stallion*), a sense boundary is construed which isolates the meaning "male" for compositional purposes. Taking this view, we would not expect *stallion* to exhibit a semantically compositional nature in all contexts.

14.3.2 The construal of category boundaries

We have been looking at boundaries between meanings. But the construal of a boundary can also be thought of in extensional terms, as a way of drawing a line between things that are in a category and things that are not. There has been a tendency to assume that words are associated with stable categories. However, it is an essential feature of the dynamic construal approach that, just as words are not associated with specific meanings, nor are they associated with specific conceptual categories, but with bodies of purport which allow variable construal in different contexts. Take the example of the category PET in English. One can find electronic devices which behave in certain ways like animals: these are sometimes referred to as *cyberpets*. If we ask whether these objects belong to the category PET, some people will answer *Yes*, and others *No*. This can be taken to indicate that different speakers construe the categories in different ways. But suppose we ask the question in (9):

(10) Is a cyberpet a real pet?

This time the majority respond *No*, because the word *real* causes the position of the category boundary to be construed differently. On the other hand, an educational psychologist consulted by the parents of a difficult child might say:

(11) I would advise you to get her some kind of pet, perhaps even an electronic one.

This will seem normal to most people, even though *pet* is used to include the electronic variety: *some kind of* and *even* cause a broader category to be construed. Another example is (12):

(12) A cat has four legs.

Few will dispute the truth of this, even though there is nothing illogical about the notion of a three-legged cat. It seems that when we interpret (11), we construe the category of cats in such a way that only perfectly formed examples are counted. A different construal of the boundaries of the category of cats is illustrated in (13):

(**13**) Cats are vertebrates.

The word *vertebrate* is a technical term, and this makes us construe a category appropriate to scientific discourse, which includes three-legged cats. Consider also (14):

(**14**) I wish I could fly like a bird.

The word *bird* here requires us to construe a category which excludes not only injured birds but also flightless birds. Notice that on the dynamic construal view, the question of which is the 'true' category denoted by *cat* or *bird*, or whatever, has no sense: the purport that the word maps onto is neutral between all the possible construals.

Boundary placement can be seen as an example of the operation of Lakoff's 'container' image-schema. Clearly, the position of category boundaries has a determining effect on sense relations such as hyponymy and incompatibility: if the category denoted by word W^1 falls wholly within the boundaries of the category denoted by word W^2, then W^1 will be hyponymous to W^2, and if the category denoted by W^2 and the category denoted by W^3 have no members in common, then W^2 and W^3 will be incompatibles. But the variability in associated categories which we have observed entails that sense relations, too, are subject to construal in context, rather than being stable properties of lexical items.

Take the case of hyponymy. Two diagnostic tests for hyponymy are first, entailment—the fact that *It's a cat* unilaterally entails *It's an animal* indicates that *cat* is a hyponym of *animal*, and second, normality in the frame *Xs and other Ys*, as in *cats and other animals*. However, there is an awkward discrepancy between the two tests: *cats and other pets* is fine, but *It's a cat* does not, in most people's judgement, entail *It's a pet*. So, is *cat* a hyponym of *pet* or not? Taking a dynamic construal view, there is no problem: *cat* is a hyponym of *pet* in *cats and other pets*, but not in *It's a cat therefore it is a pet*, and the difference is due to the fact that the construed categories are different in the two contexts. A similar story can be told about incompatibility. In *All sorts of people have used our services, students, nuns, housewives, doctors . . .*, we are encouraged to construe the coordinated categories as mutually exclusive (and therefore to construe the terms as incompatibles). But the categories construed in *X is a nun, therefore she is not a student*, are such that statement is not logically valid.

The dynamic construal view does not exclude the possibility that some construals have a **default** status, that is, they are the interpretations that will emerge if there is not enough context to guide the process of construal. Notice that this is not the same as saying that these are real, inherent meanings of words—they still have to be construed. There is, however, some uncertainty as to the criteria for deciding which readings are to be given the status of defaults. Some might feel that the reading of *cat* in *It's a cat therefore it is an animal* should be taken as the default. But why should this be? This is a rather artificial context. It is probably the case that on hearing the word *cat* out of context, most people will think of the domestic variety, which would point to the construal in *cats and other pets* as the default.

14.3.3   The construal of opposites

In most treatments of oppositeness, words are assigned to specific types of opposite. For instance, *dead:alive* are described as complementaries, and *long:short* as polar antonyms. However, the field of semantic oppositeness provides further examples of structural properties that are context-dependent, and hence a more satisfactory picture is obtained if relations such as antonymy and complementarity are regarded as holding between construals subject to constraints.

14.3.3.1   Antonyms vs. complementaries

Some opposite pairs behave in some contexts like a pair of complementaries (contradictories) and in other contexts like a pair of antonyms (gradable contraries). A typical example is *safe:dangerous*. Complementaries are recognized by the fact that negating them entails the assertion of the opposite. Most speakers will infer from (15) that it is *dangerous* to use the path in question at night:

(15) It's not *safe* to go along that path at night.

However, (16) shows *safe* and *dangerous* behaving like gradable antonyms:

(16) It used to be quite *dangerous*, but it's a lot *safer* now that they've installed proper lighting.

There is a small number of opposites that behave like *safe* and *dangerous* in that they display an unusual freedom in respect of construal type. In many cases there is evidence of conventional or cognitive constraints favouring one construal or the other. Take the case of *dead:alive*. With these a complementary construal is probably the favoured one:

(17) A: Is it dead?
     B: No, look, it's breathing—it's still alive.

However, in an appropriate context *alive* can behave like one member of a pair of gradable antonyms:

(18) You look a bit more alive than you did yesterday!

(Interestingly, this is not so easy with *dead*:

(19) ?You look a bit more dead than you did yesterday!)

The pair *married:single* show an even stronger constraint favouring a complementary construal:

(20) Are you married or single?

However, in one of Iris Murdoch's novels we find (20):

(21) Jane was very married.

This presents no problems of interpretation, but most speakers probably feel that the conventions of English are being stretched.

14.3.3.2 Direction of scale

Graded properties are usually construed in such a way that more of them is more salient, so, for instance, it is more natural to think of a scale of length than a scale of shortness. The fact that we have a scale of length correlates with the fact that *How long is it?* (rather than *How short is it?*) is the normal, neutral question for enquiring as to the linear extent of something. However, there are contexts where a construed scale seems to go in the 'wrong' direction. For instance, (22) appeared in a newspaper article about the miniaturisation of computer components:

(22) The new device is ten times smaller than anything seen previously.

And (23), in the same context, seems normal:

(23) A: Every week we produce smaller and smaller chips.
B: How small do you think you'll be able to get them?

In these examples, the scale of size is being construed as a scale of SMALLNESS rather than the more usual scale of BIGNESS/LARGENESS, and B's question in (23) is functioning as a neutral question. This reversal goes against quite strong cognitive constraints, and would not be possible unless there were special situational features. What licenses the reversal in this case is probably the 'smaller-is-better' nature of the enterprise.

14.3.3.3 Effects of calibration

Graded properties are normally construed in such a way that whether there is a standard way of measuring them can make a difference to the semantic behaviour of a word denoting the property. Take the case of *strong*:

(24) John prefers his beer and his tea to be on the strong side.

(24) is quite normal, showing that we use the same construal of *strong* for beer and tea. But there is a marked difference in normality between (25) and (26). This is because we can easily think of a way of measuring the strength of beer (for instance, the percentage of alcohol), but we do not normally assign a measurement to the strength of tea:

(25) What is the strength of this beer?

(26) ?What is the strength of this tea?

The situation is similar in the case of *hard*. There is a scientific scale for expressing the hardness of minerals, so the question *What is the hardness of topaz?* is normal in a scientific context. However, we have no readily available units for measuring the hardness of wood, so the question *What is the hardness of teak?* is somewhat peculiar.

14.4 Summary

The dynamic construal approach treats meanings and structural semantic properties such as sense and category boundaries, scale schemas, and sense relations like hyponymy and antonymy as 'on-line' construals on occasions of use, and not as inherent properties of lexical items. This approach has a number of advantages:

 (i) We are encouraged to give up the search for the 'real', 'basic', 'under-lying' meaning of words: this search has not produced impressive results. On the dynamic construal approach, there is no such thing.

 (ii) We have an explanation for the vast intuitive gulf between our vivid experience of living, situated meaning and what we get when we pick a word out of a dictionary. The dynamic construal approach brings lexical semantics much closer to actual language use.

(iii) The descriptions of sense relations and other structural properties of word meanings is greatly simplified. For instance, hyponymy and incompatibility can be given a simple logical characterization, there being no need for dubious notions like the 'para hyponymy' and 'para incompatibility' which were found necessary in Cruse (1986) to characterize the relations between *dog* and *pet*, and *nun* and *student*, respectively.

(iv) The dynamic construal approach can account equally well for context-dependent and relatively context-independent properties. Context-dependent properties are problematic for an approach that seeks to assign inherent semantic properties to lexical items. However, cases where properties appear relatively invariant under context change are no problem for the dynamic construal approach, because construal is subject to a range of constraints of different strengths, some of which are relatively transient and others of which, such as cognitive and conventional constraints, are relatively stable. Hence, the construal-and-constraints approach offers a more comprehensive account.

At the same time, the dynamic construal approach undoubtedly raises a number of questions. For instance, the exact nature of both purport and resultant construed meanings is in need of clarification—traditional semantics does not help us much here. Another question concerns the status of a conventional dictionary in this view. No one can deny the usefulness of dictionaries; but if words do not have stable meanings, what does a dictionary record? One possibility is that the main function of a dictionary definition is to help us to locate the body of conceptual content (the purport) to which the word being defined gives access. In some cases, a picture or diagram can do this more efficiently than a verbal definition. A dictionary cannot list all possible readings/construals, not even all autonomous ones, but our innate competence in construal can construct these if the appropriate purport is known. There is currently no definitive answer to these and many other questions, but ongoing research will undoubtedly bring fresh insights.

Suggestions for further reading

The first proposal within linguistics for the non-existence of fixed word meanings was in Moore and Carling (1982). For a fuller account of the dynamic construal approach, see Croft and Cruse (forthcoming). A related proposal from a relevance-theoretical viewpoint can be found in Carston (2002).

Part 3
Semantics and Grammar

Communication using isolated words is necessarily extremely limited: words need to be used together with other words. But a simple collection of words is not much use either: combinations of words need to be governed by grammatical rules. Grammar has a dual role in producing intelligible messages. First, there are rules of combination, which determine what sort of global meaning results when constituent meanings are combined. Second, the grammatical elements which articulate grammatical structures (affixes, particles, constructions, syntactic categories, etc.) carry a distinguishable sort of meaning, which contributes in a special way to the meaning of whole constructions and sentences.

In this section, which has only one chapter, we survey those aspects of the meanings of larger syntactic units which are attributable to grammar.

CHAPTER 15

Grammatical semantics

CHAPTER 15

Grammatical semantics

15.1 Grammatical meaning

In this chapter we look at the sort of meanings that grammatical elements of various kinds bear. It will be recalled that to perform their characteristic functions, any meaning carried by a grammatical element must be of an impoverished, 'thin', or very general nature, so as to permit wide collocability: typical 'rich' lexical meanings impose too many constraints on their collocants.

We shall survey the varieties of grammatical meaning, but no attempt will be made to be exhaustive (particularly typologically—most of the examples will be drawn from English). This is now a complex and well-researched area: most of the treatment will be basic and fairly traditional, as an exposition of many modern treatments requires extensive background knowledge for which there is not sufficient space here.

15.2 The meaning of major grammatical categories

Traditionally, syntactic categories are defined semantically: nouns are defined as words referring to 'persons, places or things', verbs are 'doing words', that is, they refer to actions, whereas adjectives are 'describing words'. In early structuralist linguistics such definitions were shown to be seriously flawed: (a) *punch* in *He packs a powerful punch* refers to an action, but is a noun; *seem* is a verb, but does not refer to an action; in *John shouted, shouted* describes what John did, but is not an adjective, and so on. It was recommended that syntactic categories should be defined on syntactic criteria: for instance, nouns are inflected for number, gender, and case and take articles as modifiers; verbs are inflected for tense and aspect, etc. Connections with semantics were held to be non-systematic. More recently, the question of the semantic basis of grammatical categories has been raised once again.

One approach has been to utilize the insights of prototype theory: perhaps grammatical categories are like natural categories such as BIRD and FRUIT, not definable by a set of necessary and sufficient criteria, but with fuzzy boundaries and graded typicality. We might then say, for instance, that a prototypical noun refers to a person or thing, a prototypical verb refers to an action, and so on, but that more marginal examples of these categories may not conform to these descriptions. There would seem to be some justification in this view. For instance, there are many respects in which *seem* does not behave syntactically like a typical verb: it does not occur in the passive (**happy was seemed by John*), or the progressive aspect (**John is seeming happy*). There is a certain plausibility in correlating the verb's semantic marginality with its syntactic marginality. Likewise, a semantically atypical noun like *jogging* (as in *Jogging is good for you*) is also syntactically atypical: it can be modified by an adverb (*Jogging gently is good for you*), it is unhappy with certain determiners (*this/ that jogging*), and so on.

A more illuminating and unified approach pictures the difference between nouns, adjectives, and verbs in terms of temporal stability: all languages have a way of making a distinction between persistent entities, whose properties change relatively little over time, and highly time-sensitive experiences, that is, a distinction between entities and events, with nouns encoding entities and verbs encoding events. Adjectives, if they occur, denote experiences which fall between the two poles (but not all languages have adjectives, the functions they typically have in English being performed either by nouns or verbs).

This approach, too, falls foul of the same sorts of counterexample as the traditional approach: in what sense is a punch a temporally stable entity? Once again, one can fall back on the prototype escape clause, but this does not seem entirely satisfactory. Another line of defence is to say that the characterizations do not apply directly to referents, but to conceptualizations: when we say *John punched Bill*, we conceive the punch as a time-bound happening; but when we say *The punch John threw . . .*, we reconceptualize it as something with a certain permanence, we, as it were, freeze it in mid-flight, to allow ourselves to examine it and say things about it.

Another approach takes a cognitive view and sees nouns as denoting a 'region of cognitive space' (Langacker 1991b), whereas adjectives and verbs denote 'relations', adjectives portraying the states of affairs they denote as atemporal and verbs presenting their denotations as temporal. The cognitive viewpoint here seems correct. However, the notion of a 'region of cognitive space' is not very perspicuous.

15.3 Grammatical meanings associated with nouns and noun phrases

Certain types of meaning are typically carried by grammatical elements—inflections, clitics, or markers—associated with nouns or noun phrases. The most important of these are: definiteness, number, animacy, gender, and functional roles. Definiteness is dealt with in Chapter 16, and will not be discussed here; functional roles are as much concerned with verbs as with nouns and will be discussed in the next section. In this section we shall look at number, animacy, and gender.

15.3.1 Number

Number is an inflectional category of nouns or noun phrases, which is not found in all languages. Semantically, number systems are all concerned, one way or another, with how many examples there are of some class of things. **Number systems** are not to be confused with **numeral systems**, which are linguistic devices for counting (*one, two, forty-three, one hundred and ninety,* etc.); obviously there are connections between the two, but numerals are syntactically and semantically distinct from number markers.

The number system in English has only two terms: singular and plural. We shall examine the semantics of these in a moment. A minority of languages have a three-term number system including a **dual**, used for just two things. A very small minority have four-term systems, in which the fourth term is either a **trial** (for three things), or a **paucal** (for 'a few' things). No language has a trial or a paucal without also having singular, dual, and plural; no language that has a dual does not also have singular and plural. (Of course, the meaning of *plural* is not precisely the same in a two-term system as in a three- or four-term system: *plural* in English means "more than one"; in a four-term system it means either "more than three" or "many" (i.e. "more than a few").)

15.3.1.1 Count nouns and mass nouns

English nouns are traditionally divided into two classes, count nouns and mass nouns. They can be recognized by the following criteria:

(i) Count nouns:
  (a) cannot occur in the singular without a determiner:
     *This cup/*Cup is clean*;
  (b) occur normally in the plural;
  (c) are quantifiable by *a few, many*, and numerals:
     a few/many cups; (**much cup*), *thirty cups*.
(ii) Mass nouns:
  (a) can occur in the singular without a determiner:
     Butter is good for you;
  (b) are odd in the plural (or require reinterpretation):
     butters, milks;
  (c) are quantifiable by *a little, much*:
     a little/much milk; (**many milk*).

Count nouns present something as being manifested in discrete, bounded units that in principle can be counted; mass nouns present their referent as an unbounded mass. Notice that this is a matter of conceptualization, not of objective reality: the blood referred to in *There was blood on the floor* may well have occurred in discrete drops and patches, but it is thought of as an undifferentiated substance.

What determines whether the name of something is a mass noun or a count noun? Obviously, if there is nothing to count, as with liquids and gases and many abstract notions, then the name will be a mass noun. But in the case of many mass nouns, there are observable particles of some sort: rice comes in discrete grains, and sugar in grains or crystals; even flour can be seen to consist of particles. In such cases, one determining factor seems to be the size of the particles. The cross-over point seems to be somewhere between the size of an average pea and that of a typical grain of rice (at least for English). So, we have *beans, peas, noodles,* and *lentils* as count nouns, but *barley, rice, sugar,* and *flour* as mass nouns. The boundary is not rigid: *sweet corn* and *spaghetti* seem on the large side for mass nouns; and it is worth recalling that *peas* is a reanalysed form of the earlier *pease,* which was a mass noun. Some things are referable to indifferently by mass or count nouns. Some such cases are obviously 'mass' in nature: *mashed potatoes/mashed potato, scrambled eggs/scrambled egg.* The dual use can perhaps be explained in terms of whether the conceptualization focuses on the original state of the ingredients (i.e. discrete units), or on the state of the final product. Cases where the final product is also in the form of discrete units are harder to explain: *poached eggs/poached egg.*

15.3.1.2 Secondary uses of count and mass nouns

In the above discussion it has been assumed that English nouns are 'basically' either mass or count. This has been disputed, on the grounds that the vast majority of nouns in English can be found with both count and mass uses. While this is true, it is also true that for the majority of nouns, one use is intuitively more basic than the other, and this enables us to identify two significant phenomena and enquire about their semantic correlates: basic count nouns used as mass nouns, and basic mass nouns used as count nouns.

Basic count nouns used as mass nouns
Examples:

(1) With a Lada you get a lot of car for your money.
(2) Could you move along a bit—I haven't got much table.
(3) I can hear too much piano and not enough violin.

Here, the count noun is metonymically reinterpreted to yield a mass notion: sound, in (3), working space in (2), perhaps just size in (1).

Basic mass nouns used as count nouns
Examples:

(4) Three beers/cheeses/cakes/chocolates
(5) Three wines

Mass nouns used as count nouns are usually to be interpreted in one of two ways, either as unit quantities of the continuous mass or as different types or varieties. The first type is illustrated in (4). The type of unit is partly conventionally determined, partly contextually. Thus, *three beers* probably refers to three bottles or standard glasses of beer, *three cheeses* to three spherical entities with a single rind, as the cheesemaker first produces them, etc. This mass/count alternation does not only apply to edible substances: it is observable in *not much time/they come at different times; not much space/spaces between words*, etc.

The second type is sometimes known as the **distributive plural** and is illustrated in (5). It is not immediately clear why the default interpretation of *three beers* should be "three standard quantities", whereas *three wines* normally means "three types". Perhaps it is because beer drinkers are prototypically faithful to a single brand, whereas wine-drinkers habitually match wine varieties to situations. Some languages have a special form for the distributive plural; in others the plural is only used in a distributive sense. For instance, the Arabic *ashjaar* is a plural of *shajar*, meaning "tree", but is indifferent to the number of trees, only to the number of tree varieties referred to. Something like a distributive plural can be observed in English, with words that do not usually take the plural affix, such as *trout, deer*. They can, on occasion, take the plural -*s*, and when they do the most likely interpretation is a distributive one: *the trouts of North America, the deers of Northern Europe*, etc.

The semi-mass use of count nouns. In the previous paragraph we examined some cases of the anomalous presence of the plural marker. In this section we look at the converse of this: the anomalous absence of the plural marker. The following are examples:

(6) We shot three lion last week.
     (*We shot three fox last week.)
(7) She owns three hectares of oak.
(8) There is a field of beetroot/turnip behind our house.
(9) Two rows of lettuce/*leek/*pea/*bean have been ruined.

This is not ordinary mass use, because the words in question are plurals:

(10) Those lion we saw last week have moved on.
(11) The oak on the other side of the hill are showing signs of disease.

On the other hand, there is something 'mass-like' about this usage. It seems to be confined to experts, hunters, foresters, horticulturists, and so on (as, indeed, is the use of the anomalous plural -*s*). Somehow, the individuality of the referents does not matter, only their species.

15.3.1.3 Singular nouns with (optional) plural concord

Two further number anomalies are worth pointing out. The first concerns so-called **group words**. These are count nouns which have the peculiarity that in the singular form they can take either singular or plural concord with the verb:

(12) The committee is/are considering the matter right now.

These words refer prototypically to groups of humans (my student informants find *The flock have gone over the hill* odd, but in Gray's *Elegy in a Country Churchyard* we find *The lowing herd wind slowly o'er the lea*); certainly, inanimate 'collections' do not behave in this way:

(13) *His library are all leather-bound.
(14) *The forest are leafless at this time of the year.

There is a subtle difference of meaning between the uses. With singular concord, the group is conceptualized as a unity; with plural concord, it is conceptualized as constituted out of separate individuals. Predicates which can only apply to each individual separately are anomalous with singular concord:

(15) The committee are wearing their hats.
(16) *The committee is wearing its hat/their hats.

Predicates which can only be true of the group as a whole are anomalous with plural concord:

(17) The committee was/*were formed six months ago.

It is only verbal concord which may vary: items inside the noun phrase must be singular:

(18) *Those committee are considering the matter now.

15.3.1.4 Plural nouns with (optional) singular concord

The second anomaly is the converse of the first, namely, plural nouns with singular concord:

(19) Five wives is more than enough for anyone.

This use seems to be confined to noun phrases with numerals in them:

(20) *Those wives is more than enough for any man.
(21) ?Several wives is too much for an old man.

In this usage, the quantified noun phrase is interpreted as a single quantity.

15.3.2 Gender and animacy

Gender is a classification system for nouns, which affects such grammatical matters as agreement and pronominal reference. Many different types of gender system can be found in the world's languages, some of them quite exotic (like the case made famous by Lakoff, in which one gender class includes words referring to 'women, fire and dangerous things'); but the most widespread are those which correlate to a greater or lesser degree with the sex of the referent, and the present account will be limited to these.

It is usual to make a distinction between **natural gender** and **grammatical gender**. English is usually said to exhibit natural gender (in so far as it has gender at all—it affects only pronominal reference), since the appropriate pronoun (*he, she*, or *it*) can be predicted with a high degree of success purely on the basis of the sex (male, female, or neuter) of the referent. In languages possessing grammatical gender, at least a significant proportion of cases of gender assignment are apparently semantically arbitrary, although in some cases the arbitrariness is less than it seems at first sight. Often cited as exemplifying the semantic arbitrariness of gender are the German words *Löffel* ("spoon"; masculine), *Gabel* ("fork": feminine), and *Messer* ("knife": neuter). However, in German, as in French, there is a strong tendency for words referring to male beings (especially humans) to be grammatically masculine, and for words referring to females to be grammatically feminine (there are exceptions in both languages). (Since there are no languages with completely arbitrary gender assignment, we should probably think in terms of a scale of naturalness/arbitrariness, rather than an arbitrary/natural dichotomy.)

Gender is of course intimately bound up with animacy, since prototypically, only living things can be male or female. Many languages have grammatical processes which are sensitive to animacy, or relative animacy. The American linguist William Frawley, the author of a well-known book on grammatical semantics (1992), puts forward the following scale (animacy decreases from right to left):

1st Person > 2nd Person > 3rd Person > Human > Animal > Inanimate

An examination of the English pronoun system shows that it too correlates to some extent with the animacy scale, in respect of the transition from *he/she* to *it*:

he/she only	*he/she/it*	*she/it* only	*it* only
non-infant humans, (gods, angels)	infant humans animals	(cars, ships)	things

What seems to underlie the scale of animacy is perceived potency, or capacity to affect other things (including the human mind, hence also salience and relevance) and bring about changes. What a culture regards as potent may not coincide with our notions: it is reported, for instance, that Yagua, an Amazonian language, uses the same classifier for humans, animals, the moon and stars, rocks, brooms, and fans, while the sun, spoons, and other inanimates have a different classifier. This system makes more semantic sense when it is realized that the Yagua are moon worshippers, while rocks, brooms, and fans are valued for the effects they produce (in the case of rocks, for crushing food).

15.4 Grammatical meanings associated with the verb

15.4.1 Tense

Semantically, the grammatical feature of **tense** serves essentially to locate the event referred to in the sentence with reference to the time at which the utterance was produced (although it may have other secondary functions). Only languages which encode timing distinctions by means of grammatical elements (usually inflectional morphemes or grammatical markers such as auxiliary verbs) can be properly said to manifest the grammatical feature of tense; many languages encode the timing of a designated event lexically, by means of expressions equivalent to *yesterday, last year, next week*, etc.

A distinction is usually made between **primary** (or **absolute**) tenses, which encode event time directly relative to time of speaking, and **secondary** (or **relative**) tenses, which encode event time relative to a secondary reference time which, in turn, is located relative to speaking time, thus making the relation between event time and speaking time an indirect one.

The tense systems of most languages are said to be **vectorial**, that is, the grammatical terms indicate merely the direction along the time-line from speaking time to event time, rather than how distant in time the event is (this information can of course be conveyed lexically).

There are three basic primary tenses, **past** (event occurs before time of speaking); **present** (event occurs concurrently with speaking time, or includes it); and **future** (event is projected to occur after the time of speaking):

(22) John saw Bill.
(23) John sees Bill.
(24) John will see Bill.

In the case of secondary tenses, there are nine theoretical possibilities (in each of the following, the reference time is John's arrival, and the time of Bill's action is situated relative to that):

(25) At the time John arrived, Bill had switched on the lights.
     (event prior to reference time; reference time in past)
(26) At the time John arrived, Bill switched on the lights.
     (event coincident with reference time; reference time in past)
(27) At the time John arrived, Bill was about to/was going to switch on the lights.
     (event subsequent to reference time; reference time in past)
(28) At the time John arrives, Bill has switched off the lights.

(event prior to reference time; reference time in present—can only receive a habitual interpretation)

(29) At the time John arrives, Bill switches off the lights.
(event coincident with reference time, reference time in present—can only receive a habitual interpretation)

(30) At the time John arrives, Bill is about to switch off the lights.
(event subsequent to reference time, reference time in present)

(31) At the time John arrives, Bill will have switched off the lights.
(event prior to reference time; reference time in future)

(32) At the time John arrives, Bill will switch on the lights.
(event coincident with reference time, reference time in future)

(33) At the time John arrives, Bill will be about to switch off the lights.
(event subsequent to reference time, reference time in future)

Presumably all nine secondary tense relationships can be expressed one way or another in any language; however, no language with an inflectional tense system has distinct inflections for all nine.

Some languages have what is called a **metrical** tense system, which grammatically encodes degrees of remoteness as well as direction. The most frequent type is the **hodiernal** system, which distinguishes "today" and "not today". Frawley (1992) gives the example of Grebo:

(34) Ne   du-   e   bla
     I   pound today   rice
     "I pound rice today" (the pounding may occur before or after the speech event, provided it is within the bounds of "today")

(35) Ne   du-   ə   bla
     I   pound yesterday rice
     "I pounded rice yesterday"

(36) Ne   du-   a   bla
     I   pound tomorrow rice
     "I will pound rice tomorrow"

Up to six or seven intervals may be distinguished, with the past being typically more highly differentiated than the future. According to Bernard Comrie, an authority on typological linguistics, Yagua makes the following distinctions with respect to the past in its grammatical tense system (Comrie 1985: 99):

   (i) past (today);
   (ii) yesterday;
   (iii) within a few weeks;
   (iv) within a few months;
   (v) distant past.

15.4.2 Aspect

It is important to distinguish aspect clearly from tense. Tense serves to locate an event in time; aspect says nothing about when an event occurred (except by implication), but either encodes a particular way of conceptualizing an event or conveys information about the way the event unfolds through time. It is also important to make a distinction between aspect as a semantic phenomenon, and aspect markers in a particular language, which may have a variety of semantic functions. To make things even more complicated, a lexical verb may encode aspectual information as part of its meaning, independently of any grammatical markers; this may affect the way the meaning of the verb interacts with the meanings of aspectual markers.

15.4.2.1 Basic aspectual features

From the semantic point of view, aspect is normally regarded as a property or characteristic of events and states. (There is no convenient cover term for these in English, but they are sometimes referred to jointly as 'eventualities'—we shall use 'events' to cover both, as is customary.) Events are held to fall into one of a small number of **aspectual classes**, which are defined on the basis of yet more fundamental aspectual features, themselves values on three basic dimensions: change, boundedness and duration.

Change. A state of affairs can be construed as changing or as remaining constant. An event is described as **homogeneous** if it is construed as unchanging, and **heterogeneous** if it is construed as changing. Generally speaking, if something 'happens', or 'is happening', then change is involved.

Boundedness. Some events are construed as having one or more inherent boundaries. A boundary may be at the beginning or the end of an event, but it is the final boundary which is generally regarded as the most significant. An event with a final boundary is described as **telic**, and one with no final boundary is described as **atelic**. It is natural to think of a telic event as 'finishing', or 'being completed', as opposed to merely 'stopping' or 'coming to an end'.

Duration. An event may be construed as taking time to unfold, or as occurring in an instant. An instantaneous event is described as **punctual**; an event that is spread over a time interval is **durative**. Notice that while the durative/punctual distinction is obviously not independent of objective duration, it is essentially a matter of construal.

15.4.2.2 The major aspectual classes of events

The main aspectual classes of events can be characterized using the above features.

States. **States** are homogeneous, in that no change is involved; they are unbounded, in that they have no inherent beginning or end; and they are durative, in that persistence through time is of the essence. They may be expressed in English by adjectival expressions (37), prepositional phrases (38), or stative verbs (39):

(37) Dolphins are highly intelligent.
(38) Edirne is in Turkey.
(39) Frank loves his garden.

Activities and processes. **Activities** and **processes** (which differ in respect of the non-aspectual feature of agentivity) resemble states in being unbounded and durative, but differ in that they are heterogeneous. Something is 'going on', but this is not construed as a movement towards an inherent point of completion:

(40) It is raining.
(41) We are driving northwards.
(42) I wish they would stop arguing.

Accomplishments. **Accomplishments** share the features of durativity and heterogeneity with activities and processes, but are distinguished by being telic, i.e. by being inherently completable:

(43) I'm going to mow the lawn.
(44) Let's have a game of chess.
(45) Bill is preparing lunch.

The difference between activities and accomplishments can show up in particularly striking fashion when they are combined with the verb *stop*:

(46) Mary stopped mowing the lawn.
(47) John and Bill stopped arguing.

In (46), the existence of a natural point of completion of an event of lawn-mowing induces a strong sense of unfinished business, which is completely lacking in (47). (From a strictly logical point of view, there is no reason why Mary in (46) should not have stopped because she had finished the job: the inference of incompleteness is a 'generalized conversational implicature' (see Chapter 18).)

Achievements. **Achievements** are events in which there is a transition from one state to another which is construed as being instantaneous. Achievements are thus heterogeneous, naturally bounded (by the point of transition), and punctual:

(48) John forgot everything he had learned.
(49) She arrived yesterday.
(50) They graduate next week.

Some state transitions are felt to be the beginning of a new state. This is known as the **inchoative** aspect:

(51) She was born during a thunderstorm.

(52) The new arrangements were set up last week.
(53) As soon as I saw him, I knew he was guilty.

Other transitions are construed as the end of an old state.

(54) My driving licence expired a month ago.
(55) The business went bankrupt.
(56) We soon exhausted our stocks of food.

Such transitions exemplify the **terminative** aspect.

Semelfactives. The class of **semelfactives** cannot be neatly distinguished from the others in terms of the above features: they have the same features of heterogeneity, boundedness, and punctuality as achievements. They differ from achievements in that they do not involve a transition between two states, and they are perhaps more revealingly viewed as 'punctual accomplishments'.

(57) The bomb exploded.
(58) John gulped.
(59) Mary tapped John on the shoulder.

A possible way of accounting for semelfactives using the features employed for the other four types is to say that accomplishments are initially and finally bounded, whereas in semelfactives the initial and final bounds are fused.

15.4.2.3 Some further aspectual distinctions

Perfective/imperfective. One of the most widespread aspectual distinctions is that between imperfective and perfective. In many languages there is a formal distinction of some sort whose prototypical semantic function is to signal the perfective/imperfective contrast (e.g. Czech and Arabic). In English, there is no regular way of indicating the distinction, but it is often associated with the progressive/simple alternation and can be observed in the following:

(60) I saw the chicken cross the road. (perfective: the event is viewed in its entirety and is treated as unanalysable)
(61) I saw the chicken crossing the road. (imperfective: event is viewed as taking time, allowing other events to be temporally located within its boundaries. There is no commitment as to whether the chicken successfully made it to the other side of the road, but the chicken's movement is seen as part of a complete crossing)

The perfective aspect construes an event as completed, and as an unanalysable conceptual unit with no internal structure; it is sometimes described as viewing an event holistically, without any attention being directed to constituent parts. Notice that it does not say anything about the event itself, for example whether it is punctual or durative: what the perfective aspect does is to treat the event as if its time course was irrelevant. The imperfective aspect, on the other hand, opens up the internal temporal structure of the event, taking an inner rather than an outer viewpoint, and allowing intermediate stages between beginning and end to be relevant. The imperfective aspect, like the perfective, is compatible with different event types, although durative events naturally lend themselves more readily to imperfective construal than do punctual events.

Although tense and aspect are to be rigorously distinguished, it is sometimes the case that information that is conveyed in one language by the tense system, is conveyed in another by the aspectual system. This occurs particularly with the perfective/imperfective contrast. It is arguable that Arabic, for instance, has no tense system. A sentence like *John killed* is translated into Arabic as *qatala Hanna*, whereas *John is killing* would be *yaqtala Hanna*. The verb *qatala* is not in the past tense, but in the perfective aspect; likewise, *yaqtala* is not strictly in the present tense, but the imperfective aspect. The connection between past tense and perfective aspect is that, prototypically, events that are complete are ones that happened in the past; similarly, there is a default assumption that an uncompleted event is currently in progress, hence the association between imperfective and present tense.

Perfect/prospective. The English perfect is a typical example. Consider the difference between the following:

(**62**) John read the book.
(**63**) John has read the book.

Both indicate that John's reading of the book occurred in the past. But the first sentence directs our attention into the past, to the specific time when the event occurred; the second sentence, on the other hand, directs our attention towards John's present state, or at least at aspects of it which are attributable to his having read the book at some (indeterminate) time in the past. This is the essence of the perfect: present relevance of past events. Notice the incompatibility between a perfect and a definite past time adverbial:

(**64**) ?I have done it yesterday.

and (in British English, at least) between the past tense and now:

(**65**) ?I just did it now.

Some linguists distinguish a counterpart to the perfect, but involving the future, called the prospective. A gloss of this would be: the present relevance of a future event. Consider the difference between the following:

(**66**) John will leave tomorrow.
(**67**) John is leaving/is going to leave tomorrow.

One explanation is that the first sentence can be a pure prediction, and can apply to an event which is not under the control either of John or of the speaker. The second sentence, on the other hand, implies that the event is under the control of one or the other, and that decisions and arrangements are currently complete; in other words, things are currently in a state such that, if all goes according to plan, John will leave tomorrow. This would go some way to explaining why, for instance, the following is somewhat odd:

(**68**) The sun is going to rise at 7.00 a.m. tomorrow.

Iterative/habitual. Consider the difference between (69) and (70):

(**69**) John sneezed.
(**70**) John was sneezing.

Sentence (69) is aspectually a semelfactive: it indicates a single sneeze; (70), on the other hand, denotes a series of bounded events with a relatively short time interval between them. This aspect is given the name **iterative**. The iterative aspect is to be distinguished from the **habitual**, where there is also a repetition of bounded events, but over a longer period, and with (potentially) longer intervals between occurrences, as in:

(**71**) John switches on the lights at 5.00 p.m.
(**72**) John washed the dishes every evening.
(**73**) John sleeps in the afternoon.

15.4.2.4 The aspectual character of verbs

It was mentioned above that verbs often encode aspectual information as part of their meaning. For instance, *be born* denotes the beginning of a state (inchoative), and *die* the end of a state (terminative). These verbs are sometimes said to have a particular **aspectual character**. It is instructive in this connection to examine the different 'uses' of the English **progressive** (*Mary is/ was smiling*) and **simple** forms of the verb (*Mary smiles/smiled*). It will be seen that the forms signal aspectual information, but have a different aspectual significance according to the aspectual character of the verb.

First, we shall assume that the prototypical meaning of the progressive form is to indicate that a process, activity, or action is, was, or will be in progress at some particular (perhaps implicit) reference point in time. For instance, *It is raining* indicates that the natural process of precipitation is in progress at the time of speaking, that is, it started before the time of speaking and is expected to continue after the time of speaking. *It was raining* involves an implicit reference point in the past (e.g. *It was raining when we left the house*), but the relation to the reference point is the same as in the previous example.

The effect of combining the progressive form with a verb in English depends on the semantics of the verb. With verbs denoting processes (non-intentional durative 'happenings'), the progressive has its prototypical value. A subtle difference can be detected between verbs (or expressions) which denote activities and those which denote accomplishments. The difference with the progressive can be felt with the following:

(74) He's washing the dishes.
(75) He's crying.

In (74), there is an implication that unless there are unforeseen interruptions or impediments the action will continue to completion; in (75), there is no such implicit boundary.

With verbal expressions possessing semantic characteristics other than those just discussed, the progressive takes on a different hue. We may begin with stative verbs, that is, verbs which denote a state of affairs which remains constant over an appreciable time-scale. Some stative verbs will not accept the progressive at all; this type includes a number of inanimate types like *resemble, contain, overlook*.

(76) This box contains/*is containing twenty-five matches.
(77) The flat overlooks/*is overlooking the park.
(78) John resembles/*is resembling Bill.

and also certain mental verbs:

(79) I know/*am knowing him.
(80) I believe/*am believing that to be so.

With a number of stative verbs, a feature of 'provisionality' is added to the message. This can take different forms. For instance, in (81) and (82) the contrast seems to be one of permanence vs. temporariness:

(81) John lives in London.
(82) John is living in London.

In (83) and (84), the feature appears as tentativeness, openness to correction:

(83) I assume you will do it.
(84) I am assuming you will do it.

In (85) and (86), and (87) and (88), the feature appears as doubt of the evidence of one's senses, admission of the possibility of hallucination:

(85) I hear a noise.
(86) I'm hearing a noise.
(87) I think I see something.
(88) I think I am seeing something.

In the case of punctual verbs—verbs or expressions whose default construals are achievements or semelfactives—there are two main effects, in each case modifying or extending the meaning of the verb so as to conform with the prototype. The first can be observed in (89):

(89) John is coughing.

Here we have an iterative construal—a series of punctual events is being construed as a unified durative process. The same interpretation is possible for (90):

(90) John is switching on the lights.

However, this interpretation is not available if the direct object is singular:

(91) John is switching the light on.

In this case, the punctual event is extended to include preparatory actions like going towards the switch, and in that way receives a durative reading.

15.4.3 Voice

In this section we shall look only at the three traditional **voices**:

(i) Active: *John opened the door.*
(ii) Passive: *The door was opened by John.*
The door was opened.
(iii) Middle: *The door opened.*

To understand the passive, we must first consider the nature of a prototypical transitive clause. In this, one participant, the most 'active', exerts some kind of force on a second, less active participant, resulting in some change, denoted by the verb. In the active voice, the more active participant plays the syntactic role of subject, and the less active participant plays the syntactic role of direct object. There is another difference between the two participants, besides their relative level of activity: the more active participant, the subject, is thrown into higher relief than the object, and in the basic form of the clause functions as the 'topic' of the clause: it represents the entity that the clause 'is about'. The effect of passivization is to promote the less active participant (the logical object), as it were, to the front of the stage by making it the syntactic subject, and to background the logical subject (to such an extent that it becomes an optional adjunct). The effect of the middle voice is to abolish the logical subject altogether, and construe the event as being causeless. (Even in the short passive, although the logical subject is not overtly mentioned, the event is construed as being the result of an action by an 'off-stage' agent.)

Clauses whose semantics depart radically from the prototype may resist passivization:

(92) The box contains Mary's jewellery.
(93) *Mary's jewellery is contained by the box.
(94) John resembles his brother.
(95) *John's brother is resembled by him.

(Notice that although *John resembles Bill* is too far, semantically, from the prototype for passivization to occur, it has not lost all contact with the prototype: there are still two participants, one relatively highlighted, the other relatively less prominent and functioning as a reference point.)

15.4.4 Functional roles

Consider the sentence *John opened the door*. There are two main participants in the event, John and the door. These, however, have different relationships to the act of opening: John is the doer, the agent, and supplies the force needed to open the door; the door is passive, is affected by the action, and undergoes the designated change of state. Consider, now, the sentence *John saw the door*. Again there are two participants, but at least one of these has a third possible relation to the verb. John is no longer a supplier of force resulting in the change of state of the door; in fact, he is now the entity that is affected, in that he has a perceptual experience. However, it would be misleading to say that John's experience was caused by the door, in the same sense that the door's opening was caused by John. Hence we have identified three (possibly four) different possible relationships that the noun phrase in a minimal transitive clause can contract with the verb. As a final example, consider *This key will open the door*. Here the door seems to be in the same relationship with the verb (plays the same functional role) as it does in *John opened the door*. The role of *key*, however, is a new one: the key, although it affects the door, does not supply the necessary force; it rather transmits it from another entity (unmentioned). The relationships that have been illustrated are variously called **functional roles, case roles, deep cases, participant roles, or thematic roles**.

When a wide range of languages is examined, it appears that the same roles crop up again and again, and it seems that in some sense there is a limited number of possibilities. There are many accounts of functional roles, which differ not only in what roles are recognized but also in the number recognized. None of the suggestions so far has received general acceptance. A full discussion of this topic is not possible here; what follows is merely illustrative.

It is first necessary to distinguish between **functional roles** and **circumstantial roles**, our discussion being confined to the former.

Consider the following sentences:

(96) John repaired his bicycle in the garage.
(97) John put his bicycle in the garage.

In (97), the phrase *in the garage* has a much more intimate relation to the verb than the same phrase in (96): it is part of the 'inner' structure of the clause. In (96), on the other hand, it is external to the clause nucleus. In traditional terms, *in the garage* in (97) is a **complement** (= fulfils a functional role) of the verb, whereas in (96) it is a **clausal adjunct** (= fulfils a circumstantial role). How do we tell the difference? Well, as a start, all adjuncts are optional (syntactically—i.e. omitting them does not render the clause ungrammatical), whereas all obligatory elements are complements. On this basis, *in the garage* in (97) is a complement. The major problem with this characterization concerns optional complements. We shall not delve into this matter too deeply. The following can be taken as indications of complement status:

   (i) occurrence as subject, direct or indirect object of verb;
  (ii) omission leads to **latency** (i.e. 'missing' element must be recovered from context, as with the direct object of *watch* in *Somebody's watching*).

We shall now concentrate on complements.

As mentioned above, there is no agreement as to the best way of describing functional roles, although a significant number of linguists appear to feel that there is a finite number. It would be impossible in the limited space available to give a thorough discussion of the various suggestions: what we shall do here is to go back to the earliest set of proposals, namely those of Fillmore (1968), and point out some of the difficulties. Fillmore's proposals had an elegant simplicity, but history shows elegant simplicity to be a fragile thing in linguistics. Fillmore's original list (1968: 24–5) went as follows:

[i] AGENTIVE (A), the case of the typically animate perceived instigator of the action identified by the verb.
    [**Mary** kicked the cat.]
[ii] INSTRUMENTAL (I), the case of the inanimate force or object causally involved in the state or action identified by the verb.
    [Mary used **the hammer** to break the window.
    The hammer broke the window.]
[iii] DATIVE (D), the case of the animate being affected by the state or action identified by the verb.
    [**Mary** heard the nightingale.
    The nightingale enchanted **Mary**.]
[iv] FACTITIVE (F), the case of the object or being resulting from the action or state identified by the verb, or understood as part of the meaning of the verb.
    [John cooked **a delicious meal**.]
[v] LOCATIVE (L), the case which identifies the location or spatial orientation of the state or action identified by the verb.
    [Mary vaulted **the wall**.
    John put his finger **on the button**.]
[vi] OBJECTIVE (O), the semantically most neutral case, ... conceivably the concept should be limited to things which are affected by the action or state identified by the verb.
    [Mary opened **the door**.
    The door opened.]

The following indicates the flavour of some later developments:

   (i) **Agentive**: Most modern treatments subdivide the AGENTIVE role. There are various problems. A prototypical agent is animate, supplies the energy for the action, and acts deliberately. First of all, an agent-like cause may not be animate: *The wind rattled the windows*. By Fillmore's definition, *wind* should be INSTRUMENTAL, but this does not seem satisfactory; some linguists suggested a new case, FORCE, which was distinct from AGENTIVE. (Does this apply to *computer* in *The computer is working out the solution?*) Second, there are agent-like entities which do not really supply the energy for the action, although they do supply the will, as in *The sergeant-major marched the recruits round the parade ground*. This has been called the INSTIGATOR, although it is then not clear what role to assign *the recruits* to. Finally, there are cases where the agent-like entity supplies the energy, but not the will, as in *John accidentally knocked the vase on to the floor*. A suggestion for this is EFFECTOR.

(ii) **Instrumental**: Instruments are supposed to be inanimate; what, then, are we to make of sniffer dogs in *The police used sniffer dogs to locate the drugs*? (This syntactic frame is often put forward as diagnostic for INSTRUMENTAL.)

(iii) **Dative** (sometimes called **Experiencer**): The definition for this role leaves open the possibility that *John* in *Mary threw John out of the window* is EXPERIENCER, but it does not seem significantly different from *Mary threw John's trousers out of the window* (and they coordinate without zeugma, sometimes given as a test for same role: *Mary threw John and his trousers out of the window*). One way round this is to stipulate that EXPERIENCER can only occur in connection with a process or action where animacy is crucially involved. This is clearly not the case in the above example, but is in *Mary terrified John*, and *John heard the noise*. A distinction is often made between EXPERIENCER and BENE-FACTIVE, the latter being exemplified by *Mary* in *John made Mary a cake*.

(iv) **Factitive**: This is not now usually separated from PATIENT (see below).

(v) **Locative**: Various subdivisions can be made of this role. One is a simple, static location, as in *The Ighzui inhabit a remote island in the Pacific*. Three dynamic subdivisions are possible (i.e. cases where motion is at least implied. First, we have SOURCE, as in *The lamp emits heat*; second, PATH, as in *Mary crossed the street*; and finally GOAL, as in *We finally reached the igloo*.

(vi) **Objective**: A frequent division under this heading focuses on whether the affected entity is changed by the process or action, or not. An unchanged inanimate affected is a THEME, as in *John put on his hat*; a changed item is a PATIENT, as in *Mary minced the meat*.

Two points should be made about functional roles. The first is that there are obviously many borderline and intermediate cases—one can go on subdividing until the cows come home. Clearly some criteria are needed. Since we are dealing with grammatical semantics, one criterion is that a proposed subdivision should have grammatical consequences. Again, there are two possibilities: a case role distinction can be recognized if any language makes the distinction grammatically; or a distinction can only be justified within a particular language if that language makes the distinction grammatically. It should probably be borne in mind also that necessary and sufficient definitions of functional roles are likely to be hard to come by, and that the best approach may be to characterize the prototypical cases.

Functional roles provide an approach to the characterization of syntactic functions such as subject and object. Traditionally, the subject is the 'doer' and the object the 'done to' (in the active voice), but it is easy to think of exceptions to this. A more promising approach is to establish a scale of 'activity', and define the subject as the most active participant. Fillmore's activity hierarchy went as follows:

AGENTIVE > INSTRUMENTAL > EXPERIENCER > LOCATIVE > OBJECTIVE

In English, a subject is obligatory, so if there is only one noun phrase in a sentence, it automatically becomes subject. The hierarchy explains cases like the following, where the subject has different roles, but is always the most active in the sentence:

John cut the wood with a saw.
This saw won't cut the wood.
Mary opened the door.
The door opened.
Mary saw the incident.
John frightened Mary.

There are many exceptions: for instance, a change of voice from active to passive will obviously change the rules for subject. There is not space to go into details.

15.4.5 Semantics and syntax: a case study

An important question concerning the relation between semantics and syntax is the extent to which the syntactic properties of words are determined by, or predictable from, their meanings. A substantial body of opinion holds that there is a significant degree of arbitrariness in grammar. That this is so is suggested by such elementary considerations as the obvious syntactic differences between near-synonyms, as in the following:

(98) Let's hide it.
Let's conceal it.
(99) Let's hide.
*Let's conceal.
(100) We've finished the job.
We've completed the job.
(101) We've finished.
*We've completed.

Even Langacker, who believes that grammar can only be properly understood in terms of its semantic function (i.e. every construction at every level must be seen as symbolizing some element of conceptual content), nonetheless denies that grammar can be predicted from meaning. In one sense this is obvious, otherwise all languages would have essentially the same grammar, differing only in phonetic realization. However, it leaves open the possibility that, within a particular grammar, formal choices may be dictated by meaning. We shall illustrate this point by referring to a study by the linguists Beth Levin and Malka Hovav Rappaport (1992) which takes up this position, and attempts to support it by showing a tight relationship between the meanings of a set of verbs and their complementation patterns.

Levin and Hovav Rappaport's study involves what they initially call 'verbs of removal' (although *remove* does not belong to the class), such as those in:

(**102**) John cleared the leaves from the lawn.
(**103**) Mary wiped the offending words from the blackboard.

Both of these also occur in a pattern in which the location (where the things are removed from) is the direct object of the verb:

(**104**) John cleared the lawn.
(**105**) Mary wiped the blackboard.

However, the two verbs differ in their ability to occur in a pattern where the locatum (the thing which is removed) is expressed by an *of*-phrase:

(**106**) John cleared the lawn of leaves.
(**107**) *Mary wiped the blackboard of offending words.

Wipe can occur in this pattern only if a final state is specified:

(**108**) Mary wiped the blackboard clean of offending words.

The patterns in which they occur separate these verbs of removal into two distinct classes:

I *Clear*-verbs: clear, clean, empty
II *Wipe*-verbs: buff, brush, file, mop, pluck, rake, rinse, rub, scour, scrape, scratch, shear, shovel, sponge, trim, vacuum, wipe

Remove belongs to a third class which do not allow alternative expression of their arguments:

III *Remove*-verbs: dislodge, draw, evict, pry, remove, steal, uproot, withdraw, wrench

Levin and Hovav Rappaport's task, then, is to discover the semantic features which determine whether a verb belongs to I, II, or III above. The following generalizations emerge:

    (i) *Clear*-verbs: these verbs all encode the final state of the entity being acted on, but do not encode either the manner in which the final state is achieved or the instrument which is used. Consistent with this, they are typically derived from adjectives denoting the final state: this is true of the verbs *clear*, *clean*, and *empty*, which are zero-derived from adjectives.

(ii) *Wipe*-verbs: these verbs all encode either a manner (e.g. *wipe*) or an instrument (e.g. *brush*), but do not entail that a particular state will result (as the authors point out, the fact that a blackboard has been wiped is no guarantee that it is clean). None of these verbs is de-adjectival (i.e. morphologically derived from an adjective); those, like *brush*, which encode an instrument are typically derived from the noun denoting the instrument.

(iii) *Remove*-verbs: these verbs are characterized by the fact that they encode neither a final state nor a way of carrying out the action.

It is clear from the results of this investigation that, at the very least, there is a close relationship between meaning and grammatical properties.

15.4.6 Modality

Modal expressions are those which signal a particular attitude on the part of the speaker to the proposition expressed or the situation described (typically in a statement). So, for instance, in *It's probably the case that imported versions are cheaper*, the words *It's probably the case (that)* indicate the speaker's assessment of the likelihood of the proposition *imported versions are cheaper* being true. Other modals indicate the degree of desirability (or otherwise) of a proposition becoming true: *I think you should ask John about it first*. Here the speaker indicates his assessment of the merit of bringing about the truth of the proposition *you ask John about it first*.

If we take modality to be a semantic phenomenon, it is clear that it is not exclusively grammatical in nature. Indeed, in the first sentence quoted in the previous paragraph, it is expressed by lexical means. In this chapter, however, we are concerned with grammatical meaning. As far as English is concerned, this involves the so-called **modal verbs**, such as *may, might, should, ought, can*.

15.4.6.1 Epistemic and deontic modality

Consider sentence (109):

(**109**) John should be there by now.

This has two fairly distinct interpretations:

(i) John is under an obligation to be there by now.
(ii) It is likely that John is there by now.

Interpretation (i) is said to be a **deontic** reading of the modal *should*, and interpretation (ii) is said to be an **epistemic** reading. The British linguist Michael Halliday, the leading figure in 'systemic' linguistics, says that epistemic modality calibrates the area of meaning lying between *Yes* and *No*;

whereas deontic modality calibrates the area of meaning between *Do it!* and *Don't do it!* (Halliday 1985).

It is a notable fact that grammatical modal expressions regularly have both epistemic and deontic uses, and this seems to be a universal phenomenon, not confined to English. Various suggested explanations have been put forward for this, either claiming that both are merely special cases of some more general meaning or claiming that the derivation of one from the other (by metaphor, or whatever), is so 'natural' as to be inevitable; however, none of the proposed solutions so far is wholly convincing.

15.4.6.2 Values of modals

Halliday recognizes three strengths or levels of modality: **high, median**, and **low**. In the case of epistemic modality, *high* means a high probability of the truth of the proposition; in the case of deontic modality, *high* designates a high degree of obligation. High and low values can be distinguished from median values by their behaviour with negatives. It is first necessary to distinguish between the negation of the modal and the negation of the proposition. Take the case of (110):

(110) John must leave tomorrow.

If the modal is negated, the meaning would be that John is not obligated to leave tomorrow; if the proposition is negated, the meaning would be that John is obligated to not leave tomorrow. In English, a straightforward syntactic negation results in the proposition being negated semantically:

(111) John must not leave tomorrow.

In order to express the negation of the modal, a different verb is needed:

(112) John need not (i.e. "not-must") leave tomorrow.

It sometimes happens that whether the modal or the proposition is negated by a syntactic negative depends on whether the modal is functioning epistemic-ally or deontically. This is the case, for example, with *may*:

(113) The papers may not be ready. (epistemic: "it is possible that the papers are not ready"; proposition negated)
(114) You may not leave before you have finished your work. (deontic: "you are not allowed to leave before you have finished your work"; modal negated)

High and low values of modality are distinguished from median value by the fact that there is a marked difference in meaning according to whether the modal or the proposition is negated; for a median-value modal, there is relatively little difference of meaning. In the case of high-and low-value modals, negation reverses the value, so that a high-value modal assumes a low value, and vice versa:

(115) You must do it. (high-value modal)

(116) You mustn't do it. (high-value; proposition negated)

(117) You needn't do it. (low-value; modal negated)

(118) You may do it. (low-value modal)

(119) You may not do it. (deontic: high value; modal negated)

(120) It shouldn't be too difficult. (epistemic; modal negated; median value)

(121) It should be not-too-difficult. (epistemic; proposition negated; median value)

Halliday classifies modal verbs as follows:

high: must, ought to, need, have to, is to
median: will, would, shall, should
low: may, might, can, could

15.4.6.3 Modality as deixis

Recently it has been suggested that modality can insightfully be regarded as a form of deixis with a spatial basis, with modals indicating the extent to which the speaker associates with or distances themselves from the proposition. This might have a superficial plausibility, but the arguments are far from compelling. Clearly, modality would have to be seen as a metaphorical extension of space (along the lines of *John and I are very close*). However, modal expressions which contain metaphorically extended spatial terms do not readily spring to mind (modal verbs have no overt connection with space). Moreover, one can just as easily think of modals operating on a scale of something like certainty, on the model of the scales of length, temperature, or whatever, which underlie antonym pairs. This, while perhaps ultimately having some connection with spatial concepts, would indicate a much less direct association between modality and deixis. (Another argument against a *deictic* analysis of modality (even if a spatial analysis is accepted) is that objective interpretations of modals are arguably not oriented towards the speaker.)

15.5 Adjectives and properties

Not all languages have adjectives (the functions that adjectives perform in English being covered by nouns, verbs, or some combination of these); but in those languages which have them, adjectives prototypically denote atemporal properties, that is to say, properties which are relatively stable over time, or which are construed in such a way that no account needs to be taken of the passage of time. Adjectival properties are also prototypically unidimensional, denoting an easily isolable concept, in contrast to prototypical nouns, which denote rich, highly interconnected complexes of properties.

15.5.1 Modification

The principal function of adjectives is **modification**: the combination of Adj. + Noun prototypically restricts the domain designated by the noun alone to a subpart, and designates a subset of the entities denoted by the noun alone.

There are two main positions for adjectives in English:

a long book	**attributive** position
The book is long	**predicative** position

Most adjectives can occur in both positions (there are exceptions: *The man is afraid/*the afraid man*; *the main problem/*The problem is main*). One suggestion as to the semantic correlates of this positional difference is that the predicative position attributes a relatively greater time sensitivity to the designated state of affairs. So, for instance, (122) is slightly more normal than (123), because the temperature of water is inherently changeable:

(122) Be careful, that water is hot.

(123) Be careful, that is hot water.

The normalities are reversed in (124) and (125), because softness is a relatively permanent property:

(124) Don't add too much detergent—our water is soft.

(125) Don't add too much detergent—we have soft water.

This proposal would also offer an explanation of the oddness of *an afraid man*.

Generally speaking, we would expect dispositions to be happier in attributive position and labile states to be happier in predicative position:

(126) He is calm now.

(127) ?He is a calm man now.

(128) ?He is placid now.

(129) He is a placid man now.

In this connection we may contrast *afraid*, which is a labile state, with *timid*, which is a disposition, and has a preference for the attributive position:

(130) *John is timid* is less normal than *John is a timid person*.
    John is an afraid person is less normal than *John is afraid*.

15.5.2 Gradable and non-gradable adjectives

There are two major dichotomies in the classification of adjectives. The first separates **gradable** from **non-gradable** adjectives. This has grammatical consequences, because prototypically, the degree inflections occur only in connection with gradable adjectives; if an adjective is basically non-gradable, then it has to be reinterpreted when inflected for degree (the affix coerces a reinterpretation), as in *Kate was very married* and *Mary is very alive*. These topics are treated in some detail in Chapter 9.

15.5.3 Absolute and syncategorematic adjectives

The second major division among adjectives is between **absolute** and **relative** (or **syncategorematic**) types. A simple test for this distinction is as follows: if Adj. + X (always) entails Adj. + Y, where X is a hyponym of Y, then the adjective is absolute; if there are clear cases where the entailment fails, then the adjective is a relative one. The essence of a relative adjective is that it cannot be interpreted except in connection with the head noun. So, for instance, *a black dog* is *a black animal*, hence *black* is an absolute adjective, but *a small tyrannosaurus* is not *a small animal*, so *small* is a relative adjective.

15.5.4 Order of modifiers

Adjectives have a tendency to occur in a particular order when there are several attached to one noun:

(**131**) three excellent thick sturdy old black front doors
(**132**) *sturdy thick old front black three excellent doors

There have been many attempts to account for this ordering (which is not identical in all languages, although there are general similarities). One approach describes the order in terms of general concept types:

QUANTITY > VALUE > PHYSICAL PROPERTY > AGE > COLOUR

This covers English pretty well (ignoring certain specifiable exceptions), but it leaves much unexplained. An approach that is similar in principle, but more unified, suggests that adjectives denoting more objective properties, which are less susceptible to the vagaries of personal judgement, come nearest to the noun, whereas those that are more a matter of personal opinion come furthest away from the noun. This explains why VALUE is further than COLOUR (this seems to be true of many languages), but it does not explain, for instance, why QUANTITY is the furthest, or why *long* comes before *old*. Nor does it explain why the order is as it is, rather than the reverse. Various partial explanations have been put forward, but none is comprehensively convincing.

15.6 Quantification

Quantification is concerned with expressions like

No Albanians came to the party.
Some of my best friends are troglodytes.
All aardvarks can sing the 'Marseillaise'.

The subject noun phrases in the above are **quantified noun phrases**; the sentences express a quantification.

A quantification requires a **quantifier** (e.g. *no, some, many, all*), a **restriction** (which indicates the sort of things being quantified, e.g. *Albanians*), and a **scope**, which expresses what is true of the items designated by the quantified noun phrase.

15.6.1 Quantifiers in classical predicate logic

Classical predicate logic recognizes just two quantifiers, (i) the **existential quantifier** (usually symbolized as ∃), which in its quantificational properties corresponds to such English expressions as *somebody, a cat, some book*, etc. and (ii) the **universal quantifier** (symbolized as ∀), which corresponds to expressions like *all* men, *every aardvark*, *everybody*. Some idea of the nature of quantifiers can be gained by a closer examination of these. Consider the English sentences below:

(**133**) Everybody saw Mary.
(**134**) Somebody saw Mary.
(**135**) Mary saw somebody.
(**136**) Mary saw everybody.

These would be translated into predicate calculus by means of formulae with roughly the structure of the following:

(i) For all (x), (x) saw Mary.
(ii) For some (x), (x) saw Mary.
(iii) For some (x), Mary saw (x)
(iv) For all (x), Mary saw (x).

Here, (x) is called a **variable**, because it does not have a fixed reference, and the quantifier is said to **bind** the variable. Mary saw (x) is called a **propositional function** and when (x) is given a referential value, it forms/expresses a proposition. For a sentence like *All aardvarks are left-pawed* a more complex representation is required:

For all (x), if (x) is an aardvark then (x) is left-pawed.

And for existential quantification, take An aardvark sang:

For some (x), (x) is an aardvark and (x) sang.

Now let us look at sentences with two quantifiers, for example:

(**137**) Every aardvark saw a springbok.

This sentence is ambiguous: either all the aardvarks saw a particular springbok, or every aardvark had a springbok-viewing experience, but not necessarily of the same springbok. This ambiguity can be captured by placing one quantifier within the scope of the other in two different ways. Suppose we start with the existential quantifier in the outer position, with the universal quantifier in its scope. The resultant sentence has a 'formal' translation as follows:

There exists some (x), such that (x) is a springbok and for all (y), if (y) is an aardvark then (y) saw (x).

Reversing the order of the quantifiers yields:

For all (y), if (y) is an aardvark then there exists some (x) such that (x) is a springbok and (y) saw (x).

Quantifiers interact in regular ways with negatives, and similar sorts of ambiguities can arise as with two quantifiers. Take the sentence *Alf the aardvark didn't see a springbok*. The most natural interpretation of this would be:

It is not the case that there exists a (y) such that (y) was a springbok and Alf saw (y).

Here, the existential quantifier is within the scope of the negative operator (translated as "it is not the case that . . ."). But there is another possible interpretation for this type of structure, as in *John did not see a sniper, and was shot as he crossed the road*. Here the negative is inside the scope of the existential operator:

There existed an (x) such that (x) was a sniper and it is not the case that John saw (x).

There is a similar interaction between a negative and a universal quantifier. Consider the sentence *All the aardvarks did not see Pik*. The most natural interpretation of this is once again with the negative having widest scope:

It is not the case that for all (x), if (x) is an aardvark, (x) saw Pik.

It is less natural to read this sentence with the quantifier having the widest scope:

For all (x), if (x) is an aardvark then it is not the case that (x) saw Pik.

A more natural encoding of this meaning is *None of the aardvarks saw Pik*. If we have two quantifiers and a negative, as in *All the aardvarks did not see a springbok*, there are in theory six possible interpretations, although some of them are somewhat unnatural:

For all (x) if (x) is an aardvark, then it is not the case that there exists a (y) such that (y) is a springbok and (x) saw (y).
(No aardvark saw a springbok)

For all (x) if (x) is an aardvark, then there exists a (y) such that (y) is a springbok and it is not the case that (x) saw it.
(For every aardvark there was a springbok that it did not see)

It is not the case that for all (x) if (x) is an aardvark, then there exists a (y) such that (y) is a springbok and (x) saw (y).
(Not all the aardvarks saw any springbok)

It is not the case that there exists a (y) such that (y) is a springbok and for all (x) if (x) is an aardvark then (x) saw (y).
(No springbok was seen by all the aardvarks)

There exists a (y) such that (y) is a springbok and for all (x) if (x) is an aardvark, then it is not the case that (x) saw (y).
(There is a springbok that none of the aardvarks saw)

There exists a (y) such that it is not the case that for all (x) if (x) is an aardvark then (x) saw (y).
(There is a springbok that was not seen by all the aardvarks)

When one quantifier is within the scope of another, the including quantifier is said to have **wider scope** (this applies not only to the 'classical' quantifiers just dealt with, but to *most, many, a few*, etc.). It is possible to arrange quantifiers in order of their preferences for wide scope; this at least partially determines the preferred readings of propositions with more than one quantifier. One suggestion for the order of preference is as follows:

EACH > EVERY > ALL > MOST > MANY > SEVERAL > SOME > A FEW

The effect of these different degrees of inherent tendency to have wide scope can be seen in the following:

(**138**) A springbok was seen by many aardvarks.
(**139**) A springbok was seen by each aardvark.

In the preferred interpretation of (138), *many* is within the scope of *a*, and we take it that a single springbok is involved. In (139), however, the scopes are reversed, and we assume a plurality of springboks. This is a consequence of the fact that each has the stronger tendency to wide scope, strong enough to override the tendency of a subject to take wide scope, *many*, on the other hand, is overridden by *a* in subject position.

15.6.2 Generalized quantifiers: the 'set' interpretation of quantifiers

The trouble with the classical quantifiers of predicate logic is that, first, there are quantifying expressions that intuitively belong together with *every* and *some/a*, but which cannot be expressed in the predicate calculus (*many, few, more than half*, etc.) and second, there are many whose expression is clumsy and counterintuitive. Ronnie Cann, a formal linguist, gives the following as a translation of *At least two students laughed* (Cann 1993):

There exists an (x) and a (y) such that (x) is a student and (y) is a student and (x) is not the same as (y) and (x) laughed and (y) laughed

This can be adapted for any specific number, but at some cost in plausibility.

A more fruitful way of looking at quantifiers is to say that they express relations of quantity between sets of elements. These are relations which are not concerned with the identity of any of the elements in the sets that they relate to, but only with their numbers. The relevant sets in a quantified sentence such as *Every aardvark sneezed* are (i) the set of things which satisfy the subject nominal, that is, the set of aardvarks, and (ii) the set of things which satisfy the predicate, that is, the set of sneezers. One way of accounting for the relation between these sets which is expressed by the sentence is to say that the set of aardvarks is a subset of the set of sneezers. A more general way which allows a uniform treatment of a wider range of quantifiers is in terms of cardinality, that is, the number of elements in a set, together with operators such as $=$, $>$, $<$. This gives the following interpretations:

(140) Every X is Y: "The number of elements in the set of things that are X but not in the set of things that are Y is zero."

(141) Some X are Y: "The number of elements in the set of things that are both X and Y is greater than zero."

(142) Five X are Y: "The number of elements in the set of things that are both X and Y is five."

(143) Most X are Y: "The number of elements in the set of things that are both X and Y is greater than the number of elements in the set of things that are X but not Y."

(144) Neither X is Y: "The number of elements in the set of things that are both X and Y is zero, and the number of elements in X is two."

Some of these analyses are straightforward, but some merit further discussion. Take the analysis of *most*: as it stands, it would also serve for *the majority of* and *more than half*. Is this an entirely satisfactory account of *most*? Cann (1993) suggests that for at least some speakers *most* requires a greater proportion than *more than half*: that is to say, if out of 100 aardvarks, 51 sneezed and 49 did not, this would not justify the use of *most*, but would satisfy the formula given above (and would justify *more than half*). Cann's solution is to say that the required proportion for *most* is pragmatically determined by reference to context (this should be taken to include the identity of X and Y); he incorporates a contextual proportional factor in the formula. His account of *most* can be expressed verbally as follows:

(145) Most X are Y: "The number of elements in the set of things that are both X and Y is greater than the number of elements in the set of things that are X but not Y multiplied by the contextual factor c."

A contextual factor is also needed for *many*. Cann points out that the proportion which would justify the use of *many* need not be as much as *more than half*; for instance, *Many civil servants receive knighthoods* may mean no more than that the proportion of knighted civil servants is greater than that of other comparable professions, and may still be quite a small percentage. Cann's analysis of *many* is:

(146) Many X are Y: "The number of elements in the set of things that are both X and Y is greater than the number of elements in the set of things that are X multiplied by the contextual factor c."

It should be noted, however, that the c which appears in (145) is not the same as that which appears in (146); strictly speaking, therefore they should be distinguished as c_{most} and c_{many}.

15.6.3 Conservativity

Conservativity appears to be a property of all natural language quantifiers (taking as a defining feature of quantifiers that they are syntactically determiners). Consider the following:

(147) Every aardvark sneezed.
      Some aardvarks sneezed.
      No aardvark sneezed.

In assessing the truth of these sentences, we are constrained to consider the set of aardvarks, and we do not need to consider anything that is not an aardvark. The quantified noun phrase establishes the universe of discourse. Contrast these with (148), where the truth cannot be established by looking only at aardvarks, since non-aardvarks must also be considered:

(148) Everything except aardvarks sneezed.

The quantifier phrases in (147) are said to be conservative; that in (148) is not conservative. Cann suggests that conservativity can be recognized by para-phrasability, as follows:

(149) Every aardvark sneezed.   = Every aardvark is an aardvark that sneezed.
      Some aardvarks sneezed. = Some aardvarks are aardvarks that sneezed.
      No aardvark sneezed.   = No aardvark is an aardvark that sneezed.

Notice that (148) cannot be paraphrased in this way:

(150) Everything except aardvarks sneezed. ≠ Everything except aardvarks is an aardvark that sneezed.

15.6.4 Directional entailingness

From sentence (151):

(151) Every dog barked.

we can validly infer *Every spaniel barked*, but not *Every animal barked*; we can also infer *Every dog made a noise*, but not *Every dog barked loudly*. Notice that the valid entailment goes from less specific to more specific for the subject term, but from more specific to less specific for the predicate term; more technically, the subject in (151) is **downward-entailing**, and the predicate is **upward-entailing**. The directional pattern of entailment is characteristic of the quantifier *every*, which creates a downward-entailing environment for its subject and an upward-entailing environment for its predicate. The full range of patterns is as follows:

15.6.4.1 Subject upward-entailing; predicate upward-entailing

(152) If some dogs barked, then some animals barked.
(153) If some animals barked, then some animals made a noise.
        (provided *some* is interpreted as "at least one")
(154) *If some dogs barked, then some spaniels barked.
(155) *If some dogs barked, then some dogs barked loudly.

15.6.4.2 Subject and predicate downward-entailing

(156) If no dogs barked, then no spaniels barked.
(157) If no dogs barked, then no dogs barked loudly.
(158) *If no dogs barked, then no animals barked.
(159) *If no dogs barked, then no dogs made a noise.

15.6.4.3 Subject downward-entailing, predicate upward-entailing

(160) If every dog barked, then every spaniel barked.
(161) If every dog barked, then every dog made a noise.
(162) *If every dog barked, then every animal barked.
(163) *If every dog barked, then every dog barked loudly.

15.6.4.4 Subject no entailment, predicate upward-entailing

(164) If most dogs barked, then most dogs made a noise.
        (provided *most* is interpreted not to exclude "all")
(165) *If most dogs barked, then most spaniels barked.
(166) *If most dogs barked, then most animals barked.
(167) *If most dogs barked, then most dogs barked loudly.

15.6.5 Negative polarity items

Directional entailment properties correlate in an interesting way with so-called **negative polarity items (negpols)**. These are expressions which are only normal in certain types of environment, typically containing a negative element of some kind. Typical examples are *anyone, anything, ever*:

(168) He never says anything.
        He rarely says anything.
        I haven't seen anyone.
        No one has ever reached the top.
        Few people have ever reached the top.

Compare the normality of these with those in (169):

(169) *A man has ever reached the top.
　　　*All men have ever reached the top.
　　　*Some men have ever reached the top.
　　　*Most men have ever reached the top.
　　　*Many men have ever reached the top.
　　　*He always says anything.
　　　*He sometimes says anything.
　　　*He usually says anything.

The correlation with direction of entailment is that negpols are allowed in downward-entailing environments, but not in upward-entailing environments or environments where there is no entailment. This correlation is interesting, but it does not really constitute an explanation. There are other interesting properties of negpols, such as the fact that some occur happily with questions while others do not, and the fact that some occur happily with conditionals while others do not:

(170) I didn't say anything.
　　　Did you say anything?
　　　If you say anything, you're finished.
(171) I didn't say a word.
　　　*Did you say a word?
　　　If you say a word, you're finished.
(172) It won't take long.
　　　Will it take long?
　　　*If it takes long, I'm not going to do it.

Discussion questions and exercises

1. In what way(s) is the number-related behaviour of the following English nouns unusual?

   cattle   oats   scissors   iron filings

2. Construct a set of sentences parallel to (28)–(36) in this chapter, but with the secondary tense in the subordinate clause, and the reference time in the main clause, as in:

   When John had eaten, Bill switched off the lights.

   Notice the different distribution of forms.

3. What event types are represented by the following sentences?

    (a) I'll just hang these things out to dry.
    (b) Smoke was coming out of the bedroom window.
    (c) I know that man.
    (d) Jane caught a cold yesterday.
    (e) Mary is practising for the concert.
    (f) There was a knock on the door.

4. What case roles are represented by the italicized items in the following?

    (a) *John* watched *the squirrel*.
    (b) Mary put the cup *on the table*.
    (c) *You* can taste the wine. (two possible answers)
    (d) We followed *the river* for three miles.
    (e) John drilled *a hole* in the wall, then filled *it* with plaster.
    (f) They left *London* yesterday.
    (g) *The storm* had ripped the roof off.
    (h) Mary bought *John* a tie.

5. The notion of modality is sometimes extended beyond modal verbs proper to expressions like it is possible that. Classify the following as high-, median- or low-value modals:

    it is probable that
    it is possible that
    it is unlikely that
    it is certain that

6. How would you characterize the following verbs in terms of Levin and Hovav Rappaport's three classes?

    erase drain extract sweep unload scrub

7. Which of the following are implicitly negative (examine their collocability with negpols)?

    hardly often seldom occasionally
    mostly a few far (from) near
    free (from) beware of take care to avoid

Suggestions for further reading

The most complete currently available account of grammatical semantics is Frawley (1992), which covers all the topics dealt with in this chapter in a fairly accessible way. For a fuller treatment of individual topics, the following may also be consulted:

- *Number: Allan (1986: i: 120 ff.) and Cruse (1994a).
- Tense and aspect: Dahl (1985); Kearns (2000: chs. 8, 9).
- Participant roles: Fillmore (1968; 1977); Kearns (2000: ch. 10).
- Modality: Palmer (1986); Halliday (1985).
- Quantifiers: Cann (1993); Larson and Segal (1995: chs. 7 and 8).

Part 4
Pragmatics

Part 4 deals with topics which are normally held to fall under the heading of pragmatics. The topics of reference and deixis, and conversational implicatures, dealt with in Chapters 16 and 18 respectively, belong uncontroversially here, since they deal not only with aspects of meaning not overtly encoded as the conventional meaning of any linguistic expressions but also with how language 'hooks on to' the extralinguistic world. Speech acts, on the other hand, the topic of Chapter 17, straddle the semantics/pragmatics divide somewhat uncomfortably: performative verbs arguably belong to lexical semantics, and grammatical performatives, like interrogatives and imperatives, would not be out of place in Chapter 15. However, much illocutionary force is implicated, and to that extent belongs in pragmatics. It is customary to treat the various aspects of speech act theory as belonging to pragmatics, and this convention has been followed here.

Reference and deixis

Reference and deixis

16.1 Reference

The topic of **reference** has been the cause of an outflow of gallons of recondite ink: some of the subtlest philosophical minds have grappled with it, and the debates have been contentious and inconclusive. What is put forward in this chapter is necessarily of an introductory nature.

Under the heading of reference we encounter one of the most fundamental and vital aspects of language and language use, namely, the relations between language, as a medium of communication between human beings, and the world, about which we communicate. One of the most basic things that we do when we communicate through language is to pick out entities in the world and ascribe properties to them, or indicate relations between them. Reference is concerned with designating entities in the world by linguistic means.

Right at the start we encounter deep controversies. One of these concerns the basic nature of reference. Let us take it for the moment as uncontroversial (it isn't) that one of the terms in an instance of the relation of reference is something in the world. What is the other term? The obvious choices are a linguistic expression, such as *Tom*, or *the man*, and the person speaking. It is commonplace in discussions of linguistic matters to say things like: *George Bush* (in, say, *George Bush is to visit Ireland in May*) 'refers to the current president of the United States'. Here we are putting forward an expression and a person as the terms of the relation of reference. However, there is no privileged one-to-one relationship between the expression *George Bush* and the George Bush who is president of the USA. There are doubtless hundreds (at least) of George Bushes in the world. *George Bush* referred to the current president of the USA only because some speaker intended to use the expression for that purpose on some particular occasion. Here we have a unique one-to-one relation: that between the speaker's intention to refer and the president of the USA. We shall therefore adopt Searle's (1969) position, and say that reference is not an inherent property of expressions, but is a speech act. This is not to say, of course, that the speech act of reference is unconstrained by the linguistic expressions used; on the contrary, certain expressions are specially adapted for this function, as we shall see.

Two further uses of the word 'reference' should be signalled, one of which will be occasionally adopted here, the other not. It is common to speak of the reference of a linguistic expression, meaning the things it has been used on some specific occasion to refer to. So, for instance, in a newspaper headline *George Bush to visit Ireland in May*, the reference (in this sense) of *George Bush* is the present president of the USA. This seems to be harmless, and does not lead to confusion. (If there is any danger of confusion we shall use 'referent(s)'.) Another common usage is to say that, for instance, *dog* refers to the class of dogs, and that the reference of *dog* is the class of dogs. This is contrary to our usage, and it will not be adopted. We shall follow Lyons (1968), and say that *dog* **denotes** the class of dogs, and that the class of dogs constitutes the **denotation** of dog. (There is, of course, a relation between what an expression denotes and what acts of reference it can be used in the performance of: the former constrains the latter.)

We have so far assumed that the distal term of the relation of reference is something in the world. But this, too, is rife with controversy, and goes even deeper than the controversy just mentioned. Are there, indeed, any such things as 'things in the world'? Are things not mental constructs? In which case we should specify that reference is to do with things in the experienced world, not in the objective world. Of course, we assume there is some connection between these two worlds, but the relation between referrers and the objective world is indirect. This position is compellingly argued by Jackendoff (1983), and will be assumed here to be correct, although we shall continue to speak merely of things in the world.

16.1.1 Definite reference

There are various types and modes of reference. We shall concentrate on three: **definite reference**, **indefinite reference**, and **generic reference**. There is no doubt that it is definite reference which is the most crucial for the functioning of language. (In the philosophical literature it is usually called 'singular definite reference'; for our purposes, however, there are no particular problems in moving from singular to plural.)

To open the discussion of definite reference, consider the two sentences below:

(1) The man gave it to her.
(2) A man gave it to her.

How does the meaning of sentence (1) differ from the meaning of sentence (2)? Obviously both indicate an act of giving by some adult male person (we shall ignore the rest of the sentence). The features which distinguish (1) from (2) can be set out as follows:

(a) The intended referential target is necessarily a particular entity (believed by the speaker to fall into the category MAN, but notice that the speaker can be mistaken about this and still, on some particular occasion, successfully refer), who can in principle be uniquely identified by the speaker.

This means that the speaker should be able, on demand, to give information that for them distinguishes the (man) in question from all other men. The speaker may not be able to name the man, or even give any descriptive information: for instance, what makes the man unique may be only that he occasioned an auditory experience on the part of the speaker at a particular time and place.

(b) The speaker intends that the referential target should come to be uniquely identified for the hearer, too.

This is in fact the main point of the act of reference. Once again, the information which enables the hearer to uniquely identify the intended referent may be minimal.

(c) The act of reference brings with it to the hearer an implicit assurance that they have enough information to uniquely identify the referent, taking into account the semantic content of the referring expression (or other properties of the expression which limit the search space), and information available from context, whether situational (i.e. currently perceivable), linguistic, or mental (i.e. memory and knowledge).

Searle makes a quaint distinction between a 'successful' act of reference, which requires only (a) to hold, and a 'fully consummated' act of reference, which requires also (b). (The act of reference is thus like having an orgasm: one can do it on one's own, but to be fully consummated we need a partner.) We can follow Searle, and add the following features/conditions for a fully successful act of referring (not necessarily distinctive for referring):

(d) Normal input and output conditions hold.

This just means that, for instance, speaker and hearer speak the same language, the utterance is both audible and comprehensible to the hearer, and so on.

(e) The act of reference is embedded in a more inclusive speech act.

An act of reference cannot stand on its own as a communication: *the man* communicates nothing, except when embedded in a sentence like *I saw the man*, or as an answer to a question such as *What can you see?*

(f) The speaker intends that the hearer should recognize his intention to refer by virtue of his having produced the utterance in question.
(g) Prototypically, the part of the utterance the production of which is intended to signal the intention to refer should have a form which conventionally performs this function.

In general, the identification of the referents of definite referring expressions is necessary so that the hearer can reconstruct the proposition(s) being expressed by the speaker, as these specify the arguments of such propositions. (We shall not discuss here the knotty problem of exactly what the terms of a proposition are, i.e. whether they are things in the objective world or the experienced world, or entities in the same sort of platonic realm as numbers, etc.)

16.1.2 Indefinite reference

Sentence (2) above is an example of indefinite reference. The essence of indefinite reference is that the identity of the referent is not germane to the message: that is, nothing hinges on the identity of the referent; only the class that the referent belongs to is presented as relevant. Notice that this has nothing to do with whether or not either speaker or hearer is in fact able to effect a unique identification of the referent. Suppose someone complains of extreme boredom, and in response I pick up a book and offer it to them, saying either (i) *Here, read a book*, or (ii) *Here, read this book*. What is the difference? In both cases the identity of the book may well be known to both participants. The crucial difference is that in (i) the identity of the book is not germane to the message, just the fact that it is a book, whereas in (ii) the identity of the book is presented as important to the message.

We have so far only considered the indefinite article as a signal of indefiniteness. However, all the following sentences contain indefinite expressions:

Come up and see me sometime.
I expect he's hiding somewhere.
You'll manage somehow.
Are you looking for something/somebody?
She met this sailor.
Some man gave it to him.
To make the spell work, you have to say certain words.

Consider now the following sentence:

(3) To get the automatic door to open you have to say a word.

This can be interpreted in two ways: either it is the case that any word will open the door, or a specific one is necessary. This is the classic **specific/non-specific** distinction in indefinites, which has given rise to much discussion. It is usually claimed that the distinction is operative only in certain modal contexts, for example with *want, must, have to*, and so on (the standard example is *Mary wants to marry a Norwegian banker*). It is true that there are circumstances where the difference is hard to intuit (e.g. *Mary married a banker*), but this may simply be because it is difficult to construct a context where the distinction would be relevant. It would be difficult to extend the idea of 'modality' to cover the following cases, where the distinction can easily be felt:

(4) A: How did he get the door to open?

B: He said a word.

(5) A: Why was Mary angry?

B: Because John bought a book.

The specific readings of *a word* in (4) and *a book* in (5) are very close to "a certain word" and "a certain book", respectively. (I am referring here to what I assume are central uses of *a certain X*; there are (presumably) marginal cases where the use represents the deliberate avoidance of a proper name for (presumably) non-semantic reasons, that is, the proper name, would, other things being equal, have been appropriate:

(6) I spoke to a certain person about you-know-what.

The 'specific indefinite' readings in (4) and (5) share with the meaning of the corresponding definite expression (*the word* and *the book*) the implication that the identity of the referent, as opposed to merely the class of the referent, is relevant to the situation described; what distinguishes these readings from definites is that the speaker does not signal to the hearer that the identification of the referent is essential to the message being conveyed. Notice that *this* can also function as a specific indefinite:

(7) We met this man in the pub.

This usage seems to signal that the man in question has been introduced as a topic about which more will be said; *a certain man* does not function in this way.

There has been some controversy about whether sentences like (3) are genuinely ambiguous between the two readings, or whether the specific reading is merely a contextual enrichment of the non-specific reading. This is somewhat difficult to decide. One can point to the fact that in some languages, the distinction is made grammatically:

(8) Marie cherche un homme qui **peut** lui faire l'amour douze fois par jour.

(9) Marie cherche un homme qui **puisse** lui faire l'amour douze fois par jour.

("Marie is looking for a man who can make love to her twelve times a day")

In (8), Marie knows exactly who(m) she is looking for; in (9) she is simply overly optimistic. The difference is signalled by indicative vs. subjunctive mood in the verb.

In Turkish, a difference of this kind can be signalled by the presence or absence of the direct object marker on the noun:

(10) Bir **kelime** söyledi. ("S/he said a word"; non-specific)

(11) Bir **kelimeyi** söyledi. ("S/he said a word"; specific)

But such observations are not conclusive as far as ambiguity is concerned.

If we take it that the specific indefinite is more specific than the non-specific indefinite in the same—or a similar—sense in which *dog* is more specific than *animal*, then we can apply the independent truth-condition test. Recall examples like the following:

(12) A: Does John drink?
      B: No, he'll just have an orange juice.

This shows that the specific reading of *drink* (= "drink alcohol") has independence.

The specific reading of *child* (= "girl"), on the other hand, does not pass this test:

(13) A: Was it a child who answered the door?
      B: *No, it was a boy.

We can now apply the same test to indefinites. First notice the normality of the following:

(14) A: Do you have to say a certain word?
      B: No, any word will do.

If *a word* is ambiguous, with "a certain word" as one of its readings, the following ought to be normal:

(15) A: Do you have to say a word?
      B: No, any word will do.

Clearly this is not normal, and this is evidence for the lack of distinctness of the specific reading.

At least one analysis of indefinites (Hawkins 1978) claims that the use of an indefinite implies that reference is being made to one item out of a set of similar items. Suppose A says, *I can't see to read in my bedroom* and B replies, *Take a lamp from the dining room*. This seems to implicate that there is more than one lamp in the dining room, otherwise B would have said, *Take the lamp from the dining room*. However, this is not quite true: the facts are more complex. Suppose B does not know how many lamps there are in the dining room. In that case, B will still say, *Take a lamp.* . . . That is to say, the true implicature of *a lamp*, out of context, is that a plurality of (qualifying) lamps is not excluded. A will take an implicature that there is more than one lamp only if they know (or assume) that B knows how many lamps there are. The claim Hawkins should have made, therefore, is that the use of an indefinite implicates that reference is not knowingly being made to an item uniquely defined by the linguistic expression used. If the referent is known by the speaker to be thus uniquely defined, but the particular identity is not specially relevant, then some other construction must be used, for instance, *There's a lamp in the dining room you could use.*

16.1.3 Generic reference

Now consider the following sentences:

(16) The tiger is a friendly beast.
(17) A tiger is a friendly beast.
(18) Tigers are friendly beasts.

Sentence (16) is ambiguous, with a reading which is irrelevant to our current concerns, but all three have readings which involve what is called generic reference, that is, reference to a class of referents. All of the above predicate friendliness as a general characteristic of the members of the class of tigers. None of them is inconsistent with minor exceptions, but all of them are inconsistent with the existence of a significant sub-class of unfriendly tigers:

(19) The tiger, with few exceptions, is a friendly beast.
(20) ?The tiger is a friendly beast, although there are many that are not friendly.
(21) A tiger is a friendly beast, although there is the occasional exception.
(22) ?A tiger is a friendly beast, although many of them aren't.
(23) Tigers, with few exceptions, are friendly beasts.
(24) ?Tigers are friendly beasts, although many of them aren't.

None of the above is synonymous with *All tigers are friendly beasts* or *Every tiger is a friendly beast*:

(25) *All tigers are friendly beasts, although there are a few exceptions.

There are two sorts of proposition involving generic reference as argument: either something is predicated of the whole class referred to, or something is predicated of each member of the class. These two readings available under the heading of generic reference are known as the **collective** reading and the **distributed** reading respectively. The types of generic in (16), (17), and (18) have different affinities for these two uses. The form *the X* strongly prefers the collective reading:

(26) The tiger is extinct.
(27) The tiger is a widely distributed species.
(28) ??I like watching the tiger.

The form *a(n) X* will accept only distributive uses:

(29) *A tiger is extinct.
(30) *A tiger is widely distributed.
(31) A tiger has a long tail.
(32) I like watching a tiger.

Notice that this last sentence is singular, that is to say, it expresses enjoyment of watching a single tiger. This is why it will not accept distributive plural uses (i.e. those where the basic fact involves individuals, not the species, but a plurality of individuals is necessary):

(33) The computer has revolutionized business practices.
(34) Computers have revolutionized business practices.
(35) *A computer has revolutionized business practices.

The form *Xs* will accept either use:

(36) Tigers are extinct.
(37) Tigers are widely distributed.
(38) I like watching tigers.

(Notice that in (38), the plurality of *tigers* does not fall under the scope of *like watching*—one can with perfect propriety reply: *Good, here's one for you*.)

16.1.4 Non-referential uses of referring expressions

It is as well to note that although the expression *a tiger* in many of its uses can be used in the act of indefinite reference, it is not always so used, as for instance in (39):

(39) This animal is a tiger.

Most analysts agree that this sentence does not state that there is a tiger that this animal is identical with. For instance, it does not make sense to ask *Which tiger is it?* It seems clear that *a tiger* here stands for a set of properties which are being predicated of this animal. This enables us to give a satisfying account of (one) reading of *John is a complete politician*, namely, that John has all the properties which are characteristic of (prototypical) politicians.

16.2 Definite reference

We shall henceforward concentrate on definite reference, which is arguably the prototypical type of reference.

16.2.1 Types of definite referring expression

The following types of expression are definite referring expressions in English:

   (i) noun phrase with definite determiners: *the book, this book, that book, my book, your book, his book, her book, our book, their book*;
   (ii) personal pronouns: *I, you, he, she, it, us,* they;
   (iii) proper names: *John, Mary, Paris, Gone with the Wind, Middlemarch, Notre Dame, Parsifal, Guernica*;
   (iv) certain locative adverbs: *here, there, yonder*;
   (v) certain temporal adverbs: *now, then, yesterday, next Xmas*;

(vi) verb tense: a statement like *I saw her* involves a reference to a definite time (unlike *I have seen her*).

Definiteness can also be argued to be present in some unexpected places. Consider the difference between the following two sentences:

(40) Mary's watching.
(41) Mary's reading.

These two sentences have several features in common. Neither verb makes sense without there being something which plays the role of direct object, or theme of the action: one can't read or watch, without reading or watching ***something***. Furthermore, in neither case is the theme of the action explicitly mentioned. However, there is a crucial difference between them: the hearer is required to recover (from the context) a specific direct object for *watch*, but not for *read*. We shall borrow Matthews's term and say that there is a **latent** direct object in (40). The evidence for this is as follows.

(i) 'Reading' counts as an autonomous activity. 'Watching' does not. Imagine someone (A) standing outside the closed door of a room, speaking to (B) who is inside the room:

(42) A: What are you doing?
     B(1): I'm reading
     B(2): ?I'm watching.

The reason B's second answer is odd is that A is not in a position to recover the 'missing' direct object.

(ii) *Watch* gives rise to an identity constraint in verb-phrase anaphora, whereas *read* does not:

(43) John is reading; so is Bill
(44) Mary is watching; so is Sue.

For (44) to be normal, Mary and Sue have to be watching the same thing (which could, of course, be the same television programme on two widely separated television sets); there is no need for John and Bill in (43) to be reading the same thing.

The use of a relative adjective like *tall* can be argued to involve covert reference to a reference value for underlying variable property. Thus, *Mary is tall* means something like "Mary's height is greater than X to a noteworthy extent", where X is the reference value for height.

The use of an ambiguous word such as *bank* likewise involves a kind of definiteness: in, for example, *We finally reached the bank*, the speaker intends one specific sense out of the possibilities to be operative, and intends that the hearer be able to identify the same sense, its identity being crucial to the message.

Except in the case of latency, it is not possible to convey pure definiteness, and even in such cases the search space for the intended referent is heavily constrained by selectional restrictions and so on; that is to say, it is virtually always the case that some sort of extra help is given to the hearer in selecting the intended referent(s), and this is typically overtly encoded. So, for instance, *the book* indicates that the intended referent falls within the denotation of *book* (i.e. is an instance of the concept BOOK), *he* indicates that the referent is singular, human, male, and neither speaker nor hearer in the current speech situation, *John* constrains the search to those who bear that name, and so on. The types of 'help' that speakers give to hearers can be roughly grouped under three headings: describing (e.g. *human, male, book*), pointing (e.g. *that book* is relatively distant from speaker), and naming. These are not, of course, mutually exclusive: a given expression may incorporate more than one of these. We shall now examine separately, and in greater detail, three central types of definite expression: noun phrases with the definite article, proper names, and deictic expressions.

16.2.2 Definite descriptions (noun phrases with definite article)

It has been sometimes claimed that the way definite descriptions work is to provide sufficient information to distinguish the referent from all other possible referents, that is, to render it unique (presumably in the universe). This is not of course ruled out: if someone refers to *the boil on my nose*, and there is clearly only one boil on the speaker's nose, then that illustrious object has been distinguished from all other objects in the universe. But this cannot be a general truth about definite descriptions. Consider the following three instances:

(45) A: Have you seen Pride and Prejudice?
      B: No, but I've read **the book**.

The emphasized noun phrase refers successfully, but the only descriptive information offered is that the referent belongs to the class of books, and there are billions of these in existence.

(46) A: (in restaurant) I didn't want custard on my pie.
      B: You should have told **the waitress**.
(47) A: (at breakfast in hotel on holiday in Durham) What shall we do today?
      B: I think we should go and see **the cathedral**.

In none of these cases is enough information given overtly within the definite noun phrase to uniquely distinguish the intended referent, yet they all refer successfully. How is this possible? Of course, in each of the above cases the hearer ends up in possession of enough information to characterize the referent uniquely. The question is really: what principles govern the amount of information the speaker has to provide explicitly? Sometimes this may be quite a lot:

(**48**) Could you send me the small blue book near the right-hand end of the second shelf from the bottom of the bookshelves in my bedroom?

In (45), (46), and (47), the amount of information is quite limited (even so, it is perhaps more than strictly necessary in some cases: e.g. in (45), *I've read it* would probably do), but at least in some cases it is necessary. So, for instance, *the building* would probably not suffice for (47). What we shall say is that the job of the speaker is to give enough information to uniquely specify the referent within some limited domain. Then, provided that the hearer can identify the relevant domain, the information given will suffice. So, for instance, in (45), the hearer merely needs to identify a book pertaining to something that has just been mentioned; in (46), there are thousands of waitresses in the world, but only one relevant to the current immediate situation that A and B find themselves in; a similar explanation is valid for (47), except that the situation is a broader and less immediate one. This is all very well, but merely pushes the problem back one stage: how does the hearer identify the relevant domain within which the description offered uniquely characterizes the referent? The process goes something like this. The hearer makes an ordered search through possible domains, roughly in the order: (i) immediately preceding discourse (more strictly, within short-term memory), (ii) immediate situation (currently available to senses), (iii) broader situation, (iv) memory/general knowledge. We need to assume that these are in decreasing order of accessibility (in terms of amount of cognitive work needed to activate them). So, if a qualifying referent is found in the first domain, then that is taken as the intended referent (if there is more than one qualifying referent in the first domain, the speaker has failed to refer successfully). If there is no qualifying referent in the first domain, the hearer then searches the next most accessible domain, and so on, until he finds a suitable potential referent. This account (adapted from Cruse 1980) is broadly compatible with a relevance-theoretical (RT) account (see Chapter 18).

16.2.3 Proper names

Proper names, too, have given rise to a great deal of discussion, especially within the philosophy of language. There are two diametrically opposed extreme positions with regard to proper names. One of these says that proper names have no meaning whatsoever: this is usually expressed by saying that they have extension, but no intension. That is to say, they are unlike, for instance, *the dog*, which can be used to refer to canines in the extralinguistic world by virtue of the intension, that is, the semantic content, of *dog*. Whereas a proper name like *John* can be used to refer to an individual referent, it does not do so by virtue of its semantic content, but by virtue of some other property, namely, that it is borne by the referent as a name. Imagine we have a batch of identical boxes which we may want to designate individually at some time. The most convenient way would be to stick a numbered label on each of them: we could then talk about *Box 235* and so on. It is clear that the numbers do not constitute in any way descriptions of the boxes, and have no essential connection with their respective boxes. On the view of proper names currently under examination, proper names are no more meaningful than the numbers on the boxes. They function to individuate members of large sets of similar entities, to distinguish which by means of descriptions would be either cumbersome, if sufficient details were known, or impossible, if they are not known. Hence, we find proper names used particularly for people and places.

The opposite view of proper names from the above is that proper names function as abbreviated descriptions: they stand for the sum of the properties that distinguish the bearer from all other referents, or, to put it another way, they get their meaning by association, not with generic concepts, in the way that common nouns like *dog* do, but with individual concepts. Thus, just as we say *It's a dog* entails *It's an animal*, and this is ultimately a consequence of the properties of the concepts DOG and ANIMAL, in reference to the present writer we would also say *It's Alan* entails *It's a man*, because of the relation between the individual concept ALAN CRUSE and the generic concept MAN. It might be objected here that there are many individuals who bear the name *Alan*, and hence the entailment does not hold. However, there is more than one concept DOG (viz. the part of an old-fashioned fireplace where vessels are placed), and hence, by this argument, the former entailment does not hold, either. But there is no reason why ambiguity should invalidate entailment, as long as a determinate sense is intended on the occasion of use. On this view, the only difference between the *dog* case and the *Alan* case is the greater degree of homonymy in the latter. (Notice that in a use such as *There were three Alans in the room*, the word *Alan* is not being used as a proper noun, that is to say, there is no activation of associated individual concepts; *Alan* functions in such cases as a common noun meaning "person bearing the name Alan".)

Here we have two apparently irreconcilable views. In fact, it will be argued here that both are (partially) correct. Let us first look at objections to each of the views. A standard argument against the second view, that proper names are abbreviated descriptions, is that the continuing use of proper names for reference is immune to changing conceptions of the nature of the referent: proper names have stable referential properties. We may, for instance, discover that someone we have come to think of as a gypsy princess called Toni turns out to be a Welshman: we can on such a discovery say, without a hint of contradiction, *My friend Toni isn't a gypsy princess, but a Welsh ex-miner* (notice we don't say *He's not Toni after all* nor *Toni doesn't exist any more* nor even *Toni has changed*). How is this possible, if proper names stand for an individual concept? We shall return to this in a moment.

There are also arguments against the proposal that proper names are devoid of meaning. One is that there must be an associated set of properties of some kind, which are in some way defining, or at least distinctive, otherwise one would never be able to say *No, that's not John, that's Bill*. (Notice that even after the traumatic discovery of the previous paragraph, one would still not be in a position to say *That's not Toni*: it is, on the other hand, inconceivable that the name would persist if *every* property changed.) Another argument, or at least a pertinent observation, is that many common nouns have a similar property of denotational stability in the face of modifications in the concept. These are the so-called natural-kind terms, like *water, gold, or tiger*. We shall at some time have to integrate these into our picture. A different line of argument is to point out that, for instance, it would be odd to christen a girl *John*, or *The Old Mill*, or even *Littlehampton*, nor would we expect a boy to be called *Daffodil*, or a country to be called *Mary*. We also say things like: *He doesn't look at all like a Cecil*. Why do we do this if (a) names have no semantic properties and (b) we expect to be understood?

We seem to faced with a welter of apparently contradictory facts. Yet a satisfying account of proper-name-hood should accommodate them all without strain. Let us consider in more detail how proper names work, and enquire why all languages seem to have them, and what distinctive function they serve. The question can first be considered in the light of the three ways a speaker aids a hearer in selecting the appropriate referent. It will be remembered that three main ways were postulated: describing, naming, and pointing. How does naming help the hearer? The case of naming is not fundamentally different from the case of describing where a speaker gives enough descriptive information to render the referent unique in some relevant domain. Something similar is true of the use of proper names: the speaker uses a proper name when only one referent within the most relevant domain bears it; in other words, the name renders the referent unique within the domain. In a definite description, it is the descriptive information that performs the act of selection. Searle (1969) makes a point of declaring that "bears the name John" is not an adequate paraphrase of the meaning of John. And in many important ways this is true. However, it is by means of this aspect of its meaning that a proper name refers to or selects its referent. It is clear that in most circumstances, referring by means of a proper name is much more economical than referring by means of description. In most everyday domains, there is only one John: another way of referring, however, would be necessary at a congress of Johns. It is probably an advantage, too, that proper names are, as it were, reusable. Speakers normally have a limited inventory of possible proper names (at least for people). It would be uneconomical to have a different name for everyone one knows.

Searle also stresses the importance of the fact that a proper name must be associated with a set of properties—with an individual concept of some sort, in our terms. Otherwise it would not be possible to use a proper name consistently, that is, by referring to the same individual on each occasion of use: we must have some way of recognizing that individual. The importance of the associated individual concept, however, goes even beyond that: in the act of expressing a proposition using a proper name in argument position, it is the individual concept that forms the true argument of which something is predicated. Notice, too, that a sentence like *Even John thinks that the story must be true* relies on the association of certain properties with John. It is also true, however, that we must not lose sight of the fact that changing an individual concept does not entail a change of name: the concepts associated with proper names are, in a sense, always 'interim', and liable to modification at any time. Again, this is unlike descriptions. Searle puts this forward as another functional virtue that proper names possess: their flexibility. It is useful to have ways of referring that are not tied to particular constant conceptual properties. It enables us to refer successfully to entities about which we know very little. A similar functional virtue attaches to natural-kind terms. It might be proposed that these are particularly adapted to entities whose essences are mysterious. (It is a moot point whether, for instance, STALLION and HORSE are different sorts of concept, or whether they are basically the same sort of concept, but they are attached to the words *stallion* and *horse* in different ways.)

On a rather different point, proper nouns and noun phrases with the definite article share a property which distinguishes them from other definite expressions, especially pronouns, and that is that they signal that their referents have a relatively low accessibility. This means that relatively more cognitive effort is required to bring them to the forefront of consciousness. This may, for instance, be because of low salience, or perhaps because their memory trace is fading owing to the time elapsed since the last activation. Pronouns, on the other hand, signal high accessibility. This difference shows up clearly in **anaphoric** uses of definite expressions. For instance, assuming the items in bold are co-referential, (48a) and (49a) are markedly less normal than (49b) and (50b), respectively:

(**49**) a. We saw **John** in the park this morning; **John** was wearing pyjamas.
      b. We saw **John** in the park this morning; **he** was wearing pyjamas.
(**50**) a. There was **a man** in the park this morning; **the man** was wearing pyjamas.
      b. There was **a man** in the park this morning; **he** was wearing pyjamas.

If we make 'the man' less accessible, for instance, by supplying a competing antecedent, then the definite description becomes the normal option:

(**51**) a. We saw **a man** and a boy in the park this morning; **the man** was wearing pyjamas.
      b. We saw **a man** and a boy in the park this morning; **he** was wearing pyjamas.

16.2.4 Indirect reference

Indirect reference is reference to something by means of a linguistic expression whose default use is to refer to something else. We have already encountered two species of indirect reference, metaphor and metonymy (Chapter 11). But the phenomenon goes beyond these, and includes cases which would not normally be considered to fall under either. A typical case involves characters in plays and films, and the actors who portray those characters. Imagine a situation where John and his wife, Mary, both act in a play. John plays a character called Ralph, and Mary a character called Elizabeth. In the play, Ralph and Elizabeth are lovers; the character Ralph is poisoned in the third act by Elizabeth's mother Joan (played by Mary's sister Alice), who hates him, and doesn't want him to marry her daughter. In this situation, all the following sentences (and many more similar) have valid interpretations:

(52) John is married to Mary.
(53) John and Mary are lovers.
(54) Ralph and Elizabeth are lovers.
(55) Ralph is married to Elizabeth.
(56) John is poisoned in the third act.
(57) John gets poisoned by Alice.
(58) Alice is Ralph's mother-in-law.
(59) Alice doesn't want Elizabeth to marry Ralph.

To account for this and similar cases, the cognitive linguist Gilles Fauconnier (1994) proposes an **identification principle**:

If two objects (in the most general sense), a and b, are linked by a pragmatic function $F(b\ F(a))$, a description of a, d_a, may be used to identify its counterpart b.

In the above case, there is a pragmatic function, which we can label 'dramatic portrayal', linking John to Ralph, Mary to Elizabeth, and Alice to Elizabeth's mother. By virtue of this, we can refer to actors by the names of the characters they portray, and vice versa. Notice that each of the sentences (51–8) has two distinct readings, one true and the other false, without being, in the normal sense of the term, ambiguous (there is neither lexical nor grammatical ambiguity). Another pragmatic function that licenses indirect reference is 'pictorial representation':

(60) In that photo I am only two weeks old.
(61) Jane has freckles, but in the painting her skin is like pink satin.

A pragmatic function of 'personal identity' allows us to refer to persons at an earlier stage of their life by their present functions, even though those functions did not apply at the time:

(62) My mother was only two years old when war broke out.

Fauconnier accounts for these sorts of case in terms of **mental spaces**. These are mental constructs in which alternative representations of states of affairs are held. The pragmatic functions underlie correspondences that are rather like Lakoff's metaphorical correspondences between domains, in that they connect entities across spaces. For instance, in the theatrical example mentioned above, there is a 'reality space' and a 'play space', each depicting a state of affairs, and there are correspondences which link individuals in one space with individuals in the other space. Example (62) requires a 'present time' space and a 'past time' space, the correspondence being based on the persistence of personal identity through time. The description *my mother* is obviously valid only in the present time space, but can be used to refer to the same individual in the past time space. Mental spaces have been put to a variety of uses which it is not possible to explore fully here.

16.3 Deixis

Deixis means different things to different people. For Bühler (1934), any expression which located a referent in space or time was a deictic expression. Thus, for him, *The cat sat on the mat* contained a deictic locative expression, namely, *on the mat* (the sentence also contains a tense marker, which is usually considered to be deictic). Later scholars have mostly restricted the term 'deixis' to cases where the referent is located using the current speech event (particularly the time of speaking) or one or more of its participants (particularly, but not exclusively, the speaker) as reference points. In the sentence *The cat sat on the mat*, the cat is located with respect to the mat: the mat is thus the reference point, and the speech event plays no role. In the sentence *That cat sat on the mat*, however, the cat is located not only with respect to the mat but also with respect to the speaker, *that* indicating (probably) that the cat was relatively distant from the speaker. A point of disagreement concerns the deictic status of the definite article. Some scholars consider it to be deictic, because the current context of situation is involved in referent identification. Others exclude the definite article, because it does not locate the referent on any specific parameter, relative to the current speech event. We shall, at least at first, include only expressions which truly locate a referent with respect to (some aspect of) the current speech situation. We therefore include personal pronouns, but exclude the definite article. Our key diagnostic criterion for deictic expressions will be the sensitivity of their use in designating a given referent to certain speech-situational parameters, particularly location in space and time relative to the speaker, and participatory status. Thus, someone referring to a book held by another person would say *that book*, but the holder of the book, referring to the same book, would say *this book*; referring to 8 July on 7 July, one would say *tomorrow*, but referring to the same day on 9 July, one would say *yesterday*; a speaker refers to himself as *I*, but his hearer, referring to the same person, would say *you*. We shall initially recognize five main types of deixis: person deixis, spatial deixis, temporal deixis, social deixis, and discourse deixis.

16.3.1 Person deixis

Person deixis involves basically the speaker, known as the **first person**, the addressee, known as the **second person**, and other significant participants in the speech situation, neither speaker nor hearer; these are known as **third person**. All of these, at least in English, come in singular and plural form and several are marked for case:

	Singular	Plural
1st person	*I/me*	*We/us*
2nd person	*you*	*you*
3rd person	*he/him, she/her/it*	*they/them*

In many languages, pronoun usage encodes social deixis (see below). Notice that the third person singular forms also encode gender. It is important to realize that the occurrence of gender in these forms is not deictic—that is to say, it is not sensitive to aspects of the speech situation. In other words, not all the meaning of a deictic expression is deictic in nature.

A couple of remarks are worth making on the subject of plural forms of personal pronouns. First of all, there is a kind of dominance relation holding among the terms: first person dominates second and third, and second person dominates third. This manifests itself in the following way. If the group designated includes the first person, then a first person plural pronoun must be used, even if there is only one first person and thousands of second and/or third persons. Similarly, if there is no first person in the group designated, but at least one second person, then a second person pronoun is needed. Only if neither first person nor second person is present can third person pronouns be used.

The second point concerns the **representative** vs. **true** use of the plural pronouns. The word *we* is rarely spoken by a plurality of persons: there is normally a single speaker. This speaker represents the group to which he or she refers. On the other hand, *they* usually designates a plurality of present referents. Representative use is possible, but is more uncommon (e.g. in pointing to a single person and saying *They are going to Greece for their holidays*). In the second person, the two possibilities, of representative and true use, are more or less equally likely.

16.3.2 Spatial deixis

Spatial deixis manifests itself principally in the form of locative adverbs such as *here* and *there*, and demonstratives/determiners such as *this* and *that*. English has a relatively impoverished spatial deictic system, with only two terms, usually labelled **proximal** and **distal**. Many languages have three or more terms. The most common types of three-term system subdivide the distal category. There are two main ways of doing this. The first involves a **distal/remote** distinction. (English at one time had such a system, with three terms *here*, *there*, and *yonder*.) Spanish has such a system. The other type of three-term system does not strictly depend on distance, but is closely related to the person system, that is to say, the terms can be glossed "near to me" (= here), "near to you", and "not near to either you or me" (= third person). Older analyses of Turkish proposed this analysis. It is nowadays not considered correct, however. One suggestion as to the true nature of the Turkish spatial deictics is that within the distal category there is a gestural/symbolic distinction (see below). Deictic systems with more than three terms incorporate such notions as "visible"/ "invisible", "below the line of sight"/"above the line of sight", and so on.

Let us return now to English (although many of the observations will be more generally valid). The proximal term *here* means something like "region relatively close to the speaker", and *there* means "relatively distant from the speaker". It is important to realize, however, that "relative closeness" is contextually determined. *Here* may represent an area less than the square metre on which the speaker is standing, or it could be something much vaster, such as *Here in our local galaxy cluster*. This is another species of definiteness: *here* is meaningless unless the hearer can locate the dividing line (in terms of distance) between *here* and *there*. (Paradoxically, there is no limit to how far away *here* can extend.)

The spatial deictics show a similar sort of dominance relation to the personal pronouns. We can illustrate this with *this* and *that*. The point is that the combination of *this book* and *that book* must be collectively referred to as *these books*, not *those books*. This encourages us to think of *this* as a first person deictic. (There is a small amount of evidence that *that* is ambiguous between second person and third person, in that *those* prefers to be either one or the other. I can refer to (i) *those books that you have* and (ii) *those books that John has*. If I subsequently say *Those books are very valuable*, there is a strong preference for interpreting this as either (i) or (ii), but not both together, unless you and John can be united in a joint second person reference.)

16.3.3 Temporal deixis

Temporal deictics function to locate points or intervals on the time axis, using (ultimately) the moment of utterance as a reference point. There are thus three major divisions of the time axis: (i) before the moment of utterance, (ii) at the time of utterance, (iii) after the time of utterance. The most basic temporal deictics in English are *now* and *then*. *Now* is in some ways a kind of temporal *here*, and displays the same capacity for indefinite extension. That is, it can refer to a precise instant: *Press the button—NOW!*; or it can accommodate a wide swathe of time: *The solar system is now in a relatively stable phase* (notice, however, that the phenomenon of dominance is absent from temporal deictics, as is the association with first person). *Then* points away from the present, but is indifferent as to direction, which is normally indicated contextually (*We were happy then*; *OK, I'll see you then*).

Temporal deictics depend heavily on calendric notions, if we understand that term to subsume both clock and calendar. For instance, the English terms *today*, *yesterday*, and *tomorrow* designate, respectively, "the period of twenty-four hours beginning at 12 o'clock midnight which includes the time of utterance", "the period of twenty-four hours which precedes the one including the time of utterance", and "the period of twenty-four hours which follows the one including the time of utterance". Notice that these terms' meanings include both deictic information (past, present, or future) and non-deictic information ("period of twenty-four hours beginning . . .", etc.). Only the twenty-four hour period has lexicalized deictics. For parallel references to other periods, we must use the terms *this*, *last*, and *next*. With these, there are complications (and uncertainties) according to whether the time period is referred to by means of a proper name or not. Consider, first, cases where a proper name is not used. Expressions such as *this week*, *last week*, and *next week*, *this month*, *last month*, and *next month*, *this year*, *last year*, and *next year* are all interpreted calendrically, that is to say, to take the example of *week*, *last week* means "the period of seven days beginning on Sunday (or Monday) preceding the corresponding period which includes the time of utterance" (a non-calendric interpretation would be "the period of seven days preceding the time of utterance"). Notice that *Mary is here for a week/month/year* is not normally interpreted calendrically; *Mary is here for the next week/month/year*, according to my intuitions, can be either calendric or not.

If the proper name of a period of time is used, additional restrictions come into play. Take first the names of days. The lexical items *today*, *yesterday*, and *tomorrow* have priority, so that, for instance *this Wednesday* cannot be uttered on Tuesday, Wednesday, or Thursday. *Last Wednesday* cannot be uttered on Thursday to refer to the previous day, but may be used to refer to the Wednesday of the preceding week. Speakers disagree as to whether a reference to, say, *Monday*, said on the Wednesday of the same week, should be *this Monday* or *last Monday*; a parallel disagreement applies to a reference, said on the same day, to the following Saturday—some would say *this Saturday*, others *next Saturday*. In referring to months, *this July* means "the July falling within the calendric year which includes the time of utterance", with the exception that one does not normally say (with exceptions to be noted in a moment) *this July* if one is speaking in July. With months, there is a similar uncertainty concerning the meanings of *last* and *next* as with named days.

It is of course possible, and quite normal, to say, for instance, *This July is the hottest I have ever known*, when one is still within the period designated by *this July*. However, it is important to realize that the *this* in this usage is not a temporal *this*, that is to say, it does not belong to the contrast set which includes *last* and *next*. In fact, it is an extended use of the spatial *this*, and contrasts with *That July was the hottest I have ever known*. It is therefore not a specifically temporal deictic.

It has already been mentioned that verb tense represents a type of deixis. This will not be dealt with here; it is discussed in Chapter 15.

16.3.4 Social deixis

Social deixis is exemplified by certain uses of the so-called **TV** (*tu/vous*) pronouns in many languages. It will be illustrated here using examples from French. Arguments will be presented that not all the usages of TV pronouns fall properly under the heading of deixis. One which incontrovertibly does is where relative social status of speaker and hearer is signalled. There are three basic possibilities involving two communicants A and B: (i) A addresses B with *tu*, B addresses A with *vous*; (ii) A addresses B with *vous*, B addresses A with *tu*; (iii) A and B both use the same form (either *tu* or *vous*). The basic parameter here is social status: in asymmetric use, *tu* points downwards along the scale of social status with the speaker's position as reference point, *vous* points upwards, while symmetric use signals social equality.

Turning now to instances of symmetric usage of TV pronouns, let us enquire briefly into the factors which determine whether *tu* or *vous* is used, and whether such usage can properly be regarded as deixis. One factor is usually described by some such term as 'social distance': *tu* indicates intimacy, *vous* indicates lack of intimacy, or distance. It is tempting to draw a parallel here with the proximal and distal terms in spatial deixis, and say that *tu* is proximal and *vous* distal. I shall suggest two reasons why such a parallel should not be drawn. The first is that there is no validity in an argument from reverse metaphor. That is, just because the [+intimate/– intimate] distinction would make a satisfying metaphorical extension from the [proximal/distal] distinction of spatial deixis, it does not follow that that is what it is, especially if the forms used give no support to the derivation. In the present case, there is no spatial content in literal uses of *tu* and *vous* to support such a derivation. The second reason is that the dominance relations between [+intimate] and [– intimate] are the wrong way round. Recall that *here* dominates *there*: in the case of TV pronouns used to signal intimacy (or lack of it), V dominates T. It is hard to demonstrate this in French, because there is no distinct intimate plural form, as there is in, for instance, German. But it can be shown. Imagine a group of people appointing one of their number as a spokesperson to address some individual. Suppose that the person chosen would naturally say *tu* to the person being addressed. Suppose further that the group contains individuals who would naturally say *vous* to the person being addressed. What form does the spokesperson choose? French native intuitions unhesitatingly opt for *vous*.

As a clue to another factor affecting the choice between T and V, consider the following situation. A husband and wife jointly front a news programme on television. When they are on the air, they address one another as *vous*; off-camera, of course, they use *tu*. Clearly neither relative social status nor intimacy can explain this. The deciding factor seems to be the formality or informality of the situation. It is at least arguable that this cannot be laid at the door of deixis at all.

16.3.5 Discourse deixis

Discourse deixis involves such matters as the use of *this* to point to future discourse elements, that is, things which are about to be said, as in *Listen to this, it will kill you!*, and *that* to point to past discourse elements, as in *That was not a very nice thing to say*. In a similar spirit, the *hereby* of an explicit performative sentence could be said to point to current discourse: *Notice is hereby served that if payment is further delayed, appropriate legal action will be taken.* It is sometimes claimed that certain sentence adverbs, such as *therefore* and *furthermore*, include an element of discourse deixis in their meaning, as they require the recovery of a piece of previous discourse to be understood. *Therefore* and *furthermore* could be glossed: "It follows from that" and "In addition to that", respectively (where that is a discourse deictic). A distinction can be made between discourse deixis and anaphora, although the two are obviously related. Anaphora picks up a previous reference to an extralinguistic entity and repeats it. *In John entered the room. He looked tired*, *he* refers to the same person that *John* refers to, but it does not strictly refer to the word *John* itself. It must be admitted that in reference to a case like *therefore* the distinction between discourse deixis and anaphora becomes somewhat blurred.

16.3.6 Psychological use of spatial deixis

It may be presumed that spatial deixis is the prototypic variety, and is certainly the source for much metaphoric generalization. A relatively simple extension is into what Langacker calls 'abstract space'. This is exemplified by such usages as *Here the argument runs into difficulties* or *What do you think of this idea of mine/that idea of George's?* Ideas and arguments do not literally occupy space, but it is easy to think of them as if they did. This use of deixis sometimes seems to invalidate the generalization just given above regarding discourse deixis, namely, that *this* points forwards in discourse: *2 + 2 = 4. The truth of this proposition is guaranteed by mathematical logic.* We would have to say, here, that this is not discourse-deictic (otherwise we would be obliged to use *that*), but means something like "the proposition we have in the forefront of our minds".

Another extended use of spatial deixis is to signal emotive distancing or closeness:

(63) A: Here comes Jane.
      B: I can't stand that woman.
(64) This beautiful city of ours.

16.3.7 Gestural and symbolic deixis

Some uses of deictics require for their interpretation continuous monitoring of relevant aspects of the speech situation: in the clearest cases, the hearer has to be able to see the speaker and their gestures:

(65) Put one over there and the other one here.
(66) This is the finger that hurts, not that one.
(67) Press the button when I give the word—now!
(68) I want three volunteers: you, you, and you.

These are examples of **gestural deixis**. In other cases, such minute monitoring of the speech situation is not necessary, and in general, the relevant parameters for the deictic interpretation are established over relatively long periods of a conversation/discourse. This is called **symbolic deixis**:

(69) (people at an exhibition) Isn't it interesting!
(70) Isn't this weather gorgeous?
(71) I've lived in this town for twenty years.
(72) Those foreigners are always whingeing.

In general, the difference between these would seem to be a matter of degree. However, there is one significant consequence of the distinction: it is only in the case of gestural use that the place denoted by *here* need not include the location of the speaker (e.g. *Will you please sign here, sir?*).

16.3.8 Deictic vs. non-deictic uses of locative expressions

It is sometimes claimed that certain locative expressions can be used either deictically or non-deictically. An example is the following:

(73) Mary lives in the house opposite the church.
(74) Mary lives in the house opposite.

The claim is that *opposite* is used **non-deictically** in (73) but **deictically** in (74), where it is interpreted as "the house opposite the speaker". However, this claim is at least disputable. An alternative explanation is that in (74), *opposite* has a definite zero complement (like the latent direct object in *Mary's watching*). The definite zero complement must be inferred contextually, that is, if it is not made explicit, one must always enquire *opposite what?* In some situations, the most relevant complement will be the speaker, as in (74), but this is not necessarily the case:

(75) Go along this road until you come to a church. Mary lives in the house opposite.

In (75), the most relevant complement is *the church*. In other words, there is no need to invoke deixis in such cases; they are explained by general principles of definiteness. A slightly more complex example involves expressions like *in front of*. Many objects have a 'canonical' front and back: persons, buildings, vehicles, and so on. Other objects do not have a canonical front and back: a tree, a dustbin, a lamp-post. If an object X does not have a canonical front and back, the expression *in front of X* is claimed to mean generally "situated somewhere on an imaginary line between X and speaker". If an object has a canonical front and back, then *in front of X* is ambiguous, and means either "at or near the canonical front of X" or "situated somewhere on an imaginary line between X and speaker". The former reading is claimed to be non-deictic, and the latter reading deictic. However, the same type of objection can be made as with the so-called deictic reading of *opposite*. That is to say, the so-called deictic reading of *in front of X* does not necessarily mean "situated somewhere on an imaginary line between X and speaker", but "situated somewhere on an imaginary line between X and some definite reference point to be inferred from context". Examples where the speaker is not the reference point include the following:

(76) Follow my instructions carefully. Walk slowly towards the tree. You will find the box about one metre in front of the tree.

(77) Tell John to follow the instructions carefully. He must walk slowly towards the tree. He will find the box one metre in front of the tree.

Again, no recourse to a special notion of deixis is called for, simply the principles governing definite reference. It is interesting to speculate whether all deixis can be explained away in this fashion. (For example, we might gloss the meaning of *I* as simply "the speaker", leaving the principles of relevance to select "the utterer of I" as overwhelmingly the most relevant construal in the vast majority of circumstances.)

Discussion questions and exercises

1. Identify instances of implicit definite reference points, latent elements, etc. in the following:

   (a) I would recommend the other route.
   (b) Mary will ring up and see if there's still time.
   (c) Turn left at the next traffic lights.
   (d) That's rather a lot, isn't it?
   (e) The last sit-in was much better.

2. Point out all the instances of deixis in the following, indicating what type is involved:

   (a) I understood that there would be an opportunity to meet her there later that week, and that I would be responsible for bringing the documents. At least, that's what John said.

(b) Come out from behind there at once, Smith!

(c) I met this chap at the concert, and we got talking. He said that this Xmas had been the worst he had ever spent. I'm meeting him again tomorrow.

3. Decide which of the following sentences have normal interpretations, and which have none. For those that have, specify any necessary conditions (e.g. the relative location of participants). On the basis of these data, give a concise specification of the deictic properties of bring and take.

(a) Take it here.
(b) Bring it there.
(c) I will bring it to you.
(d) I will take it to you.
(e) I will bring it to John.
(f) I will take it to John.
(g) You will take it to me.
(h) You will bring it to me.
(i) You will bring it to John.
(j) You will take it to John.
(k) John will bring it to you.
(l) John will take it to you.
(m) John will bring it to Mary.
(n) John will take it to Mary.
(o) John told me he would bring it to you.
(p) John told me he would take it to you.
(q) Did John tell you he would bring it to me?
(r) Did John tell you he would take it to me?
(s) John told me he would bring it to Mary.
(t) John told me he would take it to Mary.

4. Comment on the use of the italicized items in the following:

(a) The visitors will arrive at Edinburgh Waverley Station at 3.00 p.m. *Here* they will be met by our representative. (Assume the message originated in London.)

(b) Jackson rubbed his hands with satisfaction: he was *now* in possession of all the facts.

(c) I have been informed about your insubordination this morning. *This* is the third such incident this week.

(d) What's all *this* about you leaving next week?

Suggestions for further reading

For illuminating discussions of reference and its varieties, and definite reference in particular, see Searle (1969), Hawkins (1978), Givón (1984), and Chesterman (1991).

Further reading on deixis could usefully begin with Levinson (1983: ch. 2). See also Anderson and Keenan (1985).

Speech acts

Speech acts

17.1 Locutionary, perlocutionary, and illocutionary acts

Communication is not just a matter of expressing propositions. A 'naked' proposition, as we saw in Chapter 2, cannot communicate anything at all. To communicate we must express propositions with a particular illocutionary force, and in so doing we perform particular kinds of action, such as stating, promising, or warning, which have come to be called **speech acts**. It is, however, important to distinguish between three sorts of thing that one is doing in the course of producing an utterance. These are usually distinguished by the terms 'locutionary acts', 'perlocutionary acts', and 'illocutionary acts'.

17.1.1 Locutionary acts

Speech acts were first studied by the philosopher J. L. Austin. **Locutionary acts** were explained by Austin (1962) as follows:

The utterance of certain noises . . . certain words in a certain construction, and the utterance of them with a certain sense and a certain reference.

Notice that this conflates a number of distinguishable 'acts'; Lyons sets these out as follows (1977):

(a) produce an utterance inscription;
(b) compose a sentence;
(c) contextualize.

The first of these refers to the physical act of speaking, that is, producing a certain type of noise (or, in the case of written language, a set of written symbols). In principle, a parrot could do this. The second refers to the act of composing a string of words conforming to the grammar of some language (more or less well). (Searle (1969) groups these two together as performing an **utterance act**.) Item (c) has two components. First, many sentences contain either lexical or grammatical ambiguities. Normally only one of the possible readings is 'intended': the speaker's intention in this regard forms part of the specification of the locutionary act being performed. The second component is that any definite referring expressions in an uttered sentence normally have extralinguistic referents intended by the speaker. The assignation of these, too, forms part of the locutionary act. It can be seen, therefore, that if the sentence uttered is declarative in form, then performing a locutionary act includes the expression of one or more propositions. (Searle refers to **propositional acts**.) As far as is at present known, parrots cannot perform (b) or (c).

17.1.2 Perlocutionary acts

Perlocutionary acts are acts performed by means of language, using language as a tool. The elements which define the act are external to the locutionary act. Take the act of persuading someone to do something, or getting them to believe that something is the case. In order to persuade someone to do something, one normally must speak to them. But the speaking, even accompanied by appropriate intentions and so on, does not of itself constitute the act of persuasion. For that, the person being persuaded has to do what the speaker is urging. The same is true of the act of cheering someone up: this may well be accomplished through language, in which case it is a perlocutionary act, but even then the act does not consist in saying certain things in a certain way, but in having a certain effect, which in principle could have been produced in some other way.

17.1.3 Illocutionary acts

Illocutionary acts are acts which are internal to the locutionary act, in the sense that, if the contextual conditions are appropriate (see below), once the locutionary act has been performed, so has the illocutionary act. Take the act of promising. If someone says to another *I promise to buy you a ring* they have, by simply saying these words, performed the act of promising. Notice that it makes sense to say: *I tried to persuade her to come, but I failed*, or: *I tried to cheer him up, but failed*, but it makes no sense to say: *I tried to promise to come, but I failed*, except in the sense that one failed to utter the words, that is, to perform the locutionary act.

The same illocutionary act can be performed via different locutionary acts: for instance *I saw Jane today* and *I saw your wife today* (on the assumption, of course, that the addressee's wife is called Jane). Furthermore, the same locutionary act can realize different illocutionary acts: for instance, *I'll be there* can function as a promise, prediction, warning, and so on. It is also the case that a locutionary act can be performed without an illocutionary act thereby being performed (although Searle, for instance, denies this). For instance, in classes in elementary logic, propositions such as *All men are mortal* are often 'entertained' without anything being expressed beyond the bare proposition. The focus of the present chapter is on illocutionary acts.

17.2 The nature of illocutionary acts

17.2.1 Implicit and explicit illocutionary force

The illocutionary act aimed at by producing an utterance is known as the **illocutionary force** of the utterance. There is no communication without illocutionary force. How does a speaker convey, or a hearer understand, the illocutionary force of an utterance? We can first of all distinguish between **explicit** and **implicit** illocutionary force. In the former case, there is a specific linguistic signal whose function is to encode illocutionary force. We can distinguish two types, lexical and grammatical. The lexical type are illustrated by the following:

I promise you I will leave in five minutes.
I warn you I shall leave in five minutes.
I beg you not to leave so soon.
I thank you for staying.

The verbs *promise, warn, beg, thank* are known as **performative verbs**: they function specifically to encode illocutionary force. The grammatical type is illustrated by the following:

You wrote the article.
Did you write the article?
Write the article!

In these cases it is the grammatical form that encodes the illocutionary force.

According to what has just been said, it would appear that illocutionary force is always explicit. In the sense that every utterance encodes some indication of illocutionary force, this is probably true. However, the illocutionary force of an utterance is not always fully specified linguistically: what is not so specified is implicit. There are two main ways in which the effective force of an utterance may deviate from the overtly expressed force. First, it may differ in specificity. For instance, a number of more specific speech acts, such as promises, threats, warnings, and predictions, share the underlying feature of assertion. A declarative sentence simply encodes the force of a statement: where it functions as, say, a promise, the difference must be construed on the basis of context. The second way in which the effective force of an utterance may differ from the overtly expressed force is when it performs a different illocutionary act. For instance, *You will leave immediately* has declarative form, that is, it encodes the force of a statement; but it could well be used to issue a command. In the latter type of case, it is common to speak of **indirect speech acts**.

17.2.2 Explicit performativity

17.2.2.1 Performative verbs

Performative verbs, that is, those verbs one of whose functions is to signal specific speech acts, have certain peculiar properties which set them apart from non-performative verbs. First of all, they can generally be recognized by the fact that they can occur normally with *hereby* (we are talking here about semantic normality, that is, lack of anomaly; the result may well be somewhat stilted):

(1) I hereby undertake to carry out faithfully the duties of Royal Egg-Sexer.
(2) I hereby declare the bridge open.
(3) I hereby command you to surrender.

This use of *hereby* is not possible with non-performative verbs of speaking:

(4) *I hereby persuade you to accompany me.
(5) *I hereby recount the history of my family.
(6) *I hereby explain why I did it.

Performative verbs can be used either performatively or descriptively; in the latter use they are no different from non-performative verbs:

(7) John is always promising to do things, but he never does them.
(8) He ordered them to leave the premises.
(9) Who is going to christen the baby?
(10) He went round congratulating everyone.

Notice that in such descriptive uses of performative verbs, *hereby* is ruled out:

(11) *John is always hereby promising to do things.
(12) *He hereby ordered them to leave the premises.

The performative use of performative verbs is extremely restricted grammatically. They must be in the simple present tense. They may be active or passive; if active, then they must also be in the first person. Consider, first, active uses. Notice the following contrasts:

(13) I (hereby) promise to pay you next week.
     I (*hereby) promised to pay him the following week.
(14) I hereby declare John Smith the duly elected Member for this constituency.
     I have (*hereby) declared John Smith the duly elected Member for this constituency.
(15) I hereby warn you that legal action will be taken.
     I am (?hereby) warning you that legal action will be taken.

Similar contrasts are possible with passive uses:

(16) Passengers are (hereby) requested not to smoke.
Passengers were (*hereby) requested not to smoke.

(17) You are (hereby) warned to leave immediately.
They will be (*hereby) warned to leave immediately.
They are at this moment being (*hereby) warned to leave.

Notice that there is no grammatical restriction on descriptive use: that is to say, the use of a performative verb in, say, present simple first person active form is not necessarily a performative use:

(18) A: Are you clear about what you have to do?
B: Yes, I (*hereby) christen the baby Jonathan, then I (*hereby) congratulate the parents and then I (*hereby) confess that I am the baby's father and (*hereby) promise never to reveal the fact.

The same is true of passive uses:

(19) Passengers are (*hereby) regularly requested not to smoke.

Performative verbs are thus ambiguous in certain of their forms, and context is needed to disambiguate them. (Unresolved ambiguities are vanishingly rare.)

Performative verbs used performatively are often held to be non-truth-conditional (although there are alternative claims). Some cases seem clear enough. If someone says *I warn you to stay away from her!* it doesn't make much sense to reply *That's not true*. (Notice that in reply to *I warned you to stay away from her*, a reply of *That's not true* would be perfectly normal.) Similarly with *I congratulate you on your promotion*. Other cases are not so clear. For instance, it does seem to make sense to reply *That's not true* to *I confess that I took the money*. However, it still can be claimed that it is not the veracity of the fact that a confession is being made that is being called into question, but the truth of the proposition that forms the content of the confession. This can perhaps be seen more clearly in the following case:

(20) A: I predict that the world will end tomorrow.
B: That's not true.

Here, it might be claimed that B is not challenging the fact that A is making a prediction, but is denying the truth of what he is predicting. However, we need to be clearer about what is happening here. Take the case of *I confess . . .* If someone says something, then it is either true or false that they are making a confession. Therefore it does not make sense to say that *I confess . . .* cannot be assessed for truth-value. However, confession consists in saying certain words (although sincere confession obviously demands more), so the truth of the proposition that A is confessing is a necessary consequence of A's uttering appropriate words, among which are the words *I confess . . .* In other words, the reason we cannot say *That's not true* to someone who says *I confess . . .* is that it is necessarily true, like *Bachelors are unmarried*.

Something more needs to be said, however, about why it is acceptable to say *That's not true* in response to *I predict the world will end tomorrow*, but not in response to *I congratulate you on your promotion*, or *I warn you to leave immediately*. Actually, two reasons are involved here. First, one can only deny the truth of an expressed proposition; if the utterance in question does not actually express a proposition (other than the necessarily true performative part, which cannot be denied) then one cannot deny its truth. This is the case with *I warn you to leave*. If the utterance does express a proposition whose truth is contingent rather than necessary, the normality of saying *That's not true* depends on the relative salience of the performative part of the meaning and the propositional part. For instance, in the case of *I warn you the roads are slippery*, the important part of the meaning (for most hearers) is that the roads are slippery, not that the speaker is delivering a warning. On the other hand, in *I bet you £500 that I can get Mary to go to bed with me*, the nature of the performative act is crucial. It is therefore a matter of salience, and graded normality. Of course, it must also be borne in mind that there is a difference between saying *I warn you the roads are slippery* and *The roads are slippery* (even when uttered with the intention of warning the hearer): in the former case the speaker is constraining the hearer's interpretation, by making the intentions more explicit.

17.2.2.2 Grammatical performativity

Most languages have grammatical ways of indicating the illocutionary force of an utterance (this is not intended to be an exhaustive list):

(21) John is brave.
(22) Is John brave?
(23) Be brave, John!
(24) What bravery!

These grammatical forms perform the same sort of function that performative verbs do. Thus, the first three sentences above have an obvious relation to the following:

(25) I (hereby) state that John is brave.
(26) I (hereby) enquire whether John is brave.
(27) I (hereby) urge John to be brave.

(Interestingly, the fourth has no performative verb equivalent: *??I hereby exclaim* . . . This point will be further elaborated below.)

However, the range of choice of forms is much more limited than is the case with performative verbs, and hence the meanings are much less specific. It is therefore not possible, in general, to paraphrase the grammatical forms precisely in terms of explicit performative verbs. Let us examine more closely the four types illustrated.

Declaratives. Sentence (21) is in **declarative** form. Now, obviously, a sentence in declarative form can have a wide range of illocutionary force. Something like *He's leaving* can function to inform someone of the fact, to ask whether it is true (normally with appropriate intonation), as a promise, or a threat, or a command, or even a congratulation. Because of this wide range, doubts have been expressed as to whether declarative form encodes any sort of speech act at all (in fact the doubts in some quarters extend to interrogatives and imperatives). Austin's original treatment drew a distinction between what he called **performative sentences** and **constatives**, and declaratives fell into the latter category. Later he decided that declaratives, too, were performatives, and that there was no difference in principle between *John is brave* and *I (hereby) state that John is brave*, except that in the latter case the performative verb was explicit. It is also worth remembering that declarative sentence form has often been regarded as in some sense the 'basic' sentence form (as in early versions of transformational grammar), and it is easy to go from this to regarding it as a 'neutral' form, from which all others are 'derived'. It is therefore not surprising that it has a wide range of applicability. This notion of basicness has a parallel in lexical meanings. Compare the colour name *red* with, say, *orange*. *Red* has a wide range of 'extended' uses, as in *red hair, red earth, red wine*, many of which are not objectively red at all (in the default sense of *red*). *Orange*, on the other hand, cannot be used so freely: something described as *orange* must have a colour much closer to the prototype. However, *red* also has a clear prototype. This phenomenon is quite widespread. Take *circle* and *pentagon*. If someone says: *The mourners stood in a circle around the grave*, the circle may be very approximate indeed. But if someone says: *The mourners stood in a pentagon round the grave*, the disposition of the mourners is much more constrained. It is in this sense, perhaps, that the declarative sentence form can be viewed as basic. Being 'basic', it can be extended in ways that other forms cannot. But it nonetheless has a much more restricted, non-extended range of interpretations. And in its prototypical manifestations it commits the speaker to the truth of the expressed proposition, and thus belongs to the same family of illocutionary meanings as *assert, state, declare, claim*, etc. The various performative verbs mentioned can be regarded as specifications of the meaning of the straight declarative prototype. (The use of a performative verb also has the effect of highlighting the performative aspect of the sentence: with all grammatical performatives, the performative meaning is relatively backgrounded, but this is especially the case with declaratives.) It would be a mistake, however, to believe that every declarative, to be understood, must be 'translated' into a sentence containing one of the overt performatives. (This is no more true than a claim that, for instance, *It's red* cannot be understood unless the precise named shade of red, e.g. *scarlet, crimson, maroon, brick red*, can be recovered.) An alternative view is that the declarative form does nothing but express the proposition, and that any performative force arises in the form of implicatures. This approach, however, ignores the fact of the prototypical nature of what might be called assertiveness.

Interrogatives. All **interrogatives**, at least in their prototypical uses, express ignorance on some point, and aim at eliciting a response from a hearer which will remove the ignorance. There are two sorts of question. The first sort effectively specify a proposition and express ignorance as to its truth: these are the so-called **Yes/No questions**, because they can be so answered. So, for instance, *Is John brave?* presents the proposition *John is brave* and aims at eliciting a response which indicates whether that proposition is true or not. The other sort (**X-questions**) present an incomplete proposition, and aim at eliciting a response which completes the skeleton proposition in such a way that the resulting proposition is true. So, for instance, the question *What time is it?* presents the skeleton proposition *The time is X*, and aims at eliciting a response that provides a value for X which makes the complete proposition true. Interrogatives (of both types), too, have a wide range of non-prototypical uses; but in their prototypical uses they fall into the same sort of semantic area as performative verbs such as *ask*, *enquire*, or *demand to know*. But again, they are not, in every instance of use, reducible to one of the overt performatives.

Interrogatives are sometimes held to be a type of imperative. Thus, the meaning of *Is John brave?* might be paraphrased "Say Yes if the proposition JOHN IS BRAVE is true and No if it is false". Likewise, the meaning of *What is the time?* can be paraphrased "Give me a value for X such that the proposition THE TIME IS X is true". These paraphrases are obviously imperative in nature, and equally clearly, capture directly at least some of the meaning of the corresponding interrogatives. This analysis gives a good account of examination questions. These have the function of instructing candidates to produce a quantity of linguistic output under certain semantic (and secondarily syntactic, etc.) constraints. Notice the absolute equivalence between *What are the reasons for . . .?* and *State the reasons for . . .* in an exam context. Notice also that a form such as *State the reasons for . . .* will still be regarded as an examination QUESTION. Another interesting observation is the parallelism between *Open the door, please* and *What is the time, please?*

However, the imperative analysis deals less successfully with cases like *Now where did I leave my wallet?*, said when one is alone. It might be argued that the speaker in such a case is addressing the question to an imaginary hearer, and ordering him to give an answer. But this does not seem intuitively correct: such questions are not usually accompanied by such images. Lyons (1977) suggests that in such cases one is not asking a question but merely posing it, and that posing a question is expressing doubt or ignorance. Lyons also points to the fact that if someone says *No!* in answer to a command, one is refusing to carry out the desired action, but if one says *No* in answer to *Is John here?*, one is not refusing to answer the question, but is actually answering the question.

It is necessary to make a distinction between saying that questions are a type of imperative and saying that questions have an imperative-type component to their meaning. There is also a distinction between saying this and saying that questions prototypically have an imperative-like component. (The latter is what will be claimed here.) Notice that the strong imperative analysis omits any mention of an expression of ignorance. Such analyses rely on this being supplied inferentially in the contexts in which it occurs; likewise with the expression of a desire for the ignorance to be removed.

An alternative analysis on the lines of the imperative analysis is to say that what a question really means is an expression of ignorance, leaving the imperative component to be supplied inferentially in the contexts which call for it. This analysis handles the *Where did I put my wallet?* case, but deals less well with the examination case.

It is argued here that none of these reductive analyses accounts satisfactorily for the overwhelmingly strong intuition that the real meaning of a question, its prototype, includes at least the imperative component, the desire for the removal of ignorance, and the expression of ignorance. With this complex as central, it is easy to see other, non-prototypical readings clustering round it, forming a family resemblance structure with varying degrees of resemblance.

Imperatives. **Imperatives** resemble declaratives and interrogatives in that there is a prototypical use, whose main component is to get someone to do something, as with *Shut that door!*, and a cluster of non-prototypical uses, such as *Take another step and I'll shoot*, which manifestly does not aim at eliciting the action represented by the verb in the imperative, but rather the opposite. The negative force of this use of the imperative shows up in the (relative) normality of:

(**28**) Take another step and I'll shoot. And don't move your hand, either.

Once again, the prototypical meaning of the grammatical imperative lies in the same area as that of a set of explicit performatives, in this case, such as *order, command, enjoin, beg, beseech, request*, but, as usual, is not synonymous with any of them.

Some analyses of imperatives (for instance Palmer 1986: 29–30) argue that the strong directive force observable in, say, a military command is not a property of the imperative as such, but arises from the recognized authority of the speaker. Palmer points to the fact that *Come in!* in response to a knock on the door is not strongly directive, but is in fact a granting of permission. He suggests that the basic meaning of the imperative is the expression of a generally favourable attitude to the action indicated (if a higher-ranking military person expresses a favourable attitude to some action, a lower-ranking addressee will infer that he or she had jolly well better do it). However, this is not entirely convincing. If someone says *Peel those potatoes!* the directive force is not at all dependent on the authority of the speaker (although the felicitousness of the command is). The directive force is, however, dependent on whether the action is more likely to benefit the speaker or the hearer (see the discussion of the 'cost–benefit' scale in the next chapter). It is arguable that the prototypic use of the imperative is to elicit actions which are beneficial to the speaker: cases like *Come in!* in answer to a knock on the door, or *Have a nice holiday!*, on this view would not be prototypic uses.

With the three grammatical performatives we have looked at so far, the following characteristics are observable:

(i) They all have a range of uses which goes well beyond that of any explicit performative.
(ii) Their meanings are not identical with that of any explicit performative.
(iii) Their prototypic meanings are at the same time superordinate to, and more 'basic' than, the meanings of related performative verbs.

Exclamations. Curiously, exclamations cannot be performed by any performative verbs, although there are verbs with meanings describing such actions:

(**29**) What a lovely day it is!
     *I hereby exclaim what a lovely day it is.
     (I exclaimed what a lovely day it was.)

It seems that one does not exclaim by saying the word *exclaim*: one exclaims by calling something out in a loud voice:

(**30**) ?'How boring it all is,' exclaimed John in a barely perceptible whisper.

The word *exclaim* therefore does not encode an illocutionary act. It is too loaded with manner meaning, like *whisper*:

(**31**) ?I hereby whisper that you mustn't do that in the presence of the Queen.

What, then, *is* one doing with the exclamative form? Is it a speech act? Notice that it is truth-conditional:

(**32**) A: What a lovely day it is!
      B: Is it heck!

But it is not the primary purpose of an exclamation to inform:

(**33**) A: Tell me about your day.
      B: *What a lovely day I've had.

The encapsulated information seems to be presupposed (although one can enter the house after a day at the beach, and say *What a lovely day I've had* as a way of informing the occupants of the fact that one has had a lovely day. However, this can usually be done with presuppositions). All that is expressed is a psychological attitude to the fact. Intuitively, it is not performativizable, but it is still a mystery why not.

17.2.3 The 'performative hypothesis'

There are certain types of utterance whose properties seem to suggest that even implicit performatives have a 'hidden' or underlying explicit performative verb. This is the essence of the **performative hypothesis**, according to which every implicit performative has a 'deep' structure something like:

I (hereby) Vp you (that) S

where **Vp** is a performative verb, and **I (hereby) Vp you (that)** is optionally deletable without change of meaning. The claimed advantages of this proposal are that certain otherwise puzzling phenomena receive a natural explanation.

17.2.3.1 Reflexives

(34) The letter was addressed to John and myself.
(35) People like yourself should be given every assistance.
(36) ?The letter was addressed to herself.

On the face of it, there is no antecedent for the reflexive pronoun in (34) and (35) (notice the ungrammaticality of (36)), but if there is an underlying performative verb with a first person subject and second person indirect object, the mystery is explained.

17.2.3.2 Adverbs

(37) Frankly, I couldn't care less.
(38) What's the time, because I don't want to miss my train?

At first sight, it is not clear what *frankly* in (37) and the *because*-clause in (38) modify; however, the natural interpretation of these suggests that it is the performative verb in each case: "I tell you frankly that I couldn't care less"; "I ask you what the time is because I don't want to miss my train".

Attractive though it might seem, this analysis runs into serious difficulties, and is now out of favour. Two of the problems may be mentioned. Consider sentences (39) and (40):

(39) I hereby state that I am innocent.
(40) I am innocent.

By the performative hypothesis, these should mean the same and therefore should have identical truth conditions. But even if we admit that (39) has a truth condition (which is denied by many) it is true irrespective of whether the speaker is innocent or not; this cannot be the case with (40).

More problems occur with adverbs. For instance, there seems no reason, under the performative hypothesis, why *hereby* is not allowed with implicit performatives:

(41) *Hereby what is the time?/*Hereby it is three o'clock.

(42) I hereby ask you what the time is.

Also the interpretation of many adverbs seems to require the (underlying) presence of verbs not proposed in the performative hypothesis:

(43) Honestly, who do you think will win?

This does not mean "I ask you honestly . . .", but "Tell me honestly . . .".

17.3 Classifying speech acts

Performative verbs fall fairly naturally under a small number of headings. It is useful to group them in this way, as it enables us to gain a picture of the range of functions that these verbs perform. The classification we shall illustrate below is due to Searle. It is not a perfect taxonomy, as it is in many cases possible to place verbs under more than one heading, that is to say, the categories are not mutually exclusive. But it enables us to take a synoptic view.

17.3.1 Assertives

Assertives commit the speaker to the truth of the expressed proposition:

state, suggest, boast, complain, claim, report, warn (that)

Notice that *boast* and *complain* also express an attitude to the proposition expressed besides a belief in its truth.

17.3.2 Directives

Directives have the intention of eliciting some sort of action on the part of the hearer:

order, command, request, beg, beseech, advise (to), warn (to), recommend, ask, ask (to)

17.3.3 Commissives

Commissives commit the speaker to some future action:

promise, vow, offer, undertake, contract, threaten

17.3.4 Expressives

Expressives make known the speaker's psychological attitude to a presupposed state of affairs:

thank, congratulate, condole, praise, blame, forgive, pardon

What seems to distinguish these from *boast* and *complain* is that the attitude expressed by the latter is primarily an attitude towards the state of affairs (or the proposition). In the case of Searle's expressives, the attitude is more towards the persons involved. These do form an intuitively satisfying set, and *boast* and *complain* intuitively do not belong here.

17.3.5 Declaratives

Declaratives are said to bring about a change in reality: that is to say, the world is in some way no longer the same after they have been said. In an obvious sense this is true of all the performative verbs: after someone has congratulated someone, for instance, a new world comes into being in which that congratulation has taken place. What is special about declaratives? The point about these is, first, that they cause a change in the world over and above the fact that they have been carried out. This, again, is true of all the other verbs, but notice that in the case, say, of *congratulate*, such effects would be perlocutionary, whereas in the case of declaratives they are illocutionary. The second point is that they standardly encode such changes. So, if someone says *I resign*, then thereafter they no longer hold the post they originally held, with all that that entails. The following are declarative verbs:

> resign, dismiss, divorce (in Islam), christen, name, open (e.g. an exhibition), excommunicate, sentence (in court), consecrate, bid (at auction), declare (at cricket)

There is a finite number of explicit performative verbs in English (several hundred), but there is no reason to believe that there is a theoretically finite set of possible speech acts.

17.4 Conditions for the successful performance of speech acts

There are normally contextual conditions which must be fulfilled before a speech act can be said to have been properly performed. These are usually called **happiness conditions** or **felicity conditions**. Some of these are of course conditions on any sort of linguistic communication, such as the fact that speaker and hearer understand one another (usually speak the same language), can hear one another, and so on. The following conditions are more germane to the present chapter and are worth spelling out (after Searle).

17.4.1 Preparatory conditions

Preparatory conditions do not define the speech act, but are necessary in the sense that if they do not hold, the act has not been carried out (it is said to have **misfired**). In the case of declarative speech acts, the person performing the act must have authority to do it, and must do it in appropriate circumstances and with appropriate actions. For instance, it is not enough for someone to break a bottle of champagne on the bows of a ship, and say *I name this* *ship* **Venus**, for the ship either to acquire an official name or to change its name. A proper ceremony must be enacted, with officially recognized participants. The same is true of christening a baby. Even in the case of resigning from a job or position, just saying the words *I resign*, at breakfast, say, does not constitute a resignation: there are proper ways of resigning and channels for communicating such a decision. In the case of a promise, the hearer must prefer the promised action's accomplishment to its non-accomplishment, and the speaker must have reason to believe that the eventuality promised will not happen in the normal course of events. For a command, the speaker must be in authority over the hearer, must believe that the desired action has not already been carried out, and that it is possible for the hearer to carry it out. And so on.

17.4.2 Sincerity conditions

For **sincerity conditions** to be fulfilled, the person performing the act must have appropriate beliefs or feelings. For instance, in performing an act of asserting, the speaker must believe the proposition they are expressing; when thanking someone, one ought to have feelings of gratitude; when making a promise, one should sincerely intend to carry it out, and so on.

If the sincerity conditions are not met, the act is actually performed, but there is said to be an **abuse**.

17.4.3 Essential conditions

Essential conditions basically define the act being carried out. Thus, for a promise, the speaker must intend his utterance to put him under an obligation to carry out the act which corresponds to its propositional content. For a request, the speaker must intend that the utterance count as an attempt to get the hearer to do what is requested; for a statement, the hearer must intend that the utterance count as a guarantee of the truth of the statement; for a question, the hearer must intend that the utterance count as an attempt to elicit the appropriate answer from the hearer, and so on. If the essential conditions are not met, the act has not really been carried out.

17.4.4 Other conditions

Prototypically, the hearer should recognize the speaker's intention to perform the illocutionary act in question in uttering the words in question. This is called **uptake**. Uptake must be distinguished from **acceptance**: the fact that one refuses to accept, say, an apology or a resignation does not mean that the speaker's intention has not been recognized. Generally, uptake does not seem to be a necessary condition for speech acts, but there are doubtful cases. Take the case of boasting. Does someone boast if nobody who hears the utterance thinks it's a boast? There are indications that it *is* still a boast. First, it is anomalous to say: *?John tried to boast, but everyone thought he was just stating the facts.* Second, one can hear a statement and subsequently find out that someone was boasting: *He told me he had just lost £10,000—I didn't realize at the time that he was boasting.*

Ideally, the speaker's actions subsequent to the utterance should be consistent with the purport of the speech act carried out. Thus, someone who makes a promise should carry out the promised action; someone who orders someone else to do something should not be angry if they subsequently do it; after asking a question, one should give time for an answer to be given; someone who names a ship should not thereafter refer to it by a different name, etc. These inappropriate actions do not destroy the validity of the speech act, but they nonetheless indicate that something is amiss. They may be termed **breaches of commitment**.

Discussion questions and exercises

1. Which of the following verbs are performatives?

   bet (consider both meanings)   pray (in the religious sense)
   admire   interrogate   deplore   regret   celebrate

2. Thinking of locutionary, illocutionary and perlocutionary acts (and their components), consider what (a) a parrot and (b) a computer could reasonably be expected to be able to do.
3. Which of the following performative verbs can be classified under more than one of Searle's headings?

   complain   warn   confess   bemoan

Suggestions for further reading

For the Austin–Searle version of speech act theory see Austin (1962) and Searle (1969). A good survey of various approaches to speech acts (but not including Leech or relevance theory) is Levinson (1983: ch. 5). For a discussion of grammatical performativity, see Palmer (1986: 1.4) The views of Leech (who rejects the Austin–Searle position) can be found in Leech (1983). The outlines of a relevance-theoretical account are given in Blakemore (1992: ch. 6).

CHAPTER 18

Conversational implicatures

CHAPTER 18

Conversational implicatures

18.1 Grice's theory of implicature

We shall begin the discussion of conversational implicatures by outlining the pragmatic theory proposed by the philosopher H. P. Grice. In Grice's system, implicatures in general stand in opposition to 'what is said', as components of a more inclusive 'what is meant'. All these notions are sophisticated and controversial: the account given here is necessarily of an introductory nature. We shall take 'what is meant' to be equivalent to utterance meaning as defined in Chapter 2—that is, roughly, everything the speaker intends to convey by standard linguistic means.

18.1.1 Implicatures and 'what is said'

We can get a grip on the distinction between implicatures and 'what is said' in terms of the normal use of expressions like *X said P/X did not say P*, and the idea of contradictability: briefly, what is said (in the relevant sense) can be contradicted, agreed or disagreed with, and so on, whereas what is implicated cannot. Consider the following again:

(1) A: Has John cleared the table and washed the dishes?
    B: He's cleared the table.
    C: (i) That's not true.
       (ii) Yes, he has.
       (iii) You're right, he hasn't.

Suppose that C knows or assumes that B is in possession of the full facts. C would normally feel entitled to conclude from B's reply that B intended to indicate that John had not washed the dishes. However, that piece of information is not available for contradiction or confirmation, etc. C's comments (i) and (ii) in (1) cannot be taken to mean that John had in fact washed the dishes, nor can (iii) be confirmation that he had not. They can only apply to what B actually says: that is, comment (i) disagrees with the statement that John has cleared the table, (ii) expresses agreement that John has cleared the table, and comment (iii) doesn't make sense. Notice, too, that C would not be entitled to make the claim in (2):

(2) B said that John hadn't washed the dishes.

In other words, in terms of the distinction between what is said and what is implicated, B in (1) says that John has cleared the table, and implicates that he has not washed the dishes.

It is important to point out, however, that some parts of what is said may not have counterparts in the physical utterance: parts of utterances left unexpressed can nonetheless be part of what is said:

(3) A: What time is the train for London?
     B: 2.30.

Suppose that B consults the timetable and finds that the train is at 3.30. All the following are then possible retorts:

(4) No, it isn't. It's at 3.30.
(5) You said it was at 2.30.

In other words, what B says (in the relevant sense) in (3) is (6):

(6) The train for London is at 2.30.

By the above criteria, certain other aspects of what is meant fall outside what is said, and thus are to be considered implicatures. This is true, for instance, of expressive meaning. Somebody uttering (7) undoubtedly expresses anger, but does not *say* that they are angry:

(7) Shut that flaming door!

(8) and (9) do not constitute appropriate responses (as they would be to *I'm angry*):

(8) You have every right to be.
(9) No, you're not—you're only pretending.

We must thus conclude that the expression of anger is an implicature.

The status of presuppositions is more controversial, but there are some grounds for saying that the speaker of, for instance, (10) is not saying that someone stole the mangoes:

(10) It wasn't John that stole the mangoes.

18.1.2 Conversational implicatures

We now have a rough way of separating what is said from what is implicated. We now need to distinguish two types of implicature, conversational implicatures and conventional implicatures. It is the former type that has overwhelmingly claimed the attention of pragmatic theorists, and we shall follow this trend. The following are amongst the criteria which have been proposed to diagnose conversational implicatures. They are intended to distinguish them not only from conventional implicatures, but also from entailments. (These criteria are not entirely logically independent from one another.)

18.1.2.1 Context-dependence

An expression with a single meaning (i.e. expressing the same proposition) can give rise to different conversational implicatures in different contexts.

(11) A: Have you cleared the table and washed the dishes?
      B: I've cleared the table.
(12) A: Am I in time for supper?
      B: I've cleared the table.

In principle, the number of possible conversational implicatures of a proposition is unlimited. This criterion is intended to distinguish conversational implicatures from, both entailments and conventional implicatures. Take entailments first. There is no context in which (13) does not entail (14):

(13) John killed the wasp.
(14) The wasp died.

According to the criterion (of context-dependence), therefore, (14) is not a conversational implicature of (13). Grice regarded entailments as part of what is said. This is, however, not uncontroversial, and indeed, it is not intuitively obvious that a speaker of (13) actually says that the wasp died.

'Conventional implicatures' is the name given by some to non-truth-conditional aspects of meaning which are conventionally attached to particular linguistic forms. (Conversational implicatures are not conventionally attached to any linguistic forms.) For instance, the meaning which distinguishes *but* from *and* is of this nature, as is also the difference between *I haven't cleared the table* and *I haven't cleared the table yet*, and between *John killed the wasp* and *It was John who killed the wasp*. These differences are part of the conventional meaning of certain linguistic forms, whether lexical or grammatical, and hence they are not context-dependent—if these forms are used without the intention of carrying the meaning, then they are being misused.

Context-dependence is not a sufficient criterion on its own, because certain aspects of what is said are also dependent on context (consider, for instance, example (3) above).

18.1.2.2 Defeasibility/cancellability

Conversational implicatures are said to be **defeasible**, or **cancellable**; that is, they can be nullified by additional material without any resultant contradiction or anomaly.

(**15**) A: Did the Minister attend the meeting and sign the agreement?
       B(i): The Minister attended the meeting.
       B(ii): The Minister attended the meeting; a statement will be issued later
              with regard to the agreement.

B's first answer as it stands creates quite a strong presumption that the Minister did not sign the agreement. However, the additional material in B(ii) suppresses the implicature: we are no longer entitled, or invited, to conclude that the agreement was not signed. In the case of a conventional implicature, subsequent inconsistent material simply gives rise to anomaly:

(**16**) ?John hasn't arrived yet: I know for a fact he's not coming.
       *John killed the wasp, but it didn't die.

Although defeasibility or cancellability is one of the standard criteria for conversational implicature, it is nonetheless questionable. The reason is that adding material changes the context: there is no way of suppressing the implicature without doing this. In other words, this criterion arguably adds nothing that is not covered by the criterion of context-dependence.

   It is sometimes claimed that the criterion of cancellability does not discriminate between what is said and conversational implicatures because aspects of what is said are also cancellable. The following illustrates the sort of examples offered in support of this claim:

(**17**) I'm hoping to finish the book by Christmas.
(**18**) I'm hoping to finish the book by Christmas this year.
(**19**) I'm hoping to finish the book by Christmas, but not Christmas this year, of course.

I find this unconvincing. It seems to me that *I'm hoping to finish the book by Christmas* expresses a different proposition in (17) and (19). This simply shows that what is said is context-sensitive, not that any aspect of it is cancellable.

18.1.2.3 Non-detachability

The same propositional content in the same context will always give rise to the same conversational implicature, in whatever form it is expressed (that is to say, the implicature is tied to meaning and not to form):

(**20**) A: Have you cleared the table and washed the dishes?
       B(i): I've cleared the table.
       B(ii): I've taken all the things off the table.

Both of B's responses implicate that B did not wash the dishes. The implicature is said in such cases to be **non-detachable**. This is not the case with conventional implicatures. In the following, (21) implicates (22), but (23), which is usually considered to be propositionally identical with (21), does not implicate (22). In other words, the implicature (21) is tied to the lexical item *manage*:

(21) John didn't manage to walk as far as the crossroads.

(22) John attempted to walk as far as the crossroads.

(23) John didn't walk as far as the crossroads.

18.1.2.4 Calculability

A conversational implicature must be **calculable**, using statable general principles, on the basis of conventional meaning together with contextual information.

The nature of the calculation will be discussed below. This criterion serves to distinguish conversational implicatures from special arrangements whereby, for instance, two people agree (arbitrarily) that whenever one of them says X, they actually mean Y. For instance, a husband and wife might fix it between them that if one of them says *Have you seen anything of Clive recently?* it will mean "Let's leave in fifteen minutes". This will not be calculable, by general principles, from the conventional meaning of the utterance together with contextual information.

18.1.3 The cooperative principle

One of the most influential accounts of implicature is that of Grice (the usual source for this is Grice 1975). Grice framed his account as an explanation of certain features of conversations; it can be extended in obvious ways to other communicative situations, but we shall confine ourselves for the sake of economy to conversations. Let us think in terms of a prototypical conversation. Such a conversation is not a random succession of unrelated utterances produced alternately by participants: a prototypical conversation has something in the nature of a general purpose or direction, and the contributions of the participants are intelligibly related both to one another and to the overall aim of the conversation. By participating in a conversation, a speaker implicitly signals that he or she agrees to cooperate in the joint activity, to abide by the rules, as it were. Grice's version of what a conversationalist implicitly endorses (by agreeing to take part in the conversation) is expressed in terms of rules of conduct, and runs as follows:

The cooperative principle: Make your conversational contribution such as is required, at the stage at which it occurs, by the accepted purpose or direction of the talk exchange in which you are engaged.

This principle is elaborated by means of a set of maxims, which spell out what it means to cooperate in a conversational way.

18.1.3.1 The maxim of quality

The **maxim of quality** is concerned with truth-telling, and has two parts:

(i) Do not say what you believe to be false.

(ii) Do not say that for which you lack adequate evidence.

One could argue that the second sub-maxim entails the first: there will obviously not be adequate evidence for a false statement. We can paraphrase this maxim as 'Do not make unsupported statements'.

It may strike some that in real life this maxim is honoured more in the breach than in the observance. However, a moment's reflection should convince anyone that without a default truth-telling presumption of some sort—that is, unless we can count on at least a tendency for utterances to correspond to states of affairs—language would be unlearnable and unworkable. This does not necessarily mean that Grice's formulation is the optimum one. We shall return to this point in due course.

18.1.3.2 The maxim of quantity

The **maxim of quantity** is concerned with the amount of information (taken in its broadest sense) an utterance conveys.

(i) Make your contribution as informative as is required for the current purposes of the exchange in which you are engaged.
(ii) Do not make your contribution more informative than is required.

Imagine a conversation between a mother and daughter:

(24) M: What did you have for lunch today?
(25) D: (i) Baked beans on toast.
            (ii) Food.
            (iii) I had 87 warmed-up baked beans (although eight of them were slightly crushed) served on a slice of toast 12.7 cm. by 10.3 cm. which had been unevenly toasted . . .

Answer (i) is a 'normal' answer; (ii) gives too little information, thus contravening the first part of the maxim; (iii) gives too much information, and contravenes the second part of the maxim.

18.1.3.3 The maxim of relation

The **maxim of relation** is very simple:

Be relevant.

The point of this maxim is that it is not sufficient for a statement to be true for it to constitute an acceptable conversational contribution:

(26) A: Have you seen Mary today?
      B: ??I'm breathing.

Notice that this maxim is implicated in the maxim of quantity, which could easily be reformulated as in Levinson (1983: 106n.):

[Make] the strongest statement that can be relevantly made.

Here, 'the strongest relevant claim' is not materially different from 'as much information as is required'. The close relationships among the three maxims of quantity, quality, and relation have led some scholars to combine them into a single maxim. For instance, Levinson's version could easily be extended to:

[Make] the strongest statement that can be relevantly made that is justifiable by your evidence.

Here, 'justifiable by your evidence' corresponds to the maxim of quality. The relative 'strength' of two statements can be judged by the entailment relations between them: the stronger of the two entails the weaker. Hence, *John captured a badger* is stronger than *Somebody caught an animal*.

The maxim of relation can be understood on the everyday interpretation of the notion of relevance. But so much hinges on it, that it really ought to be more explicitly defined. Leech's version (1983) will suffice for the time being:

An utterance U is relevant to a speech situation to the extent that U can be interpreted as contributing to the conversational goals of S or H.

Relevance theorists have their own version, which will be outlined below.

18.1.3.4 The maxim of manner

The **maxim of manner** has four components:

  (i) Avoid obscurity
  (ii) Avoid ambiguity.
  (iii) Avoid unnecessary prolixity.
  (iv) Be orderly.

It is generally regarded as being less important than the others. It is largely self-explanatory, except that:

  (1) *Ambiguity*, of course, means 'ambiguity in context': it is virtually impossible to avoid potential ambiguity.
  (ii) Not everybody knows what *prolixity* means. The *Concise Oxford Dictionary* has 'lengthy, tediously wordy'.
  (iii) The 'orderliness' Grice had in mind was recounting events in the order that they occurred (if temporal relations are not explicitly signalled). A well-known infringement of this sub-maxim is:

(27) ?The lone ranger rode off into the sunset and jumped on his horse.

(Of course, there is nothing wrong with *The lone ranger rode off into the sunset after jumping on his horse*—well, not **much** wrong with it.)

18.1.3.5 The nature of the maxims

A number of points need to be made about the nature of the maxims. The first is that they are not rules, after the fashion of grammatical rules. They are much more flexible, more like guidelines. Infringing a rule of grammar leads to an ill-formed utterance; the maxims can be creatively infringed, frequently conflict with one another, and are to be followed by and large to the best of one's ability.

Grice is at pains to emphasize that the maxims are not culture-bound conventions like table manners: they are rationally based, and would hence be expected to be observable in any human society. In fact, Grice claims that similar maxims govern any cooperative activity. So, for instance, if workman A asks fellow workman B to pass him a chisel, B does not hand over a saw (maxim of quality), give two chisels (maxim of quantity), hand over a saw when none has been requested or seems necessary (maxim of relation), nor does he indicate the location of the chisel by means of a riddle (maxim of manner). This does not entail, however, that there are no cultural differences to be observed. One way in which cultures can differ is in the relative importance allotted to the maxims. For instance, a strict adherence to the maxim of quality may lead to no information at all being given. In some cultures this may come across as rudeness, and to avoid this result, it may be preferable to provide fictitious information in order to make up a seemly response.

18.1.4 How implicatures arise

It is now time to consider the question of how implicatures arise. In Grice's system, there are two main mechanisms. The first, which gives rise to what are sometimes called standard implicatures, requires the assumption that the speaker is doing their best to follow the cooperative principle, even though the result may not be the best, from the point of view of the hearer. The second mechanism involves a deliberate flouting of the maxims, which is intended to be perceived as deliberate by the hearer, but at the same time as nonetheless intending a sincere communication, that is to say, without abandonment of the cooperative principle. Let us look first of all at the first type.

18.1.4.1 Standard implicatures

In some cases, a single maxim seems sufficient to explain an implicature. Examples of this are easiest to find with the maxim of relation. One such is Grice's own example (already quoted: repeated here for convenience):

(28) A: (stranded motorist) I've run out of petrol.
      B: (passer-by) There's a garage just round the corner.

On the assumption that the speaker is obeying the relation maxim, B's reply in (28) implicates that the garage both sells petrol and is open, to the best of the speaker's knowledge; if either one or both of these were not the case, the utterance would not be relevant in this context. Another example might be the implicatures of questions in various contexts. Let us assume that the conventional force of an interrogative is to induce the hearer to produce an utterance with certain aspects of its content specified (as we saw in Chapter 17, this is not the only possible interpretation of interrogatives). A likely implicature of *What's the time?*, on the assumption that the speaker is observing the maxim, would be that the speaker did not know what the time was. However, in the context of an examination, it is not a plausible implicature of *What are the reasons for the decline of the Roman Empire?* that the utterer does not know the answer.

In most cases (probably), more than one maxim is involved. A number of implicature types can be attributed to Levinson's conflated maxim (expanded and repeated for convenience):

[Make] the strongest statement that can be relevantly made that is justifiable by your evidence.

Consider the following:

(29) A: Where's the corkscrew?
       B: It's either in the top drawer in the kitchen or it's fallen behind the piano.

The information given here is not really enough to satisfy the questioner, but if we suppose that B is doing his best to follow the cooperative principle, then we must conclude that something is preventing him from giving more. A likely possibility is that he doesn't actually know any more than he says, and to say more would violate the last clause of the (conflated) maxim.

Another related type of implicature goes under the generic heading of 'scalar implicature'. For instance:

(30) A: Have you read any of Hardy's novels?
       B: I've read some of them.

B's reply implicates that he has not read all of them. If he had in fact read all of them, in the context of the question this would have been (a) relevant information and (b) stronger than what was said, and the maxim would require it to have been given. Since the stronger statement was not made, there is an implicature that something prevents it. In this case, the most likely possibility is that it would not be true. In the following case, B would be seriously misleading the police officer (although perhaps not actually telling a lie) if he had in addition drunk five double whiskies:

(31) A (police officer): How much have you had to drink, sir?
       B (motorist): A half pint of lager, officer.

The implicature is that no relevant, true, stronger statement could be made—that is, B's alcohol intake was limited to half a pint of lager.

Yet another type of case explicable (partly) by Levinson's maxim is the following:

(32) A: What do you think of Mr X's candidacy for the post of Professor of Brain Surgery?
       B: Well, he's an excellent golfer, and a damn nice chap.

The implicature here is that surgical skill and experience do not figure amongst Mr X's qualities, otherwise they would be mentioned. However, to explicitly point out their lack would be insulting. It could be argued that the cooperative principle cannot wholly account for this, and a politeness principle is needed. This will be taken up below.

An example involving the maxims of relation and manner is the following:

(33) In order to obtain a ticket, take up a position with the feet no more than 50 cm. from the base of the machine, bending slightly from the waist towards the machine. Take a 20p coin, holding it vertically between thumb and forefinger. Insert the coin carefully into the slot indicated, and release it when inserted more than half-way. The ticket will appear in the lower left-hand slot of the machine.

(34) To obtain a ticket, insert a 20p coin into the machine.

Under normal circumstances, (33) is far more detailed than is required ((34) would be enough), and thus apparently infringes the 'avoid unnecessary prolixity' injunction. However, assuming the speaker is obeying the cooperative principle and is not given to verbosity, a possible reason for going against the relation maxim is that what is at first sight redundant information is in fact relevant; hence a likely implicature is that the situation is not normal, and the instructions must be followed to the letter, otherwise unpleasant consequences (or some such) may ensue.

18.1.4.2 Flouting the maxims

The other way in which implicatures arise is through deliberate flouting of the maxims in circumstances in which (a) it is obvious to the hearer that the maxims are being flouted, (b) it is obvious to the hearer that the speaker intends the hearer to be aware that the maxims are being flouted, and (c) there are no signs that the speaker is opting out of the cooperative principle. The hearer is thus given a signal that the utterances are not to be taken at face value, and that some sort of extra processing is called for. A weakness of these proposals is that no explanation or motivation is provided with respect to the exact nature of the extra processing. Any of the maxims may be violated in this benign way.

The maxim of quality

(35) The mushroom omelette wants his coffee with.
(36) I married a rat.
(37) It'll cost the earth, but what the hell!

In their most likely contexts of use, none of the above sentences is likely to be literally true, but equally, none of them is likely to mislead a hearer. In each case some additional interpretive process will be brought into play. In the first example, the interpretive process will be a metonymic one, and the understood message will be that the person who ordered a mushroom omelette wants his coffee served with the omelette, rather than afterwards. In the second example, the interpretive process will be a metaphoric one. In the third example, the implicatures are not so obvious, but hyperbole of this kind can implicate a relaxed, informal relationship with interlocutors.

The maxim of quantity

(38) Boys will be boys.

At first pass this gives no information at all. At second pass, we interpret the first boys in a subtly different way from the second boys. The first includes all boys, even those we thought had been tamed and could be relied on for good behaviour. The second is predicative, and presents certain stereotypic properties of boys as being innate and unavoidable.

(39) It must be somewhere.

Of course it must be somewhere. Completely pointless? Not quite: it implicates that a more determined search will be likely to result in success.

(40) Mother: What did you do last night?
     Daughter: (with exaggerated patience, elaborates a long list of totally uninteresting details)

This represents the inverse of the two previous examples, in that here, too much information is given. The implicature is that the mother is too damn curious, and overworried about her daughter's doings.

The maxim of relation

(41) A: I say, did you hear about Mary's . . .
     B: Yes, well, it rained nearly the whole time we were there.

This is an obviously irrelevant comment. Assume that A and B are having a conversation about a colleague, Mary. Mary approaches them, seen by B but not by A. The implicature is: *Watch out! Here comes Mary!*

The maxim of manner

(42) A: I'll look after Samantha for you, don't worry. We'll have a lovely time. Won't we, Sam?
     B: Great, but if you don't mind, don't offer her any post-prandial concoctions involving supercooled oxide of hydrogen. It usually gives rise to convulsive nausea.

The implicature arising from this unnecessary prolixity is obviously that B does not want Samantha to know what she is saying.

18.1.4.3 Particularized vs. generalized conversational implicatures

Grice introduced a distinction between conversational implicatures which are highly dependent on precise details of context and those which, while being defeasible, show a relative robustness in the face of contextual variation. He labelled the former **particularized conversational implicatures** (henceforth **PCIs**) and the latter **generalized conversational implicatures** (henceforth **GCIs**). Levinson (2000: 16) gives the following informal characterization:

a.   An implicature i from utterance U is *particularized* iff U implicates i only by virtue of specific contextual assumptions that would not invariably or even normally obtain

b.   An implicature i is *generalized* iff U implicates i *unless* there are unusual specific contextual assumptions that defeat it

Levinson illustrates the difference between PCIs and GCIs with an example of an utterance in two different contexts:

(**43**)   A: What time is it?
       B: Some of the guests are already leaving.
           PCI: It must be late.
           GCI: Not all of the guests are already leaving.
(**44**)   A: Where's John?
       B: Some of the guests are already leaving.
           PCI: Perhaps John has already left.
           GCI: Not all of the guests are already leaving.

Notice that the PCIs are tied to their contexts, but the GCI is insensitive to this particular change of context. In fact, the GCI 'Not all Xs are Y' is so closely bound to utterances of the form *Some Xs are Y* that most speakers will probably feel that *not all* is part of the meaning of *some*. However, the non-pleonastic nature of *Some, but not all Xs are Y* (cf. **John killed the wasp, but it died*), and the non-contradictory nature of *Some Xs are Y—in fact they all are* (cf. **John killed the wasp—in fact it didn't die*), show that *not all*, though regularly associated with *some*, does not have the status of a classical semantic component. This weaker status is taken by most pragmaticists as evidence that it is, in fact, an implicature.

Levinson (2000), building on Grice's work, suggests a division of GCIs into three types, which we shall call **Q-implicatures**, **I-implicatures**, and **M-implicatures**.

Q-implicatures

Q-implicatures are derived from the principle 'What you do not say is not the case'. Taken generally, this is obviously not true: it is intended to be applied to a salient, or relevant, set of alternatives, which generally differ in informativeness, newsworthiness, or 'strength'. Choosing a weaker member of such a set implicates the non-applicability of stronger members of the set. The scalar implicatures mentioned above fall under this general heading. The following are examples of Q-implicatures:

(45) He owns three cars.
   contrast set: one, two, three, four, five, . . .
   implicature: "not four", "not five", . . .

(46) If he's free, he'll let us know.
   contrast set: *since P, then Q; if P, then Q*
   implicature: "it's not certain that he is free"

(47) It made her ill.
   contrast set: *become ill; die*
   implicature: "she did not die"

(48) The gunman's target was the Prime Minister.
   contrast set: *have a target; hit a target*
   implicature: "the gunman did not hit the Prime Minister"

I-implicatures

I-implicatures are essentially enrichments of what is said. Levinson expresses the underlying principle thus: 'What is expressed simply is stereotypically exemplified.' (He subsequently attempts to broaden this principle in order to cover a wider variety of cases, but we will stay with the simpler version.) The basic idea is that if a hearer will normally expect something to be the case, we do not need to spell it out. The following are examples.

(49) Daddy brought me a kitten home for my birthday.
   implicature: "the kitten was alive"

(50) We went to that new restaurant yesterday.
   implicature: "we had a meal"

(51) John is going out with a nurse.
   implicature: "the nurse is female"

(52) If you want to come, I'll get you a ticket.
   implicature: "If you don't want to come. I won't get you a ticket."

M-implicatures

The principle underlying **M-implicatures** is, as it were, the other side of the coin from the I-principle, and can be expressed thus: 'Marked expressions call for marked interpretations.' In other words, there is usually a good reason for a departure from the 'normal' way of saying something. Example (33), taken as a departure from the more normal (34), illustrates this principle. The following are further examples (the sentences are from Levinson).

(53) Bill caused the car to stop.
   Simple expression for normal occurrence: *Bill stopped the car*
   implicature: "Bill did not stop the car in the normal way"

(54) The corners of Sue's lips turned slightly upwards.

Simple expression for normal occurrence: *Sue smiled*
implicature: "Sue's facial expression was not a normal smile"

All three principles can be related to Grice's original maxims; this reworking is intended to extract the basis specific to GCIs.

18.2 Politeness: principles and maxims

18.2.1 The politeness principle

There is no doubt that the cooperative principle can go some way towards explaining the generation of implicatures. But one class of implicature which receives no account under this heading concerns implicatures of politeness. For this, Leech has proposed an independent pragmatic principle, to function alongside the cooperative principle, which he calls the **politeness principle**.

Before we discuss this principle and its maxims, some discussion of politeness is in order. Politeness is, first and foremost, a matter of what is said, and not a matter of what is thought or believed. Leech expresses the politeness principle thus:

(I) Minimize the expression of impolite beliefs.

This is not an ideal formulation, as politeness does not essentially concern beliefs. However, it does have the merit of throwing the weight on to expression. Let us rephrase the principle as follows:

(II) Choose expressions which minimally belittle the hearer's status.

The sorts of thing which may be thought to belittle the hearer's status (or, alternatively expressed, 'cause the minimum loss of face to the hearer') are:

- Treating the hearer as subservient to one's will, by desiring the hearer to do something which will cost effort, or restrict freedom, etc.
- Saying bad things about the hearer or people or things related to the hearer.
- Expressing pleasure at the hearer's misfortunes.
- Disagreeing with the hearer, thus denigrating the hearer's thoughts.
- Praising oneself, or dwelling on one's good fortune, or superiority.

The purpose of politeness is the maintenance of harmonious and smooth social relations in the face of the necessity to convey belittling messages. Of course, the nature of reality—social, psychological, and physical—constrains the scope for politeness: if our world is to 'work', we must respect this reality. We can think of the cooperative principle as a restraining influence on the politeness principle.

It is worth while distinguishing between positive and negative politeness. Negative politeness mitigates the effect of belittling expressions:

(55) Help me to move this piano.
(56) You couldn't possibly give me a hand with this piano, could you?

Positive politeness emphasizes the hearer's positive status:

(57) Thank you, that was extremely helpful.

Generally speaking, we are more concerned, as social beings, with negative politeness, as breakdowns in social harmony are much more likely as a result of the expression of belittling thoughts. Another dichotomy in politeness phenomena is between speaker-related and hearer-related effects. Generally, speaker-oriented politeness involves self-belittlement, as any aggrandizement of self implies a relative belittling of the hearer. As a general rule, hearer-oriented politeness is more salient and more crucial.

Certain language expressions are specialized for polite use, such as *please* and *thank you*. These involve conventional implicatures, because the politeness is conventionally associated with the linguistic expressions. But the greater part of politeness comes across in the form of conversational implicatures, although these are arguably not propositional in nature. The overall mechanism Leech proposes for the generation of implicatures via the politeness principle is similar to that proposed by Grice for the cooperative principle. Each principle is accompanied by a set of more specific maxims.

18.2.1.1 The tact maxim

The tact maxim is oriented towards the hearer and has positive and negative sub-maxims:

Minimize cost to the hearer.
Maximize benefit to the hearer.

The operation of this maxim can be clearly seen in the context of **impositives**, that is, utterances which have the function of getting the hearer to do something (the term 'impositive' includes commands, requests, beseechments, etc.). We can roughly order impositives in terms of the cost to the hearer, greatest cost first:

Lend me your wife.
Wash the dishes.
Pass the salt.
Say 'Ah!'
Have another sandwich.
Have a nice weekend.

We can think of this as a continuous (cost–benefit) scale, although of course there is a switch-over, somewhere in the middle of the list, from cost to benefit.

How does the tact maxim work? Well, it is obvious that the linguistic form of the impositive is not going to affect the real cost or benefit to the hearer: what the maxim means is that in order to get a hearer to do something which involves a cost, a polite speaker will cast his utterance in a form which softens the effect of the impositive. Conversely, to get the hearer to do something to his benefit, a polite speaker will strengthen the impositive. What is meant by softening or weakening an impositive is, essentially, making it easier for the hearer to refuse. This can be done by increasing optionality or by increasing indirectness. These two factors cannot necessarily be clearly separated. For instance, (58) is more polite than (59), and (60) is even more polite:

(**58**) Could you wash the dishes?
(**59**) Wash the dishes!
(**60**) I was wondering if you could possibly wash the dishes.

Sentence (58) does not directly encode an imposition; its literal force is to enquire about the hearer's ability to perform the task, and leaves the impositive force to implicature. It is therefore more indirect than (59). Implicatures are inherently weaker than explicatures, so the impositive force is weaker, and a refusal by the hearer would be less impolite. Sentence (60) is even more indirect, as it does not, literally, even ask a question, but merely voices the speaker's internal musings.

Looking at impositives which correspond to a benefit to the hearer, we may first note that (61) is definitely not more polite than (62):

(**61**) I was wondering if you could possibly enjoy your holiday.
(**62**) Enjoy your holiday!

For impositives beneficial to the hearer, the situation is reversed, and the stronger impositives are the more polite. Sentence (61) is actually rather rude: it suggests that the hearer is a habitually gloomy, complaining type.

Notice that the politeness in the cases discussed does not inhere in the linguistic forms: there is nothing inherently polite in *I was wondering if you could possibly V*. Politeness is an implicature arising from a three-way interaction between explicature, the context, and the politeness principle.

18.2.1.2 The generosity maxim

The **generosity maxim** is a sister to the tact maxim, and is oriented towards costs and benefits to the speaker:

Minimize benefit to self.
Maximize cost to self.

This maxim works in a way parallel to that of the tact maxim, except that the effects are reversed. So, for instance, offers to do something which involves benefit to the hearer but cost to the speaker must be made as directly as possible, for politeness. Hence, (63) is more polite than (64):

(63) Let me wash the dishes.
(64) I was wondering if I could possibly wash the dishes.

On the other hand, politeness demands that requests for benefit to the speaker be weakened:

(65) I want to borrow your car.
(66) Could I possibly borrow your car?

18.2.1.3 The praise maxim

The maxims of praise and modesty form another natural duo, concerned in this case with the expression of positive or negative opinions about speaker or hearer. The **maxim of praise** is oriented towards the hearer, and goes as follows:

Minimize dispraise of the hearer.
Maximize praise of the hearer.

As usual, negative politeness is the more crucial, and hence the first sub-maxim is the more likely to be brought into play. The effect is to tone down any criticism or unfavourable comment:

(67) A: Do you like my new dress?
      B: *No.
      B: Well, yes, but it's not my favourite.
(68) A: Oh! I've been so thoughtless.
      B: *Yes, haven't you?
      B: Not at all—think nothing of it.

The effect of the second sub-maxim is to exaggerate praise:

(69) Thank you so much for inviting us. We had an absolutely wonderful time!

18.2.1.4 The modesty maxim

The modesty maxim is the natural partner of the previous one, being oriented towards the speaker, with the relevant 'values' reversed:

Minimize praise of self.
Maximize dispraise of self.

Praising oneself is inherently impolite, so negative politeness here is a matter of toning down self-congratulation:

(70) A: You did brilliantly!
      B: *Yes, didn't I?
      B: Well, I thought I didn't do too badly.

Positive politeness under this heading, that is, exaggerating protestations of worthlessness, tends in the direction of grovelling:

(71) Your Majesty, I am a mere worm, a disgusting toad, a dog's turd, and I deserve no forgiveness! I throw myself at Your Majesty's feet!

It is perhaps worth pointing out here the paradoxical fact that implicatures of politeness only arise when it is clear to the hearer that the speaker's utterance is not completely sincere. If someone does something very well and one tells them so, although such praise is in a sense inherently polite, and is enjoined by the maxim, it does not seem satisfactory to say that there is an implicature of politeness. The implicature is paradoxical because it indicates that the speaker's opinion is in reality less complimentary, or more critical, as the case may be, and this is of course less polite. In other words, the message "I am being polite" is itself impolite, although indirectly and therefore weakly. This kind of paradox runs through all politeness phenomena (see Leech 1983 for more detailed exemplification and discussion).

18.2.1.5 The agreement maxim

The final two maxims do not form a pair. This is not, as Leech claims, because they do not involve bipolar scales (at least one of them does), but because they are inherently relational in a way that the others are not. That is to say, agreement is a relation between the opinions of the speaker and those of the hearer. One cannot contrast an orientation towards self with an orientation towards hearer, as with praise, and benefit/cost: it does not matter whether agreement forms a bipolar scale or not. (One could argue about *agreement* (i.e. whether "disagreement" is "zero agreement", or whether there is a midpoint zero of 'no contact', with "agreement" and "disagreement" as polar extremes), but *sympathy/antipathy* (see next maxim) definitely is bipolar, with a central "indifference" representing zero between the two extremes). The **agreement maxim** is simply:

Minimize disagreement with the hearer.
Maximize agreement with the hearer.

The sub-maxims are not clearly distinct. A typical strategy is to begin with partial agreement before expressing disagreement:

(72) A: She should be sacked immediately. We can't tolerate unpunctuality.
     B: *I disagree.
     B: I agree with the general principle, but in this case there are mitigating circumstances.

18.2.1.6 The sympathy maxim

Sympathy is again a matter of a relation between speaker and hearer, and cannot, therefore, be differentially speaker- or hearer-oriented. The **sympathy maxim** has two sub-maxims:

Maximize sympathy (expression of positive feelings) towards the hearer.
Minimize antipathy (expression of negative feelings) towards the hearer.

As Leech points out, this maxim renders congratulations and commiserations or condolences inherently polite acts. Once again, however, it seems we can speak of implicatures of politeness only if a discrepancy can be intuited between what the speaker says and what he or she feels.

18.2.1.7 The consideration maxim

Leech presents the **consideration maxim** as a separate principle (the Pollyanna Principle), with, in my opinion, very little justification, as it works just like the other maxims:

Minimize the hearer's discomfort/displeasure.
Maximize the hearer's comfort/pleasure.

Negative politeness under this maxim involves the softening, by various devices, of references to painful, distressing, embarrassing or shocking events, facts, or things, etc. For instance, if someone's husband has recently died, it is more polite to say *I was sorry to hear about your husband* than *I was sorry to hear about your husband's death*, as the latter highlights the distressing event to a greater degree. Another typical manifestation of this sub-maxim is euphemism, where indirectness of various kinds is employed to avoid mention of words likely to cause offence. The following examples use a despecifying strategy:

(73) She has a lovely figure.
       *She has beautiful breasts.
(74) He exposed his parts.
       *He exposed his penis.

The following example uses a kind of frozen metonymy (at one time one had to put a penny in the door of a public toilet to get in):

(75) Hang on a minute, I need to spend a penny.
       *Hang on a minute, I need to piss.

The converse sub-maxim, concerned with positive politeness, requires one, for instance, to be more specific when referring to things the thought of which is likely to give the hearer pleasure. Thus, if the hearer's daughter, Jennifer, has just won an Oscar, then (76) is more polite than (77):

(76) That was great news about Jennifer's Oscar.
(77) That was great news about Jennifer.

18.2.2 Miscellaneous principles

Leech proposes two more principles, independent of both the politeness principle and the cooperative principle. We shall not propose additional principles, but follow the Gricean example and speak instead of deliberate flouting of the principle of politeness. There are two basic possibilities here; one can be superficially polite but patently insincere, leading to rudeness by implicature, or one can be superficially rude but patently insincere, leading to politeness by implicature. The insincerity must be indeed patent for the trick to work, and the strategy carries a certain risk that one might be taken at one's word. Leech groups the following sort of example under what he calls the **irony principle**:

(78) You're a fine friend! (with appropriate intonation)
(79) Do help yourself! (to someone who helps himself unjustifiably, without invitation)
(80) Well, thank you very much! (someone parks his car in front of your drive, so you can't get out)

The opposite sort of case comes under Leech's **banter principle** (actually both involve a type of irony):

(81) Look what the cat's just brought in.
(82) You stupid bitch! (to a close friend who's just done something daft)

The implicature here is that the relationship is so solid that politeness is not necessary, and this is of course a polite implicature.

18.2.3 General discussion

Like the cooperative principle, the politeness principle is intended to be universal—that is, not culture-dependent—in its application. However, probably even more than the maxims of conversation, the politeness maxims are given different relative weightings in different cultures, with the result that politeness phenomena in speech can have a very different superficial appearance, and a knowledge of the maxims is no guarantee that one can avoid solecisms. The relative weighting of cooperative as against politeness maxims also varies. For instance, a British hostess will probably take a compliment on her cooking something like this:

(83) Guest: Oh, Jane, that was a delicious meal.
      Jane: Thank you. I'm glad you enjoyed it.

However, a Japanese hostess in a similar situation (so it is reported) is obliged by politeness rules to deny any merit whatsoever in her efforts to entertain, so that quite long 'arguments' can ensue, with the guest praising the meal and the hostess denigrating it. This can be explained by the high weighting given to the modesty maxim in Japanese culture (and the relatively low weighting to the quality maxim, since it is unlikely that the Japanese hostess actually believes her meal to have been worthless). (The rules were, I understand, somewhat different at an earlier period in certain sections of British society, when the guest's comment in (83) would have been taken as an insult. The reason is that it would have been understood as the expression of a newsworthy proposition, that is, something unexpected! This presumably has something to do with the status of the maxim of relevance.)

18.3 Relevance theory

Relevance theory is a comprehensive pragmatic theory developed originally by the French anthropologist Dan Sperber and the British linguist Deirdre Wilson. The notion of implicature (which in a relevance-theoretical context refers only to conversational implicature) is a crucial concept of the theory. The following brief account is based mainly on Sperber and Wilson (1986), but also draws on the work of Diane Blakemore and Robyn Carston.

18.3.1 The principle of relevance

In relevance theory, the cooperative principle is replaced by the principle of relevance, and this in turn is claimed to make the separate maxims redundant. The principle of relevance has two parts (according to Carston (2002)), the first (cognitive) principle of relevance, and the second (communicative) principle of relevance:

The first (cognitive) principle of relevance
(IV) Human cognition is geared towards the maximization of relevance (that is, to the achievement of as many contextual (cognitive) effects as possible for as little processing effort as possible).

The degree of relevance of a communicated fact is governed by two factors:

(i) Contextual effects: the more of these there are, the greater the relevance of a particular fact. Contextual effects are such things as:

(a) adding new information;
(b) strengthening old information;
(c) weakening old information;
(d) cancelling old information.
   A new fact which is totally unconnected with anything already known is probably not worth processing. A new fact which, taken together with old information, allows many new inferences, is probably worth processing.

(ii) Processing effort: the less effort it takes to recover a fact, the greater the relevance of the fact. In particular, the following general points can be noted:

(a) More salient facts take less effort to access than less salient facts.
(b) Direct inferences take less effort than indirect inferences.

The second (communicative) principle of relevance (slightly modified)

(V) Every bona fide act of linguistic communication automatically carries with it, by the mere fact of its being executed, the utterer's belief in its optimal relevance.

In other words, by saying something (in the normal course of human inter-action) one is telling the hearer(s) not only that one thinks that what one says is worth the time and effort it will take to process it but also that no more easily processed utterance would give the same result.

The procedure to be followed by a hearer in interpreting an utterance is summarized by Carston (2002: 45) as follows:

Check interpretive hypotheses in order of their accessibility, that is, follow the path of least effort, until an interpretation which satisfies the expectation of relevance is found; then stop.

18.3.2 The problem of context

The proper context for the interpretation of an utterance is not given in advance; it is chosen by the hearer. The correct context is the set of assump-tions which yields adequate contextual effects compared with effort required when combined with new information contained in the utterance.

The speaker has the prime responsibility in communication: the speaker assumes certain facts about the hearer's knowledge and its organization, in particular the relative accessibility of facts. The speaker produces an utterance which will enable the hearer to make the correct inferences with minimum expenditure of cognitive effort.

The hearer's role is more passive. The hearer tries possible contexts in order of accessibility, and the first one to yield relevant inferences com-mensurate with the effort expended up to that point is the one intended by the speaker.

18.3.3 Explicature

Explicature corresponds in many ways to the Gricean 'what is said', but it is defined differently. The explicature of an utterance is closely tied to what is explicitly encoded in the linguistic form uttered, but is not identical to it. An explicature must be logically complete. For instance, if it is a statement, it must embody a proposition with a truth-value. It was pointed out in Chapter 2 that most sentences do not encode propositions. Carston goes further than this and claims, not implausibly, that none of them does. Hence, to get from what is encoded in an utterance to the explicature of the utterance, a process of elab-oration is necessary. This process of elaboration is driven by the principles of relevance. We shall illustrate four aspects of explicature where recourse to inference, guided by relevance, is required.

18.3.3.1 Disambiguation

Normal language is full of potential ambiguities, but these are only rarely noticed, because they are disambiguated by context. This disambiguation process is relevance-driven. Each of the following sentences contains at least one ambiguous word, but none of them is intuitively ambiguous, even out of context. In (84) and (85), the disambiguating information is at least partially given in the sentence, although relevance plays a part in both cases. In (84), the presence of *cheek* in the sentence predisposes us to select the reading "small dark spot on the skin" for *mole*, largely because the cognitive effort involved in creating a plausible scenario in which that particular proposition played a part is significantly less than that required to construct a scenario in which a furry animal or an industrial spy was involved. Less effort entails greater relevance, and hence that is the reading selected. In (85), the "small dark spot" reading of mole is ruled out as anomalous, but the relative difficulty of scenario construction for "industrial spy" as compared with "furry animal" ensures that the former is selected. Sentence (83) contains nothing specific to bias the interpretation towards a financial bank, but it is nonetheless the case that it is easier to envisage a scene where a financial bank is involved than one where the bank of a river is involved. This is because our memories contain records of frequently encountered scenarios which can relatively easily be retrieved.

(84) She has a mole on her left cheek.
(85) They managed to place a mole in the rival organization.
(86) I can't see you now, I've got to go to the bank.

18.3.3.2 Reference assignment

A second important role for inference in the construction of an explicature is in the identification of the referents of definite referring expressions. Obviously, context is crucial here. As an illustration, consider (87) (slightly adapted from Blakemore 1992):

(87) A: I'll make the salad dressing.
      B: The oil's on the top shelf.
      A: I can't see it.

We shall ignore the problem of identifying the referent for *the salad dressing* and move to the question of the referent of *the oil*. No oil has been mentioned up to that point, so which oil are we talking about? Relevance requires us to maximize contextual effects, and one way of doing this is to integrate an utterance with previous discourse. In the present instance, this can be done by retrieving an item of knowledge from memory to the effect that one of the ingredients of salad dressing is oil. This is known as **bridging** and is a common discourse-processing device. In this way an integration is accomplished, with satisfactory inferential consequences, by identifying the referent of *oil* with the oil needed to make the salad dressing. This is possible without any more contextual information.

But suppose, now, that A and B are in B's garage at the time of the utterance, and A is about to do some work on B's car. This context raises the possibility of an alternative referent for *oil*, namely engine oil. But notice that the referent of *oil* most likely would not change in the new context as described: this suggests that making connections with previous discourse has some kind of priority over making connections with immediate context— one may surmise that this is because it is more easily accessed. But then think of what would happen if A was actually working on the car, had the bonnet lid up, and the oil filler cap off, and A was looking around, scratching his head. Surely then we would interpret *oil* as engine oil? There must therefore be some point at which the salience (ease of access) of "engine oil" overtakes that of "salad oil", that is, when immediate situational context takes precedence over previous discourse. It seems that immediate context has to be very salient to suppress previous discourse. Clearly, too, previous discourse becomes less accessible the further back in time it is relative to the production of the definite referring expression, and presumably the easier it is for situational context to prevail.

What happens if there is no referent either in previous discourse or in immediate context (and none can be inferred by bridging)? In such a case it is possible to use general knowledge, as in (88):

(**88**) (Tourists A and B are having breakfast in a London hotel; the hotel has no tower, none has been mentioned, none is visible from where they are sitting.)
   A: What shall we do today?
   B: Let's visit the Tower. (N.B. speech has no capital letters!)

From the above considerations it seems we can state an order of preference for domains wherein a referent might be found, and this is probably the order in which they are searched:

previous discourse > immediate situation > stored knowledge

Clearly the processes of referent identification are complex and subtle, and the above discussion has no more than scratched the surface of the problem.

18.3.3.3 Enrichment

An important part of the process of constructing the explicature of an utterance is the recovery of missing components of the expressed propositions by **enrichment**. This involves fleshing out skeletal propositions, but not radically changing them (this notion is not entirely clear). Two varieties of enrichment can be distinguished: recovering missing elements in cases of ellipsis and resolving semantic incompleteness. The first of these is straightforward enough:

(**89**) A: When you've finished the dishes will you post these letters?
   B: I will.

Obviously, what B 'really means' is "I will post those letters when I've finished the dishes". Any assessment of the truth-value of B's utterance will take this as read. The missing portion can be reconstructed by grammatical rules.

The resolution of semantic incompleteness is less straightforward, at least in some cases, but the general idea is convincing enough. Usually, the missing information cannot be grammatically specified. The following are relatively clear examples:

(90) That one is too big.

Here we need to recover the standard against which size is being assessed: *too big* for what? Without this, the statement is virtually meaningless. Such examples are legion. Take (91) compared with (92):

(91) The petrol tank exploded some time after the impact.
(92) Her first suicide attempt occurred some time after her divorce.

Even if we take *some* to mean "relatively great", it seems likely to be interpreted in quite different terms in the two sentences: probably, in (91) it is to be taken as referring to minutes or even seconds, and in (92) as years. Sentence (93) is presumably to be taken as meaning that the speaker has brushed their teeth on the day of speaking, and not, for instance, at some point in their life; in (94), on the other hand, the latter interpretation could well be the speaker's intention.

(93) I've brushed my teeth.
(94) I've seen the Northern Lights.

Notice that if the last time the speaker of (93) had brushed their teeth was the day before, then *No, you haven't* would be a perfectly reasonable retort. Finally, in this connection, consider (95):

(95) The plate was hot and he dropped it.

According to Blakemore's account, the explicature here will contain information to the effect that the hotness of the plate was the cause of its being dropped. This is supported by the normality of *That's not the reason—he was drunk* as a subsequent comment.

18.3.3.4 Higher-order explicatures

According to relevance theorists, there are two kinds of (implicit) speech act **communicated speech acts** and **non-communicated speech acts**.

Communicated speech acts

Some speech acts are institutional and could not function without the existence of appropriate constitutive rules and social structures. These are communicated speech acts. They must be recognized for what they are in order to be properly comprehended. Examples are promising and thanking. Simply stating that you will do something does not of itself constitute a promise: if you subsequently do not do what you say you will do, the hearer has no grounds for accusing you of evading an obligation. Only if the utterance is intended and understood as a promise does the obligation become operative.

Non-communicated speech acts

These are acts which do not require the speaker to identify them as such in order to be successfully performed. Examples are:

asserting hypothesizing suggesting claiming denying entreating demanding warning threatening

Take the example of a warning:

(96) The path is slippery here.

To understand this fully, a hearer does not have to recover the sentence: *I warn you that the path is slippery here*. The speaker's intention is fully achieved if the hearer becomes aware that the path is slippery at the appropriate place, and derives the implicature that it might be dangerous. There is no **institution** of warning: a declarative utterance qualifies as a warning in virtue of certain intended implicatures, but these implicatures arise along with others as a result of general pragmatic processes. According to relevance theory, the specification of communicated speech acts will be part of explicature but the specification of non-communicated speech acts will not. So, for instance, if (97) represents a bet, then that must be recovered and incorporated as part of the explicature:

(97) Jane will leave the room before John arrives.

On the other hand, whether (98) is intended as a warning or not will be a matter of implicatures:

(98) The plates are hot.

18.3.4 Implicatures

The following is a sketch of the relevance-theoretical position; it sticks closely to Sperber and Wilson and to Blakemore. Consider sentence (100), which can be regarded as the full form of what was intended by B in (99):

(99) A: Why wasn't I invited to the conference?
       B: Your paper is too long.
(100) The article the hearer has written is too long to fit into a standard time-slot for the conference.

Notice that *your paper* has been disambiguated, and the reference length for *too long* has been supplied. Getting this additional information requires the use of inference based on contextual information (including general knowledge about the organization of conferences) together with the principle of relevance. Sentence (100) has a close relationship with the linguistic form of (99B): it represents an enrichment of (99B). Sentence (100) is therefore part of the explicature of (99B). Consider, now, (101) and (102):

(**101**) A: Did I get invited to the conference?
       B: Your paper was too long.
(**102**) A did not get invited to the conference.

Here, A will infer (102) from B's answer in (101), after accessing stored knowledge such as (103):

(**103**) If one's paper is too long for the conference one will not be invited.

Proposition (102), says Blakemore, cannot be regarded as an enrichment of B's utterance in (101), since there is no relationship between the linguistic form of B's utterance and assumption (102). She points out that (102) can only be inferred once the fully enriched form of B's utterance (i.e. (100)) has been retrieved. Hence (102) is not part of the explicature of (98B), but is an implicature.

Suppose someone were to ask why A does not infer (104):

(**104**) Nigel will not attend the conference.

Neither (104) nor (102) follows logically from (101B); (102) follows only when taken together with (103), an item of knowledge presumably stored in A's memory. But maybe A also has access to (105):

(**105**) If your paper is too long for the conference, you will not be invited.
      If you are not invited to the conference, there will be no papers on pragmatics.
      If there are no papers on pragmatics at the conference, then Nigel will not attend.

Why should A assume that (102) is B's intended message, rather than (104)? The reasoning goes something like this:

(i) The principle of relevance entitles the hearer to expect that they can obtain adequate contextual effects for a minimum cost in processing.
(ii) The more items of knowledge that need to be recovered, either from memory or from current situation, and the less accessible they are, the greater the processing effort.
(iii) A was able to obtain adequate effects with one easily accessible item of knowledge, and is therefore entitled to conclude that no further cognitive work was required, and to accept this as the whole of B's intended message.

The question must then be asked why B did not simply say (106) in answer to A's question in (101):

(**106**) No, you were not invited.

After all, (101B) requires more processing effort than (106) would have done. As Sperber and Wilson point out (1986: 197): 'it follows from the principle of relevance that the surplus of information given in an indirect answer must achieve some relevance in its own right.' That is to say, (101B) must produce more contextual effects than (106) would have done, and these must be sufficient to justify the extra effort that the speaker requires of the hearer. In this case a reason is given for the refusal of the paper, and this could, for instance, forestall an anticipated follow-up question.

18.3.4.1 Implicated premises and implicated conclusions

Recall the following exchange:

(**107**) A: Am I in time for supper?
       B: I've cleared the table.

B's reply does not directly answer A's question, but it enables A to recover information about mealtime scenarios and B's willingness to be put to a lot of extra trouble, which presumably includes at least some of the items in (108):

(**108**) When the table is cleared, there is no food, etc. on the table.
      For someone to have supper, food, etc. must be put on the table.
      Putting food on the table will require effort on someone's part.
      Someone who has just cleared the table will resent having to put the food etc. back.

B's reply in (107) and (108) taken together yield (109):

(**109**) A is too late for supper.

The propositions in (108) are implicated premises of B's reply in (107); (109) is an implicated conclusion. All implicatures fall into one of these categories. Implicated premises are part of the context that the hearer must construct in order to recover the implicated conclusion which is the main point of the utterance. The items in (108) play the same role in the derivation of (109) that bridging implicatures play in identifying referents.

18.3.5 Strong and weak implicatures

In relevance theory, the implicatures of an utterance come in a range of strengths, according to how much responsibility the speaker takes for them, and to how vital their contribution is to the relevance of the utterance. To quote Sperber and Wilson (1986: 199):

The strongest possible implicatures are those fully determinate premises or conclusions . . . which must actually be supplied if the interpretation is to be consistent with the principle of relevance, and for which the speaker takes full responsibility. Strong implicatures are those premises and conclusions . . . which the hearer is strongly encouraged but not actually forced to supply. The weaker the encouragement, and the wider the range of possibilities among which the hearer can choose, the weaker the implicatures. Eventually . . . a point is reached at which the hearer receives no encouragement at all to supply any particular premise and conclusion, and he takes the entire responsibility for supplying them himself.

(It is not clear what form this 'encouragement' takes. It would appear to be itself an implicature. This is a bit awkward, as it too must come in a range of strengths.)

One example from Sperber and Wilson goes as follows (1986: 194–8)):

(110)   Peter: Would you drive a Mercedes?
        Mary: I wouldn't drive **any** expensive car.

What is explicitly conveyed in Mary's utterance does not directly answer Peter's question; however, Mary might reasonably assume that Peter can retrieve the information in (111) from his general knowledge:

(111) A Mercedes is an expensive car

and using this as context (implicated premise), will derive the implicature (112):

(112) Mary wouldn't drive a Mercedes.

This would be a strong implicature—it is the main point of Mary's reply. But it cannot be everything that Mary wishes to convey, because it could have been more simply conveyed with a simple *No*. Sperber and Wilson suggest that the 'extra' consists of weaker implicatures. For instance, Peter might add (113) to the context and derive (114):

(113) People who refuse to drive expensive cars disapprove of displays of wealth.
(114) Mary disapproves of displays of wealth.

What about (115)? Can we be sure that everyone would class a BMW as an expensive car?

(115) Mary wouldn't drive a BMW.

Or, going further, would it be legitimate for Peter to use (116) to derive (117)?

(116) People who would not drive an expensive car would not go on a cruise, either.
(117) Mary would not go on a cruise.

Sentences (112), (114), (115), and (117) seem to be progressively weaker implicatures.

(It is perhaps worth pointing out that the relatively complex form of Mary's reply in (110) compared with *No* is justified without recourse to weak implicatures by the fact that it gives a reason for her refusal to drive a Mercedes.)

Sperber and Wilson suggest that 'poetic effects' are explicable in terms of richness of weak implicatures.

18.3.6 Constraints on relevance

In relevance theory, there are no implicatures corresponding to Grice's 'conventional implicatures'. Instead, these are analysed in terms of a distinction between **conceptual semantic information** and **procedural semantic information**. Some of the information coded in linguistic forms is not conceptual in nature, but functions to guide or limit the sorts of inferences the hearer is to draw. This notion of *constraints on relevance* was introduced by Blakemore (1987). Carston (2002) gives the following example (slightly altered):

(118) Ann: Are you interested in seeing *Sense and Sensibility*?
    Bob: Hmmm.
    Ann: It should be good, after all, Emma Thompson is in it.

We are concerned here with the 'meaning' of *after all*. According to Carston, *after all* 'indicates that the addressee is to process the following clause in such a way that it provides evidence or backing for some highly accessible assumption(s)'. In this case, the 'highly accessible assumptions' include the claim in the previous clause that the film should be good. The constraints operate on the clause *Emma Thompson is in it* as follows. The basic explicature of the clause is:

(119) Emma Thompson is in *Sense and Sensibility*.

The implicated premises are:

(120) If Emma Thompson is in a film, the film is likely to be good.
(121) If the film is likely to be good, we should go to see it.

And the implicated conclusions are:

(122) *Sense and Sensibility* is likely to be good.
(123) We should go to see *Sense and Sensibility*.

On this analysis, *after all* can be said not to contribute any propositional content to the implicated message. Words like *but*, *moreover*, and *therefore* can be given similar explanations. Notice, however, that the constraint is expressed in propositional terms: this approach does not give a revealing account of expressive meaning.

18.3.7 Conclusion

Providing an account of unencoded aspects of the meanings of utterances is arguably the central task of pragmatics. What has been presented in this chapter hopefully conveys some notion of the field, but it hardly scratches the surface either of the problem itself or of the solutions offered by linguistic pragmaticians, many of which are accompanied by lively polemics.

Discussion questions and exercises

1. By selecting suitable utterances for A, show how B's utterance can give rise to six different implicatures:

   A: ??
   B: Her black dress cost £500.

2. Each of the following conversational fragments is to some degree odd. To what extent can the oddness be explained by reference to Grice's cooperative principle and/or Leech's politeness principle?

   (a) A: Have you seen Peter today?
       B: Well, if I didn't deny seeing him I wouldn't be telling a lie.
   (b) A: Are you there?
       B: No, I'm here.
   (c) A: What did you do yesterday?
       B: I had a swim, changed into my swimming trunks, and went to the beach.
   (d) A: Thank you for your help, you've been most kind.
       B: Yes, I have.
   (e) A: Can you tell me where Mr Smith's office is?
       B: Yes, not here.
   (f) A: We're off to Mallorca tomorrow.
       B: I was wondering if you wouldn't mind enjoying your holiday.
   (g) A: Would you like some coffee?
       B: Mary's a beautiful dancer.
   (h) A: Would you like some more dessert, or coffee, perhaps?
       B: I'd like to go to the lavatory.
   (i) A: Thank you for a wonderful evening. The meal was delicious.
       B: No, it wasn't.
       A: Yes, really, we enjoyed it enormously.
       B: It was disgusting, and I was pathetic.
   (j) A: Has the postman been?
       B: He leant his bicycle against the fence, opened the gate, strode briskly down the path, stopped to stroke the cat, reached into his bag, pulled out a bundle of letters and pushed them through our letter-box.

3. Classify the propositions in brackets in each of the following as (i) an entailment from the explicature, (ii) part of explicature by enrichment, (iii) a particularized conversational implicature, (iv) a generalized conversational implicature, or (v) only possible by an ad hoc agreement between A and B:

(a) A: What happened to the rat?
     B: John killed it.
     ("The rat is dead")

(b) A: Who was the last one to leave the office last night?
     B: That would be either Jane or Sue.
     ("B doesn't know whether the last to leave the office was Jane or Sue")

(c) A: What's Bill's new house like?
     B: The garden's beautiful.
     ("Bill's new house has a garden")

(d) A: Did you bring the photos?
     B: I left them on the kitchen table.
     ("It's time to leave")

(e) A: Did you speak to John about the CD?
     B: It wasn't John that borrowed it.
     ("Somebody borrowed the CD")

(f) A: Shall we go to your place?
     B: My Dad's in.
     ("A and B can't go to B's place")

Suggestions for further reading

The seminal work on the topic is Grice (1975). The commentary in Levinson (1983) provides amplification and discusses some of the trickier points. Grice's intellectual heirs are of two main sorts. The so-called 'Neo-Griceans' seek to refine his system and remedy perceived weak points. The main proponents of this approach are Horn and Levinson, and their views can be sampled in Horn (1984) and Levinson (1989). Leech (1983) uses a Grice-like approach to explain implicatures of politeness, which he claims are overlooked by the standard Gricean account. A more radical challenge is provided by relevance theory. The source text for this is Sperber and Wilson (1986); a simpler introduction is Blakemore (1992). The most recent account, more advanced than Blakemore, is Carston (2002).

Conclusion

We have now completed our survey of the landscape of meaning in language. Having acquired a basic conceptual toolkit for semantic analysis, we have looked in some detail at the principal bearers of meaning in language, namely words, at their meanings, their interrelations, how they combine, how new meanings are created, in both the short term and the long term, and how grammar contributes to (indeed, is vital to) the assembling of complex meaning structures.

Of course language is not a self-sufficient, hermetically sealed system. It has to make contact with the world in which we live, one way or another. We have accordingly looked at principles and mechanisms of reference. We have also taken note of the fact that what people say typically encodes only part of their intended message, and we have looked at the principles which enable hearers to flesh out the encoded meaning to yield a much richer message.

The survey has necessarily left many details and complications unexplored, but at least we have over-flown the terrain, and picked out the principal landmarks.

We started out by relating the notion of meaning in language to the wider one of communication. It is important to emphasize that all the complexities and richness we have observed in connection with meaning phenomena exist/ have evolved because they are essential to a communication medium which is efficient and flexible and has unlimited expressive power.

All systematic aspects of meaning contribute to efficiency in storage and use: recurrent sense relations, patterns of sense extension, compositional principles. Pragmatic principles which allow many message components to be inferred rather than being overtly encoded ensure economy in use by reducing the length of utterances.

Flexibility is ensured by the fact that new meanings can either be created in response to the fleeting demands of a particular situation (nonce readings) or permanently laid down for long-term use in response to large-scale changes in the physical, social, or conceptual environment.

A recursive syntax, together with principles of compositionality, is essential to a communication medium which has universal expressive power. Probably few messages, if any, in the real world are conveyed with no loss occurring between the speaker's intention and the hearer's apprehension. However, the design of human language allows us to approach as nearly as is necessary to any point or area in semantic space.

Is the study of meaning in language of any practical utility? Well, yes, at least potentially. For instance, everyone concerned with the teaching of language can benefit from, on the one hand, being made aware of aspects of meaning of which they formerly only had a subliminal knowledge and, on the other hand, acquiring an arsenal of descriptive concepts and techniques which lend discipline and precision to thinking.

A field of endeavour where lexical semantics is of potential utility is the making of dictionaries. The theoretical concerns of lexical semantics impinge on the practical concerns of lexicography at a number of points. One is in establishing criteria for sense division—at present a somewhat hit-or-miss affair, as can be seen by comparing different dictionaries. Another is in the ordering of material in articles so as to highlight relationships. Others include: the structure of definitions, establishing criteria for deciding what collocational information to include, and the discrimination of near-synonyms (something current dictionaries are rather bad at). (It has to be admitted, however, that the 'dynamic construal' approach to word meaning seems at first sight to undermine the work of lexicographers. At the very least, the nature of the lexicographer's craft needs to be rethought.)

As a final example, mention might be made of a field whose promise is yet to be realized: and that is the electronic processing of language, whether for the purpose of machine translation, designing 'intelligent' robots capable of responding to ordinary language commands, or designing systems whereby humans can interrogate large databases in ordinary language and receive answers likewise. Progress is unlikely on any of these fronts without a deep knowledge of how meaning works in normal human interaction (even if, in the end, successful automated systems are not merely copies of human models).

The current state of knowledge about meaning phenomena is very patchy: some areas are relatively well charted compared with others. But in all domains, serious black holes of ignorance abound. Many of the fields of uncertainty involve very fundamental issues: for instance:

- How best to represent the semantic properties of a word. Should we aim for some sort of core meaning, from which variations in context can be predicted? (No one has yet come up with a satisfactory way of doing this, although as a programme it has its attractions.) Or are observed word meanings created on-line on the basis of a mass of memory traces of actual usage?
- Are there such things as stable conceptual primitives, semantic atoms? If so, what are they like? Is the task like the human genome project—almost unimaginably complex, but in principle feasible, given time and money—or

is it fundamentally flawed? (If the dynamic construal approach is correct, then semantic atoms will go the way of fixed word meanings.)

- Progress has undoubtedly been made in the understanding of metaphor, yet the true nature of metaphor, especially novel metaphor, seems still to elude the grasp of researchers.
- The constraints on possible word meanings are only partially understood.
- I have no doubt that relevance is one of the key concepts of pragmatics, but in spite of the efforts of relevance theorists, for my money the bird of relevance is still flying free in the bush.
- Finally, in this (somewhat selective) inventory of knowledge gaps, very little has been established regarding the most fundamental question of all: how does language connect with the things and events in the world around us? How does the whole system work?

It sometimes seems that everyone has been, as it were, paddling at the edge of the ocean. However, this is perhaps overly pessimistic: progress has undoubtedly been made, and will continue to be made—and the enterprise is a worthwhile one.

Answers to questions

Chapter 2: Logical matters

1. Arguments and predicates

yawn	one-place
steal	three-place (X *stole* Y *from* Z)
thank	three-place (X *thanked* Y *for* Z)
pay	four-place (A *paid* B C *for* D)
be tall	one-place
be taller than	two-place
meet	two-place
put	three-place (X *put* Y *somewhere*)
imagine	two-place (one place may be occupied by a proposition, as in A *imagined* X *stealing* Y *from* Z)
day-dream	one-place
cost	syntactically three-place, but arguably four-place semantically, like *buy, sell, pay,* etc.
understand	two-place
explain	three-place (in *John explained the problem*, there is an implicit audience for John's explanation)

2. Sentence, statement, utterance, and proposition

X was inaudible.	utterance
X was uninformative.	statement, utterance (a proposition only becomes potentially) informative when we know whether it is true or false: in itself, it tells us nothing; a statement comes with the 'epistemic commitment' of the speaker)
X was false.	proposition, statement, utterance
X was in a foreign accent.	utterance
X was ungrammatical.	sentence, statement, utterance
X was insincere.	statement, utterance

3. Propositional and non-propositional meaning

(a) Non-propositional. The desired action is the same for both, but there is a difference in expressive meaning.

(b) One answer is that these are propositionally identical, because the context of *cheaper* indicates that *get* is to be interpreted as "buy". However, it is not totally out of the question that *get* is used to mean "steal", and *cheaper* refers to the cost of getting to Gregg's, in which case the difference would be propositional.

(c) Intuitions differ here. For some, the only difference is in the attitude expressed, which is non-propositional. For others, there is no contradiction in saying *John's thin, but he's not skinny*, which suggests that *skinny* not only expresses an attitude but also denotes a higher degree of thinness, in which case there are both propositional and non-propositional differences.

(d) Propositional. Sentence (i) perhaps expresses disrespect for the writings, but passes no judgement; sentence (ii) passes a negative judgement, and can be contradicted with *It wasn't garbage*.

(e) Propositional, even if both are interpreted to refer to time. The start of a race is a more narrowly delimited time than the beginning, so (ii) could be true and (i) false.

(f) Non-propositional. There is no conceivable circumstance in which one could be true and the other false. *Yet* expresses some sort of expectation, but non-propositionally.

(g) Non-propositional. The difference is one of register.

4. Entailments

(a) No entailment. A cat may lose a leg without ceasing to be a cat.

(b) (i) entails (ii).

(c) (i) entails (ii).

(d) No entailment. On the assumption that *quadruped* denotes an animal which in its well-formed state has four legs, a cat which lost a leg would not thereby lose its status as a quadruped.

(e) (i) entails (ii), but only if we take *animal* to mean "belongs to the animal kingdom". In the more everyday sense of *animal* which contrasts with *fish, bird, insect*, etc., there is no entailment.

(f) (i) entails (ii) (with the same proviso as in (e)).

(g) Here we encounter two problems. The first concerns the status of *cyberpets*: are they pets? If the answer is 'yes', then presumably there is no entailment. But even if the answer is 'no', there is still the problem of dead pets. If *living* means "belongs to the realm of organic matter" (or some such—it is actually quite difficult to formulate), and we exclude cyberpets, then we can say that (i) entails (ii).

(h) (i) entails (ii), but only if X belongs to the realm of entities of which "dead" and "alive" can properly be predicated. *The table is not dead* does not entail *The table is alive*.

(i) First we have to decide whether (i) means that X has given up the habit, or has just put out a cigarette. There is a possibility of entailment only in the first case. But even that is arguable, because there are people who give up smoking several times during their life. Strictly speaking, all that is entailed is that there was at least one period when X did not smoke.

(j)   If Z is something like French, or mathematics, then, alas, there is no entailment. But curiously, if Z is expressed as an infinitive, as in *John taught Bill to swim*, then according to my intuitions, there is entailment.

(k)   At first sight, (i) seems to entail (ii), but this ignores the possibility of resurrection. Strictly, all that is entailed is that there was a period when Y became not alive.

(l)   In normal use, *watch* presupposes a changing stimulus, so we *watch* a game, but *look at* a painting. However, the mere expectation of change is sufficient to license the use of *watch*, so there is no entailment.

5. Relations between propositions

(a)   Contradiction.

(b)   Contrariety (John may be indifferent).

(c)   Contradiction, assuming that normal presuppositions are satisfied, e.g. that Mary understands the statement, and has an opinion about it; otherwise, contrariety.

(d)   These are converses (and are equivalent).

(e)   Contradiction (barring resurrection for wasps).

(f)   If we interpret *bachelor* as meaning "marriageable man who is not married" (thereby excluding three-year-old boys and the Pope), then there is no logical relation. If, on the other hand, *bachelor* simply means "unmarried male person", then (i) and (ii) are equivalent.

6. Logical relations

parent of	intransitive; asymmetric.
ancestor of	transitive; asymmetric.
brother of	transitive; non-symmetric (if A is B's brother, B might be A's sister).
related to	transitive (for blood relations; for relations by marriage things are not so clear—is one's brother-in-law's cousin a relation?).
sibling of	Transitive; symmetric.
friend of	Non-transitive; symmetric.
near to	Non-transitive (if A is at the limit of what can be described as *near to* B, and C is similarly disposed with respect to B, but in the other direction from A, then A may not be near enough to C to count); symmetric.
to the right of	Transitive (assuming a constant reference point); asymmetric.
far from	Non-transitive (if A and B are both far from C, they could be next to each other); symmetric.
resembles	Non-transitive; in some sense symmetric from the strictly logical point of view, but notice that while it might be acceptable to say *My brother resembles Julius Caesar*, it would be decidedly odd to say *Julius Caesar resembled my brother*.

Chapter 3: Types and dimensions of meaning

1. Types of anomaly

(a) Dissonance; notice that substitution of *not as bad as* for *better than* removes the anomaly (for discussion, see Chapter 9, section 9.2.2.3).

(b) There are two anomalies here. *What happened tomorrow* involves a dissonance; *a bad disaster* illustrates pleonasm (all disasters are bad; notice that substitution of *terrible* for *bad* removes the pleonasm, because some disasters are worse than others).

(c) The anomaly can be cured either by replacing *conceal* with the near-synonymous *hide*, or by adding a closed-set item, namely *yourself*; it is therefore grammatical in nature.

(d) Zeugma; plays on two readings of *dog*: "member of canine species"/"male of canine species".

(e) Improbability.

2. Degree of necessity

(a) Improbable.

(b) Expected. Not canonically necessary, because well-formed Manx cats do not have tails.

(c) Expected.

(d) Impossible.

(e) Natural necessity.

(f) Logically necessary.

(g) Possible.

(h) Canonically necessary.

3. Presuppositions

(a) Lesley is a woman.

(b) Lesley plays the clarinet.

(c) Lesley is an undergraduate.

(d) Lesley has caused a lot of trouble.

(e) Somebody wrote the letter.

(f) Lesley was ill; Lesley serves on the committee.

4. Dimensions of descriptive meaning

(a) Specificity.

(b) Quality.

(c) Intensity.

(d) Vagueness.

(e) Viewpoint.

5. Dimensions of non-descriptive meaning

(a) Expressive meaning (surprise?).

(b) Evoked meaning: style.
(c) Evoked meaning: field.
(d) Expressive meaning (intensity of desire; politeness); evoked meaning (register: style).

Chapter 4: Compositionality

1. Modes of combination

a forged passport	negational (assuming that such a document is not really a passport; otherwise, Boolean)
a dead cat	Boolean
long eyelashes	relative
a clever footballer	indirect/relative (ambiguous)
a high price	relative
artificial cream	negational
a former Miss World	negational
a black hat	Boolean
a brilliant pianist	indirect/relative (ambiguous)
a poor singer	indirect/relative (ambiguous)
a small planet	relative
a striped dress	Boolean

2. Conventionalized expressions

(a) *You have to hand it to him*: frozen metaphor.
     he's got guts: compositional: non-default reading of *guts*.
(b) Frozen metaphor (drawn from tennis).
(c) Idiom.
(d) Compositional: cliché
(e) Idiom.
(f) Frozen metaphor.
(g) Idiom.
(h) Compositional: collocation — non-default reading of *loaf*.
(i) Compositional: cliché.
(j) *He swallowed it*: collocation — non-default reading of *swallow*.
     lock, stock, and barrel: for those who know that these are parts of a rifle, frozen metaphor; for most of us, idiom.
(k) Idiom.
(l) Cliché.

3. Semantic constituents

A full answer is not possible here. The following are some suggestions:

(a) Fully meaningful:
     (i) *dislike, disapprove* (*like* and *dislike*, *approve* and *disapprove*, are closest to antonyms — see Chapter 9);

     (ii) *dismount, disembark* (*mount* and *dismount, embark* and *disembark* are reversives);

     (iii) *discolour, displace* (*discolour* means something like "cause to become wrong in respect of colour"; *displace* (on one reading) means "cause to become wrong in respect of place");

     (iv) (a case can perhaps be made for *disconfirm* and *dispossess*, but neither meaning is recurrent).

  (b) For most words beginning with *dis-* the prefix is not independently meaningful: *disgust, dismay, disgruntle, disturb, disport, discover, disconcert,* etc.

4. Active zones

  (a) Father's hand; son's buttocks.
  (b) Petrol tank.
  (c) Ambiguous: frames or lenses.
  (d) Unambiguous: lenses.
  (e) Handle.
  (f) Blade.
  (g) The carrying out of operations.
  (h) The drinking of it.

Chapter 6: Contextual variability

1. Distinctness of readings

  (a) Homonymous senses (these are etymologically related, but I imagine few speakers of current English can intuit a relationship).
  (b) Polysemous senses.
  (c) Different perspectives.
  (d) Different facets.
  (e) Microsenses.
  (f) Polysemous senses.
  (g) Polysemous senses; (autohyponymy: (b) is hyponymous to (a)).
  (h) Contextual modulation.
  (i) Different facets.
  (j) A difficult case: these may well be local senses on a sense spectrum.

2. How many senses?

This is quite a difficult exercise, and illustrates the problems of 'real-life' lexicography. My analysis would be as follows, but there is room for disagreement.
    There seem to be two basic meanings of *collect*:

  (A) "bring scattered or distributed items together in one place";
  (B) "pick up and take away".

A straightforward example of (A) is: (d); (e) is a straightforward metaphorical extension; (b) and (i) are distinct specializations (in (i), the direct object (presumably money) is incorporated into the meaning of the verb).

Examples of (B) are: (c), (f), (j), (k), and (n). The instances in (l) and (o) are presumably metaphorical extensions of this sense (in neither case do the recipients literally 'pick up' anything).

Readings (a) and (g) are obviously related (although distinct by our criteria), and differ from (A) and (B) in that *book* designates a location in both cases. There is an intuitive connection between these and (h), but this has to be considered separate, as there is no transitive version (*The notice board collects students*).

We have not yet accounted for (m). There is a possible connection with (A) (*They survived by collecting mushrooms from the fields and rainwater in a bucket*); but there is also a possible relation to (a)/(g) (*Rainwater collects in the bucket*). My vote would go to the former solution, but the matter is far from clear-cut.

Chapter 7: Word meanings and concepts

2. Basic-level categories

The following would be basic-level for me:

SANDAL SEAGULL DAISY GRASS BULLDOZER BUS SUGAR
DELI(CATESSEN) SUPERMARKET PETROL STATION TOWN HALL MOTORWAY
ROAD PARK CANAL POLICE STATION WINE MILK

(It is true that in one of the senses of *road* a motorway is a kind of road, but the default reading of *road* is one that excludes motorways.)

Chapter 8: Paradigmatic sense relations of inclusion and identity

1. Taxonymy

The following are related by taxonymy:

poodle:dog
cottage:house
hailstone:precipitation
boot:footwear
icing sugar:sugar

2. Meronymy

Readers will have to give their own answers to this. My judgements would be as follows:

(a) prototypic examples
   belt:buckle; jacket:lapel; fork:prong; candle:wick; door:hinge
b) non-prototypic examples
   shoe:lace; hand:vein; beard:hair; finger:tip
(c) borderline
   building:façade; bread:crumb; omelette:egg; colander:hole; potato:peeling
(d) non-examples
   bottle:cap; hot-water bottle:water; bed:sheet; cassette player:cassette

The non-examples all seem to lack the feature of integrality. The borderline cases are not sufficiently congruent in some respect. I am less sure about the non-prototypic examples: *lace* is not sufficiently necessary for *shoe*; *hand* and *vein* are non-congruent with respect to type; the *tip* of a *finger* is perhaps not sufficiently distinct; perhaps prototypic parts need to be different from their sister-parts, and that is why *beard:hair* is not prototypic.

3. Synonyms

(a) There are no absolute synonyms; all are at least near-synonyms. I would put *brave, courageous, gallant*, and *plucky* together in a group of propositional synonyms, since it seems paradoxical to assert any one and deny another. *Heroic* and *valiant* differ from the members of the first group in intensity, and therefore are not propositionally synonymous with them, since one can say *He was brave (etc.), but not heroic* but not *?He was heroic, but not brave*. Probably *heroic* and *valiant* differ in intensity, too, with the former denoting the higher degree of the quality. *Bold* and *daring* should probably be separated from the rest because the others express a degree of approval of the action qualified, hence the oddness of ?a brave/courageous/etc. *robbery*; also, *daring* indicates a higher degree of fearlessness than *bold*.

Within the group of propositional synonyms, there are nonetheless differences. For instance, a prototypic *courageous* act has a moral dimension, and requires awareness of wider issues; hence it is odd to describe a child or a dog as *courageous*, although they may be *brave*; bravery is prototypically displayed in the face of physical danger or suffering. *Gallant* is usually used of persons engaged in battle (as is *valiant*); *intrepid* is more at home in non-combatant situations (according to my intuitions, one can be *brave* without being *intrepid*, the latter indicating a lack of fear, rather than the ability to overcome fear); *plucky* expresses condescension towards the referent, but according to my intuitions is not propositionally distinct.

(b) Most dictionaries are rather bad at discriminating near-synonyms.

Chapter 9: Paradigmatic relations of exclusion and opposition

1. Types of opposition

(a) Complementaries.
(b) Incompatibles.
(c) Co-meronymy.
(d) Complementaries.
(e) Reversives.
(f) Antipodals.
(g) Antonyms.
(h) Converses.
(i) Incompatibles.
(j) Antonyms (on the assumption that (i) one can have a neutral stance and (ii) there are degrees of approval and disapproval).

2. Antonyms

far:near	polar
beneficial:harmful	equipollent
happy:sad	equipollent
brilliant:stupid	implicit superlatives
deep:shallow	polar
advantageous:disadvantageous	equipollent
fat:thin	(for the majority of my students these are equipollent)
happy:unhappy	referring to an emotional state, overlapping; in the sense of "happy/unhappy with something", privative
satisfied:unsatisfied	privative
comfortable:uncomfortable	intuitions differ: for me, they are privatives
polite:rude	overlapping
easy:difficult	polar
thick:thin	polar
rough:calm	privative (*calm* denotes the absence of waves)

Chapter 10: Word fields

There is no 'correct answer' here, but working through the sets will dispel any notion that vocabularies oblige us by falling into neat, well-structured fields. Structuring is present, but mostly in smallish fragments, and there is quite a lot of messiness.

(a) The following words (at least) must be added to the set: *tableware, glassware, table linen, crockery, cutlery, condiments*. Mostly, this set is not problematic. There is a problem, however, of how to place the likes of *breadboard, table mat, napkin ring*, and so on. Also, assuming a cake-slice is an item of cutlery, does it fall under *knife*?

(b) There are several problems with this set. One is the lack of superordinate terms, for instance, for clothes that are prototypically worn indoors on everyday occasions, like jacket, trousers, shirt, sweater, skirt; also for clothes normally worn outdoors, such as overcoat or anorak. Another difficulty is the fact that the branches of the hierarchy have a tendency to intersect. For instance, vest can fall under underwear and sportswear, sweater under knitwear and 'ordinary wear'; outdoor wear and sportswear overlap, but not completely, and so on. This is because the superordinate terms embody different classificatory principles which are not necessarily mutually exclusive (sportswear: purpose; nightwear/ slumberwear: time; underwear: position relative to body, and so on). Men's and women's clothes partially overlap (but we have no superordinate terms for them). Some items double as 'free-standing' items and parts of an ensemble (e.g. suit and jacket).

(c) In this set, taxonomic relations (like dictionary:book) must be carefully distinguished from part–whole relations (like page:book). Even so, there is a problem of intersecting branches: for instance page will come under several headings. Do we say that different microsenses are involved? Account must also be taken of facets.

Chapter 11: Extensions of meaning

2. Examples of non-literal use

(a) *a nearly overwhelming desire* — hyperbole
(b) *a quick bowl of soup* — metonymy
kick into high gear — metaphor
the principals in the cast — metaphor
(c) *a fruitless attempt* — metaphor
to cut into the heat — metaphor
(d) *room 323 is not answering* — metonymy
(e) *staring out at the night* — metonymy
(f) *the yawning three-storey drop* — metaphor
kick in — metaphor
(g) *his name was being withheld* — metaphor
withheld from the local papers — metonymy
(h) *I could practically hear . . .* — hyperbole
hear Mac squinting — metonymy (his voice betrayed an emotion which typically makes a person squint)
(i) *July . . . is an unsettling affair* — metonymy
(j) *my sleep-smudged face* — metaphor (viewing sleep as a substance)
(k) *she's probably in the book* — metonymy
(l) *mortgaged to the eyeballs* — metaphor (debt is a liquid which can drown a person)
wasn't worth a cent — hyperbole
(m) *the day [was] all heat and bugs* — metonymy

ear-splitting regularity	hyperbole (also metonymy — regularity doesn't split ears)
(n) *have me switched over*	metonymy
(o) *pleated with erosion*	metaphor
the hills rose up	metonymy
the heaving gray Pacific	metaphor

Chapter 12: Syntagmatic relations

1. Contextual selection

(a) *Going to* has as selectional preference "location". *Club* is ambiguous ("blunt instrument"/"place of entertainment"), but only one reading is a philonym of *going to*; *bank* is also ambiguous, but both readings are philonyms of *go to*. Selection is therefore by discourse coherence.

(b) *Book* has several readings, "record a sporting offence", "reserve a place at a restaurant, theatre, etc.", "engage a performer". Neither of the first two has its selectional preferences satisfied by any reading of what follows. However, one of the readings of *turn* satisfies the preferences of the third reading of *book*; there is thus a species of mutual selection. Finally, only one of the readings of *right* has its selectional preferences satisfied by the sense of *turn* compatible with *book*.

(c) *Gain several pounds* is only two-ways ambiguous, although both *gain* ("earn/win"; "put on") and *pounds* ("money"; "weight") are ambiguous. This is because for each reading of *gain*, only one reading of *pound* satisfies it, so the pairs are mutually selecting. In the case of *wear an ensemble* there is only one pair of philonyms, namely *wear* = "carry on body" and *ensemble* = "set of clothes", the reading "group of musicians" for *ensemble* being excluded by semantic clash. The reading "put on weight" for *gain several pounds* is selected because of the greater accessibility of a plausible scenario in which the whole sentence might be used.

2. Degree of clash

(a) Inappropriateness.
(b) Incongruity.
(c) Inappropriateness.
(d) Paradox (can be normalized by substituting a different period of time).
(e) Incongruity.

3. Selectional restrictions

a record X	*score, price, distance, temperature, speed*: requires some variable property that can be calibrated on a numeric scale, a high value of which is newsworthy (notice that *record kindness/ politeness/hardness* are slightly odd).
a sad X/X is sad	*woman, teacher, family*: requires a human being, or group of

human beings (?*The horse is sad*), who has enough maturity to grasp a situation (?*The baby is sad*).

film, book, poem, song, event: requires something which expresses, describes or denotes a state of affairs.

a leisurely X   *meal, tour, walk round the park, cycle ride, shopping trip*: human activity, usually involving moving about;
voluntary;
can be performed for enjoyment;
speed variable without interfering with purpose.

Can you lend me X?   *your car, a fiver, a pen, a tie, some sugar*: inanimate (usually);
fit for some specific purpose;
control transferable temporarily;
can be restored unchanged or replaced with same.

Chapter 13: Lexical decomposition

None of the following suggested analyses is fully satisfactory, and for each there are (at least) equally good alternatives:

skirt   object
clothing
worn by women
on lower part of body
attached at waist
legs not individually covered
normally visible

book   object
serves as locus of text
has many pages bound together
has cover
not part of an indefinite series appearing at regular intervals

cottage   object
dwelling
small
permanent
stone or brick

teaspoon   object
implement
cutlery
with cup-shaped concavity at one end
for adding sugar and stirring tea in cup

violin   object
musical instrument
stringed

                     played with bow
                     lowest note: G below middle C
dream   process
                     mental
                     during sleep
                     experience unreal events
kiss (v.)   action
                     physical
                     intentional
                     apply lips to something
                     functions as conventional signal

Chapter 15: Grammatical semantics

1. Number

cattle   Singular in form, plural concord: *These cattle are* . . ;
              unhappy when explicitly counted, except with classifier:
              ?seven cattle, seven head of cattle; no singular use.
oats   Plural concord: *These oats are* . . ., but (for me) more normal to express
              quantities with *much* than with *many*:
              How much/?many oats does that sack contain?
              This feed has too much/?many oats in it.
              Singular form has a distributive meaning: This is an excellent oat for acid
              soil.
scissors   Plural in form and concord: *These scissors are* . . .; singular reference (so-
              called **pluralia tanta**); needs classifier for counting: *one/two pair(s) of*
              scissors.
iron filings Plural in form, concord and reference: *these iron filings are* . . .; odd in
              singular: *?an iron filing*, but no obvious classifier.

2. Tenses

When John had eaten, Bill switched off the lights.
When John was eating, Bill switched off the lights.
When John was about to eat, Bill switched off the lights.
When John has eaten, Bill switches off the lights.
When John is eating, Bill switches off the lights.
When John is about to eat, Bill switches off the lights.
When John has eaten, Bill will switch off the lights.
When John is eating, Bill will switch off the lights.
When John is about to eat, Bill will switch off the lights.

3. Aspects

(a) accomplishment
(b) process
(c) state
(d) achievement
(e) activity
(f) semelfactive

4. Case roles

(a) *John*	agentive
the squirrel	objective (theme)
(b) *on the table*	locative (goal)
(c) *You*	agentive (*Go and taste that wine*)
	dative (experiencer) (*I can taste the wine in this sauce*)
(d) *the river*	locative (path)
(e) *a hole*	factitive
it	objective (patient)
(f) *London*	locative (source)
(g) *The storm*	instrument (or force)
(h) *John*	dative (beneficiary)

5. Modals

it is probable that	median
it is possible that	low
it is unlikely that	low
it is certain that	high

6. Levin and Hovav Rappaport's classes

clear-type	*drain*
wipe-type	*sweep, scrub, unload*
remove-type	*erase, extract*

7. Negpols

negative items: *hardly, seldom, far from, free from, beware of, avoid*

Chapter 16: Reference and deixis

1. Implicit reference points

(a) *recommend*	for what purpose?
other	than what?
route	from where to where? (cf. *road*, which has no inherent latent complements)

(b) *ring up*	who or what? (cf. *Mary is telephoning* does not have a latent direct object)
time	for what?
(c) *left*	requires an implicit orientation to be identified
next	after what?
(d) *rather a lot*	needs an implicit reference point — compared with what?
(e) *the last*	requires identification of *this sit-in*, or some such
better	than what? The one after? The one before? Something else? Better in what respect? From whose point of view? (For instance, from the point of view of the participants, a better sit-in is probably one that more people joined, and that was more disruptive.)

2. Deixis

(a) *I, her*	person deixis
understood	temporal deixis (past tense)
meet her *there*	spatial deixis (symbolic)
that week	extended spatial deixis
bringing	spatial deixis
that's what . . .	discourse deixis
said	temporal deixis (past tense)
(b) *Come out*	spatial deixis
there	spatial deixis (gestural — the distinction is sometimes hard to apply)
at once	temporal deixis (gestural)
(c) *I, We, he,* etc.	person deixis
this Xmas	temporal deixis (symbolic)
met, got, said, etc.	temporal deixis (tense)
tomorrow	temporal deixis (symbolic)

3. Bring and take

For me, the normal sentences are: (c), (e), (f), (h), (i), (j), (k), (m), (n), (o), (p), (q), (r), (s), (t).

The rule appears to be that in direct speech, *bring* requires motion towards speaker or hearer, or someone/something in vicinity of speaker or hearer, otherwise *take* is used. In indirect speech, it appears that the deictic centre may be either the reporting speaker or the original speaker. (Note that these remarks may not be valid for every reader's usage.)

4. Non-prototypic uses of deictics

(a) The deictic centre is projected onto *the visitors* (notice that they are not the addressees).
(b) The deictic centre is projected onto *Jackson*.
(c) If this was discourse deixis, one would expect *that*. Perhaps this is a psychological use of spatial deixis, implying that the matter touches the speaker personally.
(d) Similar to (c)?

Chapter 17: Speech acts

1. Performative verbs

bet	as in *I bet you £50 she refuses* but not as in *I bet he drinks Carling Black Label*
pray	as in *We pray thee O God that thou wilt deliver us*
deplore	
celebrate	as in *We celebrate our team's splendid victory!* but not as in *We celebrate Xmas at home*

2. Locutionary acts etc.

(a) parrot   produce an utterance inscription (but not compose it, or contextualize it);
no true illocutionary act possible (a parrot might possibly intend to attract attention by producing a bit of language, but that would not function by virtue of its meaning);
there may be perlocutionary effects.
(Note that there are reports of parrots using language meaningfully; if these reports are true, the above will have to be revised!)

(b) computer Clearly, a sufficiently sophisticated computer could do everything.
(Most everyday computer messages, though, like *You are running out of memory* and *Save large clipboard?*, are not composed.)

3. Classifying performative verbs

complain	assertive (according to Searle) directive? (aims to elicit some action, but this is not normally specified) expressive (expresses an attitude to a state of affairs)
warn to	directive (according to Searle)
warn that	assertive (according to Searle) directive? (aims to elicit some action, but this is not normally specified)
confess	assertive (committed to truth of confession) expressive (expresses contrition) declarative? (in the context of a police interrogation, a confession is to some extent ritualized, and could be said to 'change reality')
bemoan	expressive assertive? (speaker is committed to truth of state of affairs bemoaned)

Chapter 18: Conversational implicatures

1. Six implicatures

Everyone will have their own answers to this. Here are a few suggestions (the implicatures vary in strength):

(a) She doesn't spend much on clothes.
    (Implicature: "Yes, she does spend a lot on clothes.")
(b) I don't know if she has anything left from the £500 she won at bingo.
    (Implicature: "She has nothing left from the £500 she won at bingo.")
(c) Does she still push drugs?
    (Implicature: "She still pushes drugs.")

2. Anomalies

(a) Infringes the maxim of manner: *Avoid obscurity.*
                                       Avoid unnecessary prolixity.
(b) There is no maxim that covers this case, but there seems to be a deliberate refusal to accept the normal convention that a change of speaker involves a change of deictic centre.
(c) Infringes the maxim of manner: *Be orderly.*
(d) Infringes the modesty maxim.
(e) Infringes the maxim of quantity (gives too little information).
(f) Infringes the tact maxim by being indirect when directness would be polite.
(g) Infringes the maxim of relation
(h) Infringes the consideration maxim.
(i) Excessive adherence to modesty maxim (not really explained by the maxim itself).
(j) Infringes the maxim of manner: *Avoid unnecessary prolixity.*

3. Classifying propositions

(a) Entailment.
(b) Particularized conversational implicature.
(c) Part of explicature by enrichment.
(d) Ad hoc arrangement.
(e) Generalized conversational implicature.
(f) Particularized conversational implicature.

References

ALLAN, KEITH (1986), *Linguistic Meaning*. London: Routledge & Kegan Paul.

ALLWOOD, J., ANDERSON, L.-G., and DAHL, Ö. (1977), *Logic in Linguistics*. Cambridge: Cambridge University Press.

ANDERSON, E. S. (1978), 'Lexical universals of body-part terminology'. In J. H. Greenberg, C. H. Ferguson, and E. A. Moravscik (eds.), *Universals of Human Language, vol. iii: Word Structure*. Stanford, Calif: Stanford University Press, 335–68.

ANDERSON, STEPHEN, and KEENAN, EDWARD (1985), 'Deixis'. In T. Shopen (ed.), *Language Typology and Syntactic Description, vol. iii: Grammatical Categories and the Lexicon*. Cambridge: Cambridge University Press, 259–308.

ARGYLE, M. (1972), *The Psychology of Interpersonal Behaviour*, 2nd edn. London: Penguin.

ASHER, R. E., and SIMPSON, J. M. Y. (eds.) (1994), *The Encyclopedia of Language and Linguistics*. Oxford: Pergamon Press.

AUSTIN, J. L. (1962), *How to Do Things with Words*. Oxford: Clarendon Press.

BACH, E., and HARMS, R. T. (eds.) (1968), *Universals in Linguistic Theory*. New York: Holt Rinehart.

BALDINGER, KURT (1980) *Semantic Theory: Towards a Modern Semantics*, trans. W. C. Brown and ed. R. Wright. Oxford: Blackwell.

BARTSCH, RENATE (2002), 'Kompositionalität und ihre Grenzen', in Cruse et al. (2002: ch. 71).

BEATTIE, G. W. (1983), *Talk: An Analysis of Speech and Non-verbal Behaviour*. Milton Keynes: Open University Press.

BERLIN, BRENT (1992), *Ethnological Classification: Principles of Categorization of Plants and Animals in Traditional Societies*. Princeton, NJ: Princeton University Press.

—— BREEDLOVE, D. E., and RAVEN, P. H. (1973), 'General principles of classification and nomenclature in folk biology' *American Anthropologist* 75, 214–42.

—— and KAY, PAUL (1969), *Basic Color Terms: Their Universality and Evolution*. Berkeley: University of California Press.

BLACK, MAX (1962), *Models and Metaphors: Studies in Language and Philosophy*. Ithaca, NY: Cornell University Press.

—— (1979), 'More about metaphor'. In Ortony (1979: 19–45).

BLAKEMORE, DIANE (1987), *Semantic Constraints on Relevance*. Oxford: Blackwell.

BLAKEMORE, DIANE (1992), *Understanding Utterances: An Introduction to Pragmatics*. Oxford: Blackwell.

BOLINGER, DWIGHT (1965), 'The atomization of meaning', *Language* 41, 555–73.

BROWN, C. H. (1976), 'General principles of human anatomical partonomy and speculations on the growth of partonomic nomenclature', *American Ethnologist* 3(3), 400–24.

—— (1995), 'Lexical acculturation and ethnobiology: utilitarianism versus intellectualism', *Journal of Linguistic Anthropology* 5, 51–64.

—— (2002a), 'Paradigmatic relations of inclusion and identity I: hyponymy'. In Cruse et al. (2002: ch. 58).

—— (2002b), 'Paradigmatic relations of inclusion and identity II: meronymy'. In Cruse et al. (2002: ch. 59).

—— KOLAR, J., TORREY, B. J., TRUONG-QUANG, T., and VOLKMAN, P. (1976), 'Some general principles of biological and non-biological folk classification', *American Ethnologist* 3, 73–85.

BÜHLER, K. (1934), *Sprachtheorie*. Jena: Fischer.

CANN, RONNIE (1993), *Formal Semantics*. Cambridge: Cambridge University Press.

—— (2002), 'Descriptive models for sense relations III: formal semantics'. In Cruse et al. (2002: ch. 68).

CARSTON, ROBYN (2002), *Thoughts and Utterances: The Pragmatics of Explicit Communication*. Oxford: Blackwell.

CARTER, A. (1984), *Nights at the Circus*. London: Chatto & Windus, Hogarth Press.

CHAFFIN, ROGER (1992), 'The concept of a semantic relation'. In Kittay and Lehrer (1992: 253–88).

CHANNELL, JOANNA (1994). *Vague Language*. Oxford: Oxford University Press.

CHESTERMAN, ANDREW (1991), *On Definiteness: A Study with Special Reference to English and Finnish*. Cambridge: Cambridge University Press.

CHOMSKY, NOAM (1965), *Aspects of the Theory of Syntax*. Cambridge, Mass: MIT Press.

—— (1976), *Reflections on Language*. London: Temple Smith.

CLARK, H. H. (1996) *Using Language*. Cambridge: Cambridge University Press.

COLE, P., and MORGAN, J. L. (eds.) (1975), *Syntax and Semantics, vol. iii: Speech Acts*. New York: Academic Press.

—— and SADOCK, J. M. (eds.) (1977), *Syntax and Semantics, vol. viii: Grammatical Relations*. New York: Academic Press.

COMRIE, B. (1985), *Tense*. Cambridge: Cambridge University Press.

CORNWELL, PATRICIA (1997), *Hornet's Nest*. London: Warner.

—— (2000), *Black Notice*. London: Warner.

COSERIU, E. (1975), 'Vers une typologie des champs lexicaux', *Cahiers de lexicologie* 27, 30–51.

COULSON, SEANA (2000), *Semantic Leaps: Frame-Shifting and Conceptual Blending in Meaning Construction*. Cambridge: Cambridge University Press.

CROFT, W. A. (1993), 'The role of domains in the interpretation of metaphors and metonymies', *Cognitive Linguistics* 4, 335–70.

—— and CRUSE, D. A. (forthcoming), *Cognitive Linguistics*. Cambridge: Cambridge University Press.

CRUSE, D. A. (1980), Review of J. A. Hawkins, *Definiteness and Indefiniteness*, *Journal of Linguistics* 16, 308–16.

—— (1986), *Lexical Semantics*. Cambridge: Cambridge University Press.

—— (1990), 'Prototype theory and lexical semantics'. In S. L. Tsohatzidis (ed.), *Meanings and Prototypes: Studies in Linguistic Categorization*. London: Routledge, 382–402.

—— (1992a), 'Antonymy revisited: some thoughts on the relation between words and concepts'. In Kittay and Lehrer (1992: 289–306).

—— (1992b), 'Monosemy vs. polysemy', review article on Ruhl (1989), *Linguistics* 30, 577–99.

—— (1992c), 'Cognitive linguistics and word meaning: Taylor on linguistic categorization', review article on J. R. Taylor, *Linguistic Categorization: Prototypes in Linguistic Theory*, *Journal of Linguistics* 28, 165–83.

—— (1992d), 'Presupposition'. In *Encyclopedia of Artificial Intelligence*, 2nd edn. New York: Wiley, 1194–1201.

—— (1994a), 'Number and number systems'. In Asher and Simpson (1994: 2857–61).

—— (1994b), 'Prototype theory and lexical relations', *Rivista di linguistica* 6(2), 167–88.

—— (1995), 'Polysemy and related phenomena from a cognitive linguistic viewpoint'. In P. St Dizier and E. Viegas (eds.), *Computational Lexical Semantics*. Cambridge: Cambridge University Press, 33–49.

—— (2000a), 'Lexical "facets": between monosemy and polysemy'. In S. Beckmann, P. P. König, and T. Wolf (eds.), *Sprachspiel und Bedeutung: Festschrift für Franz Hundsnurscher zum 60 Geburtstag*. Tübingen: Niemeyer, 25–36.

—— (2000b), 'Aspects of the micro-structure of word meanings'. In Yael Ravin and Claudia Leacock (eds.), *Polysemy: Theoretical and Computational Approaches*. Oxford: Oxford University Press, 30–51.

—— (2002a), 'Descriptive models for sense relations II: cognitive semantics'. In Cruse et al. (2002: ch. 67).

—— (2002b), 'Paradigmatic relations of exclusion and opposition III: reversivity'. In Cruse et al. (2002: ch. 62).

—— (2002c), 'Dimensions of meaning II: descriptive aspects'. In Cruse et al. (2002: ch. 41).

—— (2002d), 'Paradigmatic relations of inclusion and identity III: synonymy'. In Cruse et al. (2002: ch. 60).

—— (2002e), 'Microsenses, default specificity and the semantics-pragmatics boundary', *Axiomathes* 1, 1–20.

—— (2002f), 'Hyponymy and its varieties'. In Green et al. (2002: 3–21).

—— HUNDSNURSCHER, F., JOB, M., and LUTZEIER, P.-R. (eds.) (2002), *Handbook of Lexicology*. Berlin: De Gruyter.

—— and TOGIA, PAGONA (1995), 'Towards a cognitive model of antonymy', *Lexicology* 1.95, 113–41.

DAHL, ÖSTEN (1985), *Tense and Aspect Systems*. Oxford: Blackwell.

DEANE, P. D. (1996), 'On Jackendoff's conceptual semantics', *Cognitive Linguistics* 7(1), 35–92.

DILLON, G. L. (1979), *Introduction to Contemporary Linguistic Semantics*. New York: Holt, Rinehart & Winston.

DIRVEN, RENÉ (2002), 'Structuring of word meaning III: Figurative use of language'. In Cruse et al. (2002: ch. 39).

ELLIS, A., and BEATTIE, G. W. (1986), *The Psychology of Language and Communication*. London: Weidenfeld & Nicolson.

FAUCONNIER, GILLES (1994), *Mental Spaces*, 2nd edn. Cambridge: Cambridge University Press.

FILLMORE, C. J. (1968), 'The case for case'. In Bach and Harms (1968: 1–88).

—— (1977), 'The case for case reopened'. In Cole and Sadock (1977: 59–81).

FRASER, B. (1970), 'Idioms within a transformational grammar', *Foundations of Language* 6, 22–42.

FRAWLEY, WILLIAM (1992), *Linguistic Semantics*. Hillsdale, NJ: Erlbaum.

GECKELER, HORST (1971), *Strukturelle Semantik und Wortfeldtheorie*. Munich: Fink.

GEERAERTS, DIRK (1993), 'Vagueness's puzzles, polysemy's vagaries', *Cognitive Linguistics* 4(3), 223–72.

GIBBS, R. W. (1990), 'Psycholinguistic studies on the conceptual basis of idiomaticity', *Cognitive Linguistics* 1(4), 417–51.

GIVÓN, TALMY (1984), *Syntax: A Functional-Typological Introduction, vol. i*. Amsterdam: Benjamins.

GLUCKSBERG, SAMUEL (2001), *Understanding Figurative Language*. Oxford: Oxford University Press.

GOOSSENS, LOUIS (1990), 'Metaphtonymy: the interaction of metaphor and metonymy in expressions of linguistics action', *Cognitive Linguistics* 1, 323–40.

GRADY, JOSEPH E., OAKLEY, TODD, and COULSON, SEANNA (1999), 'Blending and metaphor'. In Raymond W. Gibbs Jr. and Gerard J. Steen (eds.), *Metaphor in Cognitive Linguistics*. Amsterdam: Benjamins, 101–24.

GRAFTON, SUE (1994), *J is for Judgement*. London: Pan Books.

GREEN, REBECCA, BEAN, CAROL A., and MYAENG, SUNG HYON (eds.) (2002), *The Semantics of Relationships: An Interdisciplinary Perspective*. Dordrecht: Kluwer.

GRICE, H. P. (1975), 'Logic and conversation'. In Cole and Morgan (1975: 41–58).

HAAS, W. (1962), 'The theory of translation', *Philosphy* 37, 208–28. Repr. in G. H. R. Parkinson (ed.), *The Theory of Meaning* (Oxford: Oxford University Press, 1968), 86–108.

—— (1964), 'Semantic value'. In *Proceedings of the IXth International Congress of Linguists*. The Hague: Mouton, 1066–72.

HALLIDAY, M. A. K. (1970), 'Functional diversity in language', *Foundations of Language* 6, 322–61.

—— (1985), *An Introduction to Functional Grammar*. London: Arnold.

HAMPTON, J. (1991), 'The combination of prototype concepts', in Schwanenflugel (1991: 91–116).

HAWKINS, J. (1978), *Definiteness and Indefiniteness: A Study in Reference and Grammaticality Prediction*. London: Croom Helm.

HJELMSLEV, LOUIS (1961), *Prolegomena to a Theory of Language*, trans. F. J. Whitfield. Madison: University of Wisconsin Press.

HOCKETT, C. F. (1958), *A Course in Modern Linguistics*. New York: Macmillan.

HORN, L. (1984), 'Toward a new taxonomy for pragmatic inference: Q-based and R-based implicature'. In D. Schiffrin (ed.), *Georgetown University Round Table on*

Language and Linguistics 1984: Meaning, Form and Use in Context: Linguistic Applications. Washington, DC: Georgetown University Press, 11–42.

HUNN, E. S. (1983), 'The utilitarian factor in folk biological classification', *American Anthropologist* 84, 830–47.

HURFORD, J. R., and HEASLEY, B. (1983), *Semantics: A Coursebook*. Cambridge: Cambridge University Press.

JACKENDOFF, RAY (1983), *Semantics and Cognition*. Cambridge, Mass: MIT Press.

—— (1990), *Semantic Structures*. Cambridge, Mass: MIT Press.

—— (1996), 'Conceptual semantics and cognitive linguistics', *Cognitive Linguistics* 7(1), 93–129.

—— (2002), *Foundations of Languge: Brain, Meaning, Grammar, Evolution*. Oxford: Oxford University Press.

JAKOBSON, R., and HALLE, M. (1956), *Fundamentals of Language*. The Hague: Mouton.

KASTOVSKY, DIETER (1980), 'Selectional restrictions and lexical solidarities'. In D. Kastovsky (ed.), *Perspektiven der lexikalischen Semantik*. Bonn: Bouvier Verlag Herbert Grundmann, 70–92

KATZ, J. J. (1972), *Semantic Theory*. New York: Harper & Row.

—— (1973), 'Compositionality, idiomaticity and lexical substitution'. In S. Anderson and P. Kiparsky (eds.), *A Festschrift for Morris Halle*. New York: Holt, Rinehart and Winston, 357–76.

—— and FODOR, J. A. (1963), 'The structure of a semantic theory', *Language* 39, 170–210. Repr. in J. A. Fodor and J. J. Katz (eds.), *The Structure of Language: Readings in the Philosophy of Language* (Englewood Cliffs, NJ: Prentice-Hall 1964), 479–518.

KEARNS, KATE (2000), *Semantics*. London: Macmillan.

KITTAY, E. F., and LEHRER, A. J. (eds.) (1992), *Frames, Fields and Contrasts: New Essays in Semantic and Lexical Organization*. Hillsdale, NJ: Erlbaum.

KÖVECSES, ZOLTÁN (1988), *The Language of Love*. Lewisburg, Pa.: Bucknell University Press.

—— (2002), *Metaphor: A Practical Introduction*. Oxford: Oxford University Press.

—— and RADDEN, GÜNTER (1998), 'Metonymy: developing a cognitive linguistic view', *Cognitive Linguistics* 9(1), 37–77.

LABOV, WILLIAM (1973), 'The boundaries of words and their meanings'. In C.-J. N. Bailey and R. W. Shuy (eds.), *New Ways of Analyzing Variation in English*. Washington DC: Georgetown University Press, 340–73.

LAKOFF, GEORGE (1987), *Women, Fire and Dangerous Things*. Chicago: University of Chicago Press.

—— (1990), 'The invariance hypothesis: is abstract reason based on image-schemas?', *Cognitive Linguistics* 12(1), 39–74.

—— (1993), 'The contemporary theory of metaphor'. In A. Ortony (ed.), *Metaphor and Thought*. Cambridge: Cambridge University Press, 202–51.

—— and JOHNSON, MARK (1980), *Metaphors We Live By*. Chicago: Chicago University Press.

—— and TURNER, MARK (1989), *Beyond Cool Reason: A Field Guide to Poetic Metaphor*. Chicago: University of Chicago Press.

LAMBERTS, KOEN, and SHANKS, DAVID (eds.) (1997), *Knowledge, Concepts and Categories*. Hove, Sussex: Psychology Press.

LANGACKER, R. W. (1987), *Foundations of Cognitive Grammar, vol. i: Theoretical Prerequisites*. Stanford, Calif: Stanford University Press.

—— (1991a), *Foundations of Cognitive Grammar, vol. ii: Descriptive Application*. Stanford, Calif: Stanford University Press.

LANGACKER, R. W. (1991b), *Concept, Image and Symbol: The Cognitive Basis of Grammar*. Berlin: Mouton De Gruyter.

—— (1993), Lecture given to International Conference: 'New Trends in Semantics and Lexicography', Kazimierz, Poland, Dec. 1993

LARSON, RICHARD, and SEGAL, GABRIEL (1995), *Knowledge of Meaning*. Cambridge, Mass.: MIT Press.

LEE, DAVID (2002), *Cognitive Linguistics: An Introduction*. Oxford: Oxford University Press.

LEECH, G. N. (1974), *Semantics*. Harmondsworth: Penguin.

—— (1983), *Principles of Pragmatics*. London: Longman.

LEHRER, A. J. (1974), *Semantic Fields and Lexical Structure*. Amsterdam: North-Holland.

—— (1985), 'Markedness and antonymy', *Journal of Linguistics* 21, 397–421.

—— and LEHRER, KEITH (1982), 'Antonymy', *Linguistics and Philosophy* 5, 483–501.

LEIBNIZ, GOTTFRIED WILHELM (1903), *Opuscules et fragments inédits de Leibniz*, ed. Louis Couturat. Paris: Presses Universitaires de France.

LEVIN, BETH, and HOVAV RAPPAPORT, MALKA (1992), 'Wiping the slate clean: a lexical semantic exploration'. In Levin and Pinker (1992: 123–52).

—— and PINKER, STEVEN (eds.) (1992), *Lexical and Conceptual Semantics*. Oxford: Blackwell.

LEVIN, S. R. (1977), *The Semantics of Metaphor*. Baltimore: Johns Hopkins University Press.

LEVINSON, S. C. (1983), *Pragmatics*. Cambridge: Cambridge University Press.

—— (1989), Review of Sperber and Wilson, *Relevance, Journal of Linguistics* 25, 455–72.

—— (2000), *Presumptive Meanings: The Theory of Generalized Conversational Implicature*. Cambridge, Mass.: MIT Press.

LYONS, JOHN (1963), *Structural Semantics*. Cambridge: Cambridge University Press.

—— (1968), *Introduction to Theoretical Linguistics*. Cambridge: Cambridge University Press.

—— (1977), *Semantics*. 2 vols., Cambridge: Cambridge University Press.

—— (1981), *Language, Meaning and Context*. London: Fontana.

—— (1995), *Linguistic Semantics*. Cambridge: Cambridge University Press.

McCAWLEY, J. D. (1981), *Everything That Linguists Have Always Wanted to Know About Logic*. Oxford: Blackwell.

MACKIN, R. (1978), 'On collocations: words shall be known by the company they keep'. In P. Strevens (ed.), *In Honour of A. S. Hornby*. Oxford: Oxford University Press.

MAKKAI, ADAM (1972), *Idiom Structure in English*. The Hague: Mouton.

METTINGER, ARTHUR (1994), *Aspects of Semantic Opposition in English*. Oxford: Clarendon Press.

MOORE, TERENCE, and CARLING, CHRISTINE (1982), *Understanding Language: Towards a Post-Chomskyan Linguistics*. London: Macmillan.
MURPHY, G. L. (1991), 'Meaning and concepts'. In Schwanenflugel (1991: 11–36).
NEWMEYER, FREDRICK (1974), 'The regularity of idiom behaviour', *Lingua* 34, 327–42.
NIDA, E. A. (1975), *Componential Analysis of Meaning: An Introduction to Semantic Structures*. The Hague: Mouton.
ORTONY, ANDREW (ed.) (1979), *Metaphor and Thought*. Cambridge: Cambridge University Press.
PALMER, F. R. (1986), *Mood and Modality*. Cambridge: Cambridge University Press.
PARTEE, B. H. (1984), 'Compositionality'. In F. Landman and F. Veldman (eds.), *Varieties of Formal Semantics*. Dordrecht: Foris, 281–311.
POTTIER, BERNARD (1974), *Linguistique générale*. Paris: Klincksieck.
PULMAN, S. G. (1983), *Word Meaning and Belief*. London: Croom Helm.
PUSTEJOVSKY, JAMES (1995), *The Generative Lexicon*. Cambridge, Mass.: MIT Press.
RICHARDS, I. A. (1965), *The Philosphy of Rhetoric*. New York: Oxford University Press.
ROSCH, E. H. (1973), 'Natural categories', *Cognitive Psychology* 4, 328–50.
—— (1978), 'Principles of categorisation'. In E. Rosch and B. Lloyd (eds.), *Cognition and Categorisation*. Hillside, NJ: Erlbaum 27–48.
—— and MERVIS, C. (1975), 'Family resemblances: studies in the internal structure of categories', *Cognitive Psychology* 7, 573–605.
RUHL, CHARLES (1989), *On Monosemy: A Study in Linguistic Semantics*. Albany, NY: State University of New York Press.
SAMPSON, GEOFFREY (1979), 'The indivisibility of words', *Journal of Linguistics* 15, 39–47.
SCHWANENFLUGEL, P. J. (ed.) (1991), *The Psychology of Word Meanings*. Hillsdale, NJ: Erlbaum.
SEARLE, J. R. (1969), *Speech Acts: An Essay in the Philosophy of Language*. Cambridge: Cambridge University Press.
SEBEOK, T. A. (ed.) (1966), *Current Trends in Linguistics, vol. iii*. The Hague: Mouton.
SPERBER, DAN and WILSON, DEIRDRE (1986), *Relevance: Communication and Cognition* Oxford: Blackwell.
STERN, JOSEPH (2000), *Metaphor in Context*. Cambridge, Mass.: MIT Press.
TALMY, LEONARD (1985), 'Lexicalization patterns: semantic structure in lexical forms'. In T. Shopen (ed.), *Language Typology and Syntactic Description, vol. iii*. Cambridge: Cambridge University Press, 57–149.
TAYLOR, J. R. (1989), *Linguistic Categorization: Prototypes in Linguistic Theory*. Oxford: Clarendon Press.
—— (1996), 'On running and jogging', *Cognitive Linguistics* 7(1), 21–34.
TSOHATZIDIS, S. L. (ed.) (1992), *Meanings and Prototypes: Studies in Linguistic Categorization*. London: Routledge.
TUGGY, DAVID (1993), 'Ambiguity, polysemy and vagueness', *Cognitive Linguistics* 4(3), 273–90.
TUŢESCU, M. (1975), *Précis de sémantique française*. Paris: Klincksieck.
UNGERER, F., and SCHMID, H.-J. (1996), *An Introduction to Cognitive Linguistics*. London: Longman.

WEINREICH, URIEL (1966), 'Explorations in semantic theory'. In Sebeok (1966: 395–477).

WIERZBICKA, ANNA (1996), *Semantics: Primes and Universals*. Oxford: Oxford University Press.

WITTGENSTEIN, L. (1972), *Philosophical Investigations*, trans. G. E. M. Anscombe. Oxford: Blackwell.

Author index

Subject index